KEFAUVER: A POLITICAL BIOGRAPHY

KEFAUVER:
A POLITICAL BIOGRAPHY

By JOSEPH BRUCE GORMAN

New York
OXFORD UNIVERSITY PRESS
1971

PREFACE

Estes Kefauver was one of the great enigmas of American politics in the middle third of the twentieth century. Although he was an unflagging champion of civil liberties, the basically conservative Tennessee electorate, nevertheless, first sent him to the Senate during the postwar anti-communist hysteria and re-elected him six years later in the midst of the McCarthy era. A gentle persuader on behalf of civil rights, he three times won the endorsement of segregationist Tennessee in periods when concern over Negro progress was especially aroused: in 1948, by the Truman civil rights program; in 1954, by the school segregation decision; and in 1960, by the first wave of "sit-ins." A persistent advocate of consumer protection, he carried on a lonely battle against monopoly at a time when traditional ideals of free competition were considered increasingly anachronistic, especially by the powerful corporate interests that came to look upon him as perhaps the most dangerous threat to their profitable neo-monopolistic practices. Finally, in an era in which sheer numbers made a truly personal approach to politics difficult, Kefauver maintained, not only in his Senate and presidential campaigns but also in his day-to-day public service, a unique interest in the individual citizen, both in Tennessee and across the country. In the process, he many times by-passed and thus alienated the professional politicians, who valued above all the team player sensitive to the interests of the organization, even when there was conflict between those interests and a conscientious concern for the public interest.

Given Kefauver's approach to both the form and substance of politics, it seems astonishing, in retrospect, that he was one of the most successful politicians the country has ever produced. It astonished his contemporaries, too. Perhaps at no time in his career was this more clearly demonstrated than in his final bid for re-nomination in 1960. His Tennessee fences were thought to be in a shambles as a result of his 1956 campaign for the Democratic presidential nomination and the vice-presidential race with Adlai Stevenson a few months later. His Tennessee enemies, for the only time in his career, had united behind a single, eminently respectable, conservative candidate, who enjoyed impressive financial backing. Kefauver was finding it difficult to raise money, and his vote for the 1960 Civil Rights Act had further enraged what were assumed to be already alienated Tennesseans. As election day approached, a close call or a defeat was universally predicted. When the returns poured in, however, observers blinked in disbelief as Kefauver smothered his opponent in the most stunning victory of his career. The strongly anti-Kefauver *Memphis Commercial Appeal,* almost incredulous over his landslide victory, announced editorially that Kefauver's showing simply defied analysis and emphasized "the need for some of us to examine more closely the things that brought it about as well as the things he advocates."

It is doubtful whether the *Commercial Appeal* ever understood Kefauver any better. He was not a man who could be analyzed at a distance and, indeed, remained somewhat of a mystery even to his family and closest friends. But all who followed Kefauver's career agreed that he had a special quality, an attraction which won him the support of the mythical common man, who saw in Kefauver an honest, sincere, and unique champion of ideals and values that seemed to be ignored or taken lightly by too many others in public life.

Attempting to recapture the life and career of such an extraordinary man has been an undertaking in which I have been aided by literally hundreds of people; I have acknowledged my debt to many of them in the Notes. There are several, however, whose encouragement and assistance merit special mention.

Miss Lucile Myers of Washington, D. C., who loyally served on Kefauver's staff from his last term in the House through his entire Senate career, read all of the manuscript and was a constant source of fresh suggestions which immeasurably improved the final text.

Mrs. Tom (Martha) Ragland of Nashville, former Democratic National Committeewoman from Tennessee and trusted Kefauver lieutenant for over twenty years, also read the entire manuscript and offered many valuable criticisms.

Both Mrs. Nancy Kefauver Fooshee of Knoxville and Miss Nora Kefauver of Madisonville and New York City, sisters of Estes Kefauver, graciously discussed their brother at length during extended interviews and provided a unique perspective on his life and career.

Dr. Frank Freidel of Harvard University, friend and adviser, took both a professional and personal interest in this project and was responsible for countless improvements in both style and content.

I am also indebted to four Washington associates of Kefauver who read and criticized sections of the manuscript: Frank Brizzi (legislative assistant to Kefauver for seventeen years), Richard Wallace (administrative assistant to Kefauver from 1951 to 1959), and Mr. and Mrs. Stanton Smith (Kefauver friends and political allies among organized labor for almost thirty years, dating back to the Volunteer movement in Chattanooga in the mid-1930s).

A final word of thanks to an assortment of individuals who, each in his separate way, have put something of themselves into this book: John Dobson, Director of the Estes Kefauver Library at the University of Tennessee, who proved cooperative and helpful beyond all expectation in making research among the Estes Kefauver Papers both rewarding and pleasant; Mrs. Philip

S. McConnell and Miss Lois Bacon of Alexandria, who edited and corrected the manuscript; Dr. Ralph W. Haskins of the University of Tennessee, who first encouraged me to undertake research on the life and career of Estes Kefauver; and, finally, my wife, Bette Stubbs Gorman, whose contributions to the successful completion of this work are beyond the ability of words to convey and which can perhaps be fully appreciated only by those who, with the aid and encouragement of patient and long-suffering wives of their own, have traveled similar roads themselves.

J. B. G.

Alexandria, Va.
July 1971

CONTENTS

Illustrations follow page 214

KEFAUVER: A POLITICAL BIOGRAPHY

INTRODUCTION

Estes Kefauver was the most authentic—and most successful—maverick in American political history. Indeed, more than any other major political figure of the last generation, he remained free of the long-range sectional, partisan, and organizational commitments that furnish political security but limit the flexibility of most men in public life. Kefauver's political independence derived to a great extent from his special talent for inspiring confidence in his leadership, even among those who should logically have been his bitterest political enemies. It was a charisma strongly rooted in Kefauver's faith both in his values and in himself as a vehicle for the defense of those values.

Supreme self-confidence—indeed, a generous measure of self-righteousness—is the indispensable psychological prop of any political maverick, and Kefauver was no exception to this rule. He never doubted his right—or his obligation—to participate in the political life of his city, state, and nation. With forebears at Jamestown as early as 1624, and with every direct ancestor in America before the Revolution, his family tradition was rich with memories not only of Valley Forge but also of subsequent roles of leadership in healing the sick, preaching the gospel, and bringing law and order to the antebellum Tennessee frontier.

His parents' marriage in 1897 had joined two of the most respected families in the state—the Esteses of West Tennessee's cotton country and the Kefauvers of East Tennessee's Monroe County, at the foot of the Great Smoky Mountains, which separate Tennessee from North Carolina. It was in the Monroe County seat of Madisonville that Carey Estes Kefauver was born July 26, 1903. He was destined to be not only the biggest, strongest, and handsomest boy in town, but also one of the smartest—and certainly the friendliest and most popular—personality developments aided immeasurably by the family's pre-eminent social position in the community. Leadership roles came quickly and naturally to young Estes.

He was Madisonville's pride when, in 1920, he enrolled in the University of Tennessee at Knoxville. The Kefauver charm, intelligence, and athletic abilities led to the most impressive record of campus achievements ever compiled at Tennessee, including outstanding performances at track and football, the editorship of the campus newspaper, and the ultimate honor, election as president of the student body.

Two years at Yale Law School launched the legal career which had been Estes's dream since boyhood. Upon graduation, he returned to his native Tennessee and began practice in Chattanooga, where, within the next dozen years, he established himself as one of the outstanding—and successful—corporate lawyers in the city.

Success at the bar was matched by a marriage so notable that the *Chattanooga Times* called it the "highlight of the weddings of 1935 among Chattanooga society." Nancy Paterson Pigott, daughter of an expatriate American later knighted for his engineering feats by George VI, had first met Estes during an American tour in the summer of 1934. Their marriage in Scotland the following year was to open doors in Chattanooga society previously only ajar, and the beautiful and vivacious Nancy soon became as much of a personality as Estes himself and, in years to come, an invaluable political asset to her perennially campaigning husband.

Kefauver had vowed to a fellow Yale Law School graduate that he would "join everything in town" after setting up a law practice in Chattanooga. He did. Within a few years, Estes had moved to positions of leadership in the local and state bar associations, the Democratic party, and local public service organizations. He achieved wide prominence as president of the Chattanooga Jaycees and as chairman of both a business committee attempting to attract investment into the Chattanooga area and a Hamilton County Regional Planning Commission seeking to establish modern zoning standards in order to make possible the orderly growth and development of the county.

It was logical, therefore, that he would play an important role in establishing and leading the Volunteers, a political action group urging far-reaching changes in the structure of Hamilton County government. The local Democratic machine, threatened by the suggested reforms, blocked the Volunteers at almost every turn. Kefauver, in response, entered the political arena in 1938 as the reform candidate for a vital state senate seat; the bosses stole the election, but Kefauver won the campaign and emerged from his defeat stronger than ever. Moreover, his background as a corporate lawyer and his prestige as a reform Democrat led the newly elected governor to appoint him as state Commissioner of Finance and Taxation, a cabinet post in which he served a brief —and universally praised—stint which gave his career a momentum so great that he easily won the Democratic nomination for a vacant House seat in the summer of 1939 with the tacit approval of the same bosses who had opposed him a year earlier, including the Crump-McKellar state machine, which controlled state politics through its ability to roll up incredible majorities in Memphis for organization-backed candidates. Running in the general election as a New Deal Democrat, Kefauver overwhelmed his isolationist Republican opponent and took his seat as a freshman congressman in September 1939.

On election night, Kefauver had sat listening to favorable returns with Lee Allen, chairman of the Hamilton County Democratic Executive Committee, in a car in which the two men had toured the district that day; when it became clear that Kefauver had won, Allen turned to Kefauver and said, "Well, Estes, you're a congressman." Kefauver was quiet for a minute and then replied, "Lee, they are a dime a dozen." So they were. But Kefauver recognized his election to Congress as an opportunity "to get to the level where world affairs were decided." And, as both his supporters and enemies were to learn again and again over the next twenty-four years, opportunity never had to knock twice for Estes Kefauver.

chapter i

FACTIONALISM IN
TENNESSEE, 1940-1947

$\bigwedge$lthough Kefauver had been elected originally with the acquiescence of the Crump-McKellar machine, by 1942 signs of strain were beginning to appear.

Kefauver had been in basic agreement with both state and Southern Democrats on most issues, although his vote for anti-poll tax legislation in 1942 provoked Mississippi's racist John Rankin to point his finger at Kefauver and cry, "Shame on you, Estes Kefauver," when they met in the well of the House after the vote.[1] The poll tax issue was one on which Kefauver consistently broke with most fellow Southern Democrats. As he explained to the House in October 1942:

> . . . a basic principle of democracy is the free exercise of franchise. Democracy can only flourish when there is general and widespread interest in public affairs, and a large and free expression of the will of the people at the polls. Any restriction, such as the poll tax, that works or is employed to prevent voting, strikes at the heart of democracy.
>
> Today, we are trying to sell the representative form of government to people and nations throughout the world. To do that we must remove the shackles here at home. What a fine example we would be setting if now we would show the world

our confidence in democratic processes and remove an obstacle which disenfranchises millions of American citizens.[2]

There was widespread opposition in Tennessee to a poll tax, and Kefauver's support for its abolition was not considered a betrayal of Southern interests by the voters of his district. In fact, in 1943, 1945, and 1947, when the House passed anti-poll tax bills, Kefauver was joined each time by at least three other Tennessee congressmen in support of the measures.[3]

It was with Senator McKellar that Kefauver began to have problems that eventually led to an open break with the Crump-McKellar machine. Kefauver's early relationship with McKellar had been very cordial. In 1940, McKellar had said of Kefauver that "I believe the time will come when he will be one of the great leaders in the state." [4] Trouble began to develop because of the attitude McKellar adopted toward the operation of the Tennessee Valley Authority. McKellar was an enthusiastic supporter of the concept of the TVA, but he was upset that it remained free from his control. Because he could not directly dictate TVA policy, he attempted to control the agency indirectly through his influence on the Senate Appropriations Committee. In April 1942, McKellar tacked on an amendment, abolishing TVA's revolving fund, to a House-passed bill. The purpose of this move was to require all moneys received by TVA to go into the general fund of the Treasury and to forbid expenditures except by appropriation by Congress. By forcing TVA to come to Congress each year for an appropriation, McKellar could wield great power over TVA through his seniority on the Appropriations Committee. In 1942 McKellar was the ranking Democrat on the committee and was *de facto* chairman, due to the ill health of Carter Glass of Virginia. Since McKellar was not officially chairman, he also held on to his chairmanship of the Post Office and Post Roads Committee. Thus, until 1946, when Glass left the Senate, McKellar was, in effect, chairman of two Senate committees, a position he used to the utmost to keep the Crump-McKellar machine running smoothly. The McKellar success in

April 1942 touched off a reaction all over the Tennessee Valley by power distributors, newspapers, and civic associations anxious to have the amendment dropped by the conferees appointed to resolve the Senate and House versions of the bill. The effort was successful and McKellar was defeated. Kefauver and fellow Tennessee Democrats Percy Priest and Albert Gore led the fight in the House to block McKellar's control of TVA. Their fear was not so much that McKellar would gain greater control over TVA as that TVA would be at the mercy of conservative Congresses in the future. The opposition to McKellar was not originally personal, but his persistent efforts to control TVA through schemes that would weaken it soon made him the target of pro-TVA supporters. When, in March 1944, he was again successful in having the Senate vote to abolish the revolving fund, the *Knoxville News-Sentinel* and the *Memphis Press-Scimitar* attacked McKellar as:

> a patronage hunter, and . . . in that role . . . we find him waging a fight year after year on Chairman David E. Lilienthal of the Tennessee Valley Authority, a fight which has now become a personal vendetta . . . [and] will succeed this year unless friends of good government stop the rampaging Tennessean.[5]

Again, however, the pro-TVA forces, including one hundred thirty municipalities and cooperatives, persuaded the House to block the provision.[6] Instead of accepting the opposition to his proposal for what is was, McKellar elected to consider it a personal matter and turned against those who had fought him on the TVA issue. A principal object of his attack was David E. Lilienthal, who, as TVA chairman, patiently worked to thwart McKellar's schemes whenever necessary.[7]

Another, more direct method of controlling TVA was unsuccessfully attempted by McKellar. He wanted to require Senate confirmation of all TVA employees earning more than $3800 a year, thus making most of the skilled specialists' jobs dependent on his patronage.[8] Little wonder that George Norris, the father of

TVA, was moved to remark that "I cannot understand how Tennessee can maintain in office anyone who has such a revengeful feeling against the operation of TVA." [9]

McKellar himself was not up for re-election until 1946, but the anti-McKellar forces sought to deny renomination to Senator Tom Stewart, who usually voted with McKellar and had little political strength in his own right, depending on the McKellar-Crump machine to keep him in office. Stewart had to face the voters in 1942, and there was pressure on Kefauver to enter the Democratic primary in an effort to retire Stewart. Anti-McKellar-Crump forces tended to look to Silliman Evans, publisher of the *Nashville Tennessean,* for leadership in the fight against the machine, and Evans's personal choice was Kefauver.

In the spring of 1942, Alfred D. Mynders of the *Chattanooga Times* wrote George Fort Milton, then a consultant in Washington, of the pressure on Kefauver:

> They have been trying to get either Estes Kefauver or Phil Whitaker to oppose Tom Stewart for the Senate. . . . Estes said he would not run because he could not get away from his work at Washington to make the campaign and didn't have the money for an expensive race.[10]

Milton's reply summarized the problems faced by Kefauver if he attempted the race:

> Estes has talked with me from time to time here recently about the pressures put on him to get in that race. I have counselled him against it, for several reasons. Perhaps the most cogent of these is that Stewart is merely a "me too" for McKellar and that Estes could not concentrate on him the public odiom [*sic*] of the attack McKellar has made on T. V. A. Estes, therefore, would get the full strength of the McKellar-Crump machines against him but would not be able to offset this with the straight out pro-T. V. A. hatred of McKellar. He would be much better off fighting McKellar for the nomination than fighting Tom Stewart for it. Likewise I think that so long as Crump is there, any

primary contender against it will have a bad time. Estes has a good reputation and strength building up now in the House. He is organizing the House fight to undo the McKellar scheme which the Senate has yielded to. Estes is sure of an unopposed renomination to the House. He had better wait on trying to get a State wide choice.[11]

Evans did find another candidate after Kefauver refused to run. Ned Carmack, son of a former United States Senator from Tennessee, rolled into Memphis with a lead over Stewart, only to see a landside for the Crump candidate in Memphis ensure the renomination of the lackluster incumbent. But the campaign against Stewart was not in vain; both McKellar and Crump were convinced by the 1942 campaign that Stewart was a weak link in the organization, and their decision to dump him six years later would have a dramatic effect on Kefauver's career.

In spite of the developing feud with McKellar, Kefauver maintained good relations with Governor Prentice Cooper, who was re-elected governor in 1940 and 1942. Cooper, elected with Crump's blessing, shared the concern of the anti-McKellar forces over what the senior senator was trying to do to TVA, but he avoided a break with McKellar. Crump himself was skeptical about the wisdom of McKellar's schemes, but he also maintained his relationship with the senator.

Kefauver was unopposed in the 1942 primary and easily won re-election in November. The next two years saw a rise in the McKellar-TVA feud, but Governor Cooper managed to preserve a working relationship with most elements in the party. However, the behavior of the Tennessee delegation at the 1944 Democratic National Convention illustrated the potential for divisiveness present in the party. Two matters upset the Tennessee delegation: the first was President Roosevelt's proposed civil rights plank; the other was the question of renominating Henry Wallace for Vice-President. Although the Tennessee delegation had endorsed Roosevelt for a fourth term, the group was upset over rumors that he would demand a civil rights plank which most of the

South could not accept. In the face of this threat, the delegation wavered. A stormy caucus on July 19 was held in which strong anti-Roosevelt sentiment began to surface. Kefauver was an alternate delegate and had not expected to take an active part in the convention's proceedings. However, he found himself leading the faction which wanted the delegation to maintain its commitment to FDR. It was a losing battle, although the final decision, to withdraw support from Roosevelt until definite information on the civil rights plank could be had, was a compromise between outright repudiation and loyalty to the earlier pledge. When the text of the civil rights plank was made public the next day, the Tennessee delegation found it unacceptable, but again compromised by declaring support for FDR but not the platform.[12]

Tennessee joined the overwhelming majority of the convention in handing Roosevelt a fourth nomination, although the unit rule concealed die-hard anti-New Dealers who preferred Senator Byrd of Virginia. But if the civil rights fight and Roosevelt's renomination had been low points in the conservatives' fortunes at the convention, the battle for the Vice-Presidential nomination offered better prospects for success. The Tennessee delegation, however, was left out in the cold as the battle raged between Henry Wallace and Truman. When it had become known that Roosevelt would not force Wallace on the convention, the Tennessee delegation decided to nominate Governor Cooper. Cooper selected Kefauver, who as an alternate was technically not entitled to deliver a nominating speech, to place his name before the convention. Kefauver was elevated to delegate after a Third District delegate was persuaded to resign, allowing Kefauver to succeed him.[13]

Kefauver's speech nominating Cooper was dull and uninspired, stressing Cooper's contributions as governor to the war effort. It was hardly distinguishable from other speeches honoring favorite sons, and Kefauver had a more difficult task than most in trying to justify the waste of the convention's time.[14] Kefauver's personal preference for Vice-President was probably

Wallace, a fairly close friend, although Kefauver did know Truman "fairly well." [15] After the convention was over, Wallace wrote Kefauver, "I want to thank you from the bottom of my heart for your fine attitude toward me during the convention. I know you did what you could under a difficult situation." [16]

But there was really very little anyone in the Tennessee delegation could do for either Truman or Wallace. The Vice-President was anathema to conservatives and moderates, but Truman was obnoxious to Boss Crump. Strangely enough, Crump, himself one of the most famous machine politicians in America, objected to Truman as the product of the notorious Pendergast machine in Missouri. Although Crump's own machine had resorted to questionable practices in its early days, by 1944 it functioned smoothly and effectively within the law, and Crump tended to view himself as an effective political leader rather than as a typical urban "boss." Thus, he could, in all sincerity, attack Truman as a candidate too tainted by his machine background.[17]

When the convention finally turned to Truman, Kefauver tried to get Tennessee to join in, but Crump ordered the delegation to stick with Cooper. Thus, Tennessee voted for Cooper to the end, even after other delegations not originally backing Truman gave him their endorsement in the interest of unity.[18]

In view of Kefauver's efforts to oppose Crump-McKellar decisions on civil rights and the Vice-Presidency, it is not surprising that McKellar informed Crump, who had controlled the delegation from Memphis:

> [The Tennessee] delegation was very harmonious except for alternate Kefauver. He was present at each meeting of the delegation and . . . objected to everything. . . . [The convention] did not pay him a particle of attention. . . . He is about as stupid as they make them.[19]

Kefauver was unopposed in the August 1944 Democratic primary. "Nonetheless," editorialized the *Chattanooga Times:*

this newspaper hopes that he will be given a thumping, district-wide vote. He deserves this as an expression of approval from the people he has served so courageously and so well. . . . Assuredly, no one in the Third District needs to be told that Estes Kefauver has served his District with even more zeal than he has served the national scene.[20]

Because of his growing seniority in the House and his loyalty to the national party, and also because he faced no serious opposition in November, Kefauver was chosen as executive director of the One Thousand Club, which raised $252,055 for the Democrats in 1944. He created an embarrassing situation when solicitation letters were made public in which he had written Tennessee businessmen that membership in the Club was "all the pass they need here in Washington to go anywhere." Kefauver replied to charges of influence-peddling in a letter to the *Chattanooga Times,* denying that contributions would result in special privileges. "I have written that we wanted money and needed it," he said. The letters in question were written to three personal friends, whom he approached "because I thought they were well qualified and able and should be outstanding party leaders." Nevertheless, it was an acute embarrassment to Kefauver.[21]

With the end of the war and the feeling that veterans returning home would have little patience for machine politics and outmoded policies, progressives in Tennessee began to consider the possibility of taking on the kingpin of elected Crump-bossed officials, Senator McKellar, who was up for re-election in 1946, seeking a sixth term in the Senate at the age of seventy-seven. The most important figures in the opposition to the Crump-McKellar organization were Kefauver, former Governor Gordon Browning, Ned Carmack (who had narrowly lost to Senator Stewart in the 1942 Democratic primary), and Silliman Evans of the *Nashville Tennessean.* McKellar was very nervous about the 1946 primary and did everything possible to undermine his potential rivals, especially Kefauver. One incident that especially upset Kefauver involved McKellar's arranging for the Midget football team of the Baylor School for Boys to meet President Truman and to have a picture taken with him—after Kefauver had been told by Truman's appointments secretary, Matthew Connelly, that it "absolutely could not be done." Obviously irritated, Kefauver complained to Connelly:

> I accepted yours and the President's decision uncomplainingly but stated that when I notified the people of the decision they would no doubt have one of the Senators or one of the Congressmen intercede. I asked you if you would protect me in that eventuality and you told me you would. . . . These boys are the sons of prominent people in my District. . . . [The coach] told them I wouldn't or couldn't make this arrangement and that they had to call on someone who had influence with the White House. This is the message they are taking back to their parents.
>
> Frankly, I think it is a very shoddy way to do anyone and to say that I am embarrassed is putting it mildly. I have been here four terms and I have worked hard for the party. I spent all last summer speaking and raising money for the election of our ticket and it is disappointing to note the appreciation one receives. This incident will cause me a great deal of trouble in my District so I do not feel very much encouraged about continuing to try to fight for the President's program up here on the Hill when someone else who has not been much help to him can get considerations which were definitely denied to me.[22]

As disgust with Crump and McKellar grew, it was natural that the opposition would look to former Governor Gordon Browning, the only governor in over a decade to break with Crump. In 1945, however, he was in Europe as deputy head of Belgium-Luxembourg missions for the U.S. Army, and in January 1946 he began a one-year tour as civil-affairs adviser on the supreme commander's staff, with policy enforcement responsibilities in Bavaria. Kefauver and Carmack sought to find out Browning's political plans for 1946 and wrote him in order to avoid a split in the opposition that would doom any anti-Crump effort. In December 1945, Browning replied sympathetically to Kefauver's request for coordination of plans and wrote that "I shall be glad to see you and Ned, and if sent home through Washington will stop over for a brief visit. In the meantime feel free to pitch your tent in any direction without chance of conflict with me." [23]

All through January, 1946, Kefauver sought the advice of state Democratic leaders on the question of his running against McKellar for the senatorial nomination.[24] On January 11, Silliman Evans wrote Kefauver, "Reports and judgments continue to be very discouraging, so much so that I think I should tell you that I do not think you would serve yourself properly if you decided to undertake the task." [25]

Senator McKellar was mobilizing all the power and influence at his disposal to keep state leaders in line. His argument that he could do more for the state as chairman of the Appropriations Committee was a difficult one to counter, especially with hardboiled political leaders. Kefauver reluctantly decided not to challenge McKellar, a decision which disappointed many who felt he was the strongest possible candidate the opposition could muster.[26]

With Kefauver's decision not to challenge McKellar, Ned Carmack stepped into the race and became the candidate of the opposition. There was a general feeling that the Crump-backed governor, Jim McCord, who had succeeded retiring Governor Cooper in 1945, was much more vulnerable than McKellar, and it was suggested that Kefauver should challenge McCord for the governorship on a ticket that included Carmack for the Senate. To a Democrat urging such a course of action, Kefauver replied:

> I am tremendously appreciative of the interest of yourself and the good friends you mentioned in getting behind me for Governor, but, somehow, the place just never has appealed to me. My interests have always been in matters that have a more national application. I hope you will explain the situation to those who have been interested, and I want you to know how much I appreciate your thoughtfulness.[27]

If Kefauver had given much thought to means of retiring McKellar in 1946, the aging senator had given an equal amount of time to stirring up trouble for Kefauver in the Third District. The organization sought a candidate to oppose Kefauver in the primary, and anti-Kefauver activity became so pronounced in the spring of 1946, even after Kefauver had decided not to run against McKellar, that Milton Ochs of the *Chattanooga Times* was moved to advise Kefauver in Washington, "It would be wise for you to come here. The McKellars are after you." [28] Kefauver began to receive many letters from political leaders in the district warning him to support McKellar or face opposition in his own primary. It was sometimes difficult to distinguish between those who sincerely wanted to know why Kefauver opposed McKellar and those who wrote to let Kefauver know that his withholding of support had come to their attention and they wanted an explanation.[29] Kefauver tried to keep the issue simplified. To one constituent he wrote:

> I am sure you will remember the various kinds of prevaricator Senator McKellar called me some months ago and that together with the TVA are the reasons I could not support him and keep my self-respect.[30]

To another he wrote:

> You asked why I am opposed to Senator McKellar, and my reason grows out of his sponsorship of the two amendments to the TVA Act, which require employees of TVA, earning more than $3800, to be confirmed by the Senate. The other amendment would eliminate the TVA's revolving fund for operation. Senator McKellar has submitted these amendments every year and he now has the amendment pending which would deprive the TVA of its revolving fund. I think the TVA means a great deal to our section, and I am satisfied that these amendments would be very detrimental to its operation.[31]

In addition to the problems with Senator McKellar, Kefauver was also having difficulties with Wiley Couch, boss of Hamilton

County. A temporary truce between Kefauver and Couch broke down, and the machine leaders of the district, urged on by Mc-Kellar, looked around for a serious opponent for Kefauver. Luckily for Kefauver, the best the machine could do was W. F. McWhorter, a road machinery salesman and a newcomer to politics. Kefauver, however, was genuinely worried about his re-election prospects.[32]

McWhorter made little headway in his campaign against Kefauver, and even the anti-Kefauver leaders became disenchanted with him. He sank to attacking Kefauver for reasons as petty as that Kefauver had a New Yorker on his staff: "Kefauver couldn't get a good Tennessee boy for his office, so he got a slick-talking New York pink." [33]

In the August primary Kefauver won a landslide victory of 28,447 to 4,419, a plurality so great that there is doubt that the machine leaders opposed Kefauver at all.[34] But the Democratic primary of 1946 saw the anti-Crump forces go down to defeat once again on a state-wide basis. Carmack ran over 80,000 votes behind McKellar; Browning, still in Europe and campaigning *in absentia* against Governor McCord, ran about 13,000 votes better than Carmack. The election was not decided in Memphis, and the Crump slate would have won without Shelby County's vote; so, Kefauver had correctly evaluated the unfavorable prospects of the progressive forces. There were rumblings here and there, especially in Kefauver's own Third District, where a GI political action group rose in armed rebellion against corrupt Crump allies in Meigs County. Even Crump-backed Governor McCord dared not send troops to save his political allies, who were run out of town by reform forces which literally overthrew the county government by armed force.[35] Another Third District veterans' group—more liberal than most—announced that it would not oppose Kefauver in November "although we know he has been the beneficiary of election thefts in Polk County." Making their warning to Kefauver very explicit, they announced that they felt certain "that he will sever his connection with the Biggs-Couch machine and that he will lean further to the left in the labor movement and that he will carry out the wishes of the Political Action Committee in its national program." [36]

But Kefauver needed no urging to break with the discredited bosses in the district, and his eyes were on the 1948 senatorial primary in which he himself would take on the most powerful boss of all.

chapter ii

SOUTHERN LIBERAL, 1942-1947

During his almost ten years in the House, Kefauver became well known in his district and over the state for his defense of TVA and public power. However, at the same time, his concentration on other problems attracted notice not only in Tennessee but earned him a reputation as a hard-working public servant in official Washington and among the national press corps. A longtime Kefauver friend and supporter recalled the House years:

> I remember in Chattanooga when we first began to realize what a really outstanding congressman we had. I was active in the League of Women Voters and it was through writing letters to him and watching his record on issues that the League was interested in that I woke up to this. . . . We thought then that he was intelligent, diligent, far-sighted and genuinely concerned for the public interest. He seemed, also, unfortunately, to have a sort of professorial stiffness. I remember we used to say in those days that Estes would go far if he just had any color. It was ironical to remember this later when he was widely being depicted as all color and no substance, as a headline grabbing opportunist with no real qualifications to support his ambitions.[1]

Other than public power, the issue with which Kefauver was most closely identified during his service in the House was congressional reform. In the late 1930s and early 1940s there was an ever increasing feeling that the federal government was becoming unmanageable. What the New Deal had done to expand Washington's role at home, World War II had done to expand its role abroad. Many in Congress felt that without some significant changes in the way Congress operated—changes that minimized the waste of time due to inefficient procedures—the historic check on the executive branch would be lost. In addition, there was also the feeling that congressional procedures were, besides being inefficient, undemocratic as well. To a nation and a Congress inspired by the democratic propaganda designed to spur the war effort, the realities of the operation of Congress, especially the seniority system, stood in sharp contrast to the basic ideals of democratic government.

The most famous of Kefauver's efforts to reform Congress, the establishment of a formal procedure for direct questioning of Cabinet officers on the floor of the House,[2] had been revived periodically since it was proposed in the First Congress. It gained widespread support in the early 1940s for a variety of reasons. From the very beginning of the New Deal, there had been a significant and visible decline in the supervision of the executive branch by Congress. As long as Congress was generally in support of Administration policies, this caused little friction. However, beginning with the off-term elections of 1938, the anti-Roosevelt forces in Congress grew strong enough to challenge effectively the President's programs and to use the powers of Congress to check the alleged abuse of authority in the executive branch. The vehicle that liberals feared would be used against the Administration was the congressional committee; therefore, in an effort to prevent the harassment of Administration figures by conservative-dominated committees, Representative William Thom, Democrat of Ohio, offered a bill on December 3, 1942, to grant floor privileges to members of the Cabinet so that they could defend themselves against congressional attack. He also hoped his measure would force the appointment of competent men to the Cabinet— men who would reflect favorably on any administration by their conduct on the floor.[3]

Kefauver, who had first been exposed to the idea through Woodrow Wilson's *Congressional Government*,[4] supported Thom's bill, and on January 25, 1943, introduced a similar bill in the new Congress. When this bill failed to generate significant support, Kefauver introduced a revised version on October 19, 1943, which called for a period during which Cabinet officers would appear on the floor to answer questions posed by members of the House.[5]

On November 12, 1943, Kefauver was granted floor time to speak in favor of his proposal and to answer questions from interested House members. Rather than presenting his proposal as a guard against conservative committees' abuse of the investigative process, Kefauver stressed the efficiency of having important figures appear before the whole House instead of before several committees, the publicity that Congress would receive through its sessions with Cabinet officers, the fixing of responsibility on specific executive officers, and the general refinement of executive responsibility in response to the need to be prepared to defend policies before the House.[6]

Six days later, on November 18, Secretary of State Cordell Hull addressed a joint session of Congress, the first time since the eighteenth century that a Cabinet officer had appeared before Congress. The break with precedent had the effect of calling even more attention to Kefauver's proposal, although Hull did not, of course, answer questions from the floor.[7]

Opposition to Kefauver's innovation soon developed. The Democratic leadership, afraid that the President could be embarrassed by a question period that got out of control, was cool to the idea. So was the Republican minority, fearful that Democratic control of the House would limit its participation, since all questions had to be cleared by the appropriate committees before being asked of the visiting executive officer.[8] Also, there was the personal opposition of Speaker Sam Rayburn to allowing anyone other than members on the floor of the House.[9]

However, the Kefauver proposal received overwhelming support from executive departments, prominent citizens, respected newspapers, and public opinion in general.[10] Arthur Krock represented the typical editorial attitude of the nation's press when, in the *New York Times,* he approved the Kefauver proposal with the comment, "The need for something better is very great. Mr. Kefauver may not have the answer, or, if he has, he is not likely to be allowed to apply it. But if he has supplied a goad to reform he has done well." [11]

The *Times* formally endorsed the idea on December 6 and 22; noting that the Gallup poll showed 72% in favor and only 7% opposed, the *Times* found it "clear . . . that the arrangement is favored by every consideration of common sense." [12] The *Washington Post* saw the plan as "so sensible and so thoroughly safeguarded that it is hard to see how any Member of Congress could object to it or how most of them could fail actively to favor it. At least it is worth a trial." [13] Over two hundred fifty newspapers endorsed the proposal through their editorial columns.[14] In an effort to enlist even more support among the public, Kefauver polled over two hundred fifty leading citizens, political scientists, and educators. By the end of March 1944 he had received two hundred forty-seven favorable and only three unfavorable replies.[15]

Life magazine gave the Kefauver plan a boost when it attacked Congressional machinery generally and praised the efforts of those who were attempting to reform it:

> Perhaps the most interesting proposal is a resolution introduced by Estes Kefauver, a conscientious young Congressman from Chattanooga, Tennessee. His resolution is so shrewdly drawn that it offends no important Congressional vested interest, and seems to have a chance of passage. Short, simple and nonpartisan, it proposes merely a slight change in the House Rules.[16]

In spite of growing support from the press and public, by March 1944 the Kefauver plan had been effectively killed by the House leadership, especially Speaker Rayburn, who finally convinced Roosevelt to take the position that the matter was one for the House to decide and that it would be improper for him to interfere.[17]

Kefauver introduced and fought for similar changes in 1947,[18] but the issue received little support at that time, even though the Republican-controlled Congress might very well have seen the measure as a device through which to embarrass Democratic President Truman. In spite of Kefauver's failure to secure adoption of the question period, however, the issue had given him widespread publicity as the foremost advocate of a reform that enjoyed heavy support all across the country.

Although no specific reform was as closely associated with his name as the question and answer period for cabinet officers, Kefauver worked consistently for other changes both in congressional procedures and in general federal relationships. One reform he thought necessary because of the role in world affairs assumed by the United States as a result of World War II was a revision of the treaty-making process. Kefauver helped lead the fight in the Judiciary Committee for an amendment giving the House an equal voice with the Senate in regard to treaties. In testimony before the committee on November 29, 1944, Kefauver argued:

> In our modern legislation, no peace treaty can long be effective without other legislation, implementing legislation, to work out the details and to appropriate money. These, of course, require the approval of both Houses of Congress.
>
> Certainly if we can trust a majority of the Congress to declare war, it seems to me that with equal faith in the wisdom and judgment of the majority we can trust it to ratify a peace treaty. The Members of the House of Representatives, being closer to the people, should have a voice in seeing to it that we do not repeat the tragic errors that have been made in the past in connection with the ratifying of peace treaties.[19]

The move for revision of the ratification process made very little headway in spite of all the debate and discussion. As might be expected, the Senate was not anxious to give up any of its deliberative power to the House, placing great value on its protection of the minority from hasty action by the majority, al-

though the filibuster could still have been used to block consideration of a treaty under the Kefauver proposal. The executive
branch, making increasing use of the executive agreement and
thereby avoiding the treaty-making process altogether, gave little
support to a proposal that would theoretically have eased its
difficulties in getting treaty approval from Congress.

What is a "reform" depends, of course, on one's idea of what
is a desirable change. One "reform" that definitely did not enjoy
Kefauver's support was the drive to limit Presidential tenure
which resulted in the Twenty-second Amendment. Whatever the
merits of the amendment, the primary motive behind its adoption was the desire of conservatives in both parties to administer
a belated slap to Franklin Roosevelt.[20] Kefauver fought the
amendment in the Judiciary Committee and on the House floor,
but he and other opponents of the amendment were unable to
block its adoption. His opposition to the amendment was based
on his belief that: "In a democracy the people reign supreme.
Their latest action is always the final one, until they act again.
It is neither good sense nor good democracy to tie their hands
now, so they cannot do what the majority want done in the
future." [21]

A year later, when the fight to block the amendment was
almost over, Kefauver continued to argue for leaving the decision
on a third term to the voters when an actual case arose: "A situation may come hereafter when the best interests of the country
require continuity in the White House. It is best to trust to the
people to make a sensible decision; that is the spirit of our Constitution and our laws." [22]

Kefauver's opposition to the Twenty-second Amendment
did not, however, indicate his satisfaction with the current
presidential election process. He was a strong supporter of measures designed to correct some of the most obvious defects of the
system. After the 1944 election he expressed his concern over the
"attempted revolt of a substantial number of the Texas electors . . . [and] the intention of some of the regular Democratic electors of Louisiana and other states to vote for someone
other than their party's nominee." [23] Four years later, when the

Dixiecrat revolt threatened even greater chaos for the presidential election process, he strongly supported a move in the House to do away with the office of elector and to provide for the mathematical division of each state's electoral vote in the same proportion as the popular vote cast in each state. He felt that the change was necessary not only to make electoral votes reflect the popular will but also "to minimize the result of third party movements" which Kefauver felt would be much weaker if they could not deliver a small bloc of electors willing to bargain for concessions from major party candidates in return for support in the Electoral College.[24]

When Congress moved to reform its own procedures and allowed the LaFollette-Monroney Committee to make suggestions within narrowly defined limits, Kefauver was one of the most enthusiastic supporters of the committee's efforts, calling congressional reform "our number-one domestic problem." He was upset with the delay in adopting the LaFollette-Monroney recommendations, especially since he felt they did not go far enough.[25] When the watered-down "reforms" were finally adopted, Kefauver attacked them as inadequate, feeling that the major problems had been ignored.[26]

While the LaFollette-Monroney recommendations were being debated, Kefauver, along with Jack Levin, a government economic consultant, authored a book on congressional reform, *A Twentieth-Century Congress.*[27] In the introduction, Kefauver explained the purpose of the book:

> There is a great deal of talk in responsible quarters of scrapping the heart of the present limited Reorganization Act. The people of the United States must realize at once the importance of not only holding onto what has been gained, but of going on to complete the job of modernizing what is still antiquated and inadequate congressional machinery. That is why this book was written.[28]

A Twentieth-Century Congress was a comprehensive examination of what Kefauver and Levin felt was wrong with Congress, and, from the range of suggestions and criticisms made by the authors, readers of the best-selling book could only conclude that there was a great deal wrong. Among the most important recommendations was the abolition of the seniority system, to be replaced by the election of committee chairmen by a majority vote of the committees. Even these elected chairmen would have their power curbed.[29] Another set of recommendations dealt with the question of party responsibility. The authors urged a greater relationship between caucus and committee action and saw as desirable a party realignment reflecting a liberal-conservative division.[30] Other recommendations included a four-year term for congressmen, House representation for the District of Columbia, limitations on filibusters in the Senate, voting by electricity to avoid time-consuming roll calls, House-Senate majority approval for treaties, reduction in the number of committees, limitations on lobbyists, and enlarged and better-paid staffs for congressmen.[31] Very little in the book was new, but it was one of the few comprehensive discussions of congressional reform written for and read by the general public, and it brought Kefauver even more notice as a champion of reform. Political scientists generally praised the book and were especially appreciative that a sitting congressman offered an insider's view of the situation. Typical of their reaction was James MacGregor Burns's comment that "surely the problems of Congress would be far less serious if there were more members like Tennessee's Kefauver aware of the defects and anxious to correct them." [32]

It was also during his House career that Kefauver began to manifest his concern over the growing concentration of economic power in the United States, a concern that was to lead him during his Senate years into investigations through which he was to make his most important contributions to the national interest. Throughout his public career, Kefauver's attitude toward economic concentration and the monopolistic practices he felt were likely to follow was based on his fundamental conviction that economic concentration was one of the most powerful threats to the American democratic political system because it resulted in the gradual loss of the people's power "to direct their own economic welfare" and "when they lose this power, they also lose the means to direct their political welfare." [33] By idealizing true intra-industry competition among many relatively small producers during a period when many other economists and politicians were counting more heavily on the restraint resulting from the countervailing influences of big government, big labor, and a few giant concerns in the major industries, Kefauver appeared to many to be an anachronism, a neo-populist whose evaluation of economic concentration was hopelessly distorted by his unrealistic appreciation for a widespread distribution of economic power. However Kefauver may be labeled, and he was far more sophisticated about the problem than his enemies gave him credit for, there were many in Congress and millions across the country who shared his fears about the concentration of economic power.

Kefauver's interest in economic problems attracted him to the Select Committee on Small Business, on which he served in addition to his Judiciary Committee assignment. During the Seventy-ninth Congress, he found a forum in the chairmanship of the Small Business subcommittee to investigate economic concentration in American business. On September 29, 1946, he announced hearings to begin October 15 on steps "to reverse the trend toward economic concentration." To Kefauver the "present trend toward concentration of production and distribution of goods into the hands of fewer and larger corporations constitutes one of the gravest basic issues of our times," threatening "the continued existence of free and independent enterprise, the traditional American way of doing business." Kefauver pointed out that the investigation was "important not only to some 3,000,000 independent merchants, wholesalers and manufacturers, but is vital to all groups—business, labor, agriculture and consumers—who have a stake in the maintenance of a competitive enterprise economy." [34]

The report of Kefauver's subcommittee was so complete that it was still in demand fifteen years later. Wright Patman, the champion populist in the House, termed Kefauver's performance "magnificent." [35] Two general observations made by the report were that economic concentration was continuing due to the deliberate efforts of the largest companies and that the government was materially aiding the concentration through its favoring of big defense contractors. The subcommittee found that the 250 largest manufacturing corporations, which before the war owned 65 per cent of the country's production facilities, operated 80 per cent of all the private facilities built during the war with federal funds. It was also pointed out that 1800 companies had been swallowed up through purchase or merger since 1940, and that eighteen of the very largest corporations had bought 242 smaller concerns. [36]

To slow down the concentration, Kefauver introduced legislation to plug a loophole in the Clayton Act that allowed one company to evade the spirit of the act by acquiring the assets of a competing company without actually merging with it; the affected company might then distribute the money received to its shareholders and go out of business. The Kefauver legislation had the enthusiastic endorsement of the Federal Trade Commission, [37] and Kefauver's own Judiciary Committee issued a strong statement on July 21, 1947, backing the measure:

> The hope that the Clayton Act would arrest the creation of trusts, conspiracies, and monopolies in their incipiency and before consummation has now been blasted. New techniques have been devised to beat the rap. First, the acquiring corporation may simply buy the assets of competitors; or, second, it may buy the controlling stock and then through such control sell the assets to itself. In either case, the present Clayton Act offers no protection to the public. [38]

Nevertheless, the bill was blocked in the Rules Committee. [39] The concern evidenced in Congress for punitive labor legislation was in such contrast to the apathy toward Kefauver's amendment to the Clayton Act that Kefauver was provoked to speak out sharply on the House floor:

. . . is this Congress going to make itself ridiculous in the eyes of history by passing a stringent far-reaching bill against the problem of monopoly in labor, while at the same time ignoring the much greater problem of monopoly in industry?

Monopoly in industry is by far the more serious problem. Monopoly in industry long preceded the emergence of large labor organizations; in fact, it is the very existence of giant industrial corporations which has made almost inevitable the development of large labor organizations and, in turn, of big Government agencies to deal with the two of them.[40]

Kefauver's experience as chairman of the subcommittee investigating economic concentration in American business and his frustrations in trying to get the Clayton Act amended made him feel a greater responsibility to alert Congress and the public to the dangers of inaction. He moved far beyond the role of simply indentifying the problem and began to formulate an over-all approach to the situation. He finally came to the conclusion that nothing would be effective short of a vigorous anti-trust role by the federal government. In an article for *The American Economic Review*, he discussed his consideration and rejection of alternatives to this approach, and emphasized his belief that the choice was not, in the long run, between efficiency and a greater degree of competition; in any event, he indicated that the overriding issue was the preservation of local, smaller units of production which Kefauver believed furnished their communities a moral and spiritual support that could not be matched by giant concerns; in addition, there was always the underlying fear that great masses of people economically dependent on a few industrial giants would lose their political independence as a result of their loss of economic independence. His immediate recommendations were greater appropriations to support larger and better-trained staffs for the Federal Trade Commission and the Antitrust Division of the Justice Department, new legislation to furnish the basis for prosecution of the industrial giants, and greater use of publicity of the problem in order to educate Congress and the public.[41]

Kefauver's classification as a liberal because of his attitude toward big business was reinforced by the consistent support he gave throughout both his House and Senate years to the rights of labor and the defense of civil rights and civil liberties—except where race was involved. His attitude toward the protection of the civil rights of Negroes underwent continual modification throughout his career, both in response to the need, in the presidential campaigns, to adjust to a national constituency and as a result of the changes which were affecting every American's attitude toward Negro rights. Kefauver had always supported an end to the poll tax, which, although it affected both poor whites and poor Negroes, was basically a device to keep Negroes from voting. That opposition to the poll tax was still a politically dangerous position in most of the South in the 1940s is indicated by the fact that as late as 1947, only six (including Kefauver and four other Tennesseans) of 105 Dixie bloc congressmen voted to abolish it.[42] Another annual civil rights battle, from the 1940s until the Johnson Administration, was fought over proposals to establish a Fair Employment Practices Commission to end racial discrimination in employment. Kefauver strongly opposed the FEPC during his House years. In a letter to a constituent, he expressed his opinion that "a great deal more harm than good would be done by trying to upset long-established conditions and customs in the Southland."[43] On the House floor, he was even more emphatic:

> The FEPC is, in my opinion, a dangerous step toward regimentation. It is of doubtful constitutionality and it certainly violates the rights of the employers of our Nation. It simply would not work—especially in the South. Any effort to put such a law in operation would cause widespread difficulty which would be very detrimental to the Nation.[44]

Similarly, Kefauver opposed anti-lynching legislation, another perennial civil rights question. He attacked such legislation as an unjustified encroachment on the rights of the States. Everybody abhors lynching, and of course lynching is murder under every State law. The adoption of the bill would be a step toward making every crime a Federal offense and removing the interest and responsibility of local people in the prevention of crime.[45]

In a general evaluation of laws designed to protect Negro rights, Kefauver exhibited the paternalism so typical of Southern congressmen:

There is no real demand for antisegregation laws in the South. The Negroes of the South are not interested in this kind of legislation. They want schools, better economic opportunity, and houses. I hope their lot in these respects can be improved. It would not be in the interest of their own welfare to fan the fires of passion and disunity by espousal of Federal nonsegregation laws.[46]

When race was not involved, however, Kefauver could be counted on by the liberal forces in the House. He was a consistent opponent of the House Committee on Un-American Activities. In 1945 he opposed making the committee a permanent one but then voted for funds to operate the committee once it was decided by the House to continue it.[47] In 1946, however, he voted against the appropriation for the committee, being one of the only two from the Dixie bloc to do so,[48] and thereafter exhibited an open hostility to the committee because of his disgust with its abuse of civil liberties. In key votes revealing members' attitudes toward the committee, Kefauver voted against striking Rules Committee Chairman Adolph Sabath's remarks that HUAC "employees should themselves be investigated" and also voted against a contempt citation for the Anti-Fascist Refugee Committee.[49] In each case, Kefauver stood alone in the Tennessee delegation in his opposition. On March 9, 1948, however, in the middle of his Senate race, Kefauver voted for the HUAC appropriation.[50]

As the anti-communist hysteria gathered momentum, Kefauver stood firm against the various "loyalty bills" and was one of only thirty-six to oppose the consideration of a 1946 bill providing for a loyalty Review Board that would be prosecutor, judge, and jury of those whose loyalty was questioned. The bill provided the accused no opportunity to confront or cross-examine those charging disloyalty and used such vague standards as "sympathetic association" and "derogatory information." There was no provision for court review. Kefauver's motion to recommit the bill to provide for such review of dismissals lost 133 to 248 even though confusion over the bill prompted even a majority of the Mississippi delegation to vote with the liberal forces. The most important of the loyalty proposals was the so-called Mundt-Nixon anti-communist bill, which Kefauver publicly opposed but did not vote on when it passed May 19, 1948, in the middle of his Senate race.[51]

Kefauver was a consistent friend of labor even though he did vote to override Roosevelt's 1943 veto of the Smith-Connally Anti-Strike Bill. In a clearly pro-labor vote in 1945, Kefauver supported protecting the packing-shed workers under the War Labor Board even though a majority of both Republicans and Democrats opposed labor on this question. Kefauver also opposed the Labor Disputes Bill, forerunner of the Taft-Hartley Act, which passed the House in early 1946 only to be vetoed by President Truman. Kefauver was among the minority managing to sustain the veto. Later in 1946, Kefauver voted against excluding agricultural labor from National Labor Relations Board jurisdiction. When the Taft-Hartley Act was considered in 1947, Kefauver opposed it, voting against it in all forms and being among the small group unsuccessfully seeking to sustain Truman's veto.[52]

Throughout his House years, Kefauver was a strong supporter of Roosevelt and Truman foreign policy positions and vigorously backed Truman on aid to Greece and Turkey and on the Marshall Plan. He had no sympathy for Henry Wallace's attacks on the Administration in 1947 and 1948. Although in 1945 Kefauver had been close enough to Wallace to send him a note inviting him to "come up here and have a gamc real soon," [53] by 1947 Kefauver was openly attacking "extremists" like Wallace who were questioning the Truman containment policy and who were urging greater efforts at co-operation with the Soviet Union:

> Wallace is doing a lot of general talk about peace. He has no monopoly on desiring peace. Both Democrats and Republicans want to avert war. Many of us feel that the Marshall plan is the best and in fact the only available way to establish order in the world. It is interesting to note that the Marshall plan is being opposed by a coalition of extremely conservative isolationists like Senator Taft on the one hand, and extremists like Wallace with Communist backing on the other.[54]

While by 1948 Kefauver was the most liberal congressman of the 105 from the eleven Southern states, he was securely in the mainstream of House Democrats as a whole and was not considered enough of a political deviant to arouse the antagonism of conservative Southern Democrats, who could tolerate much as long as the proper positions were taken on civil rights issues. Even the Crump-McKellar forces, who were aware of Kefauver's record as only political enemies can be, did not consider Kefauver's extraordinary record as a liberal Southerner exceptional enough to attempt to defeat him on the issues until 1948, when growing Kefauver strength forced them to throw everything available into the effort against him.

chapter iii

COONSKIN CRUSADE, 1948

The postwar period was a time of soul-searching and self-evaluation for Kefauver that eventually led to his decision to seek greater opportunities and challenges in his career of public service than his House seat was able to provide. The result was his famous campaign for the Senate in 1948.

In the midst of this period of reflection about his political future, the Kefauver family made its own unique contribution to the postwar baby boom, as Nancy and Estes had two additions to their family in nineteen months. Their first child, Eleanor (known as Linda), had been born in 1940, but as the years passed it appeared that the Kefauvers would have no more children, and they adopted a son, whom they named David Estes, on April 3, 1946. Within the next year, however, Nancy unexpectedly became pregnant, and a second daughter, Diane, was born December 19, 1947.[1]

Kefauver also had every reason to be proud of his record in public life. He had established a reputation in the House as a hard-working and conscientious congressman, whose ties with both the Democratic leadership and the Dixie bloc were cordial enough to ensure a high degree of effectiveness on behalf of a district which had given him overwhelming support in every election. In addition, his support for labor and civil liberties as well as his efforts on behalf of congressional reform and the curbing of

economic concentration had brought him praise and respect outside the halls of Congress. In 1946, for example, *Collier's* magazine selected him as one of the ten best members of the House.[2]

But by 1947 Kefauver had decided that he would either
move up to the Senate or return to private law practice.[3] This
decision was the result of his determination that he had fulfilled
his potential in the House and that further advancement in that
body depended principally upon moving slowly up the seniority
ladder. Kefauver was only forty-four and, like many young, able,
and ambitious congressmen, was too restless to wait the ten to
twenty years for the greater power and responsibility in the
House that come only through time.

Kefauver's decision to seek the Democratic nomination for
the Senate in 1948 after he had decided against such a race in
1942 and 1946 was also based on his belief that conditions were
much more favorable to his candidacy than they had been on the
two previous occasions. In the first place, the Crump-McKellar
organization was saddled with a weak candidate for governor, the
incumbent, James Nance McCord, who had survived a relatively
stiff challenge from absentee Gordon Browning in 1946 but who
was facing a serious threat from a returned Browning in 1948.
The unfavorable reaction to a sales tax passed at McCord's request indicated that the Crump candidate for governor would
not lead any organizational sweep in the primary and, indeed,
might very well be defeated. Another factor influencing Kefauver's decision was the weakness of the expected Crump candidate
for the Senate, incumbent Senator Tom Stewart, who had been
re-elected in 1942 only because of a landslide in Crump's Shelby
County. Stewart had done nothing since 1942 to improve his lackluster image, and Kefauver believed that Stewart was especially
vulnerable on the issues. Still another straw in the wind was the
political unrest caused by the return of thousands of veterans
who were exhibiting little patience with machine practices on
the part of those who had stayed home while the veterans had
risked their lives fighting overseas. Even in counties not taken
over by angry veterans' groups, there was a feeling that the new

and widespread interest in political affairs awakened by the veterans had made traditional electoral manipulations a thing of the past. The extent to which this interest would prove a threat to the Crump-McKellar organization and, therefore, a source of strength to Kefauver remained to be seen, but in any event the prevailing mood was one of growing dissatisfaction with the methods of political bosses in general.

On the other hand, there were also developments during 1946–47 which tended to discourage a candidacy by a liberal such as Kefauver. The 1946 election had returned a Republican Congress and had demonstrated the nation's conservative mood. The anti-labor feeling and the anti-communist hysteria seemed to make a record such as Kefauver's especially vulnerable to distortion by the opposition. In addition, the popularity of President Truman sank lower and lower during 1947, and Kefauver's support for most Administration policies seemed to be flying in the face of national (and, presumably, state) trends. If 1948 appeared to be a continuation of the 1946 reaction, it made more sense for Kefauver to postpone his Senate bid until 1952, when McKellar would be in his eighties and expected to retire and when the country might have worked its way out of the conservatism that seemed both predominant and rising in 1946–47.

But, after weighing the advantages and disadvantages, Kefauver decided to go for broke in 1948. He took the unusual step of announcing his candidacy on November 9, 1947, making it one of the earliest announcements for office in Tennessee political history.[4]

The three pledges made by Kefauver in his announcement were to become lost amid the false issues and attacks on personalities that characterized the campaign, but they demonstrated Kefauver's attempt to wage a positive campaign on the real issues. In his statement, Kefauver emphasized that he would (1) "proceed on the conviction that peace is attainable"; (2) "keep on fighting hard for T. V. A. Tennesseans will be heard by a Tennessee Senator in the T. V. A. legislative battles which lie ahead"; and (3) "work diligently toward" reducing "the cost of living and" stabilizing "our economy against ruinous inflation." He touched only briefly on what was to be a major charge against him:

> I have always espoused the cause of the middle-class citizen. This course has brought and will bring charges that I am a "liberal"; that I am a "red"; that I am a "left winger"; and perhaps other political designations. Mislabeling the bottle never changes the contents. There are a few who define "Communist" as "anyone who opposes their candidates"—in other words, anyone who opposes Government by political dictation. . . . I have never believed in and I am unalterably against any "ism" except AMERICANISM.[5]

When pressed on the reason for the early announcement, Kefauver admitted that "I'm not well known to the average voter outside my own district. I want time to get acquainted." [6] Not the least of his problems was seen as having his unusual name register with the voters across the state. He discovered during the campaign, however, that "an odd name, once learned, is more easily remembered than a plain one." [7]

Within twenty-four hours, Crump had announced to the press his reaction to the Kefauver statement: "The New York headquarters of the CIO no doubt told him to announce early. Personally, I'd as soon vote for Marcantonio as vote for Kefauver." [8] Vito Marcantonio, American Labor party congressman from New York and faithful fellow-traveler, became one of the most famous political figures of the 1940s because of the lengths to which conservative political candidates would go to prove that their liberal opponents were soft on communism because they had "voted with Marcantonio." The guilt-by-association technique, perfected by Richard Nixon in his early California campaigns, was sometimes pushed to such ridiculous extremes that even votes on procedural questions such as recesses and adjournments were examined to arrive at the highest possible percentage of agreement. It was true, however, that liberals were found voting with Marcantonio on many issues for the simple reason that liberal positions were frequently more acceptable to Marcantonio that were those of conservatives, and he voted with the liberals as the lesser of the evils. As Kefauver pointed out, "If Marcantonio votes for TVA, I'm not going to vote against it just because he voted for it." [9] In addition, Marcantonio aligned himself with the Democratic leadership on procedural matters, thus giving Republicans an issue on that score. The New Yorker, therefore, became an especially familiar name wherever a liberal incumbent faced opposition from a conservative, a development that much amused Marcantonio, who enjoyed warm personal, if not political, relationships with both conservatives and liberals in Congress. Very early in the campaign, the press sought an evaluation of the Tennessee situation from Marcantonio, who disappointed the conservatives with a defense of Kefauver against the charge that he was a leftist:

> Estes Kefauver is basically a conservative southern Democrat. He does not share my philosophy. One basic test is the capitalist system. Kefauver believes in it. He would work and fight for it. I believe in a planned economy. . . . [A]lthough I have respect for Kefauver's honesty, personal integrity, and ability, I would say that at rock bottom he is a conservative. Not a reactionary, you understand, but a conservative. By my standards he could not be termed a liberal.[10]

In the early months of the campaign, however, Kefauver's problem was not refuting charges that he was a leftist but, rather, making himself known across the state. One of the familiar stories of Tennessee political folklore relates how Kefauver sought the support of Silliman Evans, editor of the *Nashville Tennessean* and leader of the anti-Crump-McKellar forces in the state. Evans reportedly told Kefauver that "I'll support you on one condition. The condition is that you go out and make yourself known in the state—that you shake at least 500 hands a day between now and election." [11] What actually happened was a little different. The anti-Crump forces were so anxious to have Kefauver run that they would have supported him under any circumstances. Indeed, their biggest fear was that Kefauver would become too comfortable in his House seat and refuse to make the race, a fear reinforced by their failure to get him to seek a Senate nomination in 1942 and 1946. It is true that Evans played an important part in developing what was to become a Kefauver campaign trademark, the whirlwind, handshaking, grass roots tour designed to put Kefauver in personal touch with as many voters as possible. Kefauver himself remembered Evans's advice as: "You'll get the managers by and by if you make [an] impression on enough people. You've got to conduct a personalized campaign, and shake hands with 10,000 people between now and June 1st when you begin your tour." [12]

Kefauver began his campaign with the realization that he could expect (and, in fact, did receive) little help from the professional politicians across the state and therefore "set out to form a campaign organization of people without a political past." [13] In the campaign, his manager was only thirty-two and his most trusted assistant was twenty-two. Heavy emphasis was placed on an appeal to women voters, since, as Kefauver explained, "I take no stock in the idea that women vote just as their menfolk say. I think there are about as many cases where the men vote the way their wives want them to. Women have political courage and independence, and these are qualities I like." [14]

A longtime friend, Mrs. Tom Ragland, resigned as an officer of the League of Women Voters to be Kefauver's women's chairman. A vice-president of the Tennessee Federation of Women's Clubs resigned that post to become Mrs. Ragland's assistant. The form letter sent out by the women's division was keyed to the apolitical attitudes of the average female voter: "Here it is spring again, and the jonquils are in bloom, and no one seems to be thinking much about politics. But I have two children and am very much interested in the worsening world situation. . . ." [15]

The Kefauver organization was built practically from the ground up. Kefauver made a preliminary tour of the state during the winter of 1947–48, seeking to find workers to run the campaign in each local area. One method of making contacts across the state was to review his University of Tennessee yearbooks and then locate the people he knew. A more informal way of establishing himself in an area was to introduce himself to a doctor or merchant, talk for a while, and then ask for introductions to likely prospects. All the while Nancy and aides recorded useful information about the people met. If possible, Kefauver would address a local civic club or speak to an assembly at a nearby high school. In these early months, Kefauver kept away from purely political topics and concentrated on introducing himself to people who could help him later in the campaign. As the campaign heated up, Kefauver's speeches and conversations became more political, but he continued his approach of going up and down as many streets as possible, trying to meet personally as many voters as possible. Soon thereafter, a short letter would be sent to each person met, reinforcing the personal contact that became the trademark of the Kefauver campaign style. Slowly, a comprehensive file on each county and important town was developed.[16]

One of the most important areas in the Kefauver planning was Boss Crump's own Shelby County. In Memphis, Kefauver had two powerful allies from the very start—*Press-Scimitar* editor Edward J. Meeman, who had been fighting Crump almost single-handedly for years, and J. Charles Poe, a lumberman who had worked under George Fort Milton at the *Chattanooga News* during the *News*-Kefauver campaigns of the 1930s and had served with Kefauver in Governor Prentice Cooper's cabinet. These two men invited one hundred independent-minded Memphis leaders to the Hotel Peabody; only forty attended, and six agreed to serve on a Citizens' Committee for Estes Kefauver. The most important of these was Edmund Orgill, head of a wholesale hardware and implement firm and a former president of the Memphis Chamber of Commerce, who agreed to serve as chairman of the Kefauver group. After some organizational work by the committee, five hundred people paid two dollars each to attend a pro-Kefauver banquet. The AFL and CIO in Memphis joined the campaign effort and women's groups began to mobilize support for "Schools for Politics," "Schools for Watchers," and "Clean Election Clubs." The Kefauver groups pushed the sale of "Kefauver Baby Bonds"—$2.00 contributions to the campaign. One lumberman advertised the bonds with the slogan, "Is your independence worth two dollars?" [17]

It was no small thing for a Memphis businessman to oppose Crump. As one unidentified man told a *Chattanooga Times* reporter, "they might find it necessary to repair the sidewalk in front of your place of business. They could keep it torn up for six months and when that was over they probably could find something else to do." Another pointed out some of the benefits of Crump rule: "I keep out of politics. . . . We have a good city and county administration. The city is well run and there are no thieves in the courthouse. We have a low tax rate, good streets and the lowest insurance rates in the country." [18]

Meeman and the *Press-Scimitar* managed to minimize harassment by Crump because of a joint publishing arrangement with the pro-Crump *Commercial Appeal,* and both were owned by the Scripps-Howard chain.[19] The Kefauver committee was not so protected, however, and, according to Kefauver, they "received threatening telephone calls and their pasts were searched for some damaging information." [20]

The Senate race was thrown into confusion soon after Kefauver's announcement when it became apparent that the Crump-McKellar organization was not satisfied with Senator Tom Stewart as its candidate for the Senate seat he then occupied. Judge John Mitchell of Cookeville announced as a candidate, and there was speculation that Stewart might retire in favor of Mitchell. But Stewart showed no interest in dropping out and announced that he would seek re-election. Therefore, by Christmas 1947 there were three serious candidates in the field, and Crump had not yet announced his support for either Mitchell or Stewart. A cursory evaluation seemed to favor Kefauver's chances in a three-man race, especially since the principal backers of both Mitchell and Stewart were drawn from the Crump-McKellar organization, and it seemed likely that they would split the organization forces and thereby nominate Kefauver.[21]

Kefauver, feeling fairly confident, commissioned a poll by Carroll Moore of Princeton to measure his support among the Tennessee electorate. He was shocked when the poll revealed Stewart in the lead with 37 per cent, Mitchell a distant second with 21 per cent, and Kefauver trailing badly with only 13 per cent. To Kefauver, "the findings . . . were so shattering that I did not show them to my campaign manager because I did not want to discourage him further." He even swore Moore, an old friend, "to secrecy and carefully stored the only known copy of the survey in my office safe. I wouldn't even tell . . . Nancy about it." [22] If Kefauver appeared to run scared in the campaign, it was because he was influenced by the poll that his staff never saw.

After giving up on convincing Stewart to withdraw from the race, Crump, in April 1948, threw his support to Judge Mitchell, although admitting, "We have never seen him, never met him." Crump decided to drop Stewart and support Mitchell for several reasons: Stewart had given only lukewarm support to the TVA, which Crump strongly supported; Stewart had been an ineffective senator who had accomplished little in his ten years in the Senate; and there was a good chance that Stewart might lose, and Crump wanted a stronger candidate. Mitchell appeared to Crump to be that stronger candidate because of the good record he had made as a judge and because he was a veteran of World Wars I and II in a year in which Crump felt a war record, which neither Stewart nor Kefauver had, would be a most valuable political asset.[23]

It was unclear at first what effect the Crump move would have on Kefauver's chances; there was a danger that Stewart might become the anti-Crump candidate in the minds of the public. Since most of the old-line machines continued to back Stewart even after Crump's defection, it was possible that Stewart might have both organization support and the anti-boss issue. Stewart had his problems, too, however. Mitchell, while making a serious bid for the nomination, clearly enjoyed less support than either Stewart or Kefauver. Since Stewart viewed Kefauver and himself as the major contenders, there was always the possibility that Crump might come back over to Stewart if he came to believe that Mitchell had no chance. But if this did not happen, Stewart's attempt to refrain from attacks on Crump would only serve to hand the anti-Crump issue to Kefauver.

Kefauver clearly had the initiative on the vital issue of support for TVA. Both Mitchell and Stewart were forced to answer charges that they had helped or would help McKellar undermine TVA. Stewart had a record of support in the Senate for the controversial McKellar amendments to hamstring TVA, and Mitchell had received the endorsement of McKellar, who followed Crump's lead in dumping his junior colleague. McKellar, who had an intense dislike for Kefauver anyway, bitterly responded to the indirect attacks on him made by Kefauver when discussing Stewart's and Mitchell's shortcomings as defenders of TVA. On the Senate floor, McKellar emotionally read one charge after another made by Kefauver, seeking to answer each one and ending his explanations with statements such as "I am sorry we have a man in Congress from Tennessee who would make such a false statement." In commenting on Kefauver's defense of TVA accounting, which McKellar had been attacking, the senior senator sarcastically asked:

> Is it not remarkable how much information and knowledge a man acquires when he serves in Congress a little while and becomes a candidate for United States Senator? Kefauver knows no more about how this money has been used than he knows about the duties of Senator or Representative, and certainly his knowledge of the duties of the services in both these places is infinitesimal.[24]

Kefauver urged the voters not to "vote merely against my opponents. I want you to vote for me." But he continually contrasted his support for TVA with the McKellar associations of his two opponents:

> For almost ten years I have made TVA my principal business in Congress. My background has been secured by long study, sym-

pathetic understanding and legislative experience. In the U. S. Senate I will put a little more of Tennessee in the Tennessee Valley Authority, and Tennesseans will not have to look to Alabama and Kentucky for a senator to speak their piece against the enemies of TVA.[25]

On the other hand, Mitchell, speaking before the Knoxville Jaycees, was embarrassed by the question of whether he would support McKellar in his schemes to control TVA. Mitchell was obviously disconcerted and finally, after stammering and hesitating, angrily replied: "Let's leave personalities out of this. I'm not in favor of impairing the efficiency of TVA." He refused to answer further questions on the subject, of vital interest to Knoxville, TVA headquarters.[26] As for Stewart, Kefauver continually reviewed Stewart's co-operation with McKellar and charged that the two of them gave the impression that Tennessee was opposed to TVA:

> Senator Stewart cannot be depended on to support TVA because he has never consistently done so. At one time or other, Senator Stewart has supported every amendment to impede and sabotage TVA. He voted to make a spoils system of TVA by requiring Senate confirmation of its top officials; he voted for the McKellar amendment which takes away its revolving fund; he protested and delayed for 100 days the building of the Douglas Dam in East Tennessee; he opposed the nomination of David Lilienthal as its chairman; and he voted against the confirmation of Gordon Clapp as Mr. Lilienthal's successor.[27]

Kefauver charged that Stewart and McKellar had played into the hands of the private power lobby, which would benefit from Stewart's remaining in office. But the lobby feared him, Kefauver argued:

> because they know the staunch fight I have put up in defense of TVA. The only ugly name I've enjoyed being called is when Purcell Smith wrote me a letter calling me a demagogue for supporting the TVA. If that's demagogery, then I'm a demagogue and

you can put it down that if I'm elected to the U. S. Senate I'll make this private power lobbyist earn his $65,000 a year.[28]

Kefauver also revived the charge of nepotism against Stewart, pointing out that he had had fourteen members of his family on the government payroll since he went to the Senate. Stewart's son had received a government salary while attending Sewanee University—a fact whose discovery had been an issue in the 1942 primary when Stewart had narrowly escaped defeat.[29]

Early in June, however, the campaign took a turn which obscured the roles of Stewart and Mitchell, and made the contest seem to be one between Kefauver and Crump. This development had its origin in the decision of the organization, made many months before, to exploit to the fullest Kefauver's liberal voting record in the House. Will Gerber, Crump's trusted lieutenant, handled the anti-Kefauver campaign and in February had written Senator McKellar for information to use against Kefauver:

> We are very anxious to get everything we possibly can to show that Kefauver has been voting right along with Marc Antonio [sic]. Would you be kind enough to get someone to check the record as far back as possible and get us a list of Bills passed in the House in which Kefauver and Marc Antonio's votes were identical. Also any other information you can give us that can be used in the ensuing campaign on Kefauver.[30]

Beginning June 10 the results of the investigation into Kefauver's record were announced in full-page ads printed in the principal newspapers of the state and paid for and signed by Crump himself.[31] The first ad and the reaction to it were easily the most important developments during the campaign and probably decided the election in favor of Kefauver. The ad is a classic example of a political smear and might have proved very damaging to the Kefauver campaign but for the clever way in which the Kefauver forces used the attack to Kefauver's advantage. In the ad, Crump sought to show that "Kefauver has been a darling of the Communists and Communist sympathizers ever since he became a member of Congress from the Chattanooga District in September 1939. His idol has been Vito Marcantonio, the oxblood-red Communist Congressman from the 18th New York Congressional District." Most of the House votes which drew Crump's fire involved the House Committee on Un-American Activities. Crump also attacked Kefauver's opposition to the filibuster and his speech before an alleged communist-front group in New York City. The ad made no attempt at subtlety, breaking up an intemperate text with boldface headings such as "How Red Is Red," "A Shameful Record," "Marcantonio's Buddy," "Championed Communist Witnesses," "Warm Supporter of FEPC," "Kefauver Slogan—'America Last,'" "As Vito Marcantonio Votes, So Votes Estes," and "Defending the 'Reds.'" Crump compared Kefauver's "pro-Communist" voting record in the face of Kefauver's denials that he did vote the party line to:

> the pet coon that puts its foot in an open drawer in your room, but invariably turns its head while its foot is feeling around in the drawer. The coon hopes, through its cunning by turning its head, he will deceive any onlookers as to where his foot is and what it is into. If the coon could talk, he would say: "You have me wrong—I have made a mistake, look at my turned head. I am sorry about my foot. I couldn't see what I was doing." [32]

Although both Stewart and Mitchell had already labeled Kefauver's record as "pink," their attacks were mild compared with the Crump ad, which reportedly cost the Memphis boss $7000 and was as vicious as any in American political history. Kefauver's first reaction was to joke that "The only thing Red about me is my redheaded wife," [33] but he was sufficiently shaken by the attack to make immediate plans to counter the effect of the ad by answering the charges in a special radio speech on June 14, copies of which were provided his workers for distribution all over the state. In the speech, Kefauver not only sought to refute the charges leveled against him by Crump but also to seize the anti-Crump issue by making the Memphis boss, rather than the Kefauver record, the major issue of the campaign. Of the ad, Kefauver said:

> This attack is neither unusual nor unexpected. It isn't unusual because Mr. Crump designates automatically anyone who opposes his candidates as either a "Red," a "Communist," a "tool of the C. I. O.," a "Thief," or some other type of blackguard. It isn't unexpected because I made the decision to run for the United States Senate here in Chattanooga; my decision was not made, nor was it announced, from Mr. Crump's Office.

Kefauver called on Crump, Mitchell, and Stewart to stop the name-calling and "stand up on their hind-legs on the same platform with me and discuss the real issues of this campaign." Recalling his many offers to debate Stewart and Mitchell, Kefauver noted that they had not accepted and "I believe that none of them have the moral courage to stand before the people and try to substantiate their accusations against me. . . . It is not good sportsmanship to make ugly accusations against a person and then refuse to meet the accused in open debate before the people."

Kefauver reminded his audience that he had sought "to make this campaign on a positive basis. . . . I had no desire to be an 'anti-'candidate. . . . Mr. Crump didn't matter to me when I announced. . . . I never uttered his name until he pulled the string" (he had had Mitchell attack Kefauver on an issue that required a mention of Crump in order to answer the attack).

Kefauver then reviewed the prestigious support he had received in Crump's own Shelby County, especially the six-man executive board: "Does anyone think that any *one* of these six, let alone *all six* would support a candidate who is the 'darling of the communists,' or anybody's 'pet coon'?"

In a reference that contained the seeds of the great public relations coup of the campaign, Kefauver commented on Crump's coon analogy:

> This animal—the most American of all animals—has been defamed. You wouldn't find a coon in Russia. It is one of the

cleanest of all animals; it is one of the most courageous. . . . A coon . . . can lick a dog four times its size; he is somewhat of a "giant-killer" among the animals. Yes, the coon is all American. Davy Crockett, Sam Houston, James Robertson and all of our great men of that era in Tennessee History wore the familiar ring-tailed, coon-skin cap. Mr. Crump defames me—but worse than that he defames the coon, the all American animal. We coons can take care of ourselves. I may be a pet coon, but I "ain't" Mr. Crump's pet coon.

Kefauver then sought to answer each of Crump's charges that he had voted the communist line. He listed the important bills affecting national defense or postwar foreign policy that he had supported and Marcantonio had opposed: lend lease, selective service, repeal of the arms embargo, the Greek-Turkish loan, and the European Recovery Program. Kefauver also explained his attitude toward the House Un-American Activities Committee:

Each year I have judged the Committee by the kind of work I thought it was doing. On occasions the Committee has taken mailing lists and made the list public with the charge they were subversive, even though the people involved had nothing to do with their names getting on the list. At times when it was smearing the names of innocent people, when its Chairman was using its file for personal purposes—making speeches and writing books for pay—and when its payroll was loaded down with relatives of the Chairman (relatives who performed no service), I voted against the Committee and against additional funds for its operation. When I thought the Committee was doing good work, I voted for it—when it didn't, I voted against it.

Kefauver's vote against citing "sixteen Communistic witnesses" for contempt of the committee for not bringing in books and records for HUAC's inspection was explained by Kefauver as a defense of civil liberties:

I could not, as a lawyer sworn to defend the Constitution, vote to punish people for contempt for failure to produce records when they did not have the records and most of them had never seen them. Especially is this true where no charge had been made against them and the Committee had failed to pursue to a conclusion the right given it by the House to require the president of the organization who had the records to produce them. . . . [T]his action clearly violated their Constitutional rights and liberties. . . . Think of placing an American citizen in jail for failure to produce a record he had never seen, or had no control over. That may be Mr. Crump's or Senator Stewart's idea of justice; it is not mine.

As for Kefauver's opposition to a loyalty bill sponsored by Representative B. Carroll Reece, reactionary Tennessee Republican, Kefauver again explained his concern for civil liberties:

The purpose of this bill was good but as presented it was too bitter a pill to swallow. It set up a Board to try all government employees on the question of their loyalty. The Board has a right to discharge as disloyal any employee without making a charge against them, without giving them a chance to face and answer their accuser. Furthermore, it prohibited any appeal from the decision of the Board. I felt it violated many sacred rights of the people involved. . . . Afterwards Congressman Reece, the sponsor, told me that he recognized that my position was sound. The bill was in such bad shape that it was vigorously attacked by most of the press of the nation and the Senate did not even think it worthy of consideration. . . . Imagine defaming a man's name, ruining him for life, placing a stigma on him and his family without giving him a chance of knowing who accuses him, what the accusations are, and with no chance of appeal. I don't like to believe that Mr. Crump or Senator Stewart would want to so flagrantly violate rules of fair play or a man's protection under the Constitution. But maybe I am wrong.

The extent to which even Kefauver was influenced by the supposed anti-labor mood of the country was demonstrated by his defensive statement that "I voted against organized labor more frequently than I have voted for it"; he then listed the anti-labor legislation he had supported, pointing out, in an uncharacteristic *non sequitur* almost admitting the validity of guilt-by-association, that "Marcantonio has always voted with the position of organized labor." But, Kefauver said, he had tried to be more objective and had opposed the Taft-Hartley Act because he feared it "might be used to destroy the organized labor movement and I did not want this to happen."

Concluding the broadcast, Kefauver declared:

> This attempted smear business does not bother me. Looking back over the history of our country one will find that on almost every occasion when a public leader tried to do something for the welfare of the plain people, he was smeared and called ugly names by the opposition. . . . But regardless of what Mr. Crump and Senator Stewart, and the Republican press (which is carrying the burden of the Stewart campaign) say, I am going to continue to vote to uphold the rights guaranteed to the American citizens under the Constitution; and, I am going to continue to work for the betterment of the average American. This is the course I think I must follow if our country is going to remain strong and free.[34]

Kefauver's counterattack on Crump probably would have attracted little attention except that it was the beginning of a shift in campaign emphasis from Mitchell and Stewart to Crump himself. From that time on, Kefauver sought to present himself as the means of breaking Crump's control of Tennessee politics. Overnight, the coon referred to by Crump in his famous ad became the symbol of the Kefauver campaign in 1948 and was closely associated with his image (much to the distress of some of his associates who thought it unsophisticated) during the remainder of his life. In order to exploit the coon as a campaign gimmick, the Kefauver campaign located a live coon and took it around with Kefauver whenever he spoke. Kefauver would introduce the coon to the crowd by pointing out that "this is a pedigreed West Tennessee coon. Notice his big bushy tail. This coon has rings in his tail, but I want you to remember I have no ring in my nose." [35]

The live coon became a pest and a bother, not only because of the routine problems involved in hauling it around but also because it became nervous and upset as a result of the noise and applause at each campaign stop. It was becoming dangerous to handle, and when a wildlife expert warned Kefauver's campaign manager, Charles Neese, that the animal would die if kept confined, the coon was released to avoid a public relations setback to the campaign; the decision was made to replace it with a coonskin cap.[36] It is unclear who first thought of Kefauver's wearing a cap, although he had mentioned the tradition in his radio speech answering the Crump attack. One of Kefauver's friends, George Clark, president of the Pioneer Bank in Chattanooga, whose symbol for years had been a coonskin cap, sent Kefauver one after reading the Crump ad. In any event, the cap was at first considered a poor substitute for the live coon, and Kefauver's first appearance in the cap at a luncheon meeting of his Memphis supporters was over the objection of *Press-Scimitar* editor Meeman, who considered the cap undignified. Neese threatened to resign unless the cap was worn, and Meeman reluctantly acquiesced. Newspaper photographers had been alerted to look for a picture they would not want to miss when Kefauver began to speak. As Neese remembered it:

> Nancy passed the coonskin under the table to the Congressman [Kefauver], as he stood to speak. He put the cap on 'midst the flashing of photographers' bulbs. There was a startled silence; a slight snickering; then tremendous applause and laughter. . . . The candidate's first words: "I may be a 'pet coon,' but I'm not Mister Crump's 'pet coon' " resulted in thunderous applause and wild laughter—and another rousing standing ovation! [37]

The immediate and overwhelmingly favorable reaction across the state to the coonskin cap symbol surprised even the staunchest Kefauver backers; as a campaign gimmick, it ranks as one of the most successful in American political history. Not only did it continually call attention to Kefauver's independence of Crump, it was a unique identification with the idealized democratic days of the frontier, when political machines such as Crump's were supposedly unheard of. It also served to blunt the soft-on-communism charge, since what could be more American than a coonskin cap? In the less than two months left in the campaign, Kefauver made an incredible 195 appearances in the cap as he traveled across the state. Kefauver backers also began wearing coonskin caps, made mostly from the limited supply of racoon coats still around from the 1920s; when that supply was exhausted, Kefauver feared that the fad might get out of control and threaten the racoon population; so, he issued an appeal that racoons not be slaughtered just to make caps.[38]

Kefauver's posing in the cap became a ritual before every speech. He called it "a sort of striptease in reverse. The audience would start chanting 'Put it on,' until I'd have to stick the coonskin cap on my head and give a big grin before they'd let me go on with my speech." [39] Then Kefauver would launch into an attack on Crump, turning the communism issue against the Memphis leader:

> Let's examine this business of Communism: Communism is a form of dictatorship under which the state controls everything. It is a relentless, one-man rulership where difference of opinion is not tolerated; where people have no liberties, no rights, no sayso in the election of their officials; where free enterprise is handicapped; where the citizens are intimidated, placed in fear; where reprisals are made for any opposition they might show to the ruthless dictatorship. I have always worked hard and fought hard to prevent this sort of thing. Now with this definition of Communism, whom does the term fit—Estes Kefauver or E. H. Crump? [40]

One of Crump's biggest mistakes in the campaign was trying to smear too many opponents at the same time. It tended to undermine the effect of his attacks on any one opponent. In Kefauver's case, there is evidence that Crump realized that he had overplayed his hand. A Memphis labor leader traditionally friendly to Crump visited the boss to ask him to moderate the anti-Kefauver attacks. When Crump replied that Kefauver was a radical, the labor leader reminded him that Crump himself had once been called the "red snapper." "You're right," Crump agreed, but he was committed to the communist issue and felt that he could not back down.[41] He apparently never had similar qualms about his vicious attacks on the anti-Crump gubernatorial candidate, Gordon Browning. Full-page ads smearing the ex-governor began to appear in July. One ad announced:

> I have said before, and I repeat it now, that in the art galleries of Paris there are twenty-seven pictures of Judas Iscariot— none look alike but all resemble Gordon Browning; that neither his head, heart nor hand can be trusted; that he would milk his neighbor's cow through a crack in the fence; that, of the two hundred and six bones in his body there isn't one that is genuine; that his heart has beaten over two million times without a single sincere beat.
>
> Browning as governor for one term converted the proud capital of Tennessee into a regular Sodom and Gomorrah, a wicked capital, reeking with sordid, vicious infamy.[42]

Crump also continued his running battle with editor Meeman of the *Press-Scimitar.* On July 7, Memphis Mayor James J. Pleasants bitterly attacked Kefauver for having "a pink streak up his back" and, viewing Kefauver as Meeman's choice, challenged the editor to appear before an impartial committee to defend Kefauver against the pro-communist charges. If Meeman failed, he was to leave town. If he succeeded, Crump would leave town.[43]

The judgment-by-committee idea quickly became ridiculous as proposals for Crump-Meeman, Crump-Kefauver, Kefauver-Mitchell, and Kefauver-Mitchell-Stewart debates were proposed. Kefauver dismissed the idea of a Crump-Meeman debate or a Meeman appearance before a committee to defend Kefauver. Replying to Crump through Meeman, Kefauver said:

> I do not want E. H. Crump to have to take his family and move from Memphis, nor do I want you to leave. It is a dictator-

ship indeed that cannot tolerate two men of differing opinions. That's Joe Stalin's way; it's not my way.[44]

Kefauver asked instead for Judge Mitchell to debate him in Memphis: "I am the best man to present my record to any group. John Mitchell, if he thinks he can represent the people of Tennessee in the Senate, should be the man to challenge it." [45]

Judge Mitchell ignored the challenge, as he and Stewart were to do consistently throughout the campaign. Kefauver, therefore, began to show up where his opponents were speaking and challenge them to debate. On one occasion, with Mitchell hurriedly leaving as Kefauver arrived, Kefauver said to Mitchell's crowd: "You people have just been hearing Judge Mitchell call me some very ugly names. You know what a hit-run driver is. Now the Judge is a hit-run speaker. I challenge him to stay here and in open discussion repeat the things he has said behind my back." [46]

Later, catching Stewart in Fayetteville, Kefauver waited in the rear of a crowd of 300 while Stewart addressed them; Stewart finished and was asked by Kefauver to remain for questions. The senator refused, and, as he left the area, Kefauver yelled after him: "If you don't stay here and debate, I know what you are." [47]

When the Memphis League of Women Voters invited the three candidates to debate the issues, only Kefauver accepted and ended up debating two empty chairs.[48]

In mid-July Stewart, observing the tremendous lift given the Kefauver campaign by the Crump attacks, began to allude to a Crump-Kefauver deal to elect Kefauver by providing him an opportunity to exploit what had turned out to be politically stupid attacks.[49] Stewart himself had begun to move closer to an open break with Crump after Crump had been goaded into declaring that he definitely would not desert Mitchell and switch to Stewart. A Kefauver county leader later recalled how " a contract for a state-wide radio program was signed—we begged the money for it, $2500—and on it we accused Crump of planning to switch. We later found we caught him just in time." [50] But Stewart never took the final step of openly attacking Crump, perhaps thinking to the very end that some agreement might be reached with his former ally.[51]

The bossism issue which Crump handed Kefauver, the exaggeration of Kefauver's voting record, and the refusal of Kefauver's opponents to debate him all acted to prevent a serious discussion of Kefauver's record, which was, in fact, far more liberal than was public opinion in the state. In spite of Kefauver's persistent demand for debates, he would have had a real problem in convincing his basically conservative audiences of the soundness of many of his positions. Especially unpopular was Kefauver's vote against the Taft-Hartley Act, and at the Hotel Peabody meeting in Memphis, he had some difficulty in explaining his vote in a way that satisfied the conservative businessmen.[52] In addition, the enthusiastic support given Kefauver by the CIO, which was very unpopular in Tennessee, concerned many voters. When Mitchell's campaign manager charged that Kefauver "is being supported almost wholly from the coffers of the Political Action Committee of the CIO," [53] Charles Neese, Kefauver's manager, was quick to tell the press:

> I am leaving tonight and returning to raise money to support the campaign. We are so badly in need of money we have had to cancel three statewide broadcasts which we had planned before the election and only have one broadcast scheduled now.
>
> I have received no CIO or PAC money of which I have any knowledge. I have not received much money of any kind. What little money we have has come for the most part out of Estes Kefauver's savings.[54]

Stewart also tried to tie Kefauver to the CIO and picture himself as the moderate in the race: "Kefauver is the candidate of the CIO-PAC and Judge Mitchell is the candidate of Shelby County. I am the only free and independent candidate and I am going to win this race with the support of those voters who believe in 100 per cent Americanism." [55]

If the Tennessee Senate race was confusing, the utter chaos

in the national Democratic party only complicated the situation, as Dixiecrats on the right and Wallace followers on the left sought to pull as many as possible away from support of Truman. Even those remaining loyal to the President wished for a stronger candidate than they expected he would be. The Crump-McKellar stalwarts were so upset with Truman that they announced that they would boycott the convention. Those who did attend voted solidly against the Humphrey minority plank on civil rights, the adoption of which set off a Southern walkout. Tennessee, however, remained in the convention and cast its vote for Senator Richard Russell on the only ballot. Neither Kefauver, Stewart, nor Mitchell played any role in the convention.[56]

Truman's politically brilliant call for a special session of Congress to enact the Republican platform furnished Stewart with a new issue. Never being known as one to unduly exert himself on behalf of his constituents, he nevertheless saw the special session as an opportunity to assume the role as the chief defender of the state against Truman's civil rights program, which Stewart called the "worst insult to the South since the Civil War." The call of duty had overcome the demands of the campaign, Stewart announced. "God being my helper, I'll drop my campaign and go back to Washington and fight this civil rights bill as long as there is a drop of blood left in my body." Kefauver called the session a "bad blunder" and said he would fight all of the civil rights provisions except the anti-poll tax and vote fraud provisions.[57]

In spite of Kefauver's opposition to FEPC and an anti-lynching bill, he received the support of most Negro voters because of his opposition to a poll tax and the filibuster and his support of federal aid to education and electoral college reform. The anti-lynching proposals were obnoxious to Kefauver because they punished the county in which lynchings occurred, embracing, in Kefauver's views, "the Nazi-like theory of collective guilt." He also pointed out how the yearly average of lynchings had dropped from seventy-five (1900–1910) to three (1940–47), leading him to "believe it is best to let humane and enlightened sentiment in the South continue its remarkable progress toward eradicating lynchings entirely." [58]

In order not to have his civil rights position turned against him, on July 29 Kefauver delivered a strong speech on the House floor against Truman's civil rights program which left his opponents no room to attack him on that issue.[59]

One week before the primary, the anti-Kefauver *Nashville Banner* and *Chattanooga News-Free Press* reported that Kefauver had been endorsed by the Tennessee committeewoman of Wallace's Progressive party. Kefauver called it "a frameup" and

a foul attempt, planned and executed by my enemies and by the petty politicians of the Wallace party, who, for the notoriety they would receive and for the purpose of creating confusion, are willing to act as stooges for those who are so desperate and grasping at straws to try to defeat me.

The endorsement cannot possibly be genuine. No member of Wallace's third party could, in good faith, support me, because I stand directly opposite to everything they stand for. The Wallace party's recently enacted platform said they were against the Truman program, the Marshall plan, selective service and universal military training. I am and have been vigorously for these programs.

The Wallace party is for anti-segregation laws, FEPC and anti-lynch laws. I am, and have always been, definitely opposed to those proposals.[60]

To add to the confusion, a University of Tennessee Wallace group endorsed Stewart because of his neo-isolationism.[61] For his part, Stewart, perhaps sensing his approaching defeat, announced a last-minute conversion to a Huey Long type of populism. He called for personal income tax exemptions to be raised to $5000 and for the social security retirement age to be lowered to sixty. Amused observers pointed out that Stewart's proposals would exempt 90 percent of those then paying income taxes.[62]

Kefauver never let up on his argument that Crump's control of state politics was the real issue. He called on the FBI to watch

Shelby County voting and announced that he would go to Memphis himself on election day to see "that the Eighth Commandment is not violated." [63] Crump responded characteristically:

> Kefauver is welcome down here, just like anyone else. We are going to have an honest election like we always do. Why, if we were going to steal the election we wouldn't be out working the way we are to get votes. It's ridiculous to say our elections are not honest.
>
> Neither Kefauver nor the FBI nor anyone else is going to create a disturbance in one of our voting places. If he does, we'll throw him out just like we would anyone else.[64]

The election on August 5 was one of the most exciting in Tennessee political history. The anti-Crump forces sensed victory, and there was intense interest in what would happen in Shelby County. In a dramatic gesture, Estes and Nancy voted in Chattanooga and then flew to Memphis, as Kefauver had promised, where they campaigned all day, shaking hands and chatting with voters to symbolize the freedom to oppose Crump which was such a novelty to Memphis voters. They then went to Nashville to await the results of the election.[65]

The election proved to be a crushing defeat for Crump and McKellar rather than a smashing triumph for Kefauver. As the first returns came in, it became obvious that Kefauver and Stewart were running almost even. There was some concern that Crump might pass a last-minute word for Stewart and thereby decide the election after all. But Crump backed Mitchell to the end, and it was, ironically, the Shelby County vote that gave Kefauver most of his margin over Stewart: [66]

	Kefauver	Stewart	Mitchell
Outside Shelby	144,170	127,140	58,421
Shelby County	27,621	2,733	37,771
Total	171,791	129,873	96,192

It is not necessarily true that Kefauver won because of the split in the organization. While almost all of Mitchell's vote would have gone to Stewart in a two-man race, there is no way of knowing how many voters supported Stewart because he appeared to them to be a means of expressing opposition to Crump without endorsing Kefauver's liberalism. For many such voters, if the choice had been narrowed to a Stewart supported by Crump and a liberal Kefauver, they might well have chosen Kefauver.

However qualified his victory might have been, Kefauver was overjoyed at the results:

> The elation that I feel over being nominated by the Democratic party in Tennessee as United States senator is tempered by a feeling of sincere humbleness. In view of the magnificent victory, the people have won in Tennessee in this election. I am grateful to all those who made possible my nomination and the confidence that they have reposed in me will not be taken lightly. I have nothing but the highest esteem for any one who may have opposed me and hope that our intra-party differences may be laid aside now in order that we may be successful in the general election.[67]

Kefauver's victory and the companion victory of Browning were hailed as beginning a new era in Tennessee politics. While there was praise for Kefauver and Browning, most of the comment focused on the defeat of Crump-backed candidates and bossism generally. The *New York Times* saw the vote as "a resounding affirmation of the faith of many that old-time bosses do not have to be tolerated, that they exist only because of the lethargy of the voters." [68] The anti-Crump newspapers in Tennessee were almost beside themselves over his defeat. The *Knoxville News-Sentinel* hailed the election as "a great day for Tennessee. After two decades of Ed Crump dictatorship, the people at last have rebelled and have taken their government back into their own hands. They did it merely by going to the polls and voting their own convictions." [69]

The real change came in Memphis; the 1948 primary was the first time in twenty-two years that Crump had lost a voting precinct in the city; Kefauver carried twenty-two city and four county precincts.[70] Never again would the Shelby County machine be successful in delivering a bloc vote to a candidate for statewide office; indeed, the machine's own days of power were numbered, and within a few years Kefauver chairman Orgill would himself become mayor. Editor Meeman described the changes in the city:

> To hear merchants in a community, standing out in front of their stores, talking politics freely and discussing community and city affairs . . . would not be unusual in almost any part of America. But it was so unusual in Memphis on the morning of August 6 . . . that people began to talk about this new freedom which had always been assured them. . . . I predict we will have the most active citizen's movement . . . of any city in the country.[71]

Nancy and Estes returned to Chattanooga on August 7, to be greeted by a crowd of 500 ecstatic supporters at Union Station.[72] On the part of those who had worked so hard in the Kefauver campaign, including Kefauver himself, there was a renewed faith in the democratic process and a feeling that once again the people had triumphed over the politicians. The excitement of the August victory, however, was tempered by the realization that yet another hurdle remained before Kefauver could move from the House to the Senate.

The immediate danger to Kefauver was that the Crump-McKellar organization would work out an accommodation with the Republican Senate candidate, former Representative and former Republican National Chairman B. Carroll Reece. Reece and Crump had had a working arrangement for years which called for the Republicans of East Tennessee to support Crump-backed candidates in the Democratic primaries in return for weak local Democratic opposition in general elections.[73] The question in 1948 was whether Crump would go along with the seemingly logical variation on the traditional arrangement and back Reece against the liberal Kefauver. If, as everyone expected, Dewey were elected President, the Crump-McKellar organization would be taken care of by Reece, who, if elected, would certainly owe his election to the organization.

Crump's inclination not to support Kefauver was strengthened by the boss's reservations about the national Democratic ticket. Crump had previously threatened not to back Truman if he were nominated, but for two months after the convention he had maintained silence on the question of support for the Truman-Barkley ticket. There was no chance of his supporting Dewey, since the national Republican civil rights position was just as unacceptable as that in the Truman Democratic platform. There seemed to be, however, a means of protesting the national Democratic civil rights position without leaving the party, by supporting Governor Strom Thurmond of South Carolina, who claimed to be a good Democrat even while drawing support away from the national Democratic ticket. In October, therefore, Crump announced his support for the Thurmond-Wright ticket.[74]

Philosophically, Crump had more in common with Reece than with Kefauver, especially their attitudes toward internal security and organized labor. But it was the civil rights program of the Democrats that upset Crump, and, in those pre-Goldwater days when Southern Republicans were champions of Negro rights, Reece had a civil rights record just as strong as Kefauver's. In addition, Crump would have forfeited his influence within the state Democratic party had he openly endorsed a Republican. So, eventually he gave Kefauver and Browning his lukewarm support.[75]

Therefore, Kefauver and Browning led a Democratic party united at least on the surface. But uncertainty about whether the many Democrats who were expected to desert Truman for Thurmond might not also fail to back the Senate and gubernatorial nominees caused Kefauver and Browning to tour the state in what was for those years an unusually active campaign before the general election.

The election in November confirmed none of the worst fears of Kefauver and Browning. Although the Republican Senatorial Campaign Committee spent $22,000 for Reece, the third largest amount in the country, grass roots Republican support never developed, and both Democratic candidates won by huge margins. Truman even won the state's electoral vote by a plurality.[76]

As Kefauver prepared to take his Senate seat in January 1949, it did indeed seem that a new day had dawned, not only in Tennessee but in the nation as a whole.

chapter iv

FRESHMAN SENATOR
1949-1950

K efauver wasted no time in establishing himself as one of the Senate's most promising freshmen. Taking advantage of the familiarity with congressional procedures gained through five House terms and still basking in the glory and security of his widely hailed victory over Crump, he was not inclined to resign himself to the relative obscurity traditionally thought proper for Senate newcomers.

One of the first orders of business for Kefauver after the election was to try to close some of the rifts opened up by the primary. Intraparty peace depended on Kefauver's and McKellar's managing to patch up their disputes, and Kefauver took the first steps to build a better relationship with the senior senator. He called on McKellar, handing him what the old man later described as "a long line of unnecessary flattery," [1] and the two men did resolve their differences temporarily. The truce lasted about three weeks, breaking down when Kefauver blocked McKellar's recommendation that a U. S. marshal who had campaigned for Thurmond be reappointed. Kefauver prevailed on the Administration to support his candidate for the job.[2]

McKellar angrily wrote Kefauver a six-page letter which

signaled the resumption of the feud. In it, McKellar blamed Kefauver for creating ill will between the two:

> Several Tennessee newspaper people have told me that you are very anxious to cooperate with me, and the intimation was that I had refused to cooperate with you. I wonder what your idea of cooperation is? Is it that you want to do all the "operating" and leave the "co" to me? [3]

Anxious to minimize Kefauver's influence at the White House, McKellar wrote Truman in an effort to undercut his junior colleague:

> I am informed that Mr. Kefauver is claiming to have helped you in Tennessee. This claim is without the slightest foundation. The papers which supported him, with one exception, were against you. . . . Since the election, he has admitted to me personally that he had not mentioned your name except in his opening speech, and in the newspaper account of that first speech, he merely said he was going to vote for you as the lesser of two evils. I am informed he is now circulating the report that the White House has given orders to look only to his recommendations in making Tennessee appointments. I do not believe this, and I think he is attempting to perpetrate a wrong.[4]

McKellar later claimed that Kefauver was responsible for the resumption of the hostile feelings between them because he had told Attorney General McGrath that McKellar had changed his mind on an appointment when really he had not. When Kefauver came to see him after that, McKellar said, he ran Kefauver "out of my office with a cane." [5] Whatever the specific cause of the dispute, it is unlikely that Kefauver could have remained on good terms with McKellar indefinitely. The old man was allegedly one of the most power-hungry and vindictive men ever to serve in the Senate, and he is said to have interpreted any opposition on patronage matters as a personal affront.[6]

In one famous exchange on the Senate floor, Kefauver and McKellar were so at odds that Senator William Langer asked "which Senator from Tennessee represents the Hatfields and which one represents the McCoys?"[7] Tempers had flared on that occasion because Kefauver wanted an additional roving federal district judge to serve both Middle and West Tennessee, and McKellar wanted the judge for the Middle Tennessee district only. Although Kefauver won in the Judiciary Committee, McKellar converted Judiciary Committee Chairman Pat McCarran and also received support from the Federal Judicial Conference after the bill had been reported to the floor; the whole Senate upheld McKellar, 60 to 19.[8]

For all the rhetoric, Kefauver and McKellar had almost identical voting records on the major issues before the Senate. On what the *Congressional Quarterly* called the ten key votes of 1949, McKellar and Kefauver differed on only one, when Kefauver voted to uphold Vice-President Barkley's ruling that cloture could be applied to a motion to consider a resolution. The ruling was rejected by the Senate, with only two Southern Democrats, Kefauver and Claude Pepper of Florida, voting in support of Barkley's ruling. Later in 1949, Kefauver was the only Southern Democrat to support a resolution (which lost, 14 to 72) to guarantee that cloture could be applied to motions to amend the Journal. But he voted against motions to apply cloture by a simple majority or a constitutional majority.[9]

The move against the filibuster was part of the general liberal concern for civil rights legislation, the prospects of which were expected to be materially advanced by Truman's 1948 victory and the Democratic Congress elected with him. In a countermove, the Dixie bloc, except for Claude Pepper, who was written off as a hopeless liberal, planned a meeting to discuss strategy. Kefauver did not attend, and it was reported that he "could not be reached." Later, Kefauver issued a statement that he had not known of the meeting, but that if he had gone it would have been to express a "different view." "Some time or other in any legislative forum, a majority must be able to express its will by a majority vote. Otherwise, democracy becomes meaningless."[10] Newly elected Senator Lyndon Johnson of Texas also kept his distance from the Southern caucus; although he attended the first meeting, he soon began to decline invitations.[11] Appreciative of Kefauver's and Johnson's relative independence of the Dixie bloc, Truman wrote Kefauver of his satisfaction "that you and Lyndon are not permanently lined up with that crowd." [12]

Kefauver's first remarks on the Senate floor dealt with an explanation of how he differed from "that crowd" in his attitude toward the filibuster:

> . . . the position I take is not an easy one for me politically, be-cause most of my colleagues from the South have been joining in this filibuster. It is not an easy position for me personally, be-cause I have a very close and affectionate relationship with my colleagues from the South, and I dislike very much to have to disagree with them. I would not do so if I did not have a very deep conviction about the matter, and I hope my colleagues from the Southern States will understand that I am doing what my conscience dictates. . . . I have a firm conviction that the neces-sity of the Senate being able to function is paramount to any single domestic issue or any group of domestic issues, because if the Senate cannot discharge its constitutional obligation our whole system of democratic Government may be doomed. . . . I wish to make it clear that I shall vote for cloture by two-thirds, and nothing less. . . . I feel that, in the case of most of the civil-rights measures, we have a good position on the merits of the controversies. As a matter of fact, I have the impression that, by relying on debate alone, by not meeting these issues on their merits, by not having some of us from the Southland take the initiative and show that we are solving our own problems, we are doing a good deal toward aligning the rest of the Nation against us. We are giving the rest of the Nation the impression that we have no defense save a filibuster. If this is our only weapon we will lose eventually. . . . We cannot stop completely the legislative process.[13]

Kefauver's position was not considered liberal by anyone outside the Dixie bloc. Southerners were urging that cloture should never be applied to debate on a motion to take up a bill.

Kefauver supported the position that two-thirds could limit debate on all matters. The "liberal" position called for a majority of senators to end debate on all matters.[14] On other questions involving civil rights, Kefauver voted with the Dixie bloc. On May 19, 1950, he was one of twenty Southern Democrats blocking the end of debate on a fair employment practices bill. On June 21 and 22, 1950, he voted with the Dixie bloc in support of amendments to the Manpower Registration Act which would have allowed men in the armed services to choose units of their own race if they desired.[15]

Although Kefauver's cautious criticisms of the filibuster attracted the most attention, his primary concern in his first months in the Senate was the by now familiar problem of the growing concentration of economic power. Kefauver's interest in antitrust matters, as well as his general House committee experience, led him to ask, in January 1949, for assignment to the Senate Judiciary Committee. There were at that time no openings, and he was assigned instead to Armed Services, District of Columbia, and Interstate and Foreign Commerce.[16] During the next six months, however, two openings occurred on the Judiciary Committee when Howard McGrath of Rhode Island resigned from the Senate to become Attorney General and Robert Wagner of New York died; Kefauver was given a Judiciary seat on August 30.[17] The antitrust expertise gained during his House service made possible one of the biggest triumphs of his first two years in the Senate when he helped to guide to successful enactment the long debated and widely supported amendment to the Clayton Act which plugged the loophole allowing the purchase of a competing firm's assets. The measure is considered one of the landmarks in antitrust legislation, and Kefauver's partnership with his former colleague on the House Judiciary Committee, Representative Emmanuel Celler of New York, on behalf of the amendment caused the legislation to become known as the Kefauver-Celler Act of 1950.[18]

Kefauver added to his credentials as an economic liberal by his prominent role in the fight to block basing point legislation in 1950. The proposed legislation sought to amend the Robinson-Patman fair trade law to permit manufacturers in several major industries to absorb freight rates calculated from a "basing point" and to quote delivered prices reflecting the adjustment; the issue was so complicated and the effects of the proposed legislation so disputed that when it was finally passed but vetoed by President Truman, its supporters did not seek to override the President.[19]

Kefauver also consistently offered amendments to increase appropriations for antimonopoly activity by the Federal Trade Commission and the Antitrust Division of the Justice Department. In 1951 he succeeded in getting $500,000 restored for the Antitrust Division but lost on a move to add $403,000 to the figure approved for the FTC. Always worried about the effects of government purchasing on economic concentration, Kefauver introduced legislation to require the government to give contracts to small business whenever possible.[20]

Very early in his Senate career, Kefauver demonstrated again that he was not afraid to take an unpopular stand when he felt that civil liberties were in danger. The Internal Security Act of 1950, usually called the McCarran Act, represented the culmination of the efforts of years by conservatives to pass a loyalty act to protect against what was supposed to be a real or a possible danger of communist subversion, both within and without the federal government. Those concerned about civil liberties agreed with the conservatives on the need to protect against sabotage and espionage, but the liberals feared that some of the language of the proposed act infringed upon freedom of speech and the right to dissent.

Most of the arguments over the bill dealt with the importance of defining terms which liberals felt were so vague that they offered conservative prosecutors and judges a means of quieting criticism of the government under the guise of protecting national security. Conservatives exhibited little patience with liberals' arguments that the loosely worded act could be abused, and expressed great faith in the common sense of officials and juries to implement the law in a way consistent with traditional concepts of individual liberty.

When the Judiciary Committee considered the bill, Kefauver supported the move to send it to the floor, even though he expressed doubts about its constitutionality.[21] During the floor debate, he was one of a tiny band who sought to define as many of the general terms of the bill as possible. One section made it a crime to commit any act "which might contribute to totalitarian government." This phrase was especially disturbing to civil libertarians, since the language called for a government prosecutor only to satisfy a jury that an act in question *might* lead to totalitarian government, even if the act itself was within the constitutional process. If, therefore, a conservative judge and jury believed that compulsory health insurance was a step toward totalitarian government, any citizen who wrote a letter to his congressman asking him to introduce legislation to that effect would be violating the act. Kefauver objected to this language because he believed it "could be used by unscrupulous prosecutors to punish people upon suspicion, hearsay, or flimsy evidence, even though their acts are protected by the Constitution." The fact that the Supreme Court would throw out such convictions did not diminish the usefulness of the act for harassing political opponents.[22]

Another of Kefauver's serious objections to the bill lay in the loose definitions of conspiracy. The bill made it a crime to conspire to establish a totalitarian government, even if the conspiracy were not accompanied by force and violence. It seemed to Kefauver and other liberals that conservatives might see elements of totalitarianism in something as moderate as Truman's Fair Deal program and therefore seek to move against political opponents who met together to plan how they could elect a majority to the House and Senate which would, through constitutional processes, effect the Fair Deal program. Kefauver's effort to strike this section was defeated.[23]

Still another obnoxious section dealt with a vague definition of what was a communist front. Senator Herbert Lehman of New York complained that "almost every liberal in America" would be covered by the definition, which was based on the principle that communist support for a position automatically tainted anyone else who happened to support that same position.[24]

The general bias against aliens and objectionable political ideas dovetailed nicely in a provision which Kefauver called "thought-controlling" and which provided for the deportation of "any alien . . . who prints, circulates, or has anything to do with the sale or circulation of any book which teaches totalitarian dictatorship." [25]

Liberals had many other objections to the bill, but conservatives easily defeated almost all moderating amendments.[26] Congress was reacting to the anti-communist hysteria that would soon make Senator Joseph McCarthy one of the most powerful men in the country. It was almost with resignation that Kefauver argued against the general tone of the bill as it moved toward final passage:

> . . . America is never going to find security in suppression; America is never going to find any security in beating down ideas. America is going to find strength only in free men who have the right to speak and think as they wish. In that connection, however distasteful some of the persons who have strange ideas or who are crackpots or whatnot may be, I think in a free government a great deal of good has come from letting them pop off whenever they want to so long as they do not advocate the use of force and violence in an effort to destroy the Government.[27]

The Senate passed the Internal Security Act by an overwhelming vote of 51 to 7. President Truman then vetoed the act, raising the same objections as had the outnumbered liberals. Congress was determined to pass the legislation, however, and the Senate overrode Truman's veto 57 to 10.[28]

Kefauver was not as much concerned about the internal communist menace as he was by a piecemeal communist takeover of the free world resulting from a lack of co-operation and co-ordination by the nations of western Europe, the United States, and Canada. He was a strong supporter of both economic and military aid to western Europe and sought to go even beyond the alliance relationship. Throughout his Senate career, he was a strong supporter of the idea of an Atlantic Union, a federal political system operating much the same way as the American federal system but with the nations of western Europe, Canada, and the United States as members.

The Atlantic Union Committee was founded in 1949 and eventually had as many as 10,000 members. It grew out of Federal Union, Incorporated, established by followers of Clarence K. Streit and based on ideas contained in his 1939 book *Union Now*. After the war, the idea of Atlantic Union gained support, and Owen J. Roberts resigned from the Supreme Court to work for the idea. He became the first president of the Atlantic Union Committee and held that office until his death in 1955.[29] Kefauver became the Union's most outspoken champion in the Senate and urged as a first step the convening of a Federal Convention to "explore how far these people, and those of such other democracies as the convention might invite to meet with them, could apply among them, in the framework of the United Nations, the principles of federal union that are embodied in our own United States Constitution." [30]

"Imagine the repercussions," Kefauver said, "throughout the West, in India, in southeast Asia, and even among the crushed millions inside the iron curtain caused by the realization that here, at last, the forces of freedom intend to stand united against the forces of slavery." In addition, he thought the meeting would "deter aggression and promote international security" by making the Russians realize how seriously the free world was taking the concept of collective security.[31]

Although the DAR attacked the idea of an Atlantic Union as a scheme to "strip the United States of its sovereignty," the plan attracted support across the political spectrum, from conservatives such as Joseph McCarthy and Homer Capehart to liberals like Kefauver, Paul Douglas, Hubert Humphrey, and Wayne Morse. By early 1950, forty senators, including such respected men as Arthur Vandenberg, John Stennis, Walter George, and William Fulbright, had sponsored or endorsed an Atlantic Union. Resolutions supporting Atlantic Union were introduced in 1949, 1951, and 1955. Not until 1955, however, did the Foreign Relations Committee hold hearings. By then the new interest in peaceful co-existence made the Atlantic Union seem less urgent, and the disruption of the Atlantic Alliance in 1956, following the Israeli attack on Egypt, undermined the close relationship between the United States and Great Britain and France which was to be the foundation of the Union.[32]

The same willingness to consider innovative improvement that had led Kefauver to crusade for Atlantic Union was also evident in the efforts he made to implement in the Senate the congressional reforms he had been urging for years.[33] In order to remove from Congress the burden of acting as a city council for Washington, he worked with Robert Taft against strong Southern opposition to get a District of Columbia home rule bill through the Senate.[34] The bill was blocked in the House Rules Committee, however. Kefauver also worked with Henry Cabot Lodge, Jr., to reform the Electoral College by dividing electoral votes in proportion to the popular vote cast in each state. He expected that the change would lead to a two party system in the South but saw that as beneficial to the region since he felt that under the current system it was taken for granted by the Democrats and ignored by the Republicans. He supported, although doubted whether it could be adopted, the goal of popular election of the President.[35]

Recognition and praise were fast in coming to Kefauver during his first years in the Senate. In 1949, a poll of newspaper correspondents covering the Senate ranked him as one of the ten best. In 1950, *Time* called him one of the "Senate's most valuable ten," and the body's "most effective symbol of the South's new progressivism." [36] The overnight fame which was to come to Kefauver as a result of the crime investigation caused his outstanding record in other areas to be overlooked or obscured, and it may come as a surprise to recall the respect in which he was held before the crime investigation was undertaken. Even by 1950 it was obvious that Kefauver's star was definitely on the rise.

chapter v

THE CRIME
INVESTIGATION I, 1950-1951

On January 5, 1950, Kefauver introduced Senate Resolution 202, calling for an investigation of organized crime in the United States.[1] Although the resolution was hardly noticed at the time, the investigation which followed and Kefauver's role in it were to have the most profound effects on his career, lifting him in a few months from the relative obscurity of a conscientious and hard-working junior senator to a position of national prominence that made him one of the most famous and respected political leaders in the nation and a serious contender for the Presidency itself.

The initiative for an investigation of crime came from the American Municipal Association. On September 14, 1949, Mayor deLesseps Morrison of New Orleans, president of the AMA, asked the federal government to look into the influence that nationally organized racketeers had on municipal governments throughout the country. Several mayors of other cities, such as Los Angeles and Portland, Oregon, asked for specific help for their cities.[2] In December, the AMA formally appealed to the Justice Department for aid against organized crime, urging that the "matter is too big to be handled by local officials alone; the organized criminal element operates across state boundaries on a national scale." [3]

Kefauver, meanwhile, had for several years been following the lengthy reports filed by crime commissions in California, Michigan, and Chicago. His interest in organized crime had grown out of his investigation, as chairman of a House Judiciary subcommittee, of a corrupt federal judge in Pennsylvania in 1945. The crime commission reports convinced Kefauver that the federal government should play a more active role in aiding local governments in their efforts to deal with local manifestations of what were suspected to be national problems, especially interstate gambling.[4] Personal discussions with Philip Graham and Drew Pearson of the *Washington Post* helped influence Kefauver's decision to ask for a Senate investigation.[5]

A complex set of pressures and counterpressures operated in the establishment of a committee and the selection of members to carry out the investigation proposed by Kefauver. He had intended that the investigation be handled by the Judiciary Committee, perhaps by a subcommittee which he would head. However, the justification for a federal investigation was organized crime's influence on interstate commerce, and immediately a jurisdictional dispute arose between the Judiciary Committee and the Interstate and Foreign Commerce Committee, which had already handled several similar investigations and seemed to have an indisputable claim to any future ones. Chairman Edwin C. Johnson of Colorado, therefore, argued forcefully on behalf of his Commerce Committee on jurisdictional grounds, and the Democratic leadership, while seeking to accommodate Kefauver, who could not have participated in an investigation handled by the Commerce Committee, opposed on political grounds giving the investigation to the Judiciary Committee. Two Republican members of the Judiciary Committee, Senators Homer Ferguson of Michigan and Forest Donnell of Missouri, were threatening to expose alleged corruption in urban Democratic organizations in the course of any investigation, and the Democratic leadership was willing to go to any lengths to keep both men off of any unit investigating organized crime.[6]

However, Kefauver had proposed the investigation, and it was traditional to allow him, if possible, to chair the group conducting the investigation. Indeed, one of the most remarkable things about the crime investigation was the consideration the Senate leadership gave Kefauver. Of course, few senators thought the crime investigation would attract very much attention, and, although participation in an investigation of crime is always politically valuable, there was, except for Johnson, no serious attempt by senior senators to seize Kefauver's idea and conduct the investigation themselves. The main concern was that the probe be kept relatively harmless by keeping Ferguson and Donnell out of it. Since Kefauver was not a member of the Commerce Committee, the problem became how to devise a way to allow him to participate in the investigation without opening the door to the Republicans on the Judiciary Committee. The solution was the creation of a special committee composed of members of both the Judiciary and Commerce Committees. This was the plan finally adopted, although the Republicans objected and made an attempt to keep the probe in the Judiciary Committee, losing on a tie vote broken by Vice-President Barkley. The resolution setting up the special committee contained the unusual provision that Barkley would appoint a five-member committee, including two Republican members, in contrast to the usual procedure which allowed the minority to make its own committee assignments. The obvious moves against Ferguson and Donnell caused Kenneth Wherry, the Senate Republican leader, to shout angrily, "Why are they doing this? Is this an investigation or a cover-up?" [7]

Barkley chose as members of the special committee the ranking Republican members of the Judiciary and Commerce Committees, Alexander Wiley of Wisconsin and Charles W. Tobey of New Hampshire, to serve with the Democratic majority consisting of Kefauver, Lester C. Hunt of Wyoming, and Herbert R. O'Conor of Maryland. The two Republican members, Wiley and Tobey, both faced serious re-election problems in 1950, and, while membership on the committee might help them at home, their opportunities to participate (and perhaps damage Democrats) were limited by campaign demands on their time. All five men were known as relatively quiet, mild-mannered, and fair men, and the attention the committee was to attract stood in sharp contrast to the personalities of the senators serving on it.

Kefauver was more a pawn than a participant in the maneuvering that resulted in the creation of the special crime committee. On principle, he had long opposed the creation of special committees, having argued that such committees were a waste of money. Only two years before, he had written "In my opinion, there is no use for a special committee. There is nothing that a special committee can do that a regular standing committee of Congress cannot do better." One of Kefauver's objections to special committees, and a charge that was to be leveled against his own special committee, was that "being a special group, the committee usually feels it has to justify its existence by doing something sensational; hence it grabs for the headlines, and its performance often degenerates into pure vaudeville." [8]

Republican charges that the committee would cover up findings politically damaging to Democrats made Kefauver go to great lengths to avoid even the appearance of partisanship in the operation of the committee. Before the investigation began, he assured reporters that he would conduct a "let-the-chips-fall-where-they-may" investigation. "As far as I'm concerned, there will be no shying away from Kansas City or anywhere else." [9] Senator Donnell had been suggesting that an investigation in Kansas City might prove especially embarrassing to President Truman.

The Kefauver Committee, as the special committee soon was called, had three responsibilities: (1) "to determine whether organized crime utilizes the facilities of interstate commerce . . . to promote any transactions" which violated either state or federal law; (2) to investigate the "manner and extent of such criminal operations . . . with the identification of the persons, firms, or corporations involved"; and (3) to determine "whether such interstate criminal operations were developing corrupting influences in violation of the Federal law or the laws of any state." A report was to be submitted by February 28, 1951, of the findings and recommendations of the committee. The report deadline was later extended to May 1, and the committee itself continued until September 1.[10]

The committee eventually held hearings in fourteen major cities: Washington, Tampa, Miami, New York, Cleveland, St. Louis, Kansas City, New Orleans, Chicago, Detroit, Philadelphia, Las Vegas, Los Angeles, and San Francisco. Over eight hundred witnesses were heard, and the resulting testimony ran to thousands of pages. In the first weeks of the crime investigation, Kefauver conducted most of the hearings with only the assistance of the staff, the other four senators on the committee staying in Washington. Eventually, he was to travel 52,380 miles on committee business and to chair hearings on ninety-two separate days. The Kefauver Committee's work was in large part Kefauver's personal achievement.[11]

The significance of the hearings lay, however, not so much in the quantity of evidence gathered by the committee as in the incredibly effective manner in which it managed to arouse an interest among great masses of people in the nature and scope of the problem of organized crime and its relationship to political corruption. Since most of the specific criminal-political relationships investigated involved urban political machines and, therefore, principally Democratic party officeholders, the investigation created a tremendous amount of ill will toward Kefauver among the Democratic organizations affected—in spite of the fact that Kefauver had discussed the potential political dangers with urban Democratic leaders attending the Attorney General's conference on crime in February 1950 and had agreed on the final program for the investigation only after receiving general encouragement from representatives of many Democratic organizations which later were to resent bitterly the effect the Kefauver investigation had in some of their cities.[12]

However, in the beginning there was little seen to fear in either the makeup of the committee or the choice of the chief counsel, Rudolph Halley, who became one of the best-known personalities associated with the Kefauver Committee. Kefauver chose him on the recommendation of New York State Supreme Court Justice Ferdinand Pecora, who had been counsel for the famous Wall Street investigation of 1933–34. Halley was a brilliant lawyer who graduated from law school at the age of twenty; he had a love for investigations, and his first investigative experience uncovered evidence that sent Boston's Jim Curley to prison. He later served with distinction on the staff of the Truman Committee, which had been so careful of political considerations that the Administration being investigated chose Truman as Vice-President in 1944. The White House and the Democratic leadership in the Senate, therefore, had every reason to believe that the Kefauver Committee would be extremely sophisticated in its use of findings that might be damaging to the party.[13]

But, since the Kefauver Committee emphasized gambling as the life blood of organized crime, it was led automatically into Democratic urban areas, where gambling and the corruption of officials necessary to protect gambling would naturally be more prevalent than in small-town, rural, Republican America. It might very well have been impossible to conduct an effective investigation of organized gambling without damaging the Democratic party, but the fact that Democrats were investigating Democrats made the public assume that the problem was at least as bad as it appeared. Kefauver himself said:

> I knew in the beginning, of course, that our investigation would carry us into more Democratic cities than it would Republican, because most of the big cities are under Democratic control. I have always felt that, while you might hurt in some local situations, in the long run it would benefit the party that recognized that a bad situation existed and tried to cure it.[14]

The problem was that the entire local Democratic party structure was affected by an investigation, and in many places the public did not associate the local Democrats with "the party that recognized that a bad situation existed and tried to cure it." It was too often the Republicans who, in spite of their own sophistication about how much "cure" could be effected, benefited when local Democrats were discredited.

The great mass of evidence the committee was to gather came almost completely from the results of already conducted local investigations. J. Edgar Hoover testified, for example, that local authorities already knew so much about local operations that they could clean up organized gambling in forty-eight hours if they wanted to. Kefauver himself admitted that most of the information revealed before the committee was already familiar to local authorities but pointed out that "the fact that certain information is known to some people and the assembly of that information in such a way that a legislative program can be based on it are two quite different things." [15]

The committee first held hearings in Miami and immediately ran into problems with elected Democrats. In Miami, in addition to exposing the laxity of several area law-enforcement officers in suppressing gambling, the focus was on the S. and G. Syndicate, bookmakers who admitted controlling concessions at two hundred hotels and grossing, by 1948, over $26.5 million in bets. The committee found that the syndicate "enjoyed cordial relationships with members of the city government and law-enforcement agencies." Independent bookies might be raided, but S. and G. "suffered little from police interference." However, in 1949, the syndicate acquired a new partner with connections to the Capone group in Chicago after developments the committee found especially interesting. In January 1949, shortly after Democratic Governor Fuller Warren took office, he appointed a special investigator, W. O. Crosby, a man tied to the Capone organization, who began to raid gambling establishments in Dade County in co-operation with Sheriff James Sullivan. Strangely, they raided only S. and G. bookies. The committee brought out the fact that a Capone associate had contributed $100,000 to Governor Warren's campaign fund in 1948. About the same time, Continental Press Service, controlled by the Capone gang, cut off service to S. and G. With the raids and the lack of wire service, S. and G. shut down for about two weeks. But when a Capone associate was made an S. and G. partner, the raids stopped and the wire service was resumed. Meanwhile, Sheriff Sullivan's assets increased, during his five years in office, from $2500 to at least $96,000 that could be traced. Although Sullivan was temporarily suspended after the hearings in Miami, Governor Warren reinstated him without an investigation, an action the committee could not understand and strongly condemned, especially after Sullivan's open attempts to block the work of the Greater Miami Crime Commission.[16]

The Miami hearings called into question the honesty and integrity of Governor Warren, and his refusal to co-operate fully with the committee ruined his political career. When he realized the damage being done to his reputation, he tried to discredit the committee. He continually attacked the committee members collectively and Kefauver and O'Conor personally. In June 1951, he threatened to go to Maryland in 1952 and campaign against O'Conor, who faced re-election then. In October 1951, at the National Governors' Conference in Gatlinburg, Tennessee, Warren called Kefauver an "ambition-crazed Caesar who is trying desperately and futilely to be a candidate for President of the United States." "I've always heard a stuck pig always squeals," Kefauver replied. Governor Warren was embarrassed when no other governor joined in his attack and was humiliated when Nebraska's Governor Peterson answered Warren with the rebuke: "I for one do not like to sit here in Senator Kefauver's home state and hear an attack on a man who has been a great American, a good Senator and has done a good job."[17] Governor Warren's attacks on the committee contributed significantly to establishing the committee's image of integrity, indicating as they did that the Democratic-controlled Kefauver Committee was not seeking to cover up evidence damaging to fellow Democrats. Warren, as might be expected, became an implacable foe of Kefauver and figured prominently in the 1952 campaign.

The connection between politics and organized crime found in Miami existed to some extent in almost every big city, but nowhere was there the potential political danger to the Democratic party as in Illinois. Senator Scott Lucas, Senate Democratic leader, faced a stiff challenge in 1950 from former Representative Everett Dirksen in an election predicted to be very close. Lucas, of course, did not expect Kefauver to keep the committee out of Chicago, but he did request that the Chicago hearings be scheduled after the election in order not to damage the ticket. The Chicago investigation got out of control, however, when a former Chicago acting police chief, Bill Drury, was murdered on September 25, while protection by the Kefauver Committee was being arranged. Within forty-eight hours, Marvin Bas, a lawyer who had been collecting evidence for the Republican nominee for sheriff of Cook County, was also murdered. The murders received nation-wide attention, and Kefauver, after winding up a preliminary investigation in Kansas City, took the investigation into Chicago, seemingly oblivious to the political dangers involved. The Democratic organization, already on the defensive, came under a heavier cloud when it became known that both murdered men had been gathering evidence against Police Captain Dan Gilbert, the Democratic candidate for sheriff of Cook County, whose eighteen years as chief investigator for the State's Attorney had resulted in not one conviction of an important mobster.[18]

The real Chicago bombshell exploded when Gilbert testified on November 1, in a closed session of the committee, that he had allowed open violations of the gambling laws and implied that his enforcement in other areas had been just as lax. Ray Brennan, a *Chicago Sun-Times* reporter, posed as an employee of the Kefauver Committee and got a transcript of the secret testimony, which the *Sun-Times* published the next day. The following Tuesday, thousands of disgusted Democrats and independents deserted not only Gilbert but the entire Democratic ticket, and Senate Majority Leader Lucas and many other Democratic candidates went down to defeat. Lucas was furious over his defeat and blamed Kefauver for it, although Gilbert had been thoroughly discredited long before the Kefauver Committee got to Chicago. After the election, when Kefauver sought to meet with Lucas about the Illinois situation, Lucas refused and turned his back on Kefauver. Lucas was to be one of Kefauver's major political enemies in the backstage maneuverings in 1952 and 1956 and never forgave Kefauver for what he thought was Kefauver's part in ending his political career.[19]

Kefauver's first reaction to the Illinois elections was to deny responsibility for Lucas's defeat. The Sunday after the election, Kefauver appeared on "Meet the Press" and said that he did not:

> think our investigation had very much to do with Senator Lucas's defeat. Senator Lucas had supported our committee all of the way through. Nobody connected him with any of the matters brought out. You refer to Sheriff [*sic*] Gilbert in particular, I imagine. As a matter of fact, the Cook County boys should never have selected him for sheriff in the first place, and they were in bad trouble with him before we came into the picture.[20]

In line with his desire to escape responsibility for the Illinois debacle, Kefauver successfully urged the prosecution of *Sun-Times* reporter Brennan for impersonating a federal official. However, when Lucas and other organizational leaders continued to blame Kefauver for the Democratic setbacks in Illinois in 1950, Kefauver and his supporters, in time, began to interpret the developments there as an example of Kefauver's putting country above party, and Lucas entered the pantheon of powerful villains brought down by Kefauver's refusal to compromise his integrity.[21]

By the end of 1950, the Kefauver Committee had completed almost seven months of hearings and investigation and had amassed an incredible amount of evidence. The pattern was the same everywhere the committee went. Local crime commissions, grand juries, crusading newspapers, and sympathetic law enforcement officers all made available everything that might be of interest to the committee, and the staff had all it could handle just organizing the information supplied to it. Even though almost all the local evidence had been made public before, there was nevertheless a shock on reviewing the accumulated evidence of years, and the Kefauver Committee made headlines wherever it went. Scandals that had been almost forgotten were rehashed, and questions unanswered from years before about political corruption and lax law enforcement were suddenly being asked again. Since the committee was responsible for publicizing so much that had previously attracted the attention of only a few, it received much of the credit that in reality belonged to local investigators. This seemingly incredible success at identifying criminal personalities and activities, combined with the tests of integrity met in the public mind in Miami and Chicago, gave the Kefauver Committee the aura of an invincible white knight stalking the land in search of evils that had come to be taken for granted. There is no doubt that one of the real accomplishments of the committee was in raising the morale of those already engaged in the fight against organized crime and in helping to enlist the support of thousands of other people who were previously indifferent to or ignorant of the problem. The public began to view the Kefauver Committee as far more than just another Senate probe, and it acquired a prestige probably unequalled by any other congressional investigation. Its unfavorable reaction to legalized gambling in Nevada, for example, was given credit, in November 1950, for swinging voters in California, Montana, Arizona, and Massachusetts against schemes to legalize gambling in those states.[22]

The public admiration and respect was not without its price, however. The Senate leadership was becoming more and more hostile to the committee for several reasons. Defeated Majority Leader Lucas had joined Kenneth McKellar in almost open hatred of Kefauver. In addition, Nevada's Pat McCarran, powerful chairman of the Judiciary Committee, was upset over the committee's observations in Las Vegas. More important, there was a growing feeling among Senate Democrats that Kefauver was conducting the investigation with little regard for the party.[23]

The White House was becoming cool to the Kefauver Committee with every new revelation that reflected on the national party organization or the President himself, although Kefauver later stated, "I never got any pressure from anyone at the White House, nor from the Democratic National Committee, though I felt sure that some things we were doing were not very pleasing to them." [24]

One of the first witnesses to appear before the committee had accused Truman's secretary from 1935–41, and 1940 campaign manager, of taking a $1000 fee to arrange a sugar quota from OPA during the war. The accusation was denied, but the committee produced a letter which seemed to substantiate the charge. In the Miami hearings, testimony revealed that an important mobster bought $2500 worth of tickets to a Democratic National Committee dinner in Florida in 1947. The Kansas City hearings did not reflect on the President personally, but the Democratic state organization, especially Governor Forrest Smith and the state treasurer, appeared to have unexplained ties to the underworld. The Kefauver Committee also delved into the former activities of the by then defunct Pendergast machine, which had put Truman in the Senate, and thereby inadvertently reminded the public of Truman's earlier associations.[25]

In spite of growing Democratic apprehensions about the committee, Kefauver succeeded in having the life of the committee extended when it became evident that the planned schedule could not be completed by February 28. No senator, however much he wanted to end the committee, would dare be caught voting against it. "Let's face it," said one Democrat, "the Kefauver committee hurts the party and the longer it keeps going, the more we'll be hurt. But we can't stop it, not while it possesses glamour. Any effort to block it would be a political blunder, maybe suicide." [26]

The extension made possible the climax of the investigation, the sensational New York hearings, which brought the Kefauver Committee unprecedented attention from coast to coast and earned it the respect and appreciation of millions who had given only passing notice to its earlier hearings.

chapter vi

THE CRIME
INVESTIGATION II, 1951

There was little reason to think that the Kefauver Committee hearings in New York City would be very much different from those held elsewhere. Political corruption and organized crime there came in larger quantities, but so did public indifference, fed by the realization over the years that every new crime commission or grand jury investigation was followed by a temporary cleanup, with politics and crime back to normal shortly thereafter.

The Kefauver Committee itself was looking forward to the winding up of its mission, for the initial enthusiasm on the part of both staff and senators had greatly diminished as routine obligations neglected in the early months of the investigation began to demand their attention.

No one realized, therefore, when the Kefauver Committee moved into New York on March 12, 1951, that its proceedings were about to become one of the spectacular events of the year. Indeed, most people considered the New York hearings the committee's major accomplishment, the week and a half there having received more national attention by far than any other hearings or investigations conducted by the committee.

What made the difference in New York, of course, was that

the hearings were carried by national television networks and for the first time brought tens of millions of people into simultaneous contact with senators, lawyers, hoodlums, and assorted other characters who were playing out a human drama so exciting and full of suspense that had it been submitted as fiction it would have been rejected as unrealistic.

Television had been used almost three years earlier in a March 30, 1948, Senate Armed Services Committee hearing on universal military training. Shortly thereafter, the House Committee on Un-American Activities hearings involving Alger Hiss had been televised. The Kefauver Committee was only the fifth congressional committee hearing to utilize television.[1]

The Kefauver Committee's first association with TV had been when local stations filmed some of the early public hearings for showing on their news programs. In New Orleans, however, the committee granted permission to Station WDSU to telecast the actual proceedings. The response was so favorable that whenever open hearings were held thereafter they were fully televised.[2]

The committee reacted to rather than initiated requests for telecasting the hearings. In fact, Kefauver, far from scheming to publicize himself and the committee through the televising of the hearings, as charged by some critics, insisted: "I didn't know that they were going to televise the New York hearings until a day or so before the hearings started."[3]

The New York hearings, which opened on March 12, were eventually carried by TV stations in twenty cities along the eastern seaboard and in the Midwest. The usual weekday morning TV offerings were so dull that on an average morning only 1.5 per cent of homes had a TV set in use. Thus, the morning hours were relatively inexpensive for commercial sponsors, and *Time* magazine supposed the selective audience interested in the hearings might also be receptive to subscription advertising on behalf of the magazine. *Time* decided to sponsor telecasts of the hearings in New York and, later, in Washington over a fifteen-day period. Additional stations and other sponsors followed, expanding the coverage as public interest mushroomed.[4]

As the scene opened in New York, viewers were given front-row seats to a Senate investigation, and a firsthand look at what was supposed to be government in operation. Actually, the lack of partisanship on the part of the members of the committee and the heavy moral emphasis in evaluating behavior and situations tended to obscure the complexities of the legislative and investigative processes. It was as if everything about the New York hearings had been designed to reinforce the simplistic concepts of American politics conveyed through thousands of high school government classes and textbooks. Good and evil, heroes and villains, black and white categorization made each specific encounter between committee and witness easy to follow. All five senators played their roles perfectly and conducted themselves with dignity, fairness, and a confidence in their mission and authority that commanded respect throughout the hearings. Kefauver, as chairman, received by far the most attention, and emerged from the New York hearings as one of the most famous men in America. Overnight, millions had become familiar with the tall, lanky forty-seven-year-old Tennessean, whose soft Southern accent exhibited just a trace of Appalachian influence and whose firm but fair direction of the hearings evoked almost universally favorable comment. The dignity and easily shocked innocence of Kefauver and the other committee members allowed millions of viewers to identify with them and reassured the public that there were still some politicians who held to the old values that so many local officeholders had apparently discarded.

Most of the questioning of witnesses was handled by Halley, who played the role of the relentless prosecutor while the senators themselves appeared in an almost judicial role. Halley's ability to force admissions of guilt or to trap in inconsistencies so many witnesses astonished and delighted the viewers, who saw criminals fumbling for words and unable to put favorable interpretations on obviously questionable behavior.[5]

Over fifty witnesses were to testify before the committee in New York, but public interest centered on a few. The opening testimony dealt primarily with gambling at Roosevelt Raceway, but the public soon became more interested in the general influence of Frank Costello, alleged boss of the New York underworld and one of the biggest stars of the New York hearings. Just as true to type as the senators, Costello and other underworld figures reacted so predictably to the committee's questions that it was almost as if they had learned their lines by watching old gangster movies of the 1930s.

The authenticity and novelty of even the most trivial proceeding caught the imagination of viewers, who quickly spread the word about the fascinating drama. Very soon viewer response to the hearings was just as big a news story as the developments at the hearings themselves.[6]

Off and on throughout the New York hearings, Costello himself appeared before the committee, and, although he was preceded and followed by scores of other witnesses, he came to symbolize the underworld the committee was seeking to investigate, and his several appearances gave him a familiarity that most other witnesses lacked. In his original appearance on Tuesday, March 13, he objected to having his face televised, singling him out still more from other witnesses; the committee agreed that only his hands would be shown. His nervous gestures conveyed the frustrations of a man who had much to hide, and his refusal to answer some questions fully and other questions at all aroused indignant outrage among the public, less interested in specific areas of questioning than in the general attitudes displayed by Costello and other alleged hoodlums. On Thursday, Costello appeared again, but claimed he was too ill to testify and walked out on the committee, while millions heard Kefauver threaten him with contempt. Costello agreed to come back on Friday, but he again refused to testify, and the committee finally voted to cite him for contempt.[7]

The panel's detailed questions about so many seemingly unrelated topics, put not only to Costello but to other witnesses appearing before the committee, gave the impression of an incredible grasp of the New York crime problem. Much of the credit for the committee's ability to maintain its momentum and inspire confidence in the investigation belonged to Halley, who was so valuable to the committee that when he had expressed a desire to leave his job as counsel in December 1950 Kefauver kept him by threatening to step down as chairman.[8]

Throughout the week, many topics had been discussed with witnesses and then dropped, sometimes after a new revelation from a principal and sometimes with nothing seemingly accomplished. Almost overshadowed by more dramatic testimony had been the refusal of John P. Crane, president of the Uniformed Firemen's Association, to testify about campaign contributions in local elections. In addition, James J. Moran, henchman of William O'Dwyer, had denied ever having collected any campaign funds for ex-Mayor O'Dwyer, who had resigned as mayor to become Ambassador to Mexico.[9]

On Monday, March 19, O'Dwyer himself testified, coming into the hearing in the role of a concerned former mayor whose experience in office would make him a valuable witness for the committee. He soon was on the defensive in trying to explain his associations with Costello, and finally admitted appointing gangsters' friends to city jobs. On Wednesday, Crane reappeared to reveal, in one of the few testimonies before the committee that went significantly beyond evidence already supplied to it, that he had given O'Dwyer $10,000 and Moran $55,000 of union funds in campaign contributions to buy favorable decisions for the union when O'Dwyer, who was then (1947) running for mayor, took office.[10]

O'Dwyer, by 1951 a high-level Truman political appointee as Ambassador to Mexico, was in the embarrassing situation of having his income tax returns checked and his testimony before the Kefauver Committee sent to the District Attorney for possible perjury action in the face of his denials of the charges leveled against him by Crane. In addition to the personal problems created for O'Dwyer by Crane's testimony, the former mayor's own testimony had called attention to the numerous links between Tammany Hall and the underworld, and shook the New York Democratic party to its foundations, leaving it defeated and demoralized.[11]

The New York investigation became the most discussed topic in the country, and to millions the crime committee members became overnight celebrities.[12] That the hearings lacked continuity and that much of the most dramatic testimony was only indirectly related to the committee's legitimate interest were ignored. Television was coming of age, and the Kefauver Committee benefited from being in the right place at the right time with a format and topic of great interest to millions of viewers.

The twelve months preceding the Kefauver Committee's hearings in New York City had seen the percentage of homes in the New York metropolitan area with TV sets rise sharply, from 29 to 51 per cent. Programs, however, were still fairly unsophisticated, and the Kefauver hearings offered a dramatic contrast to typical television offerings. In the morning hours, the hearings created seventeen times the normal viewing audience (26.2 per cent of homes vs. the normal 1.5 per cent); in the afternoon there was also a dramatic increase in viewing (from 11.6 per cent of homes to 31.5 per cent). It was estimated that an average of 86.2 per cent of those viewing television watched the hearings, and that an average of 69.7 per cent of the TV sets in the New York area were on during the hearings, twice as many as during a weekday World Series game in October 1950.[13]

The hearings and the reaction to them became recognized as events of great national significance and were analyzed and discussed in great detail in an effort to determine what they revealed about American life and values. One judgment was universal—the hearings had thoroughly captured the imagination of between twenty and thirty million viewers. *Time* magazine, one of the major sponsors of the telecasts, received 115,000 letters in reference to the hearings, almost all of them favorable.[14]

Life magazine reflected the feeling of most observers when it proclaimed its judgment that:

the week of March 12, 1951, will occupy a special place in history. The U. S. and the world had never experienced anything like it. . . . All along the television cable . . . [people] had suddenly gone indoors—into living rooms, taverns and clubrooms, auditoriums and back offices. There, in eerie half-light, looking at millions of small frosty screens, people sat as if charmed. For days on end and into the nights they watched with complete absorption . . . the first big television broadcast of an affair of their government, the broadcast from which all future uses of television in public affairs must date. . . . Never before had the attention of the nation been riveted so completely on a single matter. The Senate investigation into interstate crime was almost the sole subject of national conversation.[15]

Newspapers were full of stories of neglected housework, and deserted movie theaters and department stores; in New York, Consolidated Edison had to add a generator to supply power for all the TV sets being used, as a vast number of people tuned in on a presentation they would not soon forget.[16]

The hearings after New York were anticlimatic, although public interest showed little evidence of subsiding. On March 24 in Washington, Station WTOP-TV cut its coverage of the Washington hearings to carry the "Baptist Church Hour." The committee did not want to take viewers away from a religious program, so a channel that had intended to continue coverage of the hearings was asked to suspend its telecasting until the "Baptist Church Hour" was over. As soon as viewers discovered that neither channel was carrying the hearings, both stations were inundated with angry phone calls, and, within ten minutes, both had given in and resumed coverage of the hearings.[17]

The televised hearings of the Kefauver Committee provoked a vigorous debate among lawyers, civil libertarians, and intellectuals generally concerning the possibility of balancing the public's need and right to be informed against the rights of individuals either mentioned in televised proceedings or forced to testify before the cameras. Many who were already fearful of the abuses of congressional committees were horrified to contemplate what might be done in the future by an irresponsible committee chairman whose opportunities for abuse would be multiplied by television.

Kefauver's protection of the individual rights of witnesses appearing before his committee brought him praise from the American Civil Liberties Union:

> In contrast to other investigating committees, the Kefauver Committee has given persons attacked in testimony a right to testify personally in their own behalf; has given witnesses the privilege of the fullest aid and advice of counsel; has sought affirmatively to prevent disclosure of names of persons who might be unjustly prejudiced; and has permitted statements to be submitted. And most important, the hearings were conducted, with one or two exceptions, in an atmosphere of fairness and sober fact-finding, without resort to the hysteria and wild accusations which has marked other Congressional probes. . . . Indeed, its findings have been given wider public acclaim precisely because of the safe-guard it established.[18]

The fairness of Kefauver's direction tended to blind some to the potential dangers of widespread use of television by government. The *New York Herald-Tribune* asked simplistically why "If television can educate (and, incidentally, entertain) the whole population on crime and politics, why not take in Congress [and even] court trials of broad and legitimate interest?" *Newsweek* called for "as many Congressional hearings as possible [to be] televised." [19]

However, the majority of observers expressed grave reservations about the practice of televising government proceedings, although many praised the restraint of Kefauver and the members of his committee.[20] One of the biggest fears was that politicians might tend to emphasize the sensational and the entertaining rather than what was relevant to the investigation. Since the crime investigation telecasts had had commercial sponsorship, there was the danger that a politician who faced sponsor cancellation might liven up the proceedings in order to stay on the air and reap the political benefits of wide exposure. Another concern of critics of the telecasts was that unsubstantiated charges against a person might be seen and heard by millions who did not stay tuned long enough to hear the charge answered. In short, the temptation to play to the galleries that was present in any congressional investigation would become almost irresistible if the politicians and witnesses involved knew that millions were watching. Although there was an appreciation for the public interest in crime awakened by the Kefauver Committee and a sympathetic understanding of the contribution that properly safeguarded telecasting of government proceedings could make to the education of the public, the over-all judgment of the intellectual community was that the dangers far outweighed the possible benefits.[21]

Kefauver himself had long been troubled by the threat to civil liberties posed by congressional investigations generally and showed a keen awareness of the potential dangers in the added element of television. "I did my best during the course of our proceedings," he said, "and I hope the record will show I succeeded, to maintain a calm and judicial attitude. . . ." He welcomed constructive criticism regarding the telecasts and the conduct of his committee and, indeed, became one of the champions in the Senate of establishing rules of procedure for congressional committees which would protect individual rights. On August 24, 1951, Kefauver and ten other senators, citing abuses by Senator McCarthy, introduced a resolution to protect victims of congressional attacks, whether they came on the floor or in committee sessions. Although no action was taken, Kefauver continued to write about and call for such a code throughout his career, stressing the need for an opportunity for persons mentioned in hearings to have limited rights of cross-examination during committee hearings and the unlimited right to submit documents in rebuttal to testimony. He even went so far as to urge that the *Congressional Record* be opened to denials by persons mentioned during floor debate or discussions, and called in all cases for advance notice to be given to persons named so that rebuttal statements could be received simultaneously with the attacks.[22]

The most prominent comment by the legal fraternity on the telecasting of the Kefauver Committee hearings came from the Federal Bar Association of New York, New Jersey, and Connecticut, which expressed concern lest "the glaring melodrama" of TV's lights and cameras obscure the search for truth.[23] The many contempt citations voted by the committee, however, soon brought into the federal courts not only the much-debated issue of the limits of the congressional investigative power but also the novel question of telecasting. The best-known case involving the use of television, *U.S.* v. *Kleinman et al.*, upheld the position that in some situations the mere fact of televising the proceeding created an improper atmosphere.[24]

Like many other congressional investigating committees, the Kefauver Committee was criticized for demanding that witnesses answer questions that might incriminate them or face contempt citations from the committee. How to run an investigation without in effect trying hostile witnesses has always been a problem for congressional committees, and the fate of contempt citations voted by the Kefauver Committee does not indicate much success in observance of the Fifth Amendment. Of the first twenty-two contempt cases arising from the crime hearings, not one was upheld; all were dismissed after trial in federal district courts or reversed on appeal.[25] By 1953, 45 citations had been disposed of; the results showed 3 convictions, 22 acquittals, 10 dismissals, and 5 convictions reversed on appeal.[26] One interesting slip that indicated the ease with which an investigator could assume the role of a judge or prosecutor occurred when Frank Costello objected to being televised. Senator O'Conor replied that "under the circumstances, then, it is the view of the committee, Counsel, that the defendant [*sic*] not be televised, or the individual who is here, the witness, not be televised at the time." [27]

As the May 1 deadline for the committee approached, Kefauver came under heavy pressure to ask for yet another extension or even to make the crime committee a standing committee of the Senate. He was very much opposed to another extension, not only because the crime investigation had made it necessary for him to neglect his constituents but also because he felt that the investigation had accomplished all that it could or should. "I'm not in favor of carrying on the Committee in the active way we have functioned in the past," he told *U.S. News and World Report* in April. "I think if the people get the idea that we're going to solve their problems, they may depend too much on us to wash their dirty linen. Now that they are interested, I think it's a good time to let the people go forward." [28]

He also felt that Congress had enough information about the problem to pass effective legislation, and the need was not more testimony and investigation but "a period of study and reflection" to make intelligent use of that which had already been gathered. But there were strong pressures to continue the committee, especially from Republican Senator Alexander Wiley. The compromise finally worked out called for an extension to September 1 and an additional $100,000 for the committee, bringing to $315,000 the amount eventually voted for the crime investigation. Kefauver refused all requests to stay on as chairman, but did give in to pleas from the Democratic Policy Committee that he stay on the committee. Senator O'Conor became the new chairman, and Kefauver attended few sessions as a committee member.[29]

Although Kefauver said he resigned as chairman to devote his attention to "international gangsters" by giving his "full time and energy to working for passage of the Atlantic Union resolution," he also looked forward to resuming a more normal life after more than a year of constant travel and disruption. Nancy was overjoyed at his decision to end his participation in the crime investigation. "We've missed him at home," she said. "For several days our life revolved around the TV set. And we were forever wiping smudges from the screen left by the children 'touching daddy.' " The Kefauvers' fourth child, daughter Gail, had been born in 1950 and had only a limited acquaintance with her father until he stepped down as chairman of the crime investigation.[30]

Since the Kefauver Committee had made its members nation-wide celebrities, it was perhaps natural that they would be in demand for television shows, motion pictures, books, and magazine articles, in addition to the less glamorous lecture circuit. The degree to which Halley and the five senators cashed in on these opportunities raised many eyebrows. In the middle of the New York hearings, Kefauver appeared on "What's My Line," donating the $50 won to the University of Tennessee, a gesture evoking favorable comment in view of the extracurricular activities of many of the witnesses before the committee. He also announced that he was thinking about writing a book.[31]

It was only the beginning. In early April, while he was still chairman of the committee and before the official report had been completed, *The Saturday Evening Post* carried a four-part series supposedly written by Kefauver entitled "What I Found in the Underworld." [32] Although the question of Kefauver's authorship was never raised, most of the text was written by Sidney Shalett, a professional ghostwriter, and contained such vulgar descriptions of gangsters as "a gorilla outfitted by a Bond Street tailor and fresh from a beauty parlor" (Tony Accardo) and "a contemptible little punk" (Mickey Cohen).[33] An anecdote that rocked Washington was Kefauver's revelation that he had been offered bribes "in six figures" for the Democratic National Committee, two unpaid secretaries for his own staff, and an offer to handle literature mailings or hold a fundraising cocktail party—all from a man "peripherally involved in the investigation." [34] If the offers were true, then Kefauver was violating a law which called for a three-year sentence and a $500 fine for not revealing a bribery attempt to law enforcement officers.[35] The fact that the matter was never pursued indicates that his overzealous ghostwriter tried to dramatize some minor incident or else fabricated the story.

The criticism in Washington, however, focused on the propriety of authoring the series for commercial publication before the official report was released.[36] To a Washington state judge who wrote him criticizing the timing of the articles, Kefauver explained:

> As you know, a magazine such as *The Saturday Evening Post* has a closing date on most articles several weeks in advance of publication. While our committee report should have been out in advance of the *Saturday Evening Post* articles, a delay unfortunately prevented this from happening. I hope there was no harm done from this and I don't believe there was.[37]

Since Kefauver had previously criticized a chairman of the House Committee on Un-American Activities for "using its file for personal purposes—making speeches and writing books for pay," [38] it is difficult to understand why he did not go to greater lengths to avoid similar criticisms of his own behavior.[39]

Kefauver also became in great demand on the lecture circuit and reportedly made $20,000 before January, 1952. Meanwhile, he lent his name and spent some time editing a book on the investigation written by Shalett entitled *Crime in America,* which made the *New York Times* bestseller list for twelve weeks between July 28 and October 14, 1951, once achieving #4 position on the list. The book was also serialized in over one hundred newspapers, netting Kefauver $8400 by November 1.[40]

One spinoff from the Kefauver Committee telecasts was a CBS-TV series, "Crime Syndicated," which paid the committee members and Halley to talk or narrate each week's story. Kefauver made only three appearances on the show and donated his payments to the Cordell Hull Foundation for World Peace. Somewhat more stagestruck were Senator O'Conor (28 appearances) and Halley (18 appearances), and criticism grew with each fresh example of how politics could lead to show business.[41]

Hollywood was less interested in cashing in on the crime investigation than was television, but Kefauver was signed up to do the introduction for "The Enforcer," starring Humphrey Bogart, and the epilogue of "Captive City." For the latter, he received $2000 plus 2 per cent of the net, all of which he turned over to the Hull Foundation.[42]

There was little objective analysis of the work of the crime committee. Kefauver was to become a controversial political figure in the years ahead, and observers tended to be influenced by their general opinion of him. Although millions of people assumed that the Kefauver Committee had made a dramatic breakthrough in the war against organized crime, informed observers tended to be more reserved in their evaluations of the committee's contributions. There is no doubt, however, that the committee could take credit for some real accomplishments. According to a press release of the Bureau of Internal Revenue in July, 1954, there were 46,000 investigations made by the Special Rackets Squad of the Bureau (later renamed the Special Activities section of the Intelligence Division), "which was activated as a result of recommendations made by the Kefauver Committee." Most of the investigations themselves "concerned persons either cited by the Kefauver Committee . . . or were corollary to an out-growth of the exposures of the Crime Committee." In addition, "866 cases have been referred to the Department of Justice for indictment, involving 941 defendants, amounting to $225 million in assessments and penalties." Of these, 593 had resulted in convictions. By 1957, taxes and penalties recovered had reached $336 million, and 874 convictions had resulted from government prosecutions, most on criminal fraud charges.[43]

Perhaps the Kefauver Committee's greatest achievement was inspiring others to carry on or begin the fight against organized crime, although one commentator expressed the view that "it is not clear whether the ultimate effect of the committee's work will be to 'clean up' gambling or merely to produce a cynicism about our political life infinitely more dangerous than gamblers' campaign gifts to the politicians." [44] Generally, however, the Kefauver Committee had a healthy effect on the communities in which it held hearings. From the very beginning, local law-enforcement officers who had been shown by the committee to be lax in fulfilling their responsibilities had been fired or had resigned in response to public opinion. In addition, more than seventy local crime commissions were established, and many others expanded their investigations as a result of the Kefauver Committee hearings.[45] Kefauver himself saw the principal achievement of his committee as the:

> bringing out of the present methods and techniques of organized criminals and showing their moral, economic, and political influence upon the American people. . . .
> The spotlighting of local crime is an important by-product. Many citizens did not appreciate the sinister influences in their communities. Now that they know the facts, they are doing something about it. . . . These fellows [racketeers] cannot operate under the spotlight of public information. They have been shown and the public has been shown that their insidious operations and influence can be exposed. This fact alone will do much to deter them in the future.[46]

Kefauver's emphasis on the responsibility of the local community for solving its own crime problem was consistent with the positions he had taken throughout his career, but it appeared to critics an easy escape from the responsibility of dealing with the situations he had exposed. Kefauver and other members of the committee received hundreds of letters from persons asking for an investigation of conditions in their areas. His standard reply was that the people themselves should act and should expect nothing more from the federal government than the reduction of "organized crime to a local operation so that local communities can cope with it." He saw "95 per cent" of any cleanup dependent on "local interest." [47]

What, then, was the role of the federal government in the fight against organized crime? Kefauver felt the first step was to establish a Federal Crime Commission to "coordinate and bring together and avoid duplication in the investigative services of the Federal Government." The Commission would "be the liaison group with good law-enforcement officers in all of the investigative agencies of the Government, keep up a study of new techniques and the new ways that racketeers and criminals operate so as to advise Congress about it." The Commission should "have a standing committee . . . as its counterpart in the Congress, to work with the commission about new legislation that may be necessary, and to be in a position with subpoena power to make a particular rare investigation when one was necessary." The specific federal legislation he felt should be passed immediately dealt with curbing the use of wire services used primarily for gambling purposes, requiring more detailed tax records by racketeers and stiffer penalties for narcotic law violations, and preventing the infiltration of legitimate business by racketeers.[48]

One suggestion he flatly rejected was the legalization of gambling. He felt "it produces nothing except more corruption." He stressed that he was "not out to crusade against gambling as such" but was concerned about any organized gambling because of the economic importance it had on crime in general, furnishing the capital to launch other criminal activities and making possible the graft necessary to buy official protection of those activities.[49]

Between 1951 and 1957, the Kefauver Committee and the heir of its records and responsibilities, the Commerce Committee, submitted a total of 221 legislative proposals to Congress. Few were ever enacted into law. One law which did grow out of the Kefauver Committee hearings was the federal gambling stamp, which Kefauver opposed, feeling that it might have the effect of quasi-legalizing gambling. The legislation requested by the committee in its May 1 and September 1, 1951, reports, however, made little progress through the legislative mill. Kefauver complained in September 1951, that not one of his committee's recommendations, which had been pending for months, had been enacted into law.[50]

In spite of his problems in guiding his committee's proposals through Congress, Kefauver had emerged from the crime investigation as an important national hero. The American Municipal Association, which had played a crucial role in initiating the investigation, was well satisfied with the results and had nothing but praise for Kefauver's direction of the committee.[51] Honors poured in on Kefauver from cities, civic clubs, and national associations. He was chosen Father of the Year for 1951 because of his "high principled leadership" of the committee which "dramatically aroused public consciousness and morality." [52] A poll in the fall of 1951 of 128 newspaper correspondents covering the Senate ranked Kefauver second only to Paul Douglas.[53] A poll of political scientists gave the same result.[54] In *Look* magazine's poll of about a thousand members of the television industry for its annual TV awards, the Kefauver Committee hearings won two honors: best public affairs program and special achievement.[55] The hearings also won an Emmy from the Academy of Television Arts and Sciences for special achievement, "for bringing the workings of our government into the homes of the American people." [56]

It was symbolic of the boost that the crime investigation had given Kefauver's career that he accepted the Emmy in February 1952 over the telephone from New Hampshire, where he was snowbound in the middle of his campaign for delegates which he hoped would help gain him the 1952 Democratic nomination for President of the United States.[57]

chapter vii

HAT IN THE RING I
1951-1952

Although Kefauver's campaign for the 1952 Democratic presidential nomination was perhaps the inevitable outgrowth of the warm public response to the Kefauver Crime Committee, the chaotic state of national politics in 1951 provoked discussion about and consideration of so many possibilities for both major party nominations that it came as a real surprise to many that Kefauver emerged in January 1952, as the most active contender for his party's nomination.

Holding the center stage as the 1952 presidential election approached was the incumbent President, Harry Truman, who, after being counted out, had rallied the Democratic party to a dramatic victory in 1948. His victory, however, did not result in the implementation of his "Fair Deal" program. If anything, the liberal domestic program urged by the President stiffened the opposition to him among most Republicans and drove more Southerners into the arms of their already rebellious Dixiecrat brothers.[1]

Adding to Truman's political troubles was the public's growing reaction against the high taxes which many people thought were unnecessarily carried over from the Second World War. The cost of living was steadily and swiftly on the rise. Continual uncovering of government waste, influence-peddling, and security leaks also played a part in discrediting the Administration.[2]

The outstanding issue, however, was the war in Korea. What had appeared to be a great victory against communist aggression after the dramatic Inchon landing became a stalemate with the intervention of the Chinese in late 1950. Boys were being killed, and many Americans wondered for what purpose, as the "limited war" showed no signs of ending. The removal of General MacArthur and the permanent decision to confine the war to Korea were decisions upsetting to Americans conditioned to expect military victory, and inevitably led to a further undermining of confidence in the Truman Administration.[3]

Kefauver had supported Truman's Korean policy from the beginning and praised "President Truman and the Democratic party for having the courage to put strength into the United Nations by stopping the first aggression in Korea. If they had gotten by with the first act of aggression, we would have another and another and another." [4]

Kefauver was by 1951 one of the most respected and popular Democratic leaders, and the Administration drafted him to help answer MacArthur's criticisms of government policy. In December 1951, Kefauver delivered in Seattle a strong attack on MacArthur, calling him a "defeatist" and a "Monday morning quarterback" who did not understand the United Nations' role in Korea. The prestige acquired by Kefauver during the crime investigation gave him a base of political security from which to answer MacArthur that few other elected Democrats enjoyed. But Kefauver himself became increasingly unhappy with what appeared to be both a military and political quagmire and was on occasion mildly critical of the Administration. In May 1951, he pointed out that MacArthur had impressed Americans with a "plan and aim" for the war, whereas the Administration had "become bogged down in technical arguments, and has no vision or star to hitch a wagon to." It was this feeling that no end was in sight that bothered Kefauver most, and, although he never made the Korean War an issue in his campaigns within the party against Truman or Truman-backed favorite sons, he did temporarily urge a threat of greater military force in the hope of influencing the communists to accept an end to the fighting. He was never able, however, to outline an approach to the war that both satisfied himself and provided a clear alternative to the current policy. And he remained a staunch defender of Secretary of State Dean Acheson, whom so many Administration opponents made the scapegoat for foreign policy setbacks.[5]

Kefauver's meteoric rise in public esteem coincided with Truman's decline in popularity, and it was inevitable that Kefauver would figure in speculation about the Democratic ticket in 1952. Although Truman would have served almost eight full years by the time his current term expired, he was exempt from the provisions of the Twenty-second Amendment and could have constitutionally sought another term had he wanted it. But Democratic party leaders, even those who were solid supporters of most Administration programs, were questioning whether Truman should be the nominee in 1952, even if he were willing. The results of public opinion polls seemed to raise grave doubts. The confidence of the public in the President, which had been judged as 26 per cent of the electorate in February 1951 had sunk to 24 per cent in June. By September it had climbed to 32 per cent, but December showed a decline to 29 per cent. As January 1952 opened, his rating fell to 23 per cent.[6]

These polls could be partially dismissed with the reminder that the polls had been wrong in 1948; but to the political realists they had sobering implications. The polls also began to show how the President would do in a contest with three possible Republican nominees, Taft, Warren, and Eisenhower. All three outdistanced the President.[7]

As the President's political troubles began to be taken more seriously and doubt began to be expressed about his seeking another term, interest focused on other available Democrats who might seek or accept the nomination in 1952. Among the most prominently mentioned were Vice-President Alben W.

Barkley of Kentucky; Chief Justice Fred Vinson and Justice William O. Douglas of the United States Supreme Court; Governor Adlai Stevenson and Senator Paul Douglas, both of Illinois; and Kefauver. With the exception of Douglas and Kefauver, all were part of the Democratic establishment in 1951–52. Senator Douglas, however, did not choose to seek the Presidency, either before or after Truman's announcement that he would not seek re-election.

Kefauver had all the ingredients necessary for a Presidential campaign in 1952. The Democratic machinery in Tennessee was in the hands of his faithful political ally, Governor Gordon Browning, with whom he had campaigned successfully against the Crump machine in 1948. In addition to his image as the man who overthrew boss rule in Tennessee, Kefauver also had an even more valuable political appeal as the leader of the crusade against organized crime in the United States. With the country especially sensitive to bossism and corruption, political analysts naturally saw in Kefauver a candidate who would be least tainted by the general charges against the incumbent Democratic Administration.[8]

Although the crime investigation had given Kefauver's Presidential prospects a crucial boost, he had been mentioned as a possible 1952 candidate as early as 1949. But even the pre-New York hearings of the Kefauver Committee had elevated him only to the category of possible alternatives to Truman. In the early part of 1951, the rising Democratic star seemed to be Senator Douglas. A poll of Democratic leaders announced on March 11 indicated that Kefauver had irritated several important figures in the party by his conduct of the crime investigation, which several saw as Kefauver's would-be vehicle to the national ticket.[9]

The televising of the New York hearings, however, transformed Kefauver into a genuine national hero and vastly heightened his availability for the Presidency.[10] His Presidential ambitions were a subject of great interest to "Meet the Press" panel members on April 1. Kefauver termed the suggestion that he would seek the Presidency "ridiculous," saying that "nobody ever thought of me for President and certainly I never thought about it myself. I just want to be a United States Senator if I can, and if I can't be that I want to go back to Tennessee and be a country squire." [11] But Kefauver was riding a wave of popularity and public esteem that showed no signs of subsiding even after the dramatic New York hearings began to fade in the public memory.

Kefauver's triumphal return to Chattanooga in late April was the occasion for the announcement of the first Kefauver-for-President Club, but Kefauver kept his distance from the group and directed his staff to do the same, saying, "I am very flattered. Who wouldn't be? But the only thing I expect to do anything about is my race for re-election in 1954." In a radio interview in June, Kefauver insisted that he had "no intention of running for the Presidency and I'm not doing anything about it." He did not think "anyone from the South would have a chance, and if a Southerner did have a chance, there are many people down there more deserving than I am." In August, Kefauver-for-President petitions were circulated in Oregon, but he asked for a halt to such activity on his behalf.[12]

Any lingering doubts about the political value of having been associated with the crime investigation were resolved in November, when political amateur Halley, running as a reform candidate of the Liberal party for President of the City Council in New York, scored a stunning upset victory over the major party candidates. Kefauver had stayed out of the campaign until late October, when he defended Halley against a charge that he had continued to practice law while conducting the Kefauver Committee investigation. Kefauver's strong commendation of Halley certainly strengthened the dislike for Kefauver by the New York Democratic organization.[13]

Also in November, Kefauver's public attitude toward seeking the nomination began to change. He now averred that he was not running for President, but added that he was not "running from the opportunity of running," and a state-wide

Kefauver-for-President headquarters was opened in Nashville. On November 29 he announced to pro-Kefauver California Democrats that he would know by February 1 whether he would be a candidate in 1952. Less than a week later, when asked whether there was any possibility that he would challenge President Truman for the nomination, Kefauver replied: "If I decide to seek it, I will go on notwithstanding. I don't think the President will announce his intention until shortly before the convention." A Kefauver campaign for the nomination looked sure enough by early December that the two most popular and highly respected members of the House from Tennessee, Representatives Albert Gore and Percy Priest, the latter then serving as Majority Whip, announced that they would support Kefauver over Truman if he chose to challenge the President.[14]

Although Douglas continued to have powerful support,[15] his refusal to consider the nomination left Kefauver as the most widely discussed alternative to Truman, especially as the Republicans made it more obvious that corruption and scandal in the Truman Administration would be major issues in 1952. Many felt that only a candidate with Kefauver's credentials could successfully answer the expected Republican attacks, an opinion believed to be shared to some degree by the President himself, and the press hinted that a reconciliation between Truman and Kefauver was being worked out in late 1951.[16] In any event, Kefauver had practically decided to try for the nomination, and the first major steps toward financing a national campaign were taken in December, when a group of approximately 250 Tennessee businessmen pledged $1000 apiece to a Kefauver-for-President drive.[17]

Just as Truman dominated Democratic politics in 1951–52, so did Senator Robert A. Taft of Ohio play a similar role for the Republicans. The leader of the conservative Republican forces, he had sought the nomination in 1940 and 1948 but had been outmaneuvered by the liberal faction of the party on both occasions. The election of 1952 was to be his last futile attempt to win the office his father had occupied forty years before.

Although he was outside the mainstream of Republican thinking, being to the right of the majority of Republican officeholders on domestic issues and neo-isolationist on foreign policy, he was loyally supported by most of the party machinery at the national, state, and local levels. He saw himself as the man who could beat Truman, whom he wanted to face in 1952; he firmly believed that "me too-ism" was the cause of recent Republican defeats at the national level. However, Taft was hurt by polls that showed he was the weakest of the major Republican possibilities for 1952.[18]

In spite of Taft's weak appeal to non-Republican voters, the only major stumbling block to his nomination was the unknown political factor of General Dwight D. Eisenhower. If Eisenhower refused to participate in politics or was beaten by the Ohio Senator for the Republican nomination, Taft could lead the conservative wing of the party to the control that had long been denied it.

Dwight D. Eisenhower's unique political strength in 1951 is almost without parallel in American history. Throughout the year, the European Commander of the forces of the Western Alliance was courted openly by powerful figures in both parties, including the titular leaders, President Truman and Governor Dewey of New York. The reason was simple: General Eisenhower was the most popular living American. In addition, he was the most popular figure among both Democrats and Republicans.[19]

While Eisenhower was interested only in the Republican nomination, he was not interested enough to come home permanently and campaign for it. He felt that his duty was in Europe, and he intended to remain there. This attitude created a frustrating situation for his liberal Republican backers, for not even the most optimistic thought that Eisenhower could get the Republican nomination without leading the fight for it. A sincere draft was almost impossible in the face of the fierce Taft activity.[20]

Truman was left in the position of not being able to make

a decision on re-election until he could be certain of the Republican nominee. He felt that he would be the strongest possible Democratic candidate and, thus, had a duty to run for re-election if Taft were the candidate, since everything possible must be done to prevent an abandonment of the Roosevelt-Truman foreign policy, which Eisenhower would continue but Taft would not.[21]

As 1951 drew to a close, therefore, the non-Dixiecrat Democrats and the liberal Republicans seemed paralyzed by the inactivity of Truman and Eisenhower. It became increasingly evident to prospective candidates for the Democratic nomination that inaction on their part would result in a July convention controlled by the Truman Administration, which would see to it that the President was renominated if he desired or that his personal choice was the choice of the convention. History offers few exceptions to the rule that an incumbent President controls his party's convention. Any premature move by a serious candidate for the nomination would offend the President's well-publicized pride and naturally destroy the possibility of White House support, or, at least, neutrality. Thus, candidates who were thinking about seeking the nomination refrained from taking any stand which put them in a position of opposition to the President.[22]

However, continued inaction obviously would result in an abandonment of opportunities to gain public and delegate support through the most democratic of delegate selection methods, the presidential primary. To seek votes and delegates for oneself would naturally imply that an alternative was being offered to the "draft Truman" delegates who would simply be stooges controlled by the state machines, which worked closely in harmony with the Administration in almost all states having primaries. In states not having presidential primaries, the machines could operate even more efficiently, with the lip-service to democratic methods being unnecessary.

By 1952, some form of presidential primary was conducted by sixteen states and the District of Columbia, thus giving voters a chance to elect about one-third of the delegates to the major party conventions. The influence of the primaries on the convention outcome could, however, be decisive if the primary results showed a general and significant rank and file support for a candidate. Since organizational support could not be won away from Truman unless it was seen, by means of primary campaigns, that another Democrat was the choice of the party, it was imperative that a candidate who planned to buck the Truman plans for a subservient convention take his case to the people via the primary route.

For a candidate to travel this road to the nomination successfully would require an all-out effort at every opportunity. Such a campaign in the presidential primaries would have to be planned as soon as possible and begun without delay, since an organization would have to be assembled to combat the entrenched state machines.

Because it was the first to be held in 1952, the New Hampshire presidential primary took on increased importance. The election itself was to be held in March, but the filing period ended in early February. If a serious challenge to the President developed within Democratic ranks, it might make itself known by late January. Thus, developments concerning the New Hampshire primary were watched with great interest by the politically alert across the nation.[23]

On January 9 it was reported that the national Kefauver-for-President headquarters in Washington was canvassing Democratic leaders in New Hampshire to feel out sentiment in regard to a primary race by the Senator. This news was considered surprising, since President Truman had not announced his plans regarding re-election.[24]

The Kefauver headquarters was contacting Democrats whose names were associated with Democratic party politics in any way, an attempt to get the support of the Democratic establishment in New Hampshire that was almost entirely unsuccessful. In late 1951, National Committeeman Emmett J. Kelley of Berlin had been asked privately by the Democratic National

Chairman to arrange a delegation which could be held for President Truman. Kelley had agreed to do so and had passed the word down Democratic channels that the organization Democrats should avoid any tieup with a campaign that might challenge the President's control over the New Hampshire delegation. Some of the "organization" Democrats, however, were sympathetic to a potential Kefauver candidacy, and one, Mayor Laurence M. Pickett of Keene, informed the Kefauver forces of a man who might be interested in helping Kefauver—Hugh Waling, who had been postmaster in Keene several years before. Although Waling was almost completely without influence in the New Hampshire Democratic party in 1952, he was, nevertheless, drafted by the Kefauver group to head the campaign because time was running out and organizational Democrats were refusing to buck the state machine.[25]

Waling was on his own in attempting to round up potential delegate candidates. The national Kefauver headquarters was desperate enough to give him free rein and did not exercise any control over the candidates procured. Despite the fact that Waling began early in January and worked right up until the deadline, February 9, he was able to get only fourteen people who would consent to run as Kefauver candidates, and ten alternate positions were forfeited. But in the early days of January, even this degree of success was encouraging since Waling was further handicapped by the lack of a public announcement by Senator Kefauver that he was seeking the Presidency.[26]

The "state machine" that took orders from National Committeeman Emmett J. Kelley was in a state of unprecedented ineffectiveness and decay. The industrial towns did have Democratic organizations of some vitality and frequently won local offices; but state-wide the party was completely disorganized. It would take little effort to upset what little control was then exercised by the party leaders over the rank and file.[27]

On January 23 Kefauver announced his candidacy for the Presidency, regardless of Truman's decision on re-election. Immediately, the Kefauver organization took steps officially to enter delegate candidates in the New Hampshire primary. The Kefauver announcement was the climax of weeks of frustration over Truman's intentions, intensified by the growing momentum of the unofficial Kefauver campaign. In late December, Kefauver had observed that "Right today I have a better chance of becoming President than I had of becoming Senator when I decided to run." His confidence was strengthened by the support that continued to build with every new hint or suggestion that he was thinking of making the race. When he and Nancy attended the Sugar Bowl game between Tennessee and Maryland on January 1, he was almost swamped by people from all over the country who wanted to meet him.[28]

Truman's attitude toward Kefauver underwent a superficial change in the opening weeks of 1952 as the President sought to give Kefauver the impression that he might eventually get Administration backing for his Presidential drive, but this supposed change of heart was only a coverup to delay Kefauver's entry into the Presidential race. Truman had once thought very highly of Kefauver, but the rumblings from Democratic urban organizations damaged by the Kefauver Committee, and Kefauver's suggestions that Truman could do more to clean house in the federal government, had caused the President to become antagonistic. "The junior Senator from Tennessee is *persona non grata* at the White House these days," Charles Neese, Kefauver's 1948 campaign manager, had written to a friend at the close of the crime hearings. The President did not watch the televised hearings, and his interpretation of what the Kefauver Committee had achieved was highly influenced by Democratic politicians' complaints about the alleged damage to the party wrought by the hearings. The press commented on Truman's "openly derisive attitude" toward Kefauver and reported that Truman believed Kefauver was standing around waiting for presidential lightning to strike him.[29]

In early January there were rumors that Kefauver might be appointed Attorney General or put in charge of Truman's announced cleanup of the executive branch. If these were trial balloons to see if Kefauver would lend his prestige to the Truman Administration, they failed. Kefauver announced that he would consider neither job. "I have other things in mind," he hinted. To the question of whether he was making a play for the Vice-Presidency, Kefauver answered that "I have no feelings toward the vice-presidency. Later on, if I should decide to run for President, I would not do it with the expectation of ending up in the vice-presidency." [30]

The attention given Kefauver as a possible presidential candidate did not sit well with more senior Democratic senators, who had long been jealous of the headlines he had captured during the crime investigation. When he walked onto the Senate floor on January 8 for the opening of the session, he was practically ignored by most Democratic senators and finally walked over to the Republican side of the aisle, where he was greeted more warmly.[31]

That Kefauver and his supporters wanted to come to some accommodation with Truman was only logical. On January 6, Representative Wayne Hays, a Kefauver supporter in Ohio, had conferred with Truman in an attempt to learn the President's plans regarding re-election, so that he could lead a campaign for Kefauver in Ohio if the President did not run. Truman had replied that the decision was made, but that he was not yet ready to announce it.[32]

Yet the Truman plans had become more and more evident in the early days of January. The President and the Democratic National Committee had asked Senator Hubert Humphrey of Minnesota to run as a favorite son in that state's primary, a move endorsed by Kefauver but obviously designed to hold the Minnesota delegates for the Administration. Three days later, on January 11, the New Hampshire Democratic machine had filed candidates favorable to the President in that state's primary.[33]

In one last effort to come to an accommodation with the President, a move encouraged by *Nashville Tennessean* publisher Silliman Evans, a close friend of both Truman and Kefauver, Senator Kefauver visited Truman on January 15. Kefauver had been trying to see the President for ten days. At the twenty-five-minute conference, Kefauver "did not ask support, receive the promise of any, or conclude any specific agreements with the President," according to the exclusive story carried by the *Chattanooga Times*. Truman was said to have told Kefauver that he favored the development of outstanding young men in the party, such as Kefauver, and had no objection to a Kefauver candidacy, which Kefauver had told the President was a matter still undecided.[34]

The hints of a Kefauver candidacy became even stronger after the meeting with Truman. To a reporter Nancy confided in early January:

> I have a feeling he will run, and if he does I certainly plan to campaign at his side.
> I can't honestly say that being first lady appeals to me very much. However, I would try to do the best job I know how to do with the big responsibilities of the job.[35]

On January 19, she let the cat out of the bag. When asked if Kefauver was planning to run for President, she replied, "Why yes, I guess he is." [36]

By mid-January there were Kefauver-for-President organizations set up in forty-six states, and the only thing remaining was an official announcement by the candidate himself. After a short vacation in Miami Beach, Estes and Nancy returned to Washington for the press conference which would kick off one of the most ambitious and exhausting campaigns for the Presidency ever conducted in American political history.[37]

The announcement ceremony on January 23 was very low key, and Kefauver placed much more emphasis on achieving world peace than on attacking crime and corruption. There was very little in the announcement itself to which Truman could have taken exception. However, one of the post-announcement questions indicated that Kefauver would not overlook what was really his most valuable issue, even at the cost of irritating the President:

> Q. Senator, do you think the present Administration has done as much as it might have done to stamp out corruption?
> A. No, I do not think so. I do think some good things have been done, but I think much more must be done. More stress must be put on morality and clean government in the Federal Government, and we must take the leadership in showing the way and giving the inspiration to local people to help them clean up their criminal conditions.[38]

President Truman's news conference the next day indicated his displeasure with the Kefauver announcement.[39] The entry of Kefauver into the contest resolved a dilemma for Kefauver but created an imposing problem for the President. Should he refrain from participation in the primary fights, hoping that his political allies would be able to crush anti-Administration rivals? It was possible that Truman's abstention would result in Kefauver's sweeping the primaries and forcing the convention to accept a candidate not approved by Truman, for fear of appearing to ignore the will of the Democratic voters. On the other hand, the President could wade into the primary battles in an attempt to use his personal prestige to smash his rivals only at the risk of being defeated and discrediting his leadership at home and abroad. In any case, the deadline for filing in New Hampshire was approaching,[40] and the pattern set there would be significant. The deadline that had forced a Kefauver announcement would also force a Truman policy decision.

chapter viii

FROM CHALLENGER TO
FRONT-RUNNER, 1952

The New Hampshire Democratic presidential primary of 1952 furnished Kefauver with his first opportunity to test his basic appeal as a presidential candidate. Even more important, the campaign techniques used and the issues raised during his campaign there set the tone for his entire pre-convention drive for the nomination.

The primary consisted of two separate elections. One, included for the first time in that year, pitted actual presidential aspirants against each other. A victory in this more publicized contest offered no reward beyond the publicity gained. A second part of the primary featured delegate contests. The victors would take seats at the national convention and cast the votes of the state on all issues before the convention, including the nomination of candidates. It was possible for a candidate to win the preference contest and yet win no delegates or only a fraction of the delegation. While a candidate could do nothing to keep delegate candidates from running and bringing his name into the election indirectly, he did have some control over the other half of the primary, the popularity contest, or presidential preference election. Anyone had the right to withdraw his name from this contest if he acted within ten days of the filing which entered him, no matter who had taken the original action.[1]

At the time of Kefauver's announcement, Truman had not been entered in the preference primary in New Hampshire, although some delegate candidates had filed favorable to his nomination. However, on January 30, almost at the last minute and without White House consultation, Truman backers in New Hampshire filed the petitions necessary to enter Truman in the preference primary.[2] The pressure was now on the President to decide whether to remain in the primary and battle Kefauver, or to withdraw within ten days and have no contest there. Kefauver could claim no victory if he ran without opposition, and the delegate races would probably go to the better-known, machine-backed pro-Truman candidates.

At a news conference on January 31, Truman announced that he would withdraw his name from the New Hampshire primary. In remarks that were to be used against him later with a considerable degree of success, Truman said that he considered presidential primaries to be "eyewash" and that he could have the nomination if he wanted it, without going into the primaries.[3]

The national response to this evaluation was mixed. Editorial reactions generally upheld the President's analysis, although most urged that something should be done to remedy the situation. Most also pointed out that primaries could have some impact, especially if the electorate were aroused by remarks such as those made by the President, whom *Life* described as speaking "with more candor than discretion." [4]

Republicans were quick to seize on Truman's remarks. Governor Sherman Adams of New Hampshire issued a statement which declared, "In effect, the president has said that the people's choice is not important. Instead, he announces that he controls the choice to be made by a rubber stamp convention to which he will dictate what to do." [5]

Republican leaders around the country echoed Adams's sentiments. Some Democrats were quick to disassociate themselves from the President's supposed position on primaries. Senator Paul Douglas of Illinois, the champion of the presidential primary idea on a national level, called for more voter participation in the presidential selection process and strongly defended that which then existed. Senator Hubert Humphrey of Minnesota, the Administration-backed favorite son in Minnesota's presidential primary, also disagreed with the President.[6]

Of course, the Democrat whose best chance for the Presidency seemed to lie in successful primary campaigns was quick to come to their defense. Kefauver issued a statement declaring:

> I feel that primaries are a very necessary way for the people to express themselves for their party candidates.
>
> I think the selection of party candidates—like those in the general elections—ought to be as democratic as possible in order to give the people an opportunity to express themselves.[7]

The reaction in New Hampshire to Truman's withdrawal was more negative than it was elsewhere. The home of the first presidential primary of the year considered the "eyewash" statement a personal insult.[8] The fairly objective *Concord Daily Monitor,* published in the state capital, was unusually aroused in its comment entitled "The Boss Is Insolent":

> What the President was saying is that he is the boss of a national political machine, held together with the patronage and favors bought with taxpayers' money, and that this machine will do whatever he bids, regardless of what is best for the people, or of what the people themselves may think best. . . .
>
> What the President was saying is that the sovereign state of New Hampshire can go to hell.[9]

Other New Hampshire newspapers expressed similar views.[10]

Although the full political implications of the President's remarks were not immediately evident, the public was not likely to receive such utterances warmly, no matter how realistic they might be. A Gallup poll prepared at the time of Truman's press conference showed that 73 per cent of the American people thought that a nation-wide system of primaries should replace the convention system, which many people accused of being dominated by political bosses. Another poll showed that 53 per cent of the public thought that the "people" did not have enough influence in choosing candidates.[11] Truman's declaration that he could have the nomination if he wanted it would, therefore, hardly appeal to the public. Kefauver thus accidentally found himself, to the degree that he was seen as the alternative to Truman, a vehicle for expressing dissatisfaction with Truman's position on primaries.

Truman's withdrawal from the New Hampshire contest would have in no way technically affected his delegate candidates. They did not have and did not need his permission to run "favorable" to him. Practically, however, there was the danger that Truman's statement would react against them, and fear of this made them insist that Truman stay in the race.

Because of consideration for the reaction of the public and especially for the predicament of the New Hampshire Democratic machine, President Truman reversed his position on February 5 and announced that he would allow his name to stay in the primary. His telegram to the New Hampshire Secretary of State asking to be left on the ballot was a carefully worded, almost humble explanation of what he had "intended" the week before:

> . . . I had thought it would be better for my name not to appear on any ballot at this time as a candidate for President until I am ready to make an announcement as to whether I shall seek re-election. But the chairman of the Democratic National Committee and many good Democrats in New Hampshire are of the opinion that my name should be left on the ballot. At their suggestion, therefore, I shall not ask you to take my name off the list.[12]

Thus, the battle was joined in New Hampshire between the President and Kefauver. It remained to be seen how successfully Kefauver could make use of the apparent advantages handed him by the President's political bungling. Besides the obvious benefits accruing to Kefauver in being the alternative to a man whom many thought had told New Hampshire to "go to hell," the senator had positive appeal as a foe of bossism and corruption in government. The *New York Times,* in its editorial hailing Kefauver's announcement for the Presidency, gave an indication of the general regard felt for the senator around the nation:

> He has earned the cordial dislike of many a professional politician of his own party as an "upstart" who has managed to elbow most of his seniors out of the limelight, and by a device that no one had thought of using in such a way before. Far worse, he is credited with playing a large part in the defeat of one or more old-school Democrats by the timing of his crime-and-politics exposures. This is the cardinal sin for which the machines are not likely to forgive him.
>
> But this is where his strength lies, too. To many Americans, sick of the corruption they hear about so often, and tired of the inability or unwillingness of the Administration thus far to take adequate measures against it, Mr. Kefauver stands as a courageous fighter for clean government.[13]

Kefauver had not dodged the touchy question of corruption in the national Democratic Administration, even in the days when he was hoping for White House support. On January 5, he had recognized that corruption would be a major issue in 1952, and he had warned that "how potent an issue it will be will depend on how fast the Administration cleans up conditions so that people will know that they are being fully corrected. The Administration is working toward that end. I might say that more can be done in that direction." [14]

There can be no doubt that corruption was a major concern of voters in 1952. A Roper poll of February 1952 showed that 52 per cent of the American people believed that there was widespread corruption in Washington among high officials. A poll taken at the same time showed that 58 per cent believed that Truman knew about corruption before it was announced;

only 28 per cent thought that scandal in his Administration came as a surprise to the President. The benefit to Kefauver, as an alternative to the President in the primary election, was obvious, especially when his image as a crimefighter was in such contrast to the view of the Administration held by the public.[15]

But Kefauver did not choose to base his campaign in New Hampshire on an open attack on the Administration; to do so would have almost assuredly cost him the nomination, whatever the outcome in New Hampshire. During his first trip to the state, he had emphasized that:

> I am not in New Hampshire to criticize President Truman, or anyone else. I have a record of my own, and I have progressive ideas of which I think citizens of this country approve. It is these ideas and my record which I intend to tell New Hampshire voters about.[16]

Nevertheless, it was obvious that he represented a means of protest against the President. The *Concord Daily Monitor* outlined the possibilities of the Kefauver candidacy in an editorial entitled "Dilemma for N. H. Democrats":

> Harry Truman is not in high favor with the members of his own party. . . .
> On the other hand there is no rash of alternative candidates, because it is assumed that the President can get himself renominated if he wants to. The single exception is the Senator who won fame, and sometimes fortune, as a television crime busting star, a man who has defied Democratic political machines before, having himself been elected to the Senate by beating the notorious Crump machine.

The editorial went on to observe that Senator Kefauver himself was not a "great man." Ignoring an impressive legislative record of thirteen years, he was cited for a lack of "imagination or initiative," and his role in the crime investigation was written off as "fate." What was significant was that Kefauver "could serve as a place for protest votes to go. If enough did, it would be anything but 'eyewash.' It might set off a Democratic revolt." Such a revolt would not result in Kefauver's being nominated, but it would encourage other good men to get into the race and prevent Truman from naming his own successor. Concluding, the editorial called for New Hampshire Democrats to put "country above party" and support Kefauver.[17]

Although by early February the Kefauver forces had been able to get the senator on the preferential ballot and round up enough delegate candidates to fill the slate, the campaign had not yet really gotten off the ground. Kefauver's personal appearance in New Hampshire on February 10 was the beginning of a serious and organized campaign to carry the primary for him. The occasion was a Nashua Chamber of Commerce dinner; at the banquet, Kefauver met and won over several men and women who were to be pillars in his primary campaign. This Nashua-based Kefauver group soon merged with the original group headed by Hugh Waling, and a state-wide organization was established by late February.[18]

Kefauver made two trips to New Hampshire in addition to the Nashua engagement. He first arrived to campaign actively on February 13 and stayed until February 20. His second tour began on March 4 and lasted until the votes were counted.[19]

The strategy of the Kefauver forces was very simple. They planned to ride on the senator's national reputation and stress the fact that he was an active candidate who cared enough about New Hampshire's endorsement to come to the state and work for it. To emphasize Kefauver's interest in the state, it was decided to adopt the person-to-person technique that had proven so successful in Kefauver's 1948 campaign for the Democratic nomination for the Senate. The campaign in New Hampshire, with its emphasis on traveling extensively over the state and meeting as many Democrats as possible, became the model for future presidential primary campaigns, not only by Kefauver but by other announced candidates for the Presidency.[20]

Because of Kefauver's national stature and his sincere interest in the people he met, he gave a tremendous psychological boost to New Hampshire Democrats, who were extremely appreciative of all the attention they were getting, especially in a state where Democrats got very little attention at all. People were amazed, for example, that a United States senator would spend Sunday afternoons visiting with them earnestly seeking their views on important national and world problems. Kefauver went to great lengths to demonstrate his interest in the voters. He would go to the top floor of factories and shake every hand on every floor, introducing himself by saying, "I'm Estes Kefauver, and I'm running for President. I'd appreciate your vote." If he heard that someone was a Democrat, he would make a special effort to meet him even if it involved a seemingly incredible investment of time and energy. Because of previous neglect, it was "just as big a thing as if the President of the United States had come to call" to New Hampshire Democrats to have Kefauver solicit their support.[21]

Informal gatherings became the trademark of the Kefauver campaign. Tea parties, church breakfasts or fairs, visits to homes of sympathetic Democrats, tours through factories, and canvassing on the street were typical of the methods used to expose Kefauver to New Hampshire voters. Democrats who had never had any formal contact with the party except to cast a Democratic vote on election day suddenly found themselves considered very important people by the hard-working Kefauver, who considered a group of five to be a "good crowd." He amazed his supporters by his tremendous energy and drive, and would campaign from early morning until late at night, never losing his personal charm.[22]

As the Kefauver campaign progressed, it was able to interest more and more people who had shown little or no interest in politics before their involvement in the Kefauver race. Almost all of the Kefauver workers among New Hampshire Democrats were amateurs, since the senator had little luck in winning important professionals away from the organization. After the campaign got rolling, it was relatively easy to get rank and file support. As one worker put it, "I liked his courage and dedication, and it was easy for me to want to help him." "We had the best product in the world to sell," said another.[23]

Nancy campaigned with her husband and made a tremendous hit in the state, setting a pace for candidates' wives to follow in the future. She avoided issues and stuck to subjects of general interest to women in the audiences and along the scheduled routes. Her activities helped win the Kefauver campaign wide newspaper coverage by the heavily Republican press of the state. Of course, Republicans had no intention or desire to build up Kefauver as a Presidential candidate who would be elected in November; but this was of no concern to them at that time, because Kefauver was given little chance of either beating Truman in New Hampshire or winning the nomination. In early 1952 Kefauver was seen primarily as a means of discrediting Truman. In addition, the activities of Estes and Nancy had interest that hit the grass roots. In comparison with the typical local news story, their routine campaign appearances were major news items. A national figure paying attention to New Hampshire was news in itself; and, coupled with Truman's indifference, it was dramatic.[24]

As February passed, the Kefauver candidacy was steadily gaining publicity and support in the state. The fact that Kefauver was an announced candidate who had come to New Hampshire to ask for votes, coupled with his favorable public image, was beginning to produce significant results for his cause, although no one would suggest that Kefauver or his delegate candidates had even a remote chance of winning any part of the primary.

The Kefauver activity, however, had the result of spurring the state machine to take previously unplanned steps to roll up the impressive majority it desired for the President. On February 22, National Committeeman Emmett J. Kelley, an ardent Truman supporter and delegate candidate, announced that the Truman Democrats would wage an active campaign to offset growing pro-Kefauver sentiment. "We'll give them a show if that is what the people expect," Kelley commented, on announcing the Truman campaign plans. Inadvertently dramatizing the under-dog role of Kefauver, Kelley declared that "state Democratic leaders, practically all of whom are on the Truman bandwagon, will leave no stone unturned to guarantee a victory for President Truman in the primary." Since Truman was not yet an active candidate for the nomination, he would not appear in New Hampshire. Deciding that an absent "nobody" could no longer campaign satisfactorily against an active "somebody," the ma-chine decided to bring in nationally known Democrats to aid the pro-Truman forces.[25]

This ploy might have had the effect of reminding New Hampshire voters that, after all, Truman was the President of the United States, and, in spite of what might be wrong with affairs in Washington, he had to lead the nation for almost another year. Did New Hampshire Democrats have a higher duty to save their President the embarrassment a defeat for Truman would bring? This was a sobering argument. As former Navy Secretary John L. Sullivan told an audience of five hun-dred at the University of New Hampshire on March 4: "In my opinion if the Democrats of New Hampshire fail to give a vote of confidence to our President, the effect in Europe will be very bad indeed and the news, when it reaches the Kremlin, will be the best news it has received in a long while." [26]

The Truman Democrats in New Hampshire in 1952 had announced that they would "call on those who have already an-nounced their support of" Truman. Scott Lucas, the former Senate Majority Leader, who blamed Kefauver for his 1950 de-feat by Everett Dirksen, was such a man, but it would have been politically inept to furnish the Kefauver forces with a walking example of the opposition to their candidate of those sinister forces of the underworld with which the ex-Majority Leader had allegedly been allied. The Truman forces had enough to do in New Hampshire without adding this liability, but they agreed to Lucas's request to participate in the organization's campaign against Kefauver. It did not take Lucas long to embarrass the

Truman camp. On March 5, he made a crack about the Kefauver Committee, terming it a "televised road show." He accused Kefauver of being a publicity seeker and using his Senate office to advance his own personal and political interests.[27]

Lucas had misjudged the reaction of the American people to the Kefauver investigation. At the time of Lucas's attack on the Kefauver Committee, the *Public Opinion Quarterly* was preparing to publish an article which showed that 94 per cent of enrolled party members in the United States had a favorable impression of the Kefauver hearings.[28] In light of his own association with the hearings, it is easy to imagine what political capital could be made of Lucas's appearance in New Hampshire and his subsequent attacks on Kefauver. The Kefauver campaign organization was quick to issue a statement on the Lucas visit:

> The action of Mr. Kelley in bringing in Ex-Sen. Scott Lucas into New Hampshire for the avowed purpose of discrediting the Kefauver Crime Committee would be funny, if it wasn't so tragic. . . . To allow Mr. Lucas to come into the state under his sponsorship and make such an unwarranted attack was political stupidity.[29]

Senator Kefauver personally announced that he considered it "regrettable that former Senator Lucas should make a personal issue of the work of our crime committee." In any event, the public should know "that we of the Senate Crime Investigation Committee would do our duty to get the facts and let the chips fall where they may." This had been done and would be done without "trying to punish or defend anybody." Kefauver noted that often the task of trying to accomplish a difficult job conscientiously "brings one bitter and powerful enemies. Their wrath follows one to distant places, even all the way from Illinois to New Hampshire." Kefauver also expressed surprise that the New Hampshire State Committee would bring Lucas into the state "to try and punish a member of the committee which rendered the country a very valuable service." [30] If Scott Lucas was an example of the kind of man selected from the national scene to speak on behalf of the President, what were New Hampshire voters to think?

Even so, every political analyst predicted a Truman victory in the preference election and close to a clean sweep in the delegate races. The Associated Press survey of March 7 showed that Truman was expected to get from 65–75 per cent of the vote, with most observers predicting a 70 to 30 edge for the President. The delegate races were expected to be somewhat closer because in parts of the primary there were more pro-Truman candidates than places on the slate to fill, with the result that the Truman vote would be scattered.[31]

Although the professional public opinion surveys indicated a Truman sweep, more informal straw votes indicated that support for Kefauver was strong and increasing as the election approached. Nevertheless, on March 11, a Truman victory of some degree was taken for granted. As voters went to the polls, they read that Senator Kefauver planned to spend election day campaigning but that President Truman was reported as showing not the least interest in the primary. Kefauver went to Epsom to attend Town Meeting Day, a social event as well as a time for voting and conducting the town's business. By "just elbowing with the common folks" Kefauver captured 50 of the 57 votes cast in the Democratic presidential primary in Epsom.[32]

As decisive results began to be reported from across the state on election night, both the Truman and Kefauver camps were shocked to see that Kefauver was running even with the President in the preferential race and that all of the Kefauver delegate candidates were running well ahead in the delegate races. As the night wore on, Kefauver moved slowly out in front of the President, building up a slight but ever increasing lead. The delegate candidates pledged to Kefauver were piling up huge pluralities. By 11 o'clock it was clear that Kefauver had scored a tremendous upset, winning all parts of the primary. His victory was the result of strong showings in all parts of the state. Rural areas gave him proportionally greater support than urban areas, but he carried the three largest cities, Manchester, Nashua, and Portsmouth.[33]

The New Hampshire primary turned the 1952 Democratic political situation upside down. The President had been rejected by a majority of his own party in a New England state that preferred a Southern, freshman United States senator to the titular leader of the national party—a man who had almost unanimous backing from higher officials of the state Democratic party and organized labor. It was inevitable that every aspect of the campaign would be analyzed to discover what had accounted for such a phenomenon and what long-range significance it might have.

To those closest to the secene, the explanation of Kefauver's victory was simple. He had been an announced candidate who had come into New Hampshire asking for support, which he had won because of the reputation he carried into the state and because of the personal campaign style that exposed voters to his charm and sincerity. No protest against Truman was seen; it was entirely a personal victory for Kefauver.

The nation's press, however, viewed the vote as a tremendous blow to the prestige and political future of the President. Most newspapers echoed to some degree the conclusions of the New York *Daily News* that:

> the New Hampshire primary may be eyewash, as Harry says all primaries are. Certainly it doesn't mean that Truman is out as a Presidential candidate. . . . As of this moment, Truman obviously has a bad case of political B. O. Also, his political slip is showing, and may conceivably be down around his ankles by convention time.[34]

Although President Truman publicly ignored the results of the primary, privately he was reported to be bitter. He blamed "selfish New Hampshire party leaders" and Democratic National Committee Chairman Frank McKinney for getting him into such a predicament, but emphasized that the New Hampshire primary would have no bearing at all on his decision regarding re-election. However, on March 29, about two weeks after the vote in New Hampshire, President Truman broke his long silence and announced that he would not be a candidate for re-election in 1952.[35]

The boost given Senator Kefauver's candidacy by his victory in New Hampshire was enormous. With his victory and the Truman withdrawal, he became the frontrunner for the Democratic nomination; as the only announced candidate with a national organization actively working for his nomination, he had a tremendous lead on all other possible contenders. His success would depend on how swiftly other hopefuls filled the vacuum created by Truman's withdrawal and silence on a possible successor. In any event, Kefauver's campaign in New Hampshire and the resulting publicity and comment upon the results there earned him the status of "a major contender for the Democratic nomination" among political observers.[36]

The New Hampshire primary was a landmark in the national political career of Senator Kefauver. It was his first political victory outside of Tennessee and demonstrated his appeal to rank and file Democrats in a state where all he had working in his favor were his national reputation and his personal campaign techniques. The boost given his national campaign for the presidency can hardly be overestimated. Before New Hampshire, he had been just another candidate; but, after the vote, he emerged as a real challenger of the President for control of the convention and the nomination. It was not without reason that he considered his New Hampshire victory to be the most important breakthrough in his efforts to capture the nomination.[37]

chapter ix

THE PEOPLE vs. THE
POLITICIANS, 1952

In his campaign to capture the Democratic nomination for President in 1952, Kefauver placed more emphasis than any other candidate in American political history on demonstrating his widespread grass-roots appeal in the available presidential primaries. In the three months that followed his surprise victory in New Hampshire over President Truman, Kefauver was to take part in more than a dozen other primaries, concentrating more heavily on some than others but never altogether avoiding a primary because of a judgment that he would not win. Incredibly, because of an unusual set of circumstances affecting Democratic hopefuls for 1952, Kefauver was able to move from one success to another, with each victory, and even his one important setback, further strengthening the belief of his followers that their candidate was truly the popular choice of the Democratic rank and file. Kefauver's failure to receive the nomination, therefore, was to come as an especially bitter disappointment not only to his dedicated supporters but even more so to the candidate himself.[1]

That those who opposed Kefauver's nomination could point to most of his primary victories as practically meaningless because of the lack of effective opposition was not Kefauver's fault. He never expected to be handed the easy victories that he achieved in so many states, and, indeed, would have welcomed an opportunity to campaign against those candidates who were later to benefit from the reservations attached to his string of victories.

In his primary campaigns, Kefauver was aided until early spring by President Truman's continued silence on his own plans for 1952—a silence that kept potential candidates hoping for Truman's eventual endorsement waiting in the wings until important filing deadlines had passed. When the President finally did announce on March 29 his intention to retire, the momentum of the Kefauver campaign discouraged some who might have challenged Kefauver in remaining primary contests.[2]

During Kefauver's exhausting campaign to take his candidacy to the people, millions got a firsthand look at the man about whom they knew little other than his role in the Senate crime investigation. Kefauver's performance on the campaign trail, with its emphasis on the average voter rather than on state and local Democratic leadership, reinforced his established image as the soft-spoken crusader for clean government, who was now taking on organized politics in the same way that he had previously taken on organized crime. On the campaign trail, Kefauver was at his best when talking informally with individuals or small groups, or when spontaneously answering questions from reporters. He was at his worst when delivering a prepared speech. Perhaps nowhere was the contrast more visible than during the Kefauver appearance on the CBS-TV series, "Presidential Timber." Kefauver's wife and father were also there, and the folksy, informal exchanges during the preliminaries were extremely effective in communicating the man-of-the-people image that was so much a trademark of the Kefauver campaign. The last segment of the program, however, featured Kefauver practically reading a prepared address, which, although not without interest itself, was delivered in such a dull manner that even the pro-Kefauver audience appeared almost put to sleep.[3] Kefauver's formal speeches had never seemed effective to the oratorical connoisseurs among the journalists covering the American political scene; one reporter spoke of Kefauver's delivering "his speeches [in the Senate] with all the gusto of one who is seeing the text for the first time." But it was difficult for the sophisticated newsmen from national wire services or radio and television networks to appreciate the appeal to the average voter of Kefauver's fumbling style. One newsman spoke of a Kefauver speech in South Dakota as "a drab speech to a drab little audience. But afterward they crowded around him with genuine enthusiasm. Something had happened. They got it. I didn't." [4]

Even among his family and close friends, Kefauver remained throughout his life a man who defied simple analysis. He was unpredictable and complex, and appeared even more so because he rarely confided his most personal hopes and fears to those around him. Charles Neese, Kefauver's administrative assistant, spoke of riding with another Kefauver assistant one day and asking, "Do you understand him [Kefauver]?" "No," his companion replied, "do you?" "No," Neese answered. [5]

The times that Kefauver's closest friends saw him angry or upset were rare; he kept his feelings to himself and struck some people as being as uninterested in listening to their small talk as he was in participating in it. Others, however, found him intensely interested in the most trivial discussions. Nancy once told an interviewer that her husband was "not much interested in individuals," and Charles Bartlett, who knew Kefauver as well as any journalist, spoke of "his disposition to sink into a shell of contemplation in the midst of lively conversation." [6] But he was generally considered one of the friendliest men in public life. Those who found Kefauver difficult to communicate with sometimes interpreted his reticence as a defense against being forced to define his positions or to reveal his lack of understanding of complex issues. Professor Paul Buck of Harvard recalled the difficulty a roomful of intellectuals in Cambridge once had with Kefauver, who kept passing the questions on to someone else, seeking opinions rather than giving them. [7]

If, as some of Kefauver's critics charged, he was a scheming and ambitious politician who put the advancement of his career ahead of issues, principles, or the welfare of the Democratic party, it was not evident to those closest to him. Even in the middle of the 1952 primary campaigns, when Kefauver's time was at a premium, one reporter was moved to comment that "If there is one feeling you get from watching Kefauver in action, it is that there is 'plenty of time.' " [8] Rather than seeing his successes as the result of his own ambitious planning, he seemed to assume, almost naïvely, that whatever victories he achieved were due as much to the moral superiority of his campaign as to the personal efforts of his supporters or himself.

In any event, whether in spite of his personal campaign style or because of it (a question unanswered because of the lack of primary opposition), Kefauver, in the spring of 1952, was reaping the benefits of having been in the right place at the right time to fill the leadership vacuum in the Democratic party. His campaign was rolling smoothly and, by committing himself to entering most of the presidential primaries, he had ensured continuous, extensive publicity for himself; because of the lack of opposition in most of the primaries, he was practically guaranteed that it would be favorable publicity. Those interests in the Democratic party that might logically want to block his nomination seemed to lack both leadership and an alternative candidate. Truman's personal choice to succeed himself was Governor Adlai Stevenson of Illinois, but the President's attempts to turn Stevenson into an avowed candidate got nowhere. The President did not immediately turn elsewhere, and Administration efforts to elect pro-Administration slates of party regulars who would follow the President's lead when he eventually did decide which candidate he would support were generally unsuccessful in primaries where the delegate selection was closely tied to a presidential preference election, as it had been in New Hampshire. California, Ohio, South Dakota, and Wisconsin featured serious delegate contests between pro-Kefauver and pro-Administration forces, and in the four primaries Kefauver amassed 1,692,163 votes (and 133½ delegate votes) to a total of 716,204 votes (and 24½ delegate votes) for the pro-Administration slates.[9]

In several states, however, Kefauver was content to enter only the presidential preference part of the primaries, leaving the delegate contests to the party regulars. In most cases he won these contests practically by default, garnering headlines but few delegates. In Illinois, Maryland, Massachusetts, New Jersey, and Oregon, for example, Kefauver received 990,877 of the 1,142,528 votes cast; his success in these preference elections was not reflected in delegate voting at the convention, however; he received the support of only 11½ of the 128 unbound delegates, although Oregon and Maryland primary rules committed those states' 30 votes to Kefauver on the first ballot. Kefauver's unofficial write-in campaign in Pennsylvania netted him 93,160 of the 174,775 votes cast there, and, even though he received 22½ votes on the first ballot in the Pennsylvania delegation, all 70 of the state's votes fell into line behind Stevenson on the crucial third ballot at the convention.[10]

Four other primaries offered results that were interpreted differently by pro- and anti-Kefauver forces. In Minnesota, Kefauver was at first entered in the primary but he later withdrew in favor of favorite son Senator Hubert H. Humphrey. The Minnesota Democratic organization was genuinely sympathetic to Kefauver and indicated to him that if he would not divide the party there by challenging Humphrey, he could expect favorable consideration if Truman did not seek reelection. Minnesota's behavior at the convention indicated that Kefauver had indeed worked out some accommodation with the organization. However, in the face of his victories by default elsewhere, Kefauver's opponents could point to Minnesota as an example of his reluctance to challenge a strong rival when he had the opportunity. Kefauver's 20,182 write-in votes there, in spite of his call to his supporters to vote for Humphrey, led professional political analysts in Minnesota to believe that Kefauver "probably would have given the party organization serious trouble" had he run against Humphrey.[11]

It was in Nebraska that Kefauver scored his only victory against an announced candidate for the nomination. Senator Robert Kerr of Oklahoma had announced his candidacy on

March 31, two days after Truman's withdrawal and only twenty-four hours before the Nebraska voting. Kerr, however, had been spending and organizing in Nebraska for weeks as a stand-in for Truman. Kerr's support by old line leaders, coupled with obviously heavy campaign expenditures for billboards, posters, radio and television shows, and 300,000 copies of a campaign newspaper, handed Kefauver the politically valuable role of the underdog. The Kefauver campaign seemed to be run on a shoestring and relied on Kefauver's by-now famous personal campaign style to offset the Kerr advantages of great wealth and organizational support. Kefauver stressed to Nebraska voters that he was "not an orator or a great speaker" and just wanted "to meet people, and discuss . . . issues with them." He and Nancy were so effective on the campaign trail that Kerr later quipped, "If I run again I'll have to learn to square-dance and ride a bicycle." His wife added, "And get a redheaded wife, too." Nebraska Democrats gave Kefauver a resounding 64,531 to 42,467 victory over Kerr on April 1.[12]

It was the Florida primary, however, that furnished Kefauver's opponents with the strongest evidence that Kefauver was not invincible at the polls. That Kefauver entered the Florida primary at all was courageous in light of his opposition there by one of the most professional Southerners of them all—Georgia's Senator Richard Russell.

Although Russell had remained loyal to the Democratic ticket in 1948, he had become thoroughly disenchanted with Truman by 1952 and had hinted strongly that he would bolt if Truman sought re-election.[13] Russell, like Kefauver, had announced his candidacy before Truman's withdrawal and had welcomed Kefauver's challenge to Truman in New Hampshire as a means of breaking the President's hold on the national party. When Kefauver shocked the nation with his surprise upset of Truman in New Hampshire, Russell immediately wired his congratulations.[14] But Russell entertained no thoughts of eventually supporting Kefauver for the nomination.

The Florida primary was the only one that Russell was to

enter, although he sought to avoid presenting himself solely as the Southern candidate at the convention. A victory over Kefauver in Florida won only by appealing to the worst fears and prejudices of Florida voters would have eliminated Russell from serious consideration for a place on the national ticket. On the other hand, a defeat in his only primary race would have cast grave doubt on the strength he might add to the ticket in the South.

When Russell first announced his decision to enter the Florida primary, he had no reason to believe that he would not easily defeat any challenger. He had the support of the entire Florida congressional delegation of eight representatives and U.S. Senators Spessard Holland and George Smathers. When it became known that Kefauver would oppose Russell in Florida, the Georgian also picked up the backing of Governor Fuller Warren, who had become a bitter enemy of Kefauver as a result of the Senate crime investigation of 1950–51. In addition, Governor Herman Talmadge of Georgia offered his campaigning services in rural northern Florida, where thousands of voters had either been born in Georgia or had close family ties across the state line.[15]

In spite of Russell's impressive array of support, Kefauver almost immediately put him on the defensive, causing some of the Georgian's supporters to feel that only by distorting Kefauver's record could they counteract the significant and growing Kefauver strength in the state. Kefauver had taken the initiative by going into Florida with an impressive series of victories in all parts of the country and by contrasting his national effort with Russell's sectional appeal. If Russell was not a serious candidate, as Kefauver suggested, then those who saw Kefauver as the anti-Truman candidate were only helping Truman if they voted for Russell in Florida. In addition, the solid line-up of state Democratic leaders against Kefauver again awakened the sympathy for the underdog that had become a standard Kefauver campaign weapon. Furthermore, the attempted smear against Kefauver by Russell supporters cost Russell voters among thoughtful people in Florida and among liberals across the country.

Even Russell himself was guilty of distortion at times, as when he warned of Kefauver's support for Atlantic Union that "it will be a blow to the cause of liberty around the world to submerge the sovereignty of the U.S. with other nations." He neglected to note that some of the most conservative men in public life were enthusiastic backers of the Union as a means of unifying the anti-communist bloc.[16] Senator Smathers was one of the most obvious Russell supporters to appeal to the worst instincts of Floridians. Among other things, he described Kefauver as "soft on communism," a line that was having great success elsewhere in the country.[17]

One of Kefauver's most valuable issues in Florida was the support of Russell by the discredited Governor Fuller Warren. Although Russell disavowed Warren's personal support,[18] the governor went to such lengths to attack Kefauver that at times the contest seemed to be between Kefauver and Warren. Warren's original contention had been that Kefauver's Crime Committee attacks on him "were made pursuant to a deal he [Kefauver] entered into with political enemies of mine in Miami whereby he would smear me in return for their promise to try to deliver to him for President the votes of Florida's delegates to the Democratic National Convention. . . ."[19] This argument fell flat in the face of the strong Russell support by much of the anti-Warren faction in the Florida Democratic party. Kefauver knew a good issue, however, and repeatedly stressed his "hope to win Florida's support for the Presidential nomination despite the active opposition of Governor Fuller Warren and the racket-element." A frustrated Russell could only complain that "Senator Kefauver is running in Florida against Warren. I had not heard that any candidate by that name was in the race."[20]

Russell also sought to ridicule Kefauver's role as underdog. "I have noticed my opponent in the role of underdog," Russell told Florida Democrats. "He has referred to the machine being against him. . . . He is doing pretty well with his operation. I read where he has 12 rooms in a hotel four blocks from the White House. I hope that is as close as he gets. . . ." [21] Russell also attacked Kefauver's frequent absences from Washington, in contrast to Russell's own important contributions there:

> I understand my opponent has been here and addressed you. . . . He's a member of the Armed Services Committee of which I am chairman. He is more fortunate than I in being able to stay away from Washington to present his candidacy. I have not been able to do that because I have certain specific legislative responsibilities. . . . We would have been glad to have him with us to work . . . on important matters.[22]

It was the civil rights question that posed the greatest danger for Kefauver in Florida. A move toward Russell's more conservative position would alienate support in the North and West. Strangely, Russell did little to exploit his advantage in Florida on this issue, perhaps because he did have serious hopes for a place on the national ticket. Kefauver got by with reiterating his opposition to FEPC and avoided stronger statements that would have haunted him later.[23]

In the South, of course, Kefauver's Tennessee background was an asset, and both there and elsewhere he had argued that "the South has been on the defensive politically for entirely too long." It was through him that the South had a real chance to elect a native son to the Presidency. To charges that he was too liberal for the South, Kefauver could point to NAACP dissatisfaction with his civil rights position.[24]

But Kefauver had little success in Florida or elsewhere in the South in winning over the professional Southerners. Southern leaders generally echoed the view that Dixie senators had of Kefauver, that he was unreliable on civil rights; his liberalism on other issues also acted to alienate those Southerners who, in any case, felt it more important to take a position on a candidate popular at home, with reluctant acquiescence in the eventual nominee seen necessary for the sake of party harmony.[25] Therefore, Kefauver's support in Florida came principally from areas (especially Miami) that were unhappy with the rural conservative elements that dominated Florida politics. And, although the primary results on May 5 gave Russell a 367,980 to 285,358 victory, Kefauver's strong showing against overwhelming odds was considered more than enough to keep him in the front of the Democratic pack.[26]

Kefauver's other primary venture that turned out badly was in the District of Columbia. There the contest was between Kefauver and Averell Harriman, who enjoyed Truman's support in the District. The Administration forces used Kefauver's Southern background and an ambiguous registration procedure (which a local political scientist criticized as leaving "room for many election irregularities") to roll up a thumping 14,075 to 3,377 victory for Harriman in predominantly Negro Washington.[27]

Whatever reservations might be attached to the statistics, Kefauver had demonstrated impressive support in the available presidential primaries against such opposition as had offered itself. Although *Life* magazine had described Kefauver after New Hampshire as "simply the first Democrat to capitalize on the yearnings of a great part of the electorate for change, any change," [28] the undeniable fact was that of those votes that were cast directly for candidates' names or pledged delegate candidates, Kefauver had an overwhelming majority:

Kefauver	3,166,071
Russell	369,671
Stevenson	78,407
Truman	62,345
Kerr	42,467
Harriman	14,075 [29]

It was not without reason, therefore, that the Kefauver campaign for the nomination in 1952 became the classic example of how presidential primary victories do not automatically lead to the nomination itself. An exhaustive study by Johns Hopkins political scientists Paul David, Malcolm Moos, and Ralph M. Goldman of the 1952 major party nominations examined the paradox and arrived at the general conclusion that:

> though seeming to run well from the inception of his campaign in the visible public contests, Kefauver's strategy failed to team his single shot victories in some of the primaries with the necessary strength in depth either among the delegates themselves or among a sufficient number of state and local party leaders who could deliver delegates at the national convention.[30]

Kefauver's fatal lack of success with the party professionals was not due to unacceptable positions on the major issues. Indeed, Kefauver on occasion spoke against the party's enemies when he had every political reason to remain silent. In Senator Joseph McCarthy's home state of Wisconsin, for example, Kefauver unequivocally denounced McCarthyism when so many others were ducking the issue:

> McCarthyism represents one of the greatest threats to our nation today and to our freedom. . . . Due to this guilt-by-association technique and smear technique used for political purposes, McCarthyism is forcing a lot of our people into conformity of thinking. I think McCarthyism is one of the greatest problems facing America today. I abhor the whole tendency of McCarthyism.[31]

Later, in a joint TV debate with Kefauver in Wisconsin, Republican hopeful Harold Stassen described Kefauver as soft on communism "because he doesn't want to outlaw the Communist party in the United States and is against McCarthy without waiting for the truth of charges of Communist invasion in Government to come out." Kefauver replied, "We must protect ourselves, and the best way to do that is not to stifle freedom of speech but to get after the social and economic conditions that breed communism." [32]

Even on the less dramatic issues, an examination of Kefauver's record indicates that he was anything but a maverick. In

1952, for example, he voted with a majority of Senate Democrats 95 per cent of the time.[33] But Kefauver was caught between presenting himself as an alternative to Truman or a Truman-picked successor and, on the other hand, not attacking the Administration so strongly that party leaders would decide that he was damaging the party in an attempt to promote his own interests. It is a problem that challengers of Presidents for control of parties have never been able to solve in American political history, and Kefauver was no exception.

Kefauver's biggest issue, his concern about and experience dealing with organized crime and corruption of public officials, necessarily presumed that the Truman Administration was not doing enough in this area. There was only a fine line between pointing out that more needed to be done and asking why the Administration was not taking the needed steps. The conclusion of many Democratic professionals was that Kefauver was furnishing the Republicans with ammunition for the general election when he insinuated that Administration opposition to him was due in part to the unholy alliance between racketeers and the political bosses who made up an important part of the President's base of support.

Politicians who for any reason opposed Kefauver's bid for the nomination were vulnerable to his charge that they were *de facto* allies of the criminal elements that feared a Kefauver victory. Since Kefauver already felt very much at home in campaigning against bossism generally, it was perhaps irresistible to merge the issues and present himself as the fighter for clean government taking his case to the people via the primaries and contending against the criminal-political forces depending on boss rule to maintain their power in the Democratic party and in the country.

Kefauver had long called for both parties to withhold patronage from local politicians with links to known criminals: "If they find they are not the proper kind of people, they could refuse them patronage and recognition and, of course, that would be a terribly big blow to their operations." [34] How seriously one took the threat of a criminal-political alliance helped to determine the importance attached to the anti-corruption appeal of Kefauver's campaign. The *New Republic* viewed Kefauver sympathetically because of its belief that "the prospect of a President who might strike at the roots of these arrangements by injecting the federal government into the main stream of law enforcement horrifies those who have thrived under the old system." Others, however, including many of those termed "bosses," saw the crime and politics issue as a campaign gimmick. New York's "Boss" Flynn reacted typically when he announced his determination not "to let these people come in from the outside and besmirch New York City without saying something about it. . . . There is no connection in any shape or form between the Democratic Party in the Bronx and gangsters or organized crime. . . . It is unfair to have them come in and picture New York as a hell hole for . . . headlines." [35]

Kefauver's reply to such blasts was to remind voters that "the boys in the smoke-filled rooms have never taken very well to me," [36] a ploy that scored well with voters but raised doubts in the minds of professional politicians whose support he would need to win the nomination. To the extent that he placed undue emphasis on bowling over party regulars by demonstrating overwhelming rank and file support in the primaries, Kefauver misunderstood the perspective of the professionals. "I can't wait for the professional politicians," [37] he had complained in December 1951, before the start of his campaign. Many of them, in turn, saw Kefauver as a threat to their positions of power within the party, especially when he seemed to make them the issue. "I know what it is to face a strong organization out to get me," he had said in New Hampshire. "But the final decision rests with the people, and I am out for their support." [38] But Democratic urban bosses are only indirectly influenced by national rank and file support for a candidate for the nomination. As Theodore H. White so well expressed it:

> They want a strong President, who will keep a strong government, a strong defense, and deal with them as barons in their own baronies. They believe in letting the President handle war

and peace, inflation and deflation, France, China, India and foreign affairs (but not Israel, Ireland, Italy or, nowadays, Africa), so long as the President lets them handle their own wards and the local patronage.[39]

Truman was a politician who knew how to play the game to the satisfaction of the urban leaders, and the hostile attitude of the Democratic National Committee toward Kefauver throughout his primary campaigns and the convention itself reflected both the President's personal opposition and organizational doubts about Kefauver. Kefauver said publicly that "the National Committee is supposed to keep a hands-off policy in relation to candidates, and, as far as I know, is doing that. I ask no favors . . . and this is as it ought to be." [40] However, a Kefauver lieutenant later wrote more realistically of the Kefauver campaign's problems with the National Committee:

. . . Frank McKinney, who was then chairman, did everything in his power to withhold committee information from us and to prevent us from using the facilities of the Democratic National Committee. The situation was so bad that members of the committee staff were fearful to be seen in our company and on a number of occasions I actually had to meet secretly with them in hotel rooms in order to get information from them. A committee mailing list, which we needed very badly and which should have been given to us without question, had to be "lifted in the dark of night" for our use.[41]

In spite of the obvious coolness of the Administration to his candidacy, Kefauver refrained from openly attacking Truman. When asked, "What, really, do you offer the voters who oppose Truman?" Kefauver stressed that "I am not running my campaign on the basis of opposing President Truman. I am appealing for and getting support on my own program, and, of course, most of my supporters are the ones who have supported President Truman." [42] If nominated, he said:

I think I have to run on the general principles of what our party has stood for. If that be the Truman record, I think I'd run on most of President Truman's record. There are some points of difference, points on which I disagree, but the general purposes of the foreign policy and the domestic program, too, of President Truman and President Roosevelt I voted for and, of course, I stand for.[43]

Kefauver later evaluated his attempt to maintain the façade of party harmony as a mistake: "It would have been better to have made a definite break with President Truman. As it was, I criticized the shortcomings of the administration . . . but still tried to avoid a final and conclusive break with him. My campaign would have been stronger and I would have lost nothing. . . ."[44]

In any event, Kefauver's most definite criticisms of the Truman Administration focused on means rather than ends. While Kefauver agreed with the firing of General MacArthur, he felt that "the way the thing was done was rather unfortunate." Truman's objective of fair employment was commendable, but "much could be done with a voluntary commission on the federal level. I think it is an educational process and until you do have the educational process it is going to be a difficult matter to legislate." Taft-Hartley "was gotten up in a spirit of vengeance to penalize labor" but "some corrective legislation was necessary," and Kefauver could not support Truman's call for total repeal. On Korea, Kefauver thought "the President did the right thing in going into Korea" but expressed disapproval of the stalemate there. The Truman loyalty program was a good one; "however, procedures ought to be worked out to give the person accused every opportunity to clear his name." Truman's foreign policy was generally sound, but "we should anticipate the difficulties and do more about them in the foreign field before they break upon us. Our foreign policy should be more dynamic and not be swerved to the extent it is by what the Communists do or don't do." Truman had the power to seize the steel industry, but Kefauver disagreed on the need: "I think all possible arbitration, negotiation and conciliation should have been resorted to in order to make a settlement."[45]

In spite of Kefauver's later feeling that he should have broken more definitely with Truman, the course he did follow was sound because it kept the door open for reconciliation if Kefauver actually did get the nomination. In any event, it is difficult to see how Kefauver could have broken radically with Truman and, at the same time, have taken positions consistent with his own record of twelve years in the House and Senate.

In addition to Kefauver's problems with the conservative South, the Administration, and the urban bosses, he also achieved only limited success with many of the professional liberals, who questioned his stature and experience, as well as his support among the minority groups so influential within many Northern and Western delegations.[46] While Kefauver might have been acceptable to them, they really were more impressed with Adlai Stevenson, who was finally to yield to requests that he accept the nomination. Stevenson's eventual support came from a variety of sources, some of which slightly preferred Stevenson over Kefauver, and others who feared above all the nomination of the Tennessean. Kefauver supporters were later to confuse the distinctions between groups making up the Stevenson coalition.

Another great disappointment of the Kefauver camp lay in the failure to enlist the support of Southern progressives generally. Southern liberals such as Senator William Fulbright of Arkansas and especially Alabama's New Deal Senators Lister Hill and John Sparkman did not rally around Kefauver, and the defection of Hill and Sparkman to Russell, with whom they had been anything but politically compatible, was especially discouraging to Kefauver hopes in the South. The fact that Hill and Sparkman had to pay with a Russell endorsement for a loyalist Democratic victory over the Dixiecrats for control of the Alabama state organization did not lessen the fact of Kefauver's meager showing among Southern delegates.

Kefauver did very poorly in winning endorsements from fellow senators in spite of the generally high regard in which many of them held him. Few Democratic senators wished to offend the Democratic White House by backing a candidate who was generally considered anti-Administration. Only maverick Paul Douglas of Illinois, who had little political clout even in the Illinois delegation, formally endorsed Kefauver. His integrity and image as a liberal champion made him perhaps the most respected member of the Senate among Northern and Western Democrats, and there is no doubt that his endorsement of Kefauver was of tremendous psychological value.[47] "Some of the politicians, bureaucrats and king-makers may not like you, because they know they cannot control you," Douglas said in his endorsement statement. "But the people are for you. Let the voice of the people be heard." "Paul, bless your heart," was Kefauver's reply on hearing about Douglas's support.[48]

Whether or not the people were for Kefauver is open to dispute. The case that they were for anyone else is obviously weak. It is impossible to determine to what extent Kefauver was a vehicle for protest against Truman in the early polls and in the New Hampshire primary. It is similarly difficult to evaluate his later primary victories against little or no opposition. And finally, the last polls taken before the convention do not take into consideration the support that Stevenson might have had if he had been an announced candidate and had received the widespread publicity that would surely have resulted from a declaration of candidacy. However, taking into account these reservations, every measure of public opinion indicated consistently strong and growing Kefauver strength in the months before the convention. In the spring of 1952, for example, Kefauver was named as one of the ten most admired living Americans in a poll conducted by Elmo Roper. No other Democrat receiving any mention before or at the convention as a successor to President Truman was on the list.[49] A Gallup poll of February 1952, taken before the New Hampshire primary, showed Kefauver giving Truman a scare among Democrats with the support of 21 per cent to the President's 36 per cent. Kefauver actually outdistanced the President among independents, 36 per cent to 18 per cent.[50] Post-New Hampshire polls showed Kefauver running better than Truman against both Taft and Eisenhower.[51] Finally, a Roper poll of June 1952 [52] showed Kefauver as far and away the favorite of those Democrats expressing a preference:

Kefauver	33 per cent
Barkley	10
Stevenson	9
Russell	8
Harriman	5

Whatever Kefauver's shortcomings might have appeared to be to various groups in the party, the fact remained that someone would eventually have to be nominated, and when viewed alongside other available Democrats, Kefauver compared favorably. Averell Harriman of New York was considered too liberal and had never held an elective office. Vice-President Barkley was too old at seventy-four to deserve serious consideration, although he, in fact, did have widespread support and was rumored to be Truman's second choice. Senator Russell was too conservative for the North and West. Only Governor Stevenson of Illinois seemed to stand in Kefauver's path to the nomination. However, he consistently refused all requests to announce as a candidate but did leave the door open to a draft. In spite of some irritation at having to seek the candidate instead of being wooed themselves, Democratic leaders had for months expressed their preference for Stevenson, and informed opinion had been predicting his eventual nomination.[53]

But, based on Stevenson's public and private reluctance to become an announced candidate or even to say whether he would accept the nomination, the Kefauver camp could look optimistically to the Democratic convention, scheduled to meet in late July. One month before the convention opened, an Associated Press survey gave Kefauver a substantial share of the committed delegates: [54]

Kefauver	257½
Russell	161½
Harriman	112½
Kerr	45½
Stevenson	41½

Another 611½ delegates were either uncommitted or pledged to favorite sons. These delegates held the key to the nomination, and there was no reason why Kefauver could not hope for eventual favorable consideration from a large number of them.

The Republican nomination of Eisenhower in early July, coupled with Stevenson's continued reluctance and Truman's continued silence, gave Kefauver a clear field to demonstrate the kind of campaign he would wage if selected to face the Republican ticket in November. He spoke of Eisenhower as "the unwitting tool of the few greedy men who have long sought to control this country's economy." Eisenhower was "nominated by Wall Street," and "if they were to win, they would take our country back to the dark days which brought us to the verge of disaster and from which we were rescued by the far-seeing program which they would seek to destroy today." [55]

Kefauver also began to seek reconciliation with offended urban leaders. "As time has gone on," he said confidently almost on the eve of the convention, "more and more city leaders were thinking in terms of winning elections and less of aggravation." [56]

As the Kefauver campaign organization faced the final test in Chicago, it could look back on an operation that had grown from an almost amateurish Tennessee-based effort into the most co-ordinated and efficient candidate-oriented organization at the convention. But when compared with the serious campaign organizations of other years, it left much to be desired, as Kefauver himself recognized. Kefauver recruited as titular campaign manager Gael Sullivan, who had been a protégé of both Mayor Ed Kelly of Chicago and Robert Hannegan, longtime Democratic professional. Sullivan had at one time served as executive director of the Democratic National Committee and left a $60,000-a-year job with the Theater Owners of America to direct the Kefauver campaign. His contribution to the campaign is something of a mystery. Mrs. Tom Ragland, in charge of the state headquarters in Nashville of the Kefauver-for-President effort in Tennessee and a member of the Tennessee delegation to the convention, could recall "no leadership, guidance or direction" by Sullivan "either before or during the convention." Even though the campaign gave some appearance of being a national effort, it remained largely a Tennessee-staffed and Tennessee-financed operation. Tennesseans and ex-Tennesseans contributed approximately 67 per cent of the campaign funds. Even the modest campaign cost of $477,445.57 exceeded contributions by almost $40,000.[57]

The Kefauver campaign relied too heavily on Kefauver himself, and his general personal appeal too many times substituted for the sustained cultivation of delegates and powerbrokers that might have wrung commitments from crucial kingmakers. Kefauver later spoke of spreading his efforts too thin, spending a great deal of time in Texas, North Carolina, and Massachusetts, where by virtue of the political machinery he did not have much of a chance of getting delegates in the first place. Kefauver also spoke of the ineffective public relations of his campaign which "could have been improved with more funds and with using the funds I had for one topnotch director rather than having it all under the direction of volunteers. . . ." [58]

Even so, when the convention met, Kefauver's nomination was a distinct possibility. Early in the convention, Kefauver's hopes were boosted even more when Vice-President Barkley, generally regarded as President Truman's second choice, withdrew as a candidate after being vetoed by organized labor as too old. But Stevenson's appeal was greatly enhanced by the very favorable impression he made on the delegates in his welcoming address as the host governor.[59]

The convention management, even when serious doubt remained that Stevenson would agree to accept the nomination, was openly hostile to Kefauver, and his interests were ignored by the small group which controlled the machinery of the convention. Jack Norman, Tennessee State Democratic Chairman, was finally provoked to complain bitterly that "the whole national committee is against Senator Kefauver. They have deliberately and I say maliciously done everything they could to cut this delegation and to keep us from getting tickets so we could make a big demonstration when Kefauver's name is presented to the convention. I am thoroughly disgusted with the treatment we have gotten." He claimed that Illinois had received 700 tickets and Tennessee only 56.[60]

Permanent Chairman Sam Rayburn used every parliamentary trick possible to block any move that was regarded as favorable to Kefauver and did it in such a way that the millions of TV viewers and radio listeners tuned in were unaware of the Speaker's bias.[61] The most astute move by Rayburn was to arrange a roll call on the seating of the Virginia delegation, which had not given the required loyalty pledge that the convention's nominees would be on the ballot in Virginia as the Democratic nominees. The convention, spurred on by the co-operating Kefauver and Harriman delegates, was heading for a liberal victory, when important pro-Stevenson leaders switched to a pro-Virginia stand in hopes of strengthening Stevenson's appeal as a compromise candidate. The vote was 475½ to 650 against Virginia when the Illinois delegation suddenly changed its vote from 45 to 15 *against* to 52 to 8 *for* the seating of the Virginia delegation. Illinois took this position in spite of the fact that it was contradicting the stand taken in 1948 by both Adlai Stevenson and the Illinois delegation of that year. Jake Arvey, boss of the Illinois delegation, later explained the switch:

> It suddenly dawned on us what was happening. The strategy of the Kefauver backers and the Northern liberal bloc was to try and make impossible demands on the Southern delegates so that they would walk out of the Convention. If the total Convention vote was thus cut down by the walkout of delegates who would never vote for Kefauver, then the Tennessee Senator would have a better chance of winning the nomination.[62]

Other pro-Stevenson delegations tended to follow Illinois.[63] After all switches had been made, Virginia won, 650½ to 518. Kefauver's steadfast support for the loyalty oath turned out to be one of his greatest political blunders. By causing Tennessee to cast the only Southern votes against the seating of Virginia, he not only handed his future Tennessee opponents an emotional issue to use against him for years, but he made it much more difficult to present himself as a candidate who could unite the party. Contrary to Arvey's analysis, Kefauver's support for the loyalty oath destroyed any chance he had for eventual Southern switches to him; until then Kefauver was the second choice of many delegates who planned to support Russell until he had no real chance for the nomination. When the convention went on to seat the challenged delegations from South Carolina and Louisiana, it was clear that the Kefauver forces had lost whatever initiative they had once had. Paul David, Malcolm Moos, and Ralph M. Goldman, writing of the loyalty fight in their study of the 1952 nominating process, concluded:

> In retrospect, it seems clear that Senator Kefauver had no real chance for the nomination after the struggle over party loyalty ended with the seating of Virginia, South Carolina, and Louisiana. By that time and at least for the brief remainder of the convention, Kefauver had become isolated as the candidate of a bitter-end faction, opposite in its point of view to the southern faction and angrily at outs with the convention management. This was a political fact, regardless of the philosophical merits of the positions assumed by the opposing parties; and the fact was documented by the stiffening attitudes of the middle-of-the-road delegates toward the Kefauver candidacy during the remainder of the convention.[64]

Kefauver himself blamed the blunder over the loyalty fight on his lack of "an advisory staff in Chicago to decide upon policy matters." The staff he did have was:

> not set up to meet, and we had an awfully hard time with communication between our floor managers. This caused an error in sizing up the so-called loyalty oath. Our original plan was to support a loyalty pledge only for States where a contest was involved, which in that case would have been Texas and Mississippi. We were told that the Moody resolution had been agreed to all the way around and before we had found out differently, several of our delegates had made speeches for it. There was nothing left to do then but go along.[65]

The success of the Eisenhower backers with a "fair play" resolution at the Republican convention two weeks before probably led the liberals at the Democratic convention to overestimate the surface appeal of supporting a position which simply called on Southern Democrats to give the voters of their states a chance to vote for the nominees. The moderates and conservatives won out because they were able to rally behind the façades of Southern nationalism and party harmony. When it appeared that Stevenson might then get the nomination because of Southern support, Harriman and Kefauver liberals were forced to move in Stevenson's direction in order to have maximum influence with the probable nominee.[66]

Whatever hope Kefauver had for rallying his forces by a successful floor fight to strengthen the anti-crime plank of the platform was ruthlessly demolished by Rayburn's refusal to allow a Kefauver-backed amendment on the floor until after the platform had been adopted. Although the amendment was properly submitted, Rayburn allowed its advocates only one minute to discuss it, announcing to the convention that it did not matter anyway "because the platform has already been adopted." [67]

As rumors of an impending Stevenson nomination grew, Kefauver called a press conference in which he called attention to "an increasing amount of resentment among the delegates against the political bosses and against drafting an unwilling candidate." But he vetoed any attack on Stevenson himself. At a campaign breakfast, a Kefauver supporter had yelled, "Ask Stevenson about Alger Hiss," whom Stevenson had defended. "That's exactly the kind of thing I want you to keep from saying," Kefauver quickly cautioned.[68]

Kefauver was put in nomination by Tennessee Governor Gordon Browning in a stilted speech that called attention to Kefauver's crime fighting record and the supposed opposition to him by those who feared honest federal law enforcement:

> We love him because of the enemies he has made and some of the enemies that he has today are rather vocal here. They are of the ones who, because of the policy he followed, object to a

molestation of their ancient solitary reign in having clandestine connection between politics and crime in America.[69]

Kefauver's nomination was seconded by Boston Mayor John Hynes, California's James Roosevelt, and Alaska's Governor Ernest Gruening.[70]

The first ballot gave Kefauver the lead with 340 votes, followed by the still reluctant Stevenson with 273, Russell with 268, and Harriman with 123½. Nine other men received scattered support. The second ballot saw Kefauver gain 22½ to 362½; Stevenson picked up 51½ to 324½; Russell also gained, receiving 294.[71]

During this hectic day of July 25, the Kefauver hopes for the nomination were dashed when Governor Stevenson finally agreed to accept the nomination if he were offered it. This was followed by an immediate switch of Harriman's support to Stevenson and the withdrawal of most favorite sons. The third ballot gave the nomination to Stevenson with 617½ votes, 1½ more than a majority. Kefauver and Russell, however, each received a substantial vote on the last ballot, 275½ and 261, respectively.[72]

Although much was later made of Truman's last-minute intervention on behalf of Stevenson,[73] the fact is that the President simply climbed aboard a bandwagon that already included such independent forces as Harriman, Humphrey, and Governor G. Mennen Williams of Michigan, who had switched his state to Kefauver after the first ballot and to Stevenson on the third ballot.[74] The Stevenson nomination was one of the most unusual in modern American political history. Stevenson did not seek support and, in fact, discouraged those who sought to win him the nomination. The motives of those backing Stevenson varied greatly, of course, but Stevenson was more than a stop-Kefauver candidate. To a substantial number of delegates, he represented the best that the Democratic party could offer in 1952. And while President Truman and certain anti-Kefauver leaders welcomed Stevenson as an alternative to Kefauver, their ability to force their choice on the convention was limited, and Stevenson's nomination, with their support, tended to make them look much more powerful than they really were. In fact, it is doubtful whether anti-Kefauver leaders could have assembled a successful coalition on behalf of any candidate other than Stevenson.[75]

Kefauver was one of the last to find out about the impending switch to Stevenson on the third ballot.[76] When it became obvious that Stevenson would be nominated, Kefauver and Paul Douglas entered the convention arm in arm and sought to gain recognition for a withdrawal in favor of Stevenson. Chairman Rayburn refused to allow an interruption of the roll call, a discourtesy which Kefauver later termed "the most aggravating personal humiliation that those who ran the convention tried to heap upon me." [77] Eventually, he was allowed to offer his support to Stevenson before the convention and issued a call for party harmony.[78]

Experienced politician though Kefauver was, he was not prepared psychologically for the hectic events of July 25. The day had seen him at his height, when he led the convention voting on two ballots; but the turn of events that led to his defeat later that night and into the early hours of the next morning put him under intense emotional strain. Senator John Sparkman, who was to be chosen later that day as the party's Vice-Presidential nominee, remembered seeing Kefauver, his wife Nancy, and Kefauver's father in the parking lot in the early hours of July 26, after the third ballot was over. All were extremely upset, and Nancy and Kefauver's father were crying. It was one of the few times in his life that Kefauver was not in full control of his emotions. Almost forgotten was the fact that it was Kefauver's forty-ninth birthday.[79]

Whatever the explanation for Stevenson's nomination, Kefauver and his supporters remained convinced that the nomination had been stolen from Kefauver by Truman and bosses who felt that they could not control Kefauver.[80] Kefauver himself later wrote:

the boss-run convention machinery had me stopped. . . .
What happened? I had aroused the implacable enmity of cer-

tain politicians, including some defeated hacks and various political yeomen who were taking orders implicitly from the outgoing Truman administration. . . .

Being thus committed to "stop Kefauver!" these "machine stalwarts," who were all-powerful behind the convention scenes, disregarded what the people and largest bloc of delegates said they wanted.[81]

Immediately after Stevenson's nomination, however, Kefauver assumed a much more philosophical attitude about his defeat, saying that he felt "no bitterness" toward the party bosses who had caused his defeat. Had he given up the idea of the Presidency? "Oh, no," he replied.[82]

All the political assets that Kefauver had which made him a serious contender for the Presidency naturally caused him to be discussed as a possible running mate for Stevenson. He was too hurt by his defeat to get excited about the possibility, but he did not rule it out when reporters cornered him after Stevenson's nomination. "I haven't been offered the place and I really don't believe I would want to accept it," he replied to the obvious question. "I haven't talked to Nancy. I don't know Governor Stevenson's attitude about it." [83]

Kefauver's eighty-one-year-old father, still upset the next day over the convention's treatment of his son, voiced one opinion of the Kefauver camp: "Let him [Stevenson] take the nomination and to hell with it." He was very much against his son's taking the Vice-Presidential nomination "to put the ticket over." After such a convention, the senior Kefauver concluded, "they [the Democrats] haven't got a chance. Eisenhower will be the next President." [84]

Of those seriously considered for Vice-President, Kefauver, Senators John Sparkman of Alabama, William Fulbright of Arkansas, and Mike Monroney of Oklahoma received the most attention by party professionals advising Stevenson. Although the Kefauver Committee investigation in Chicago had contributed to the Republican recapture of the Illinois House in 1950, and a 1951 Kefauver Committee probe had uncovered a link between gambling interests and a Stevenson staff member, who was then forced to resign, Stevenson, according to Jake Arvey, "held the Tennessee Senator in high regard. I believe Stevenson never would have agreed to be our nominee if he thought Kefauver could have united our party." [85] But Sparkman emerged as the choice of the professionals. Sparkman's selection, in spite of Senator Russell's irritation with his role in drafting the platform, was generally explained as resulting from Truman's veto of Fulbright and Russell's veto of Kefauver. In addition, Truman and Stevenson adviser Scott Lucas had no desire to honor Kefauver in any way.[86]

Kefauver, therefore, left the Democratic convention with nothing but a campaign deficit. "I'm not worried about it," he told reporters. "Several good friends of mine have indicated they will help to get it released." All in all, he had "no regrets" over his course of the past few months. "It was a glorious experience. Certainly going over the United States as we have will make me a better Senator. I have increased confidence in our great people." [87]

Kefauver's 1952 defeat for the nomination had been even harder for his family and supporters to accept because they were keenly aware of Kefauver's personal investment of energy and dedication in an effort which they saw as basically a crusade for clean government. All the sacrifices made by the candidate, his family, staff, and closest supporters seemed to have been robbed of significance by the "bosses" in Chicago. Kefauver's family had never been excited by the campaign. Very early the children had been turned against reporters and photographers when their kitten was killed in the uproar attending a March "See It Now" program.[88] In spite of Nancy's distaste for campaigning, she had given the campaign her fullest attention and was one of Kefauver's greatest assets. Even Kefauver's bitterest opponents had nothing but praise for her. She was a charming and gracious member of Kefauver's team and was called upon to endure more exhausting and boring campaign activities than any other candidate's wife in American political history. Her finest hour was at the Women's National Press Club dinner in Washington, where she substituted for her husband alongside other announced candidates. Although she was hesitant about speaking, she stole the show. After earnestly explaining her husband's desire to become president for the opportunity to serve that it offered, she confessed that "as for me, the prospect of the presidency is not an entirely pleasant one. Does any wife and mother really want to give up the greatest thing in the world—the private joys of regular American family life?" Senator Russell was moved to comment to the gathering that "Kefauver's chief accomplishment is that he outmarried himself to such an extent. His wife is his most dangerous secret weapon." [89]

Kefauver's defeat for the nomination was for him more than just a routine political setback that can be expected now and then in even the most successful political career. It was a personal tragedy because it caused Kefauver to doubt his whole philosophy about the inevitability of the ultimate triumph of the will of the people, which he associated with the "good" and the "right." Throughout his years in the House and Senate, Kefauver was reluctant to engage in the arm twisting and wheeling and dealing so much a part of any legislative process. He had believed that if people understood which was the right course, they would follow it. He had great faith in reason and education, and put more emphasis on persuasion than on bargaining; he never gave up on trying to win over those antagonistic to him, since he felt that such an antagonism must be based on misunderstanding. [90]

Feeling that he had gone to the people and won their overwhelming endorsement, it was difficult for him to accept the possibility that the majority of Democratic delegates had rejected him. The only explanation was that they had not been allowed to choose freely, that they had been intimidated by the bosses who feared a Kefauver victory. If so, how did this fit into Kefauver's concept of the Democratic party as the party of the people, in contrast to the vested interests which controlled the Republican party? If the Democratic party was also controlled at the top, was there any hope for democratic, representative government? In addition, the agonizing question remained of whether Kefauver himself had somehow failed the cause which he led. If his candidacy had been so right, how had he managed to lose to a reluctant candidate who had to be begged to take the nomination? These were questions on which he would dwell during the next few months, as he sought to find meaning in the events that had raised his expectations for and of himself to dizzying heights only to destroy them by a discouraging defeat that shook his faith not only in the system but in his ability to function effectively within it.[91]

chapter x

OUT OF THE LIMELIGHT
1953-1954

Kefauver's discouraging defeat in the 1952 Democratic presidential nomination proceedings would have been easier for him to accept had his return to Tennessee been in the role of the victim of a power play engineered by the discredited Truman Administration and corrupt city bosses. However, Tennesseans' unfavorable reaction to their delegation's vote on the seating of the Virginia delegation far overshadowed any sympathy aroused by Kefauver's mistreatment by the convention bosses. In less than a week, Kefauver's political stock, which on convention eve had been so high in the state that it was considered suicidal to oppose his bid for the presidency, had declined to such a point that even his renomination for the Senate in 1954 was no longer taken for granted. The challenge of the next two years would be to rebuild the eroded political base in Tennessee, without which there could be no future campaigns for national office and, indeed, no re-election to the Senate. But the emphasis on Tennessee had to be balanced with a concern for national issues that reflected Kefauver's desire to seek national office in 1956.

The outcry from Tennessee over the vote on Virginia was loud and clear. The Tennessee delegation in Chicago and Kefauver's office in Washington were swamped with letters and telegrams expressing disgust and dismay that Tennessee had "betrayed" her sister state of Virginia. The Dixiecrats in Tennessee overnight had been handed a powerful emotional issue, and the fact that the Stevenson forces voted for the seating of the challenged Virginia delegation made Kefauver seem even to the left of the Northern governor who became the nominee. Kefauver's enemies at home immediately began using the Virginia vote as a weapon against Kefauver's ally, Governor Gordon Browning, already facing a difficult renomination fight in the upcoming Democratic primary. He was now forced to answer charges that he had been "a stooge for left-wingers" in Chicago.[1]

Browning had been the leading anti-Crump figure in Tennessee since 1938, but after his election in 1948 he proved to be a disappointment to the progressives. He seemed to support Tennessee's "right-to-work" law and had further estranged labor by crushing a strike in a foreign-owned plant in East Tennessee. He had also shown no initiative in reforming Tennessee's inequitable tax structure. Gratitude among liberals for Browning's 1948 role in ending Crump's control of Tennessee politics soon began to wear thin.[2]

In the 1950 Democratic primary, Browning faced only a half-serious protest candidate who gave him a fairly close race in what would normally have been a runaway second term victory. With Crump's acquiescence in a second term the governor was able to win, but only 267,855 to 208,634.[3]

In 1952, however, anti-Browning forces had an attractive young candidate, Frank Clement, to oppose the governor. Although Clement enjoyed Crump's endorsement he also had broader support and was a far cry from the Bourbon candidates formerly fielded by the Crump organization. The Browning-Clement race was considered a toss-up until the Democratic convention controversy over the Virginia delegation erupted. At the convention Kefauver had been led to believe that the South had agreed to the rules that would have excluded Virginia, and so instructed Browning to speak against the state's seating. The misinformation about the Southern position, plus the switch of Stevenson delegates, served to isolate Tennessee, and the situation proved acutely embarrassing to Browning supporters, who had assumed that the governor's role as delegation chairman backing Kefauver would enhance his chances in the Democratic primary. Browning, however, did not try to evade responsibility for the vote on Virginia; he defended the stand of the Tennessee delegation as "a case of Senator Kefauver's interests versus the city bosses." [4]

As the Tennessee Democratic primary moved into the last week, Kefauver was finally forced to respond to the anti-Browning charges that the governor had betrayed the South. Kefauver could not remain neutral while his faithful ally at Chicago went down to defeat, and he spoke of how, "following my defeat at the convention, it was my intention to come to Tennessee to rest and be with my family—and not to inject myself into the political campaign now going on in the state." All along he had planned to vote for Browning but now felt compelled to do more because:

> I find that Gordon Browning is being blamed and an effort is being made to damage his campaign for re-election because of those votes he cast as chairman of the delegation upon consensus of the delegation as a unit in Chicago. It is unfair and unjust that he should be criticized or that his campaign should be prejudiced by the vote of the Tennessee delegation. These votes were cast on my suggestion and in an effort to help me. . . . He stood by me in Chicago. Today I stand by him.[5]

Kefauver's belated efforts were not sufficient to save Browning. Clement won the nomination, 302,491 to 245,166. The primary results did contain some good news, however, Representative Albert Gore, longtime Browning and Kefauver ally in anti-Crump campaigns, defeated six-term Senator Kenneth McKellar, who by 1952 was too feeble to campaign.[6] For the remainder of Kefauver's life, he was to enjoy the previously unknown benefit of working with a friendly and co-operative fellow senator from Tennessee, replacing the hostile McKellar, whose personal vendetta against Kefauver had dissipated both his own and Kefauver's effectiveness in the Senate.

After the emotional strain of the Chicago convention, Nancy and Estes had returned to Tennessee for a rest and then decided on a trip to Europe in late August in connection with a meeting in Berne, Switzerland, of the Inter-Parliamentary Union. Once the meeting was over, they began a tour of Europe. One highlight of the trip was a reunion in London with Nancy's family, who had come down from Scotland. While in England, she was surprised to be hailed by the British press as a hometown girl who had made good in America.[7]

But the European trip did not lift Kefauver from his depression over the events of July, and the couple decided to return to the United States. As Nancy told a friend, "I love Europe, but this trip was awful. He [Kefauver] was in no mood for a vacation, anyway, and wasn't thinking about what we were seeing. So I said, 'You better go back home and campaign for Stevenson.' " [8]

The Kefauvers returned to the United States in late September, in the middle of the uproar over the secret expense fund of the Republican Vice-Presidential nominee, Richard Nixon. Kefauver did not join the attack on Nixon. "I've known Mr. Nixon both in the Senate and the House," Kefauver told reporters, "and I'd be very much surprised if he did anything wrong." Kefauver did think the fund a "bad precedent" which he could not condone, but he was more interested in using the incident to support his call for a nation-wide system of primaries which would give voters and the press more time to examine the records of those being considered for national office.[9]

While in Europe, Kefauver had discounted the importance of the presidential election as far as American foreign policy was concerned. He told the North Atlantic Council that although "the Democratic party is more united on the Atlantic community than the other party . . . I don't think the result of the Presidential election will make much difference." [10]

Domestic policy was another matter, and his speeches while campaigning for Stevenson reflected Kefauver's concern over reactionary influence within the Republican party. He questioned how Eisenhower could call for "a change" when he had his arms "both literally and figuratively" around "some of the greatest obstacles to change that this nation has ever known. . . . We want some changes all right, but we do not want to change to the policies of the party of isolationists abroad and reactionaries at home to get them." [11]

Eisenhower's ambivalence toward Wisconsin Senator Joseph McCarthy bothered Kefauver and other liberals. Kefauver attacked the double standard that allowed Eisenhower to praise McCarthy and still announce that the nation could "never accept the condemnation of men and women without a full hearing and a fair trial." "The General then tells you he has not changed," Kefauver exclaimed. "Well, the two statements are just incompatible. Somebody has changed and I don't believe that it is Joe McCarthy. And, if you elect General Eisenhower, you will be adding respectability to McCarthy and what he stands for." [12]

Many of Kefauver's speeches attempted to answer the charges that his own campaign had raised against the national Democratic Administration. He made the point over and over that Democrats themselves had uncovered what corruption had been found in the Truman Administration and that Republicans would not have known there was "a so-called mess in Washington if we Democrats hadn't told them about it." [13]

Kefauver, as a strong believer in a bipartisan foreign policy, was annoyed at Eisenhower's attempt to play politics with the Korean War, especially after Eisenhower had supported the major Truman policy decisions on the war for over two years. Reacting critically to Eisenhower's announcement that he would go to Korea if elected, Kefauver urged him:

to go now, tonight. Let's not even wait for tomorrow. It is more important than the whistle-stop tour in which he is engaged. If

the General has a feasible solution, why didn't he mention it in
the last two and a half years? . . . The Korean war should not
be a matter of politics. But since General Eisenhower has made
it so, perhaps he had better call in his ghost writers and find out
what he would do if he fails to win a truce. The American people
ought to be told if among his alternatives is the widening of a
war which might eventually again involve almost all of mankind
in a bloody struggle.[14]

Certainly one of Kefauver's major contributions to Stevenson's campaign was his effort to rally his pre-convention supporters to the Stevenson-Sparkman ticket. The disenchantment with
Stevenson among Kefauver supporters was widespread. One survey conducted in September and October in eleven Western
states showed that of those for whom Kefauver had been their
first choice for President, 44 per cent intended to vote for Eisenhower, 46 per cent for Stevenson, and 10 per cent intended not
to vote at all.[15]

Kefauver was prominently mention as Attorney General
in a Stevenson cabinet, but he told Stevenson's advisers that
"there's no use discussing it, because I'm not interested." [16]
Kefauver's main concern was to leave no doubt that he had
united behind the ticket and that he had done everything possible
to elect Stevenson. His three-week campaign, taking him into
over half the states, did much to counteract the negative feeling
toward him among party regulars and no doubt served him well
in his 1956 Democratic nomination campaign.

Eisenhower's landslide victory in November included even
Kefauver's Tennessee, which the Republican presidential ticket
carried for the first time since 1928, by a margin of about 2400
votes out of almost 900,000 cast. There is little doubt that many
Kefauver supporters there and elsewhere welcomed an Eisenhower victory as confirmation of their belief that the American
voter did in fact want a change in Washington which Truman's
choice, Stevenson, did not offer. While not claiming that Kefauver would have defeated Eisenhower, Kefauver supporters
remained convinced that he would have run a much stronger

race and would have almost certainly preserved Democratic majorities in the Senate and House.[17]

Kefauver spoke highly of Stevenson's campaign, calling it "brilliant . . . setting forth the Democratic side with clarity" and serving "the nation well by fully discussing the issues on a high plane." But he was reluctant to recognize Stevenson as the spokesman for the party, although admitting that "as a matter of custom, Governor Stevenson as the defeated nominee is the titular head of the party. However, he has no right of or in himself to dictate or determine party policy. That is for a policy committee—the National Committee and its executive committee, and perhaps others." Those who were looking for hints of a 1956 Kefauver try for the nomination could certainly read significance into Kefauver's unwillingness to rally behind Stevenson's leadership during the next four years.[18]

When the Eighty-third Congress met in January 1953, Kefauver, now senior senator from Tennessee, moved up several notches on the seniority ladder. He was more than ever a celebrity of the Senate, always surrounded by autograph-seekers and well-wishers wanting to meet him. However, the Republicans controlled Congress, and Kefauver was simply one of many liberals trying to make the best of the most reactionary Congress since 1947–49. His crusade to replace the convention system with national presidential primaries got nowhere,[19] and he and other Democrats soon settled back to await the results of the first Republican control of both the White House and Congress since 1929–31.

One of the few changes resulting from Republican control of the Senate that liberals could welcome was in the chairmanship of Kefauver's own Judiciary Committee. North Dakota Republican William Langer, who was far to the left of the Republican mainstream in the Senate on almost every issue except foreign aid, replaced reactionary Democrat Pat McCarran of Nevada. Langer was one of the last of the agrarian radicals and saw the complicated economic issues of the 1950s in the same terms as did his populist-progressive predecessors. For him Wall

Street was still the enemy of the people, and he intended to use his Judiciary Committee chairmanship to carry on the fight against big business. One of his most important acts was the establishment of the Antitrust and Monopoly Subcommittee of the Judiciary Committee; the business-oriented Republican majority in the Senate was so frightened at the prospect of Langer's stirring up trouble for big business that Republicans prevented even one penny from being appropriated for the subcommittee. It was appointed, nevertheless, and Kefauver became a minority member.[20]

During the 1953 session, Kefauver continued to demonstrate his party regularity on the issues before the Senate. A survey of all Senate votes of 1953 which found a majority of Republicans and a majority of Democrats on opposing sides, showed Kefauver voting with his party on 93 per cent.[21] Any ill feeling he might have had toward the Truman Administration was certainly not evident in Kefauver's reluctance to go along with Republican and Southern Democratic attempts to "uncover" scandal in the previous administration. When, for example, a Republican-controlled Armed Services subcommittee blamed "a needless loss of American lives" in Korea on an ammunition shortage caused by the Truman Administration's "unconscionable inefficiency, waste, and unbelievable red tape," Kefauver was the only subcommittee member, Democratic or Republican, to dissent from the report. He explained his reluctance to sign the report as based on his belief that "American families which have suffered losses in Korea have sustained grief enough without sustaining added grief which this type of statement brings, when the statement is based, as the committee acknowledges, on conflicting testimony between various Army generals." [22]

One of the Republicans' major battle cries during the years of exile from 1933 to 1953 had been in defense of states' rights against the ever-encroaching power of the federal government. Early in Eisenhower's Administration there was a sincere effort to reverse the trend somewhat, until Republicans became used to the fact that they need not fear so much a federal government they controlled. But in 1953 Republican sensitivity to states' rights was still strong, as demonstrated by the tidelands oil dispute. The controversy revolved around whether the states or the federal government held title to oil produced on off-shore lands. The Supreme Court had ruled that the federal government controlled the off-shore deposits, and by 1953, almost $63 million was held in escrow pending a congressional settlement. The Republicans had promised during the campaign of 1952 that they would support a return of the off-shore oil to the states. Although the Republicans talked in terms of states versus the federal government, only three states stood to gain significantly from the Republican stand—California, Texas, and Louisiana.[23]

Since return of the oil lands to the states required an act of Congress, liberals favoring retention of federal control were put in the position of attempting to block legislation in Congress, especially in the Senate, by the same methods they had consistently condemned over the years when used by opponents of civil rights legislation. Kefauver participated in the liberal attempt to block the bill and delivered one of the longest speeches of his career (6 hours, 26 minutes) on April 20 in an effort to delay the legislation. Senator Wayne Morse of Oregon, then an Independent, was one of the few liberals to admit that opponents of the bill were, in fact, filibustering. He said that while he was against the filibuster, "we are going to use it in order to protect the people's interest in cases where it needs to be protected." Senator Herbert Lehman of New York, when answering conservatives' questions about his previous opposition to filibustering, offered to drop the tidelands oil debate and take up a rule change to abolish filibustering if the conservatives were serious about their opposition to it.[24]

Liberal efforts to block the return of the oil lands to the states were not successful. Even attractive proposals to earmark oil revenues for federal aid to education or for retirement of the national debt did not gain enough support to block the surrender of federal control. In any event, Kefauver's prominent association with the fight to save the oil lands for the federal government did not hurt him in Tennessee. The Tennessee legislature, representing a much more conservative Democracy than Kefauver's, endorsed his stand 70 to 15.[25]

Another Republican effort to harness the federal government was the proposed Bricker Amendment to the Constitution, which would have restored the Senate's control over agreements with foreign countries. Conservatives in both parties had been disturbed by the increasing use by the executive branch of executive agreements, especially when such agreements were thought to have been too favorable to the Soviet Union during the war years. Although the Eisenhower Administration originally favored some constitutional amendment to reaffirm the Senate's power to advise and consent, it soon moved to a position of neutrality and then opposition to the specific wordings supported by a majority of senators. Kefauver became the leader of the anti-Bricker forces in the Senate, and although he failed to block the amendment in the Judiciary Committee, he and others did raise enough doubts on the Senate floor about its desirability and application that it failed to receive the required two-thirds support, but only by the narrowest of margins; the vote was 60 to 31. Kefauver opposed the amendment because he believed it "would leave the United States only partially sovereign. . . . The President would no longer have control over foreign relations, since the Congress could regulate his conduct of such affairs down to the last detail." This would upset the "constitutional division of powers between the legislative and executive branches of the government, which has worked so well for 164 years." [26]

Probably nothing Kefauver did during the Eighty-third Congress was more popular in Tennessee than his tenacious defense of the TVA against the real and alleged attacks of the Eisenhower Administration. In spite of Eisenhower's pledge in the 1952 campaign that "under my Administration T. V. A. will be operated at maximum efficiency," the Republican Administration's coolness toward TVA soon became evident. One of the Eisenhower Administration's first moves had been to call for a reduction in the TVA appropriation from the Truman budget request of $254 million to $191 million. Eisenhower himself attacked the idea of the rest of the country developing an area which then drained off their industries, provoking Kefauver to term it "regrettable" that Eisenhower had "displayed an alarming lack of knowledge of T. V. A." [27]

Every anti-TVA statement by an Administration figure was answered quickly and strongly by Kefauver, who, along with other Tennessee Valley senators and congressmen, began to sense the development of a major threat to TVA. When Clarence Manion, reactionary chairman of Eisenhower's Intergovernmental Relations Commission, called for TVA's sale to private industry, Kefauver termed it "just another example of what those being appointed to the various 'study' commissions by the Eisenhower Administration have in store for public power," and saw it as representative of the Administration's hostility toward TVA.[28]

As the first year of Republican government neared an end, Kefauver was still withholding judgment on the Eisenhower Administration. The White House seemed confused, and Kefauver spoke of Eisenhower as "a poor quarterback for the new Republican team. He can't make up his mind what play to call." The President's indecisiveness was beginning to irritate both the left and the right, and Senator Joseph McCarthy began to speak of Eisenhower as no improvement on Truman.[29]

One of the most unfortunate results of Republican control of the Senate from 1953 to 1955 was the elevation through the seniority system of the irresponsible McCarthy to the chairmanship of the Government Operations Committee, which served as a perfect forum for his crusade to purge the federal government of real or imagined security risks. Even the more enlightened Democrats and Republicans were unsure of how potent an issue was the "soft-on-communism" charge manipulated so successfully by McCarthy in the early 1950s, and few wanted to criticize him unnecessarily. Kefauver was one of the least intimidated by McCarthy and had strongly attacked his methods throughout the 1952 campaign. The 1953 Republican subversive hunt, led by McCarthy but joined in by some other Republican chairmen, appalled Kefauver, who wrote Senate Democratic Leader Lyndon Johnson of his concern over:

> the excesses to which the various committees of Congress have gone in the fields of so-called subversive investigations. They have made us all look ridiculous by their headline-grabbing tactics—by the frantic efforts of various chairmen and heads of executive departments to get into the "act." Our personal liberties actually are not safe under the present arrangement and neither is this the most effective way of detecting and exposing subversive activities.[30]

McCarthy's success with the guilt-by-association technique panicked Democrats in the summer of 1954 into attempting to remove the communist issue once and for all by outlawing the Communist party. The move was generally considered an attempt to save Senator Hubert Humphrey's Senate seat, as well as to demonstrate to the country that Democrats were as anticommunist as their Republican colleagues. Kefauver had grave reservations about the legislation. He tried to point out that if the Communist party were outlawed, the registration provisions of the 1950 Internal Security Act would not apply because registration would amount to self-incrimination. He believed that control of the communists could be more effective if prosecutions were based on the failure to register under the old act rather than on an application of the thirteen criteria listed in the 1954 bill which supposedly could determine membership or participation in the Communist party. Kefauver feared above all else that the new act would become the basis for prosecuting people for having certain beliefs, since the criteria were based on the guilt-by-association approach to identifying subversives.[31]

The Eisenhower Administration and FBI Director J. Edgar Hoover also opposed outlawing the Communist party, although their opposition was based more on practical considerations than on a concern for civil liberties. But in the Senate, Kefauver was alone in his determination to oppose to the end making mere membership in the Communist party a crime. In a most courageous move he cast the only vote against the motion, adopted 81 to 1 on August 17, to make Communist party membership a felony. For the rest of his career, he was attacked by opponents for being the only member of the Senate to vote against outlawing the Communist party, although the final version of the bill, which he supported, did, in fact, deny certain legal privileges to the party. It would have been very easy to avoid the roll call or to go along with the majority, but Kefauver was determined to be recorded in defense of civil liberties.[32]

Others began to reconsider the position taken by the Senate, and in the Senate-House conference resolving the differences between the subversive control bills passed by each, the provision so offensive to Kefauver was dropped. Even so, there was still strong support for the original language when the conference report came before the Senate on August 19. Kefauver's pleas to reject the stronger provisions were directed mainly at the Democrats who had allowed themselves to be stampeded by the soft-on-communism charge:

> The Democratic Party, although it has reason to be irked and grieved by the communism charge hurled against it, cannot afford to be a party to unsound legislation in an effort to retaliate. Our Democratic Party is the traditional defender of civil liberties— we have fought efforts to deprive men of freedom of thought, religion, and speech. It will destroy our party to abandon this concept no matter how aggravating the situation may be. A grievous wrong inflicted upon us by the Republicans does not justify our inflicting an even greater wrong upon the protections given our people by the Bill of Rights.[33]

The more moderate position prevailed and the conference report was adopted. On the final vote, Kefauver joined seventy-eight other senators in a unanimous vote for the compromise subversive control legislation.[34]

For the most part, however, Kefauver played only a minor role on the national scene during the Republican years 1953 and

1954. During his fifteen years in the Senate, these two years were unique as a period of relative obscurity for him. He had been front-page news since mid-1950, but by 1953 the crime investigation and his drive for the presidency had both run their course, and there was no new national forum which drew special attention to him. In addition, there was the sheer physical exhaustion and emotional strain of the presidential drive, to which he could finally yield in the months that followed the convention. Furthermore, the Republican victory of 1952 had temporarily shifted attention away from the Democrats generally, as well as removed them from positions through which they had previously exercised the power and responsibility that go with control of Congress and its committee structure. But, more importantly, Kefauver was inclined in 1953 and 1954 to play down his image as a possible presidential candidate and concentrate instead on rebuilding his shattered Tennessee fences in preparation for his renomination campaign in 1954, in which he expected to be fighting for his political survival against a host of enemies who had every reason to believe that Kefauver's liberal record and his alienation of the most vocal defenders of the Southern way of life had made him vulnerable to a more conservative challenger.

chapter xi

RE-ELECTION, 1954

A s Senator Kefauver faced re-election in 1954, he had good reason to be somewhat apprehensive about his prospects. His identification with Northern liberals at the 1952 Democratic convention had been very unpopular in Tennessee and had further served to call attention to his generally liberal voting record during his first term in the Senate. The defeats of Senator Claude Pepper of Florida and Senator Frank Graham of North Carolina in 1950, and the bitter opposition developing in Alabama in 1954 against Senator John Sparkman, indicated that Southern progressives were on the defensive all across Dixie. It was difficult to determine whether the national swing to the right of 1952 would continue into 1954, but, in any event, the May 1954 Supreme Court decision against segregated schools ensured that Southern voters would be especially sensitive to issues they related to defense of the Southern way of life against the onslaught of liberals and left-wingers in Washington. And, since Kefauver had been nominated in 1948 only by a plurality over his two more conservative opponents, it could be argued that he had never enjoyed the support of a majority of Tennessee Democrats and that a conservative challenger acceptable to all anti-Kefauver elements would stand an excellent chance of defeating Kefauver, especially if his liberal record could be made the issue and not be obscured as it had been in 1948 by the anti-Crump crusade.

The strongest candidate mentioned as a possible opponent for Kefauver was incumbent Governor Frank Clement, whose popularity was at its peak in 1954. Although Kefauver and Clement were both progressives, they headed opposing, although somewhat overlapping, factions among Tennessee Democrats; a primary fight between them would have pitted Tennessee's two best-known Democrats against each other and would have deeply divided the party. But, after the governor's term was extended in 1953 from two to four years, Governor Clement decided to seek a second term, and the greatest threat to Kefauver's re-election was removed.[1]

However, there was no chance that Kefauver would be without opposition in the Democratic primary. One of the first moves was by a group of approximately thirty conservative businessmen who were determined to have Kefauver defeated in 1954 and who sought out prospective opponents for him. Former Senator Tom Stewart, whom Kefauver had defeated in 1948, was one of their favorites, but he declined to make the race. They got a similar refusal from Kefauver's good friend, former Governor Prentice Cooper. With their search for an eminently respectable conservative candidate coming to naught, they were forced to consider lesser-known figures in the state.[2]

As it turned out, however, the initiative in the effort to defeat Kefauver was taken out of the hands of the businessmen. Early in 1953, Representative Pat Sutton, from the Sixth District in Middle Tennessee, began to make public his interest in opposing Kefauver's renomination. In February, Sutton visited the legislature seeking support, and, in May, he announced his candidacy, a full fifteen months before the primary.[3]

Sutton, a heavily decorated veteran, had first been elected to the House in 1948 and had thereafter enjoyed a cordial relationship with Kefauver. It was with some surprise, therefore, that Kefauver learned of Sutton's plans to challenge him. The general reaction of Kefauver associates was amusement that Sutton considered himself of sufficient stature to be a serious threat. Sutton's record in the House had been undistinguished, and he had even been selected by a national magazine as one of the nation's worst congressmen.[4]

It was inevitable that Sutton would consult with the businessmen seeking an anti-Kefauver candidate. The meeting was Sutton's idea; the businessmen attempted to determine his position on all the major issues and were dissatisfied with only one or two of his answers. His war record was attractive, although one businessman commented that "a man who got as many medals as Sutton did must either be reckless or foolish." [5] Doubts were expressed about Sutton's ability to raise money for the campaign, and the group unsuccessfully tried to talk him into withdrawing in favor of another, as yet unselected, candidate. Sutton refused, expressing his determination to stay in the race even if the group did field another anti-Kefauver candidate. Since unity of the anti-Kefauver forces was essential if Kefauver were to be defeated, and since no other attractive anti-Kefauver candidate had been found anyway, the group reluctantly gave Sutton their endorsement.[6]

Even before Sutton's campaign officially opened, it was obvious that he had been very much impressed by the apparent success of the smear tactics employed by Senator Joseph McCarthy of Wisconsin. In January, 1954, he told a *New York Times* reporter:

> Personally, I like the senior Senator. I have visited in his home and he has visited in mine. But I am against him politically because I don't like his record in Washington.
>
> The senior Senator has consistently voted as a left winger against the loyalty oath in the Government, and he has voted against wire tapping to catch the Reds.[7]

In April, Sutton officially opened his campaign on the same note. He journeyed to Kefauver's hometown of Madisonville and launched into a vicious attack on the Senator, challenging him to debate and calling him a "coddler" of communists.[8]

In spite of the real opportunity to benefit from what was generally assumed to be widespread dissatisfaction with at least part of Kefauver's record, Sutton's campaign had limited success in attracting significant support from even those thought most likely to welcome opposition to Kefauver. By June of 1954, a poll commissioned by Kefauver showed that the Senator was favored by 51 per cent of those polled, Sutton by 11 per cent, with 38 per cent undecided.[9]

Sutton, however, had planned a dramatic appeal to the electorate in the last two months of the campaign, through the use of the "talkathon," a marathon television appearance lasting several hours and featuring statements of support, speeches, and question and answer exchanges between viewers and the candidate. The talkathon was claimed as the brain child of Robert G. Venn, a Miami television consultant, who had seen the possibilities for overnight publicity via television for otherwise little-known candidates. Venn's association with Florida Senator George Smathers's television smear campaign against Senator Claude Pepper in 1950 caused Kefauver to take Venn seriously. The talkathon technique was expensive and was embarked upon only after Sutton gave his backers and Venn assurances that right-wing Texas oil millionaire H. L. Hunt had pledged $150,000 to defeat Kefauver.[10]

The first talkathon featuring Sutton was held in Knoxville on June 19. Sutton appeared continuously before the cameras for 26½ hours and immediately became the hottest topic of conversation in the Knoxville area. Sutton scored well against Kefauver with the viewing audience, largely because he was able to distort Kefauver's record without fear of immediate contradiction. His credibility was not yet questioned and viewers, therefore, tended to take seriously the loose charges which were thrown out with such earnestness and self-confidence.[11]

In Memphis, Sutton's backers attempted to measure the effects of their candidate's talkathon performance there. Two professional surveys, one conducted a day before the talkathon and a second conducted two days later, showed that recognition of Sutton had increased from 35 per cent to 68 per cent, while the percentage able to identify him as a candidate for the Senate had gone from 9 per cent to 45 per cent, in contrast to only 41 per cent who so identified Kefauver. Two other talkathons were held, in Nashville and Johnson City, but one in Chattanooga was cancelled because of a lack of funds.[12]

The talkathon format would have been a challenge to any candidate utilizing it. The long hours of extemporaneous speaking before a live microphone and a television camera necessarily resulted in greater opportunities to blunder in ways that a shorter, more reasoned and organized appearance would have obviated. Furthermore, the physical strain of such a performance inevitably led to a fatigue which limited the candidate's ability to weigh his comments before speaking. Given Sutton's basic strategy of smearing Kefauver with half-truths and distortions (a strategy whose success depends on carefully evaluating to what extent the truth can be stretched before the credibility of the source itself is undermined), it is debatable whether the talkathon was the best format for the Sutton campaign, in spite of its apparent success in publicizing his candidacy. One of Kefauver's best issues in the last six weeks of the campaign became Sutton's basic irresponsibility, allegedly demonstrated during the talkathons.

The obvious expense associated with the talkathons gave Kefauver the opportunity to raise the question of who was financing Sutton's campaign. Nothing redounded more to Kefauver's benefit than the suggestions, rumors, and allegations that Sutton was being used by unsavory anti-Kefauver elements in an effort to retire the liberal, crime-fighting senator.

The most widespread allegation about Sutton's backing involved the charge that criminal elements, angered by Kefauver's role in the 1950–51 crime investigation, had marked him for defeat. As early as January 1954, *L'Italia* of San Francisco reported:

> It is rumored in Chicago, with considerable probability of accuracy, that large sums of money have been sent into the state of Tennessee for the purpose of defeating the election of Senator

Kefauver. . . . Whoever has relatives, friends or acquaintances in Tennessee should enlighten them by means of letters, newspapers and telegrams in order to try to stop a repulsive and criminal effort in a dishonest election campaign financed by the underworld to prevent the re-election of Kefauver to the Senate of the United States.[13]

The vehemently pro-Kefauver *Nashville Tennessean*, attempting to picture Kefauver's re-election campaign as an important battle in the never-ending crusade against organized crime, reprinted the *L'Italia* story, quoted Bible Belt hero Billy Graham praising the Kefauver Crime Committee, and warned editorially of the "imperative need . . . to watch for the 'outside' money said to be coming in and to find out how the invaders would 'place' it to best advantage. . . . If there are any persons in the state who are willing to handle blood money for political gain—to sell out to the New York and Chicago mobs—there is a plain duty to see that they are exposed." [14]

Sophisticated observers of the Tennessee political scene were inclined to discount as campaign propaganda the charges that organized crime was out to "get" Kefauver. It came as a genuine shock to many, therefore, when Kefauver was able to piece together two associations between the Sutton campaign and organized crime. Admittedly, the links were weak, but they were sufficient to raise honest doubts about Sutton's backing and to re-emphasize Kefauver's role as a crime-fighter. The most important revelation came when Nat Caldwell of the *Tennessean* staff went to New Orleans to investigate General Air Transports, a company that had furnished a helicopter for Sutton's use in the campaign. The vehicle was a tremendous attention-getter and attracted a crowd wherever Sutton landed, but it, like the talkathons, had raised questions about Sutton's financing. Caldwell found, with help from Kefauver's old friend, New Orleans Mayor deLesseps Morrison, that the helicopter had been purchased only two days before it had been flown to Memphis for Sutton's use. Further investigation showed that one of the stockholders of General Air Transports was Charles Murphy, accountant and secretary of a New Orleans club owned by Frank Costello, the famous underworld figure questioned by the Kefauver Committee. No evidence was ever obtained to link Murphy directly with the helicopter, but the guilt-by-association so often practiced against liberals began to operate against Sutton. As a result, the chairman of the board of General Air Transports was moved by the threat of bad publicity to comment publicly on the helicopter, something he might not have done without allegations of underworld revenge against Kefauver. "I don't believe any of our officials ever saw Mr. Sutton," he told the press. "My understanding is that our first contact about renting the helicopter came from Dallas, Texas. I don't know for sure where the first cash money for delivering the plane to Memphis came from. But I understand that came from Dallas too." This explanation proved of little value to Sutton, since it still emphasized the attempt by non-Tennesseans to influence the primary results.[15] Kefauver never determined exactly who paid for the helicopter. "I am satisfied that the money is coming from H. L. Hunt at Dallas," he wrote Mayor Morrison. "I wish in some way we could prove it." [16]

A second effort to link organized crime to Sutton's campaign was based on the identification of talkathon director Robert Venn as "a one-time associate of Mickey McBride, who ran the wire service providing the gambling syndicate with information." Venn had been general manager of radio station WMIE in Miami, one of whose owners had been McBride, who also owned Continental Press, the gambling wire service disbanded as a result of the Kefauver investigation. Kefauver himself had carefully noted only the facts of Venn's relationship to McBride, leaving his audiences to draw their own conclusions. The *Nashville Tennessean*, however, got carried away by the connection, and wrote so strongly of Venn's mobster ties that Venn successfully sued the paper for alleged damage to the commercial value of the talkathon.[17]

Although the charges of gangster influence within the Sutton campaign were based on almost insignificant evidence, the fact remained that Sutton had lost the initiative. One source reported that Sutton replied angrily to suggestions of his alliance with criminal elements by retorting that he "would rather have the backing of criminals than the support of 'left-wingers' who believe in overthrowing your government and mine." While denying that he had gangster support, he found them preferable to "left-wingers" because "they [racketeers] will take your money from you, but they won't take your country away from you." [18] Kefauver, on the other hand, sought constantly to remind voters of the crime investigation and requested statistics from the Bureau of Internal Revenue to demonstrate the success of the probe.[19] The murder in June of Albert L. Patterson, the crime-fighting Democratic nominee for Attorney General of nearby Alabama, was generally blamed on the underworld and further served to reinforce Kefauver's suggestions that intervention in politics by organized crime was a real threat. Kefauver called attention to the fact that Patterson had been one of his "best friends" and a supporter of Kefauver for President in 1952.[20]

Sutton's principal attacks on Kefauver indicated that he believed the Senator's major weakness was the liberalism which found Northern allies but few sympathizers among Southern legislators in Washington. Sutton claimed to be presenting Tennessee voters with a "clear decision. . . . The issues of this campaign have been clearly drawn. On one side, you have conservative Democratic thinking, and on the other side, you have an advocate of left-wing thinking. I am a Jeffersonian and Jacksonian Democrat. Kefauver is the fair-haired hopeful of the left-wingers." [21] On liberals generally, and on Kefauver specifically, Sutton attempted to heap blame for the communist menace both at home and abroad; in addition, the Supreme Court decision of two months before against segregated schools gave Sutton the opportunity to link Kefauver with a decision which was hailed by liberals but which had aroused and frightened white Tennesseans. In short, liberals such as Kefauver were responsible for everything that was wrong with America. It was McCarthy's message, but Sutton was not as effective as his Wisconsin model.

Calling attention to Kefauver's aloofness from the Dixie bloc, Sutton described Kefauver's "only friends . . . in the U. S. Senate [as] left wingers [such as] Paul Douglas, Humphrey, Lehman and Morse, and if you will name me more . . . I will buy you a good hat." [22]

Kefauver's role as a Southern maverick worried even his own supporters; Mrs. Martha Ragland remembered a meeting of Kefauver backers in the fall of 1952 convened to "assess his situation and presumably to advise him. Barret Ashley of Dyersburg in West Tennessee said: 'Estes, you are going to have to get more in line with the South. Can't you be more like the other Southern Senators?' There was that pause, and then Estes said, 'Yes—I can—if I disregard everything I have ever believed in.' There was no more advice along that line." [23]

Kefauver was pictured as the darling of the left: ". . . some of the people who are behind Estes Kefauver . . . I don't consider Americans," Sutton charged. "Just reading a list of activities of some of these people would take 15 minutes." [24] Sutton's attacks soon forced Kefauver to defend once more his votes against the House Un-American Activities Committee, which had been such an issue in the 1948 primary.[25] Vito Marcantonio, who earlier had been used so often by conservatives in their guilt-by-association attempts based on comparison of voting records, again emerged from obscurity.[26] When half-truths were not sufficient, outright fabrications were substituted. For example, Sutton announced on the Memphis talkathon that "in 1950, Donald Hiss, the brother of the traitor of our country, Alger Hiss, donated $10,000 to Estes Kefauver's campaign for the presidency of the United States of America." On hearing of Sutton's allegation, Hiss laughed and denied giving "a penny" to Kefauver "at any time." [27]

Sutton also disapproved of Kefauver's support of foreign aid, saying that "we have kept people overseas up long enough, and it is time they become self-supporting." He was "for taking the United States out of the United Nations and taking the United Nations out of the United States." He objected strongly to Kefauver's role in defeating the Bricker Amendment and equated Kefauver's support for the Atlantic Union with a lack of sensitivity for American sovereignty and national security.[28]

Kefauver accepted the challenge: "My opponent says that I am an internationalist. This he says in derision, but it is one of the few truthful statements he does make in this campaign." Kefauver enthusiastically admitted identification with the UN, NATO, the Greek-Turkish loan, the Point Four program, and "all those measures which have either slowed Communists, stopped them cold or thrown them for a loss in the war which rages cold and hot in this mixed up world." [29]

The greatest concern of white Tennesseans in the summer of 1954 was the long-range significance of the Supreme Court's May decision against school segregation. The Court had not yet announced how the decision was to be implemented, and, therefore, the possible resolution of the issue was left in such doubt that the wildest fears of white Tennesseans were open to exploitation. It was perhaps natural that Sutton, as it became more and more obvious that his campaign was heading for defeat, would begin to emphasize more strongly Kefauver's record as a Southern progressive on matters that could be tied to the civil rights question.

The emotional issue of Tennessee's "betrayal" of Virginia at the 1952 Democratic convention was again recalled, and Sutton quoted Senator James Eastland of Mississippi as having termed Kefauver a "renegade Southerner." There was no doubt that Kefauver's 1952 attempt to present himself as a national candidate had left him vulnerable to the charge that he had been more interested in winning Northern delegates than he had in defending the civil rights position of most Tennessee Democrats. Kefauver's problem was to establish a civil rights position which would enable him to win re-election in 1954 without damaging his future with Northern and Western liberals. Sutton detected some ambivalence and spoke of Kefauver's posing as "a great American when he comes to Gibson County" but jumping "right into the arms of the left-wingers when in Washington." [30]

Kefauver and Sutton agreed on the desirability of maintaining segregated schools. But, while Sutton spoke emotionally of his opposition to "Negro and white children attending school together, or of legislation forcing them to do so," Kefauver calmly expressed his hope that separate but equal schools could be maintained at the local level. There was never a hint of defiance in his remarks on the Supreme Court's decision, and he spoke, instead, of his belief that "if outside agitators will stay out and local people deal with their own problems, we can solve this problem satisfactorily in the South." [31]

Unable to force Kefauver into a corner on the segregation issue, Sutton searched Kefauver's record for damaging statements. The best he could do was a quote of Kefauver by the Baltimore *Afro-American* of June 17, 1952, which Sutton unashamedly altered by adding the italicized phrase:

> I assure you I will do more than talk—*there will be no segregation.* I will do something about starting a program of education and persuasion which would do more to break down the artificial barriers that separate us one from the other than anything that has yet been done.[32]

The *Chattanooga Times* immediately pointed out the inaccuracy and voiced its opinion that "Tennessee has never before seen a political campaign in which a major candidate was so completely careless with the truth as is Pat Sutton. He even puts words in his opponent's mouth which the opponent never said." [33]

Kefauver was clearly uncomfortable with the segregation issue and sought to focus on other issues. He attacked Sutton's pledge to do what he could to alter the decision: "There is not one thing a member of the Senate can do about that decision," Kefauver repeated over and over, "and anyone who tells you that he's going to do something about it is just trying to mislead you for votes." Kefauver stressed that "it's just deceit, pure deceit, on the part of my opponent to be talking like this. And it's dangerous, for in doing so he seeks to recklessly stir up racial prejudice just for what he thinks will gain a few votes for himself." [34]

In any event, Kefauver called it "ridiculous for my opponent to be telling you all he is going to do as a senator, when as a congressman for three terms, all he was able to do was have one bill—just one—enacted into law. And what was that one bill? It was, ladies and gentlemen, a bill to regulate boxing contests and exhibitions in the District of Columbia." [35]

Negro leaders had no trouble choosing sides between Kefauver and Sutton. Whatever was left to be desired in Kefauver's civil rights record, Walter White of the NAACP saw "the fight in Tennessee . . . [as] between the Dixiecrats and the liberals. It is therefore very important that Tennessee be one of the states of concentration in our current registration and voting campaign." [36]

Other groups lined up predictably. Organized labor was solidly behind Kefauver, who was one of only two senators with 100 per cent labor ratings facing re-election in 1954. Reports for that year filed by five important national labor political action committees showed that Kefauver was second in receiving financial support from labor.[37]

Sutton had expected to receive the enthusiastic endorsement of Memphis Boss Crump, the object of Kefauver's 1948 crusade against bossism. Crump, however, surprised politicians across the state in March 1954, when he commented on Kefauver's record in a statement so favorable that he seemed to be close to an open endorsement of Kefauver for renomination:

> . . . I am filing no brief for Kefauver; however, to be honest and fair, I must give him credit for two things, to wit: [he has been] a strong supporter of TVA, which means everything to Memphis, Shelby County and Tennessee; and, further, as chairman of that committee (Senate Crime Investigating Committee),

he opened the door to some very ugly things in America, which proved helpful in many places while, in others, the door no doubt closed.

Any assistance from anyone to curb corruption is desired by all right thinking people and most certainly [is] very commendable.[38]

Crump never explained his objections to Sutton, whom so many of his former allies were backing. It may have been the anti-TVA attitude of several prominent Sutton backers, or sympathy for Kefauver's efforts in the crime investigation. Perhaps it was Crump's old antagonism toward Northern urban bosses manifesting itself on behalf of Kefauver, who was generally considered their enemy at the 1952 Democratic convention. In any event, Sutton found it incredible that Crump would not want Kefauver defeated, and claimed his support. Crump denied it. "We're not asking our friends to vote for either candidate and we'll maintain that position throughout election day." That Crump's dissatisfaction with Sutton was real was made painfully obvious when the congressman was refused a police escort during a visit to Memphis.[39]

The reactionary Republican organization, centered in East Tennessee, was ready to re-establish its traditional alliance with the Dixiecrats. The *Knoxville Journal*, published by the Republican state chairman and considered the most influential voice of Tennessee Republicanism, called for Republican support in the Democratic primary for Sutton:

Under the circumstances, the logic of politics appears to dictate that Tennessee Republicans give all the aid and comfort possible to Sutton's primary candidacy, on the theory that Kefauver's retirement from the Senate is a matter of national, as well as state, importance.

If it turns out that Sutton is not able to overcome Kefauver's entrenched position in the Democratic Party, then, looking toward November, there will be a second chance to do the job in a teaming up of Sutton Democrats and Republicans behind a Republican candidate.[40]

Republican support for Sutton was certainly not based on the congressman's record during the first two years of the Eisenhower Administration. Kefauver ranked last among Senate Democrats in support for Administration positions in 1954, and Sutton ranked last among House Democrats.[41]

Kefauver was successful in picturing Sutton as a junior version of Joe McCarthy. The Army-McCarthy hearings in 1954 had made the public more sensitive than usual to the smear technique, and Sutton soon found himself on the defensive as the press insisted on details to substantiate his wild charges. Kefauver compared Sutton to Senator Jenner of Indiana, Senator McCarthy, and the *Chicago Tribune*. "Like these others, my opponent offers nothing, smears everything." The weathervane *Knoxville News-Sentinel* agreed: "One McCarthy in the Senate is enough. If we're going to have a Democrat for senator, by all means it should be Estes Kefauver and not Pat Sutton." The real McCarthy was too busy defending himself against censure by the Senate to honor the pledge he had made in 1952 to go into Tennessee and help defeat Kefauver.[42]

Sutton's campaign presented Kefauver supporters in Tennessee with the ideal challenge; pessimism about Kefauver's chances was almost the indispensable element in rousing the Kefauver organization. Inclined to view a victory of good over evil as necessarily hard-won, the Kefauver campaign thrived on reports that Dixiecrats, gangsters, home-grown reactionaries, and Texas oilmen had ganged up on their hero. National reporters covering the story went away from Kefauver headquarters with the feeling that Kefauver was in serious trouble and was especially crippled by a lack of funds. Those Kefauver supporters around the country who were not reached by the *New York Times* and the *New Republic* might be moved to action by the widely syndicated columns of Kefauver's good friend, Drew Pearson, who gave special emphasis in his columns during the summer of 1954 to renominating Kefauver. Whatever the source of information that Kefauver needed help, Kefauver supporters, and liberals generally, around the country responded to each report by inundating Kefauver headquarters with small contributions. Even the *Reader's Digest* intervened by running a homespun piece by Kefauver entitled "The Best Advice I Ever Had," which he submitted with the comment that "this will help me tremendously if it comes out in the August issue. . . . I hope you will get [it] in shape so I will not look immodest." The *Reader's Digest* article did, in fact, hit the newsstands two weeks before the primary.[43]

Kefauver's most effective appeal in his hour of need, however, was to fellow Tennessee Democrats. Perhaps no one who has ever served in Congress heeded better the classic advice to legislators to "answer your mail!" Not only did Kefauver effectively answer his mail, but he went out of his way to find excuses to write letters or postcards to voters. One Kefauver associate estimated that by 1954 50,000 Tennesseans considered themselves personal friends of Kefauver.[44] He campaigned the year round in his congressional district after 1939, in the state after 1947, and in the nation after 1951. Seeking friends and supporters became a way of life, and he invested his time and energy in effectively representing the interests of all who sought his help. For many voters around the country, Kefauver was their contact in Washington, and they many times came to him, bypassing their own senators and congressmen. Throughout his career, Kefauver was able to communicate to his supporters, in Tennessee and around the country, a feeling that he was counting on them to help him go back to Washington against what always seemed to be overwhelming odds. One New Hampshire supporter of Kefauver told of how Kefauver's friends in that state would make a point of cornering tourists in cars with Tennessee license plates to thank them for electing a man like Kefauver, making sure that each tourist went away with a feeling of pride in having Kefauver in the Senate.[45]

This feeling of having a personal interest in Kefauver's reelection was impossible to measure prior to election day and accounts in part for the predictions of close elections in both 1954 and 1960, when, in fact, Kefauver rolled up staggering pluralities over his primary opponents.

It was especially easy for Kefauver to rally his forces when circumstances made it seem that principle was at stake. Thus, Sutton, who would have had no easy time against Kefauver under any circumstances, unwittingly, by his irresponsible statements and his unsavory coalition of backers, became the necessary foil in 1954 for Kefauver's continuous crusade for honest and progressive government. Kefauver summarized the issues of the primary campaign in a speech that made reference to all those aspects of the Sutton campaign that brought out the best in Kefauver's dedicated followers:

> There has been a lot of talk in this campaign about internationalism, and I must comment that my opponent in the Democratic primary, while no internationalist, is certainly a cosmopolitan.
>
> Now he has himself a Republican campaign manager imported from Arkansas in the person of Bob Snowden.
>
> He has a helicopter from New Orleans, partly owned by a former associate of the notorious Frank Costello and partly financed by Texas oil.
>
> He has a publicity director from Florida in Robert Venn, a onetime associate of Mickey McBride, who ran the wire service providing the gambling syndicates with information.
>
> In his corner he also has a Republican national committeeman —Guy Smith—from Knoxville, who is urging Republican voters through his Republican newspaper to vote in the Democratic primary for him.
>
> My opponent's support seems to come from everyone except Tennessee Democrats.[46]

On August 6, Tennessee Democrats gave Kefauver an overwhelming victory that surprised the most optimistic Kefauver backers. Kefauver received 440,497 votes to Sutton's 186,363, and carried ninety-one of the state's ninety-five counties. An overjoyed Kefauver was quick to interpret his victory as a mandate to "go on working for 20th century goals" and a repudiation of "the doctrine of fear and suspicion as an antidote for [the] Communist peril." The *Washington Post* headlined Kefauver's smashing victory for politically conscious Washington, which had been awaiting the Tennessee vote as an indication of whether Kefauver had retained the support at home essential if he were to seek the Democratic presidential nomination in 1956.[47]

Just as in 1948, there was an attempt to forge a Dixiecrat-Republican coalition behind a Republican candidate. The most widely mentioned Republican prospect was Ray Jenkins, successful Knoxville lawyer, who had achieved prominence in 1954 when he had been brought to Washington to serve as chief counsel for the Army-McCarthy hearings. Jenkins came to the capital as an admirer of Senator McCarthy, but soon became disgusted with McCarthy's attempt to manipulate him. As early as May, *Newsweek* reported him to be "sick of Washington, disgusted with the hearings, and not interested in being a senator," although his disclaimer left the door open to a later change of attitude.[48]

After it began to appear that Sutton was picking up support against Kefauver via the talkathons, Jenkins said he would not "definitely close the door, lock it, and throw away the key" but would make a definite statement soon. If he did run, Jenkins said, he would welcome the support of McCarthy. Since the televising of the Army-McCarthy hearings had made Jenkins a familiar face across Tennessee, it seemed that a battle of political TV stars was shaping up.[49]

Jenkins finally announced that he would not run. The Republicans nominated him anyway, but after Kefauver's crushing victory over Sutton, Jenkins refused to make the race and was replaced on the Republican ticket by Nashville lawyer Tom Wall, who was not expected to be, and in fact, proved not to be, serious opposition for Kefauver, who easily defeated him in November, 249,121 to 106,971.[50]

The challenge of 1954 had been met; with his fences repaired at home, Kefauver could now afford to redirect his attention to the national political scene and his ambitions for national office.

chapter xii

LOYAL OPPOSITION, 1954-1955

By late 1954, Kefauver and other prominent Democrats became more and more vocal in expressing their growing disillusionment with the Eisenhower Administration. Part of the explanation for the rise in partisan rhetoric lay, of course, in the fact that the 1956 election was less than two years away, and Democrats who wanted to be considered spokesmen for the party began to enunciate criticisms of Eisenhower as part of their maneuvering for power within the party. In addition, however, there were other Democrats who had given the Republican Administration the benefit of the doubt during the President's first months in office but who no longer maintained their silence once they identified objectionable trends among Eisenhower's foreign and domestic policies.

Although Kefauver had doubted that Eisenhower's election would result in any significant changes in America's foreign policy, he soon found Eisenhower's Asian policies disturbing. Kefauver had given the President high marks for settling the war in Korea but thereafter became more and more concerned that Secretary of State John Foster Dulles would blunder into a new Asian war over either Formosa or Indo-China.

As the French military situation in Indo-China began to deteriorate in 1954, pressure built among rightwing Republicans for some significant American intervention to prevent the loss of the French colony to communism. Privately, Kefauver was skeptical about the possibility of blocking a communist takeover of all of Indo-China and preferred that the United States not commit itself to defending the area.[1] He was completely opposed to any action by the American government to maintain French rule in southeast Asia. In mid-April, a few weeks before the French defeat at Dienbienphu, Kefauver called for an American endorsement of independence for Indo-China, with resolution of the disputes over the mechanics of setting up new governments in the area left to the United Nations.[2] He repeatedly expressed his fear that the U. S. would intervene unilaterally to support French control, and urged instead, "We . . . must completely disassociate ourselves from the old colonialism in Asia." [3] The dilemma facing the U. S. seemed to lie in having to choose between intervention on behalf of colonialism, and a passive neutrality that would result in a Communist take-over in Indo-China. In spite of his dissatisfaction with French colonial rule in Indo-China, Kefauver, nevertheless, analyzed the war there as essentially a "struggle against the aggression of communism" rather than as a nationalist uprising against colonialism. Even so, Kefauver argued that containing communism was not solely the responsibility of the United States. If the United States did, in fact, seriously consider involvement in Indo-China, Kefauver hoped "that the governments of all the free nations of that part of Asia are included in our counsels. We can only hope that decisions involving increased intervention, if made, will be carried out in the framework of the United Nations. What is most important, however, is that the American people be told the truth and all the truth." [4]

When the decision against large-scale American intervention became known in June, Kefauver tempered his approval of the announcement with a renewed expression of his concern that the United States might yet repeat the French mistake in Indo-China:

> For the time being, we have avoided open intervention. At the moment, we are employing merely a creeping intervention. Yet

often of late we have been warned that we might be compelled to take a fully active part in this conflict; and if recent history is any criterion, we would soon be taking the major part in that war.[5]

Although the Vietnam mess was to fester for years and finally to become, in the 1960s, the focus of American involvement in southeast Asia, the powder keg in the Far East in 1954 and 1955 seemed to be Formosa. The constant exchange of epithets between Communist China and the American-backed Chinese government on Formosa was simply another round of the civil war which had raged for over thirty years. While the volleys of abusive rhetoric were unsettling, the real fear was that the Communists would renew the shooting war by an attempt to capture the "off-shore" islands still controlled by the Nationalists almost under the guns of the Communist mainland. Quemoy and Matsu were the most famous of the islands, and the debate centered on the question of whether the United States had an interest in their defense. Kefauver opposed any commitment by the United States to defend the islands and, in early 1955, urged limitations on an Administration-backed resolution giving Eisenhower almost a blank check to act in the Formosa situation. Kefauver pleaded futilely for a UN role in the crisis. Warning that "war may come out of the present situation," he urged that the "Senate should . . . get the resolution in such shape that it will result in the least possible chance of war, and still maintain our honor." [6]

He tried to amend the proposed Formosa Resolution to limit U. S. defense to Formosa and the Pescadores Islands, between Formosa and the mainland; his amendment to that effect was defeated, 11 to 75. On the final vote on a companion Mutual Security Treaty with China, Kefauver was one of the minority who opposed the pact, which was approved, 64 to 6.[7]

The Eisenhower Administration loosely defined the U. S. commitment to Chiang's government, presumably to allow maximum flexibility if and when an attack did take place. Kefauver

suggested that the situation was being arranged in order to provide a justification for an attack on China:

> There are forces in Eisenhower's Administration so powerful
> and apparently so eager for a war with China that they are be-
> coming almost impossible to resist. That the United States should
> be plunged into war over Matsu and Quemoy ought to be un-
> thinkable. Yet there are those in high places who are plotting
> to bring such a war about, whatever the risk.[8]

Kefauver saw "no moral basis whatsoever for keeping the
United States' position cloudy in so far as Quemoy and Matsu
are concerned." [9] The only explanation could be an attempt to
drag the United States into an Asian war. In a major speech on
the Senate floor, Kefauver strongly attacked the Administration's
handling of the Formosa situation:

> The remarkable thing about this plotting and planning for war
> is that the plotters and planners must know that the vast majority
> of the American people are against them. The mood of America,
> no matter how warlike some of our leaders wish to make us
> seem, is deeply pacific; and, as a matter of fact, we know that
> we are not going to have any allies, or substantial allies, if we
> get into a war over Quemoy and Matsu.[10]

Two days later Wisconsin Senator Joseph McCarthy bitterly attacked Kefauver:

> . . . the ghost of Neville Chamberlain arose day before yesterday
> on the floor of the United States Senate. I thought we had seen
> the last of the Chamberlain tradition when the Acheson-Marshall-
> Truman cabal was voted out of power. I thought we had seen
> the last of appeasement, retreat, and surrender. But the spirit of
> Neville Chamberlain—of Munich—is evidently very much alive.
> The Senator from Tennessee has proved himself a most worthy
> heir of the Munich tradition.

Kefauver's speech proved, according to McCarthy, that the
Democrats were indeed the party of appeasement. He did agree

with Kefauver, however, on the need to define clearly American commitments to Formosa in order to prevent the present confusion from leading to a war caused by Communist miscalculation of America's will to defend Formosa.[11]

Kefauver replied briefly to the personal attack:

> That . . . is the type of statement too often indulged in by some persons during these days. Instead of answering arguments on their merits, they call names, attach labels to certain persons, and try to make odious comparisons. So I am not surprised. But I should say to the junior Senator from Wisconsin I have never owned an umbrella.[12]

In spite of his caution about committing American military forces and his reliance on the UN as a major peace-keeping influence, Kefauver, perhaps paradoxically, was a staunch supporter of preparedness and was generally critical of the Administration and the Pentagon in defense matters only when he felt they had not asked for enough. On one occasion, he explained his support for an increased Army appropriation by emphasizing his determination "that this country not be left holding the sack in the event of an all-out defense emergency. . . . Where the security of our country is involved, I believe our people would gladly bear the cost of having too many tanks rather than too few." His record showed consistent support for taking no chances on being inadequately prepared militarily. For example, Kefauver voted with the majority in 1956 on a close 48 to 40 vote to increase Air Force funds by $800 million above the figure requested by the Administration. Similarly, he was with a minority in 1954 that lost (38 to 50) on a motion to increase the Army appropriation. The previous year, he had also been among a minority favoring an increase in the appropriation for the Air Force.[13]

However important Kefauver's criticisms of Eisenhower's foreign and defense policies might have seemed to the senator himself, it was Kefauver's involvement with domestic issues that attracted the most attention and garnered him the headlines which were so important in preparing the way for a bid for the Presidency in 1956. Kefauver's critics were cynical about the sincerity of the senator's interest in the topics on which he focused between 1952 and 1956, and one journalist accused Kefauver of "prospecting for publicity" with his eye on the 1956 nomination.[14]

Whatever his motives, there was universal agreement that he was able to wring maximum political benefit from his limited opportunities. The 1954 elections returned control of Congress to the Democrats and gave Kefauver a chairmanship for the first time since the crime investigation. After January 1955 he headed the Juvenile Delinquency Subcommittee of the Judiciary Committee, on which he had served prominently during the previous session as the ranking minority member. Under Kefauver, the subcommittee continued its year-old series of investigations of violence and sex in motion pictures, television, and publications. These hearings brought Kefauver very favorable publicity as a foe of influences that the popular mind identified as at least partially responsible for the alleged corruption of the nation's youth. America had overnight discovered juvenile delinquency, and studies, analyses, and recommendations became favorite pastimes of all those groups that focus on what seems to be the major problem of the season. Kefauver, therefore, was politically fortunate in being in a key position to benefit from the sudden interest in the topic. And while the investigations of the Juvenile Delinquency Subcommittee never caught the public imagination to the same extent as had the crime investigation, they had the advantage of avoiding the politically sensitive relationships whose handling had so antagonized Democratic organizational leaders in 1950–51.[15] Furthermore, since Kefauver described juvenile delinquency as "a symptom of the weakness in our whole moral and social fabric" and saw it as the result of not "a single cause but . . . many," [16] he was able to justify a wide range for the investigations of the subcommittee and, his critics charged, provide himself a forum from which to seek publicity that would aid a 1956 campaign for the Presidency.

The juvenile delinquency investigations were analogous to the crime hearings in that both featured a parade of witnesses earnestly attempting to solve an extremely complicated problem by attacking what seemed to them to be a few simple causes. Both sets of investigations called attention to sensationally shocking situations without clearly establishing a definite link between the conditions exposed and deficiencies in current statutes. Just as everyone had been against crime, so everyone was against juvenile delinquency; and comic books, TV, motion pictures, and allegedly pornographic materials were closely examined in an attempt to determine the principal causes of the problem.

The key question, the link between juvenile delinquency and the crime, violence, and sex dramatized in movies, radio, books, and TV, was never answered, and the subcommittee wound up the months-long hearings with the admission that no definite cause and effect relationship had been established. To critics of the subcommittee, it seemed that little had been accomplished beyond a series of favorable headlines for subcommittee members.[17]

Although Kefauver had thrown himself into the work of the Juvenile Delinquency Subcommittee, the fact remained that there had been little opportunity there to deal with important national issues and to maintain his position as a spokesman of the Democratic party. However, the Eisenhower Administration soon handed Kefauver an issue, the so-called Dixon-Yates scandal, that did propel him into the forefront of Democratic critics of the Administration.

The role of opposing the Dixon-Yates attack on TVA was made to order for Kefauver. His identification with TVA and public power generally had been, more than any other issue, the foundation of his political career. The break, in the early 1940s, with Senator McKellar had come primarily over the senior senator's attempts to control TVA. Moreover, Senator Tom Stewart's support for McKellar's schemes had been one of the major reasons why Kefauver challenged him in the 1948 primary. If anything, Kefauver was considered overzealous in defense of

TVA. Critics charged that Kefauver knocked down straw opposition to the Authority in an effort to identify more strongly with a position that was almost universally popular in Tennessee. In any event, from the very beginning of Eisenhower's Administration, Kefauver had warned of an Administration plot against TVA and had sought to rally opposition to what he alleged was a developing attack on public power across the country. One political enemy of Kefauver had complained in 1953 that "The TVA is not in danger. I think this whole business . . . is a scheme to put Kefauver back in the Senate. And I'm afraid it is going to succeed." [18]

Kefauver's defense of public power proved to be only a minor issue in his re-election campaign in 1954, but he had, nevertheless, left no doubt in the minds of Tennesseans that he would vigorously oppose any weakening of TVA by the Eisenhower Administration. As 1954 had opened, with control of Congress expected to hinge on a small number of key contests, Kefauver had warned that enemies of public power had "many friends in the government" and that some of these, especially those who had forgotten that public power "is a traditional American policy," will be "electrocuted at the polls, or at least seriously shocked." [19]

In spite of Kefauver's warnings, it appeared that public power generally, and TVA particularly, was losing favor in Congress. Part of the explanation lay in the fact that for the first time in TVA's history, the Executive branch was not in sympathy with TVA expansion. In fact, there was substantial doubt that Eisenhower would honor his 1952 pledge not to disturb existing TVA facilities. It was true that Eisenhower, reacting in 1954 to charges that he was seeking to destroy TVA via Dixon-Yates, had pledged:

> I am prepared to support the T. V. A. as it now stands, with all the strength I have, and anyone who says this [Dixon-Yates] is any attempt to destroy the T. V. A. is, to say it in the mildest way I know, in error.[20]

However, Emmet John Hughes remembered that Eisenhower, at a Cabinet meeting in 1953, had expressed the wish that "By God, if ever we could do it, before we leave here I'd like to see us *sell* the whole [TVA] thing, but I suppose we can't go that far." [21]

In any event, the ambivalence of the Eisenhower Administration toward TVA naturally strengthened the hand of those in Congress who were already antagonistic to TVA and who no longer faced White House pressure on behalf of the Authority. The private utilities, sensing a unique opportunity to block or reverse TVA expansion, made an attack on the Authority a major legislative goal when the Eisenhower Administration took office. The political activity by the utilities became so pronounced that Kefauver, in May 1954, called attention to the fact that the National Association of Electric Companies had spent twice as much on lobbying efforts as any other interest group seeking to influence legislation. A top lobbyist for the utilities hailed a slash in TVA funds as his major accomplishment, and the *Nashville Tennessean* reported that more than half a million dollars had been spent by the utilities in an all-out attack on public power.[22]

Given the fears of public power groups, it is understandable that they would be especially sensitive to actions by the Administration that seemed to indicate a shift in attitude toward TVA and that they would naturally place the worst construction on the relationship between opposition to TVA within the Administration and the well-known support for the Republican party by private power interests. To supporters of TVA, any Administration attack on TVA would not be seen as the result of legitimate political pressures on a Republican Administration but, instead, of a devious plot against the public interest by selfish private utilities. What remained was for the Eisenhower Administration to furnish TVA supporters with a concrete proposal affecting TVA which provided the maximum opportunity for misunderstanding and misinterpretation. Such a situation was created by the Dixon-Yates scheme.

The Dixon-Yates controversy grew out of an attempt by TVA to provide for a projected power shortage in the Memphis area. President Truman's last budget had sought funds for a TVA-owned steam plant at Fulton Landing, Tennessee. The Republican Congress, having criticized TVA as socialistic for twenty years and feeling that TVA should not be expanded further, especially to provide power through non-hydroelectric facilities, turned down the request. In 1954, TVA asked for eight new steam generating plants, a request denied by the Eisenhower Administration with the suggestion that TVA instead redistribute 500,000 to 600,000 kilowatts then assigned to an AEC plant at Paducah, Kentucky; AEC could replace the power through arrangements with private sources.[23]

The Eisenhower Administration's philosophical commitment to allowing private enterprise to supply additional power in the Tennessee Valley led the Administration to negotiate with Edgar H. Dixon, president of Middle South Utilities, and Eugene A. Yates, president of the Southern Company, both of whom headed private power companies interested in providing power to the TVA system, whose distribution area was adjacent to those of their own companies. The two men co-operated on a plan, the "Dixon-Yates proposal," which was submitted to the AEC in February 1954.[24]

The arrangement was somewhat complicated. The power to be furnished to TVA by Dixon-Yates was theoretically to replace that used by the AEC at Paducah. Therefore, although the Dixon-Yates power was to be fed into the TVA system at Memphis, Dixon-Yates sought to contract with the AEC (and not TVA), since the Dixon-Yates power was being purchased by the AEC to replace what it would continue to take from TVA. The reason for this complicated approach to supplying power in the Valley was obvious—AEC was under Administration control and TVA was not; and a TVA still controlled by pro-public power directors could hardly be expected to approve a direct arrangement with Dixon-Yates which might establish the principle that private power would supply future Valley needs.

The TVA objected to the plan on June 22, and the battle was joined. For the next year, the arguments over the Dixon-Yates contract intensified, and the continuing debate kept Kefauver and other Valley legislators occupied in an effort to force abandonment of the project. Tennessee, the state most affected by an assault on TVA, was fortunate in having both its senators in key positions on committees where the Dixon-Yates scheme could be attacked—Kefauver, as a member of the Antitrust and Monopoly Subcommittee of the Judiciary Committee, and Gore, on the Joint Committee on Atomic Energy. In 1954, Kefauver was aided on the Antitrust and Monopoly Subcommittee by the maverick Republican chairman of the full Judiciary Committee, William Langer of North Dakota, who also chaired the Antitrust and Monopoly Subcommittee. Normally, the Republican majority on the full committee and on the subcommittee would have blocked Democratic attempts to embarrass a Republican Administration's power policies, but Langer was an outspoken champion of public power and turned the Antitrust and Monopoly Subcommittee into a forum for opponents of Dixon-Yates. In July 1954 he joined Kefauver and Democratic Senator Harley Kilgore of West Virginia in a three-man majority which adopted a resolution recommending that Dixon-Yates "should not be consummated and no further negotiations be had until the Committee has had time to complete its hearings and submit its report." Republican leader William Knowland of California had long been exasperated by Langer's lack of concern for party loyalty and had, earlier in 1954, pointed out Langer as an example of what was wrong with the seniority system. It was not unexpected, therefore, when the Republican leadership denied Chairman Langer's request for funds for an Antitrust and Monopoly Subcommittee probe of Dixon-Yates. Kefauver, sensing a cover-up, immediately charged the Republican Policy Committee with denying "us funds because it doesn't want an investigation of monopoly and anti-trust matters to be made." Undeterred by his own party's opposition, Langer announced that the probe would go ahead anyway, even if he had to pay the expenses himself.[25]

Critics of Dixon-Yates focused on several aspects of the plan. Public power advocates, of course, were upset that the TVA system would not be supplying additional power needs in the Valley; but, in addition, there were two other major objections to the plan. One was the very favorable return at very little risk anticipated for the private power group operating the steam plant to be built by the Dixon-Yates group, which had received the nod for the contract without competing for it. A second major objection centered on the role in drawing up the Dixon-Yates proposal of Adolphe H. Wenzell, an unpaid consultant working at the Bureau of the Budget on TVA matters while simultaneously serving as an officer of the First Boston Corporation, through which Dixon-Yates financing was to be handled.[26] Although Kefauver and other Dixon-Yates critics made much of the secrecy and rumors of windfall which plagued the Dixon-Yates proposal, their fundamental objection was that its acceptance would be a blow to public power.

The Antitrust and Monopoly Subcommittee held hearings on Dixon-Yates from September 28 to October 30, 1954, raising doubts about the proposal in the months before the mid-term elections. Although Republican Langer was Subcommittee chairman, he gave Kefauver full rein to use the hearings to discredit the contract.[27] However, in spite of much rhetoric in Washington, Dixon-Yates became an issue very slowly and at first only in states where public power was an especially popular issue, for example, Oregon. On September 27, Kefauver, speaking in Portland, attacked the Eisenhower Administration for abdicating "federal responsibility for power supply" with the result that "the government has officially abandoned to the whims of a little group of power barons . . . the opportunity to decide how much power will be produced and what they will charge for it . . . without the benefit of yardstick comparison."[28] Such charges were helpful to Democrats in public power states, and there is little doubt that the Dixon-Yates issue became a critical factor in giving Democrat Richard Neuberger an upset victory in his race for the United States Senate in Oregon in November, a victory that turned control of the Senate over to the Democrats in January 1955.

Although Dixon-Yates had been submitted to the AEC in April 1954 and had faced vehement opposition for months, there was little reason to think that it would not eventually win congressional approval; the contract cleared hurdle after hurdle in the fall and winter of 1954. The AEC approved the contract on November 10, and on November 13, the lame-duck Republican majority on the Joint Atomic Energy Committee approved it by a 10 to 8 party line vote. On January 11, 1955, the SEC approved the securities arrangements in the contract.[29]

Although Dixon-Yates opponents had been attacking the contract for months, they had made little progress by December in creating a political issue out of the proposal. A Gallup poll published early in the month showed that only 37 per cent of those polled had heard of Dixon-Yates, and only 10 per cent thought it was a bad idea; 8 per cent favored it, and 82 per cent were undecided or had no knowledge of it.[30]

But opponents of Dixon-Yates had been at work, and their efforts began to show results. In mid-November, the Senate Democratic Policy Committee had voted to make opposition to Dixon-Yates a party position. Kefauver hailed the decision and called it "the height of irresponsibility for the White House to permit the A. E. C. to sign this contract now." Kefauver also worked hard to put the AEC on the defensive. When AEC Chairman Lewis Strauss said that consumers would be the victims of the failure of Dixon-Yates to go through, Kefauver accused him of "telling us that we had better withdraw our opposition or he'll take our power away from us." Answering the alleged threat, Kefauver announced that "we in the Tennessee Valley region do not easily submit to blackmail and this is as good a time for Admiral Strauss to find out as any." [31]

The expectation that Eisenhower would in some way attack TVA made the Dixon-Yates proposal seem much more sinister than it really was. The fact was, as James Reston pointed out in the *New York Times*, that the Truman Administration had been responsible for two similar deals, involving much more money, and one involved Edgar Dixon. Therefore, there probably would have been little chance of blocking the contract had opponents not continually raised the charge of conflict of interest and pictured the contract as part of a general attack on public power. On the other hand, the Eisenhower Administration played into the hands of Dixon-Yates opponents by seeming to cover up questionable procedures in the negotiations leading to the contract. Exploitation of Administration fumbling of the public relations associated with Dixon-Yates was greatly aided by the Democratic congressional victories in November 1954. The narrow majorities the party won gave it control of the important Joint Committee on Atomic Energy, as well as strengthening the hand of Dixon-Yates opponents on the Antitrust and Monopoly Subcommittee.[32]

The chairmanship of the Antitrust and Monopoly Subcommittee was considered enough of a prize that Harley Kilgore, who became chairman of the parent Judiciary Committee in January 1955, sought to block Kefauver's accession to the subcommittee chairmanship. Although Kefauver had been an original member of the subcommittee and had been the most active member in the two years of its existence, Kilgore's prerogatives as committee chairman gave him the right to reorganize subcommittees, and he exercised his power to name himself as Antitrust and Monopoly Subcommittee chairman. Kilgore was not interested in blocking a Dixon-Yates probe but was concerned that Kefauver might be able to strengthen his position for the 1956 Democratic presidential nomination by a spectacular performance as subcommittee chairman; since Kefauver was also chairing the Juvenile Delinquency Subcommittee, the prospect of Kefauver as chairman of two subcommittees that gave him continuous favorable publicity was more than senior Democratic senators could accept. But, since Kilgore was interested in turning Kefauver loose on Dixon-Yates, he finally, in June, gave in to urgings from Senator Gore that a special panel, headed by Kefauver, be appointed from the Antitrust and Monopoly Subcommittee to look into Dixon-Yates. Langer and Joseph O'Mahoney of Wyoming, both staunch public power advocates, were also named to the panel. Kilgore, however, kept firm control of the full Antitrust and Monopoly Subcommittee.[33]

Throughout early 1955, Kefauver had maintained his steady attack on Dixon-Yates. Although he considered "the manner in which the contract was arrived at, the sloppy negotiations, the unsuitable site, the additional cost to the government, the lack of protection for the government, the suppression of competing bids, [and] the guaranteed return to the contractor" as all "very serious objections to the . . . deal and . . . enough for any prudent business administration to throw it out," he saw "the real significance" to be the fact "that in future years the private utilities again will be dictating their own terms to municipalities and rural electric cooperatives, who have been showing the country how the electric business can be and should be conducted." [34]

Kefauver scoffed at the notion that Dixon-Yates was an example of free enterprise, as opposed to the socialistic TVA. "Two of the important elements of a free enterprise contract are missing," he pointed out, "competition and risk. This contract was awarded, by order of the President, in the absence of competing bids, and in the face of evidence of suppression of competition. You may be told that there is some risk involved, but the only risk is in cancellation of the contract, and there the Dixon-Yates combine will be awarded handsome cancellation fees." [35]

The climax of the Dixon-Yates dispute came in the summer of 1955. On June 27 the special Antitrust and Monopoly Subcommittee panel on Dixon-Yates, headed by Kefauver, opened hearings on the contract.[36] When the panel was denied access to Budget Bureau files, Kefauver complained in the Senate of an effort "to conceal and hide the true facts," especially the role of Adolphe Wenzell of First Boston. Just as the issue of conflict of interest was beginning to heat up, the first sign came that the Administration was having second thoughts about Dixon-Yates. On June 30, Eisenhower asked the Bureau of the Budget to re-evaluate Dixon-Yates in light of a June 23 announcement by the City of Memphis that it preferred to build its own generating plant rather than accept power from Dixon-Yates. Kefauver hailed the decision, putting the worst possible construction on the Administration move. "The Dixon-Yates contract was bad enough to begin with," he charged. "As it went along, it became outrageous, bordering on corruption." The logical next move, according to Kefauver, was cancellation of the contract. On July 11, his wish was fulfilled, and the Dixon-Yates contract was cancelled.[37]

Kefauver and Gore were overjoyed at the news of cancellation.[38] Kefauver heard the news at his Antitrust and Monopoly hearings on Dixon-Yates and immediately received the plaudits of his fellow subcommittee members for his role in getting the contract cancelled.[39]

He and other opponents of Dixon-Yates immediately sought to interpret the cancellation as evidence that the Administration had been "caught" in a scheme designed to favor private utilities at the expense of the public interest. President Eisenhower, however, saw the decision of the City of Memphis to build its own generating plant as an acceptable alternative to the Dixon-Yates proposal because it was in line with his announced policy of local responsibility for power. In any event, cancellation of the contract was only a partial victory for its opponents—the principle had still not been established that TVA expansion was an accepted national commitment and would continue even under a Republican Administration.[40]

Undaunted by the opposition to Dixon-Yates, conservatives were as determined as ever to press for an end to the expansion of public power. Many, in fact, would settle for nothing less than a dismantling of federal power programs. Dean Clarence Manion, for example, reacted angrily to the criticisms of Dixon-

Yates, which he considered a halfway measure at best, and argued that ". . . the federal government *must* sell the power-producing facilities of the entire country. If that be treason to the TVA brand of socialism, then Senator Kefauver can once more make the most of it." [41]

Under these circumstances, critics of Dixon-Yates could not afford to be satisfied with mere cancellation of the contract, but, instead, needed to so discredit the Dixon-Yates proposal that the Administration would surrender on the principle of TVA expansion. Cancellation, therefore, did nothing to blunt the attack on Dixon-Yates, and, indeed, served to spur on TVA supporters in their drive to embarrass the Administration over the proposal. As Senator O'Mahoney pointed out on hearing the news of the cancellation: "I think this is only the first step . . . intended to wreck . . . the whole system of public power. . . . We must find out what was the source of this drive, and we must follow it into every department of government. Unless we do that, we will be turning this Government back to Wall Street and taking it away from Washington." [42]

Post-cancellation hearings before Kefauver's special panel resulted in a flood of unfavorable publicity for Administration figures connected with Dixon-Yates. The probe uncovered attempts to influence SEC and Budget Bureau decisions without public knowledge of what pressures were being brought to bear on behalf of Dixon-Yates, a common enough occurrence in Washington, but made to appear especially sinister in this case by a former Budget Bureau Director's denial that he was aware that Wenzell was associated with Dixon-Yates's financial agent at the time he was advising the Budget Bureau on the government's role in Tennessee Valley power decisions. The chairman of the First Boston Corporation, the financial agent in question, was "at a loss" to explain the denial. Wenzell himself furnished a good example of the reactionary thinking that public power advocates feared had too much influence on the Republican Administration. He made his attitude toward TVA abundantly

clear in an appearance before Kefauver's panel on July 8, three
days before the cancellation of the contract:

> Senator Kefauver. I suppose you would agree, Mr. Wenzell,
> with another distinguished man who stated that TVA was "creep-
> ing socialism"; is that correct? Doesn't that sum up your attitude?
> Mr. Wenzell. Well, I would add to that at the rate they were
> proposing to go ahead, I would call it galloping socialism.[43]

Evidence of cover-up and Administration intervention in
the SEC hearings involving Dixon-Yates financing provoked
Kefauver to label them "a fraud and a sham," and Edgar Dixon's denial that he knew Wenzell more than "casually" elicited
from Langer the opinion that "I believe you are lying right
now." "Assistant President" Sherman Adams also came under
heavy criticism from Kefauver because of his refusal to testify
about his role in the Dixon-Yates negotiations; Kefauver was
totally unsympathetic to Adams's argument that his position in
the Executive branch gave him immunity from the panel's investigation.[44]

The critical attitude of the three-man, bipartisan panel was
reflected in a report, issued August 22, 1955, accusing the Eisenhower Administration of "contempt of Congress and its constitutional powers" through the use of "devious, indirect, and improper administrative practices. . . . One of the shameful things
about the Dixon-Yates deal is the way the President's staff has
played fast and loose with the facts even where he is concerned." [45]

Apparently the Eisenhower Administration decided that,
whatever the validity of the charges of conflict of interest against
Adolphe Wenzell of the First Boston Corporation when advising the Bureau of the Budget, some tightening of regulations
for businessmen serving the government without compensation
was in order. In December the President issued an executive
order setting down procedures to be followed in such cases.

Kefauver interpreted the move as recognition by the Administration that the criticisms raised by Dixon-Yates opponents were valid. "It's about time the Eisenhower Administration decided that government consultants should have the same high standards of conduct as other government employees," he said in response to Eisenhower's new regulations. "That's what we tried to tell the President over a year ago in connection with the Dixon-Yates deal." [46]

The Dixon-Yates controversy greatly enhanced Kefauver's national reputation as well as his prestige within the party as a spokesman for an important Democratic policy position. Furthermore, his ability to wring political mileage out of Dixon-Yates, and the favorable press he had received as chairman of the Juvenile Delinquency Subcommittee, suggested to many that he might be the kind of issue-oriented candidate the party would have to field in 1956 if it hoped to recapture the White House from the Republicans. As 1955 drew to a close, Kefauver began to receive more and more attention as a possible candidate in 1956. Those who hoped that he was considering another try for the nomination were not to be disappointed.

chapter xiii

HAT IN THE RING II
1955-1956

Kefauver's bid for the 1956 Democratic presidential nomination came as a surprise to few observers of the national political scene. It was generally accepted that he had long been bitten by the presidential bug and that his 1952 defeat had done little to discourage his ambitions for the White House. Even in the shock and disappointment following Stevenson's nomination in 1952, Kefauver had left no doubt that his interest in the Presidency was still very much alive.[1] And, while his legislative record between 1952 and 1956 was hardly a series of personal triumphs, he had managed to capture enough headlines through the juvenile delinquency and Dixon-Yates hearings to remain an important national figure and to confound those who saw his success with the crime investigation as a fortuitous accident which he would find impossible to repeat to the extent necessary to trigger a widespread public response to another presidential campaign. Furthermore, his smashing renomination victory in August 1954 reaffirmed the home state support considered such an essential ingredient of availability.

By late 1954 serious speculation about 1956 began, and Kefauver played the game according to tradition. In October he told a Madison, Wisconsin, audience that it was "unlikely" that he would seek the Presidency in 1956 but that he was "not going to close the door." A month later, while he admitted that Stevenson had "the best chance" for the Democratic nomination in 1956, Kefauver remained silent on his own plans, although cautioning against premature predictions by pointing out that "it is very difficult to say just what is going to happen." Two days later, a Chattanooga-based pro-Kefauver youth organization launched a drive to get 10 million signatures on a petition calling for Kefauver's nomination in 1956. In spite of this and other activity on his behalf, Kefauver, in late December, announced predictably that "I am not a candidate and have no plans for becoming a candidate." Stevenson was "a fine man and is way out in front right now." Furthermore, Eisenhower "will be a difficult man to beat." [2]

As Kefauver himself was very much aware, his road to the Presidency in 1956 was blocked by two presumably overwhelming obstacles which would have discouraged a less determined man. In the first place, President Eisenhower was proving to be one of the most popular Presidents ever to occupy the White House. Secondly, most Democrats seemed to feel either that Adlai Stevenson deserved the 1956 nomination or that he was, in fact, the party's strongest candidate. In eary 1955, there was good reason to argue that Kefauver, who would be only fifty-three in 1956, could easily defer to Stevenson and then seek the nomination in 1960, when the supposedly invulnerable Eisenhower could not seek re-election. Eisenhower's showing in public opinion polls certainly indicated an uphill battle for any Democrat in 1956; in the eighteen months between January 1955 and July 1956, the President averaged a 72 per cent favorable response from the public on the question of approval of his performance in office; average disapproval was only 16 per cent.[3] Furthermore, in early 1955, both Stevenson and Kefauver ran far behind the President in trial heats matching possible 1956 opponents: [4]

Eisenhower	57 per cent		Eisenhower	60 per cent
Stevenson	40		Kefauver	34
Undecided	3		Undecided	6

Although in public Kefauver remained properly reluctant to seem too anxious to seek the Presidency, he set about to overcome political liabilities which would otherwise weaken his appeal in 1956. One of his major political disadvantages as he approached both the 1952 and 1956 Democratic conventions was the feeling that his limited experience in dealing with foreign affairs had not given him the background necessary to handle the complex international responsibilities of the Presidency. His repeatedly unsuccessful efforts to gain assignment to the Senate Foreign Relations Committee after 1952 had deprived him of the most obvious opportunity to offset partially this reservation about his political experience. Even without the Foreign Relations assignment, however, Kefauver became one of the most articulate Democratic foreign policy spokesmen for such important positions as opposition to the Bricker Amendment and support for the United Nations, foreign aid, and collective security.

Kefauver's most obvious attempt to broaden his understanding of world problems before the contest for the 1956 Democratic nomination was the extended world tour he undertook in the fall of 1955. Trips abroad were nothing new to Kefauver, of course; the fall before, for example, he and Nancy had traveled extensively across Europe and the Middle East. But the 1955 trip, with stops in seventeen countries and discussions with numerous foreign political leaders, was the most comprehensive foreign tour of his career and was obviously directly related to his impending campaign for the Democratic nomination.[5]

The trip began with Kefauver's attendance at a meeting of the Interparliamentary Union in Helsinki, Finland, in August. From there, Kefauver traveled to Russia "to see for myself what is going on in the Soviet Union." [6]

The highlight of the Russian stopover was a two-hour visit, along with four other senators, with Khrushchev and Bulganin. Kefauver found Khrushchev an "unpolished individual, a complete extrovert, but very intelligent, always confident of himself and his position," with "many of the personality aspects of a high-pressure super-salesman." Kefauver's general evaluation of the top Russian leaders was that they "know what they want to do, know how to do it—and ARE doing it." Kefauver was impressed with the extent to which Khrushchev was attempting to loosen the tight controls on the Russian people and urged him to end, as a goodwill gesture, censorship of foreign press dispatches. Khrushchev pointed with pride to what he called "a good beginning in relaxing censorship" and cautioned that "everything cannot be done overnight." [7]

Kefauver's Russian tour also included stops in Kiev and Stalingrad. He then left Russia for a visit to Poland, where he "found much friendliness for the United States among the Polish people, some of it outspoken pro-Americanism." Had his visits to Russia and Poland convinced him that the announced Communist interest in peaceful co-existence was sincere? Kefauver remained skeptical. "I prefer to reserve judgment," he told reporters in Poland. "I don't think the little I have seen is enough to decide whether there has been a basic change in Communist policy or whether what is going on is merely a technical maneuver." [8]

From Poland, Kefauver traveled to Hungary, Czechoslovakia, and Yugoslavia (where he met with and praised Tito). Stops in Austria, Lebanon, Pakistan, India (and a meeting with Nehru), Vietnam (including an interview with Diem), Singapore, Malaya, Korea, Japan, and Hong Kong rounded out the trip. The swing through the Far East caused Kefauver to revise his previously held opinion that the battle to prevent an eventual Communist takeover of southeast Asia was all but lost. He was especially impressed by the quality of leadership in the emerging Asian countries but was disappointed with the "bitter resentment toward the West" that he encountered. He came away with the feeling that the United States should maintain its restrictions on China in order to force the Communist government to come to final terms in Korea and to stabilize the political situation in the countries on China's periphery. He hoped for an eventual rapprochement with China, but that would depend

A) The Anti-Crump leaders (from left to right): Gordon Browning, Silliman Evans of the *Nashville Tennessean,* and Kefauver (Credit: Kefauver Library).

B) Estes and Nancy prepare to enter the House chamber for Estes's swearing-in ceremony, September 21, 1939 (Credit: Wide World Photos).

C) The Kefauver family Christmas card, 1950 (from left to right): David, Estes, Linda (holding Gail), Nancy, Diane (Credit: Kefauver Library).

D) The highlight of the Crime Investigation (the third day of the New York Hearings). Senator Frank Tobey (R-N.H.) and Senator Herbert O'Connor (D-Md.) are to Kefauver's right; Rudolph Halley is to Kefauver's left, addressing Frank Costello (far right), the Committee's most famous witness (Credit: Wide World Photos).

E) The Kefauver-Harriman liberal coalition plans its strategy during the 1952 Democratic Convention (from left to right): Gael Sullivan (Kefauver's campaign manager), Representative Henry Jackson of Washington, Kefauver, Paul Fitzpatrick (Chairman of the New York delegation), Harriman, Representative John Carroll of Colorado, and Representative Franklin D. Roosevelt, Jr., of New York (Credit: Wide World Photos).

F) Former President Truman joins in the applause for Nancy and Estes as the 1956 Democratic Convention prepares to hear Kefauver's speech accepting the vice-presidential nomination. Kefauver has just been introduced by House Speaker Sam Rayburn, who is partially hidden (Credit: Wide World Photos).

G) Stevenson and Kefauver discuss campaign schedules, during the 1956 presidential campaign (Credit: Wide World photos).

H) Estes and Nancy on the campaign trail strike a familiar pose for reporters (Credit: Kefauver Library).

I) Kefauver refers to a chart illustrating the fantastic profits earned by Schering, as the drug investigation opens, December 1959 (Credit: Wide World Photos).

SCHERING CORPORATION
PURCHASE PRICE 1952, AND PROFITS
AFTER TAXES, 1952 – JUNE 1957

☐ ANNUAL   ☐ CUMULATED

$MILLIONS
35

25

20

15

10

0

PURCHASE
PRICE
MARCH 1952

1952   1953   1954   1955   1956   57
                    PROFITS   MOS

J) Kefauver and President-elect Kennedy conclude a discussion of Justice Department appointments, December 8, 1960 (Credit: Wide World Photos).

on, above all else, "peace in Korea." "Then," Kefauver said, "we can talk." [9]

Kefauver returned to the United States in mid-October, after an absence of over six weeks, to find the political situation very much different from that which he had left in August.

Democratic prospects for 1956 had remained basically unchanged throughout the summer of 1955 and into the fall. Stevenson was regarded as having a "commanding lead" for the nomination but little chance of beating Eisenhower. But, whatever Democratic discouragement might have been felt over the President's overwhelming popularity in his first two and one-half years in office was suddenly re-evaluated in September 1955 when Eisenhower suffered a heart attack that was expected to result in his retirement from the White House after one term. Kefauver had been in Bombay when he learned of the President's illness. The senator had immediately termed it "a great misfortune that he [Eisenhower] is ill at this time" and hoped that when Eisenhower recovered "he will run for election." Democrats could afford to toss bouquets Eisenhower's way since his retirement would have made the co-operation of the Democratic Congress with the President an issue in the party's favor in a campaign against the expected Republican heir, Vice-President Richard Nixon.[10]

Overnight, the Democratic nomination was worth fighting for, but Democratic professionals continued to move to the man who was thought to have the best chance to return the party to power—Adlai Stevenson. In a poll of state Democratic Central Committee members in October, Stevenson received the support of 82 per cent, Kefauver only 9 per cent, and Governor Averell Harriman of New York, 4 per cent. A December poll of Democratic governors, state chairmen, and National Committee members showed 76 backing Stevenson, 5 for Kefauver, 3 for Harriman, with 42 favoring others or declining to express a choice.[11]

There was no doubt that Stevenson would make the race. The extent of opposition from other Democrats had remained the unanswered question throughout most of 1955. Kefauver was considered Stevenson's most likely rival for the nomination, but his periodic explanations of why he might not run solidified Stevenson's role as the frontrunner and left Kefauver open to the later charge that he had decided to run only after Eisenhower's heart attack, while Stevenson had been willing to face the popular incumbent before the health issue made Democratic chances look brighter. In late October, however, Kefauver seemed to indicate that the upturn in Democratic fortunes had not altered his extreme reluctance to embark upon a campaign for the nomination. He explained that "I have four kids that need their parents at home" and, furthermore, "I've bled all my friends white and you can only do that so often." [12]

Stevenson's official announcement in mid-November that he would seek the Democratic nomination brought only the comment from Kefauver that he considered Stevenson "a good friend, a nice guy and a good man." Although Kefauver had two days earlier replied to a reporter's question as to whether he would run in 1956 with "I think so," he withheld an immediate announcement. Instead, he went out of his way to consult party leaders about his candidacy. When asked if he was getting more encouragement than he had received in 1952, Kefauver smiled and replied, "Certainly, I didn't get any encouragement in 1952." [13]

As it turned out, Kefauver's public hesitation did have the advantage of allowing Stevenson to become considered such an overwhelming favorite that party professionals flocked to Stevenson's support and thus gave Kefauver the familiar underdog issue to use against the 1952 nominee. By late 1955, Stevenson was considered as good as nominated by political observers, and a *Life* story on Democratic politics entitled "It's Adlai versus Stevenson for the Democratic Nomination" summed up the prevailing opinion that Stevenson was in full command of the situation.[14]

It was in this atmosphere that Kefauver announced his candidacy on December 16. He later said that his final decision on seeking the nomination had come only six days before,[15] but to politically sensitive Washington it seemed the inevitable result of four years of planning and calculation.

The formal announcement was fairly low key. After an opening statement, which Russell Baker of the *New York Times* said was "read . . . in the halting, diffident manner of a poor man's son proposing marriage to the richest girl in town," Kefauver answered questions on national issues predictably, and the campaign began very much as it had in 1952, with the obvious substitution of Stevenson for Truman as the man whose control Kefauver sought to challenge. Kefauver made it clear that he was depending heavily on good showings in the primaries to influence party leaders to support him as the choice of the party's rank and file. He would not, however, attempt to enter almost every primary, as he had done in 1952. Although he said he would enter as many as he could, he cited "the limiting factor of my work in the Senate, the amount of money available for campaigns and the possibility of conflicting dates" as making it necessary for him to be more selective than he had been four years earlier. Since Stevenson had already announced that he would enter at least five primaries (California, Illinois, Pennsylvania, Florida, and Minnesota), reporters were especially interested in which primaries Kefauver might clash with the frontrunner. Kefauver announced that he would definitely oppose Stevenson in California and might enter the contests in Florida and Minnesota.[16]

Kefauver's campaign organization felt somewhat defensive that their candidate had not agreed to challenge Stevenson in every possible primary, and, in addition to Kefauver's lack of time and money, the strain of too many primary campaigns was cited as a reason for limiting his pre-convention grass-roots campaigning. As Jiggs Donohue, Kefauver's national campaign manager, pointed out, "We don't want to kill him. We want to elect him." [17]

Although Stevenson was obviously the Democratic hopeful that Kefauver would have to displace if he hoped to capture the nomination, Kefauver declined invitations from reporters to comment on what he saw as the basic differences between Stevenson and himself:

> I do not expect at this time to try to point out the—any difference, or the differences between the attitudes, for instance, of Mr. Stevenson or Harriman or Lausche or others, on public issues, as compared with my own position.
>
> These gentlemen are all vocal and speak frequently, and whatever differences that will come up in the future, I'm certain the press and the public will be quick to discern them.[18]

Kefauver's approach, therefore, was more positive than it had been in 1952, when he had served as a vehicle for anti-Truman sentiment. This necessarily meant less emphasis on the crusading image, which obviously required a candidate or a policy against which to crusade. The new Kefauver image was in response to the distress felt by Kefauver's advisers over widespread criticisms that Kefauver was too much form and too little substance, and that his political strength was based on a personal campaign style that worked with the average unsophisticated voter but did not succeed with professional politicians and hid a fundamental lack of understanding of the complexities of major national issues. Typical of this view of Kefauver was an early endorsement of Stevenson for the Democratic nomination by *Newsday*, which, in October 1955, explained its choice of Stevenson over Kefauver as based partially on its evaluation of Kefauver's popularity as due to "his outward trappings" rather than to an understanding of his political philosophy.[19]

One of the first victims of the new image-building campaign by Kefauver advisers was the coonskin cap, which had first been associated with Kefauver during the famous 1948 campaign against Boss Crump. Kefauver strategists were inclined to let the cap be quietly forgotten until the Davy Crockett fad swept the country in 1955 and called attention to another, earlier coonskin-capped hero who had been "born on a mountain top in Tennessee." Advice on how to handle the Kefauver-Crockett relationship was mixed, and Kefauver himself exhibited the indecision within his camp over whether to drop the crusading, coonskin cap image or to ride the Crockett fad to a new emphasis on Kefauver's independence and integrity. Although Kefauver still identified with the cap at the time of his announcement to the extent of throwing one in the "ring" repeatedly for reporters, he thereafter reluctantly disassociated himself from it.[20]

The passing of the coonskin cap symbolized Kefauver's switch from an all-out campaign against the bosses to a balanced campaign seeking key primary victories and also soliciting support from professionals. His hopes for professional support far exceeded that which he was able to line up, and caused him occasionally to slip back into the role of crusader against bossism, but he cultivated the professionals much more than he had done in 1952. When asked in January why he thought he had a better chance for the nomination in 1956 than he had had in 1952, he credited his improved prospects to the fact that he had gained many more friends among the "professional politicians, if you want to call them that." [21]

The professionals, however, never warmed to Kefauver. It was almost out of character for him to worry very much about them, and most of them knew it. Theodore H. White quoted a Democratic urban leader explaining his objections to Kefauver:

> Kefauver? Look, let me explain him in terms of my own governor. When I decided to nominate him, I called him in and said, "Today, I'm the boss. But when I nominate you and you're elected, you'll be the boss because you're governor. I'm putting a gun in your hand and you can shoot me with it." Now, you see, with Kefauver, you could never be sure he wouldn't take that gun, turn around, and shoot you.[22]

What limited success Kefauver did enjoy in enlisting professional support was due as much to local rivalries as to any response to Kefauver as a candidate. For example, in Florida,

Kefauver was able to enlist the support of Mayor Haydon Burns of Jacksonville, who was involved in a struggle with an opposing faction which supported Stevenson. In New Jersey, Kefauver won the support of the discredited Hague organization, which automatically opposed the choice of the Kenny machine, which was supporting Stevenson.[23]

Kefauver never fully understood the lack of enthusiasm for him among party leaders, who were able to withstand the personal appeals that worked so well with voters, but he finally found himself having to risk everything on primary victories and acknowledged that the professionals would "come around" only "if I could show them I'm the best vote getter. . . . They'll take me if they think I'm the one they can win with." [24]

Kefauver's problems with the professionals at least had the advantage of being good for exploitation as a "bossism" issue. Kefauver's problems back home, however, offered nothing but frustration to the Kefauver organization. In contrast to the overwhelming support Kefauver had enjoyed in his home state during his 1952 campaign for the Democratic nomination, in 1956 anti-Kefauver Tennesseans felt strong enough to attempt to openly undermine the Kefauver campaign in the state that had re-elected him to the Senate by a landslide less than two years earlier. Anti-Kefauver newspapers scoffed at his presidential ambitions in a way unheard of in 1952. The conservative *Nashville Banner,* for example, took notice of Kefauver's December announcement of candidacy with a one-line editorial under the title, "Extra, Extra," which jeeringly commented, "Kefauver announces. So what?" [25]

The mixed reaction in Tennessee to Kefauver's presidential campaign was due to a large extent to the fact that vehicles for anti-Kefauver feeling were available in 1956 that had not been in 1952. Although Kefauver had been renominated and re-elected to the Senate by landslide margins in 1954, his running mate on the Democratic ticket, Governor Frank Clement, had won even more overwhelming victories in August and November. His August primary victim had been Kefauver's 1948 ally, ex-Governor Gordon Browning, whom Clement had first defeated in 1952 in the reaction in Tennessee to the state's Democratic convention vote against the seating of the Virginia delegation. Although Clement and Kefauver had many mutual supporters, the core of Kefauver's strength was the old anti-Crump forces; Clement, on the other hand, had enjoyed Crump's support in both 1952 and 1954. The Democratic voters of 1954 had been extremely selective, giving both Kefauver and Clement, who by this time headed opposite factions, overwhelming victories in the primary.[26] Strangely enough, both Kefauver and Clement had been more liberal than their opponents, but the inertia of the traditional antagonisms of their organizations toward each other, as well as the clashing personal ambitions of the two leaders, made a political alliance between the two impossible, and Clement's backers were not inclined to aid any Kefauver campaign for the Democratic nomination. Furthermore, junior Senator Albert Gore, who had traditionally been allied with the anti-Crump forces, was increasingly his own man and sought to bridge the Clement-Kefauver rivalry in a way that would enhance his own prospects for national recognition. Since both Clement and Kefauver had made no secret of their White House ambitions, and Gore was receiving attention from those anti-Kefauver forces who considered the Bible-toting Clement to be too unsophisticated for serious consideration, Tennessee was in the unusual position of providing three leaders who figured in the speculations about 1956.

It would be misleading to give undue credit to anti-Kefauver forces outside the state for engineering the build-up of Clement and Gore in order to stop Kefauver. As early as the fall of 1954, both Clement and Gore were, along with Kefauver, in great demand at party dinners all over the country, principally because all three had firsthand experience with the Dixon-Yates issue, which was a popular subject with Democratic audiences. It was estimated by some Democratic leaders that the Tennessee trio accounted for about one-third of the speeches given by national Democrats on behalf of local tickets during the 1954 campaign. By March 1955 the rival ambitions of the three were so well known that an article about them was entitled "Too Much Talent in Tennessee?" Similarly, when Democratic National Chairman Paul Butler visited Knoxville in July, he praised Clement, Gore, and Kefauver for "all . . . doing a tremendous job for the Democratic party." [27]

In spite of the fact that Kefauver was by far the most important Tennessean on the national scene, Governor Clement's power as head of the party in effect gave him control of the delegation to the 1956 convention. Since he himself had set his sights on the Vice-Presidency in 1956, with a later presidential bid, he sought to use his ability to damage Kefauver in Tennessee to win commitments from Stevenson backers for second place on the ticket. For a while, those seeking to block Kefauver were willing to give Clement just about anything within reason. His opposition to Kefauver played a part in his election as chairman of the Southern Governors Conference in October 1955 and enabled him to win the fulsome praise of both ex-President Truman and Speaker Sam Rayburn on separate visits to Tennessee.[28]

Clement endorsed Stevenson for the Democratic nomination even before Stevenson formally announced his candidacy. Clement's action immediately stirred up a hornet's nest in the state Democratic party among Kefauver backers as well as among those who, as a matter of state pride, reacted against an endorsement of Stevenson over a popular Tennessean generally regarded as a major contender for the nomination. Negotiations between Kefauver supporters and the governor began on how to avoid a bitter split in the party. Although there were periodic announcements of agreement by the two factions,[29] the fact was that the Tennessee situation was never resolved to Kefauver's satisfaction.

By mid-January of 1956 Kefauver was ready to begin his campaign in earnest, and the outlook could hardly have been bleaker. The week before, Stevenson's managers had issued a statement claiming 723 votes were already pledged to Stevenson on the first ballot—more than enough for the nomination.[30]

Kefauver, however, had one last hope—a series of primary victories over Stevenson that would so demonstrate the preference of the rank and file for Kefauver that party leaders would have no choice but to desert Stevenson and rally, however reluctantly, behind the popular choice of the party.

chapter xiv

KEFAUVER vs. STEVENSON 1956

Although Kefauver's 1956 campaign for the Democratic presidential nomination began by following almost exactly the script of the 1952 contest, the climax of the 1956 battle was not to be in the convention, as it had been four years before, but in the primaries, where Kefauver had always argued that it should be.

Kefauver had little to lose, of course, since without a series of impressive primary victories there was no reason for the party to question what seemed to be the inevitability of Stevenson's eventual nomination. The extent of Stevenson's growing strength was indicated by a survey in February which indicated that one-third of all Democratic senators had endorsed Stevenson for renomination, with none publicly favoring Kefauver; similarly, a Gallup poll of about the same time showed that Democratic voters across the country preferred Stevenson over Kefauver: 51 per cent to 18 per cent.[1]

The uphill battle which could be won only by going to the people against the party leaders was psychologically made to order for Kefauver. In addition, and especially fortunate for Kefauver, the early primary challenges were in states where his initial prospects for success were strong enough to allow his personal campaigning efforts to ensure the victories so important in providing the momentum to make later victories in less friendly territories seem at least possible. It was hoped that the charismatic Kefauver image of the 1952 campaign could be re-created: the candidate through which the rank and file could challenge the centralized control of party leaders.

Much to the delight of the Kefauver organization,[2] the first presidential primary of 1956 was that in New Hampshire on March 13. New Hampshire Democratic voters were thought to be the most pro-Kefauver in the country, outside Kefauver's own Tennessee, and it was of enormous psychological benefit to the national Kefauver effort to be able to launch a primary-oriented drive in the state where a presidential primary victory was most likely. Kefauver's strength in the state was due not only to fond memories among the rank and file of his successful campaign against Truman four years earlier but also to the fact that many of the amateurs who had entered politics to aid Kefauver in 1952 had remained involved and by 1956 held positions of power within the party. Their personal loyalty to Kefauver had remained strong, and they were ready to give him all-out support in the primary there. Under these circumstances, it was not surprising that Kefauver entered a full slate of pledged delegates and announced plans to stump the state on their behalf as the first step in a series of primary campaigns in which he hoped the Democratic rank and file would rally to his support.

Adlai Stevenson, as the frontrunner, was faced with a difficult decision in New Hampshire. He was aware of the Kefauver strength in the state but was bombarded with advice from old-line Democrats that Kefauver was really not as strong as he appeared and that Stevenson had an excellent chance to derail the Kefauver primary express before it ever got started. The thinking of anti-Kefauver leaders was that Kefauver's 1952 primary victories, in New Hampshire as well as elsewhere, were due to dissatisfaction with the Truman Administration and to the lack of a viable alternative to Kefauver as a means of expressing that dissatisfaction. Thus, Stevenson, who easily led other Democrats in public opinion polls, would not suffer from the same disadvantages that Kefauver's 1952 opposition had faced. Especially vocal among those urging Stevenson to take the plunge in New Hampshire was Henry Sullivan, Democratic National Committeeman from the state, who had been a key Kefauver lieutenant in 1952 but had endorsed Stevenson for 1956. In addition, almost every other big name among New Hampshire Democrats came out for Stevenson.[3]

Stevenson's solution to the New Hampshire dilemma was to acquiesce in a well-organized write-in campaign on his behalf in the preference election, as well as to field well known delegate candidates favorable to his nomination, who would run without his public endorsement. Thus, New Hampshire Democrats would have the opportunity to vote for Stevenson if they wished. If a Kefauver victory still resulted, it could be explained away as due to Kefauver's personal campaigning against the absent Stevenson. Anything short of a Kefauver runaway could thereby be interpreted as indicating Kefauver's weakness in an election which the Stevenson forces had virtually conceded to the Tennessean.

The New Hampshire results on March 13 were, on the whole, very encouraging to the Kefauver campaign. His slate of delegates led the better-known Stevenson delegates by comfortable if not overwhelming margins, and Kefauver himself swamped Stevenson, 21,701 to 3,806. The Kefauver forces spent only $5,754 in giving Kefauver his crucial first primary victory. The biggest boost to the Kefauver campaign was, of course, the candidate himself, who, according to Henry Sullivan, "came in here and campaigned as if he were running for alderman, with all that handshaking and all." Whatever reservations might be attached to the Kefauver victory in New Hampshire, the fact remained that the Kefauver campaign had done better than expected, while Stevenson's poor write-in vote, in contrast with the huge write-in vote in the Republican primary for Nixon as Vice-President, raised doubts about whether the enthusiasm of party leaders for the 1952 nominee was shared by the rank and file.[4]

Almost before the dust had settled in New Hampshire, Kefauver and Stevenson met again, one week later, in Minnesota. Kefauver had hesitated about entering the Minnesota primary, since the Democratic organization there, headed by Senator Hubert Humphrey and Governor Orville Freeman, was solidly behind Stevenson. At the press conference in mid-December at which Kefauver announced his candidacy, he had avoided making a commitment to oppose Stevenson in Minnesota, conceding that "things are pretty well stacked against me, apparently, in Minnesota." Two days later, on "Face the Nation," Kefauver hinted that he might give the Democrats of Minnesota a choice in spite of the odds and pointed out that "some people in Minnesota seem to resent a little bit the fact that all the organized political machinery did come out for one person, which makes it very difficult for the voters to have a choice, because that kind of freezes other people out." [5]

One of the factors which finally influenced Kefauver to attempt an upset in Minnesota was the timing of the primary, which was scheduled between New Hampshire, which Stevenson had decided to write off, and Wisconsin, which Stevenson had declined to enter because of Kefauver strength among Wisconsin Democrats. In mid-February, sensing a real chance against Stevenson in Minnesota, Kefauver announced that he would budget seventeen days to the Minnesota primary instead of eleven, as originally planned. [6]

Kefauver's Minnesota appeal was based primarily on two contrasts between himself and Stevenson. First, Kefauver embarked upon a very personal campaign effort, attempting, as usual, to meet as many voters as possible, while Stevenson contented himself with prepared addresses to formal gatherings. Secondly, Kefauver continually reminded voters that he did not have the support of party leaders and implied that it was somehow a reflection on Stevenson that the Democratic organization in Minnesota was solidly behind the 1952 nominee. Kefauver's references to organizational support for Stevenson became so irritating to Governor Freeman that he was finally provoked to attack Kefauver for the use of what Freeman considered to be a false issue of bossism. "I have a real deep, personal resentment over this," Freeman told the press late in the campaign after yet another Kefauver reference to bossism. Freeman revealed that, contrary to hindering Kefauver's Minnesota campaign, he had offered to help Kefauver select responsible delegate candidates once Kefauver had made the decision to oppose Stevenson. In gratitude, Freeman said, Kefauver apparently decided that it was "politically advantageous to open an attack upon the DFL [Democratic] party and its leadership in a bid for voter sympathy. It's part of a political technique. It's political demagoguery. It's not true and he knows it." [7]

Stevenson also joined the attack on Kefauver, accusing him of the highest political crime, dividing the party. Kefauver replied that his purpose in Minnesota was not to divide the party but to "give the good people of Minnesota their right to pick their candidates freely." Kefauver's emphasis on the "free choice" issue contrasted sharply with his earlier announced interest in talking "about the issues" and saving "our fire for the Republicans in the fall." [8]

As Kefauver made his first campaign tour through Minnesota in February, a Minneapolis *Star* and *Tribune* poll showed that Minnesota Democrats favored Stevenson over Kefauver 59 per cent to 24 per cent. Another poll, published on the eve of the primary, showed Kefauver gaining dramatically, but still trailing Stevenson, 52 per cent to 39 per cent. [9]

Primary results on the night of March 20 confounded all predictions and sent shock waves through the Democratic party around the country. A massive turnout of voters (432,608, as compared with 128,096 in 1952) gave Kefauver an upset victory over the heavily favored Stevenson, 245,885 to 186,723. Political observers were almost unanimous in analyzing the primary as perhaps fatal to Stevenson's chances for the nomination, although doubting that Kefauver would be the long-term beneficiary, because of the well known opposition of Democratic leaders to him. Pro-Stevenson Democrats, however, were quick to seize on the explanation that the huge increase in the Democratic primary vote was due to thousands of Republicans who voted in the Democratic primary in order to knock out the Democratic frontrunner, whom they felt had the best chance of defeating Eisenhower in November.[10]

Kefauver himself apparently accepted the analysis that many Republicans did vote in the Democratic primary, but he did not admit that they voted for him for ulterior reasons or that they voted for him at all. He saw "the size of the vote" in heavily agricultural Minnesota as indicating "that many independents and Republicans have realized that only through the Democratic program can a justifiable and equitable farm program be obtained." However, since Kefauver had favored higher farm price supports than Stevenson, it would have been natural for Republicans and independents concerned enough about falling farm prices to vote in the Democratic primary to choose Kefauver over Stevenson.[11]

The charge that he was being used by the Republicans was especially irritating to Kefauver, and when stories began to circulate that Kefauver was receiving campaign donations from Republicans, he vigorously denied them: "I know of no Republican money being spent for me, and my associates know of none. It looks as if Mr. Stevenson is laying the groundwork for another alibi." Kefauver campaign adviser Howard McGrath added that the charges being made against Kefauver made Stevenson sound "like a man in the first stages of panic."[12]

However inviting the explanation that Republicans had invaded the Democratic primary, not all observes were willing to dismiss Kefauver's victory as a Republican plot to derail the Democratic frontrunner. Many analysts, including several of Stevenson's own advisers, agreed with *Time* that:

. . . the key factor in Estes Kefauver's spectacular victory was the difference that Minnesota Democrats found in the two candidates. In Adlai Stevenson many Minnesotans saw a precise talker without much to say, a philosopher whose philosophy did not clearly emerge—a man they did not really like or even understand. In

Estes Kefauver they saw a big, friendly, folksy politician whose comfortable generalities were easy to take and whose warm hand was easy to shake. As reporters combed over the bones of the Minnesota contest, one voter after another spoke of Kefauver as "a down-to-earth man of the people." [13]

Theodore H. White similarly analyzed "the core of his [Kefauver's] magic" as:

the ability to make almost anyone—in overalls, miner's hat or housedress—feel that politics is you. Out of his enormous zest and enjoyment for politics, he communicates the idea that politics is fun; that you, the individual he is talking to, have a role to play in it; that, specifically, this year as he seeks the grand office of the Presidency, he needs you; you count.[14]

Others, however, were more critical of Senator Kefauver for adopting, and the voters for responding to, a campaign technique that stressed personal contact and a general approach to the issues at the expense of a serious attempt to educate and inform the voters about the complex problems facing the country and the candidates' ideas on how to deal with them. Typical of this view was an editorial in *Christian Century*, which complained that:

Alongside Mr. Stevenson's critical, intelligent, balanced discussion of the issues, the senator's recklessness discredits Kefauver as a serious statesman. American political life and standards would be tragically the loser if such campaigning cost us the counsel and criticism of Adlai Stevenson. We will do well to distinguish always between those who seek to contribute something to high office, and those who seek what high office has to contribute to themselves.[15]

Stevenson himself was shaken into admitting, however, that "I have not communicated successfully." The 1952 nominee, who had been considered practically nominated on March 1, was still surveying the damage done to his campaign by New

Hampshire and Minnesota when, two weeks after the Minnesota vote, Kefauver ran up 330,665 votes in winning, uncontested, Wisconsin's pledged delegation, at a total cost to the Kefauver organization of only $41. By early April, to Stevenson's dismay, it appeared that Kefauver was on his way to a primary sweep matching the spectacular performance of 1952. He had, in eighty days, traveled 37,000 miles through eighteen states, won all three primaries held, amassed 598,251 votes to Stevenson's 190,529, and won 62 pledged delegates to Stevenson's four.[16]

Within the course of a few weeks, therefore, the fight for the Democratic nomination had become, once again, wide open. The respect accorded overnight to the Kefauver campaign moved Joseph Donohue, Kefauver's campaign manager, to joke that:

> We've been lonesome in the Kefauver camp for a long time. Before New Hampshire, hardly anybody would speak to us. After New Hampshire we got a polite "How do you do." After Minnesota, they really acted as if they were happy to talk to us. Since the Wisconsin vote some people are so polite it's embarrassing.[17]

There were other signs that the Kefauver campaign was making significant inroads into Stevenson's support. The first Gallup poll taken after Kefauver's three primary victories indicated that in one month Democratic voters had shifted dramatically to the extent that Stevenson's 51 per cent to 18 per cent lead over Kefauver among Democratic voters before New Hampshire had dwindled to 39 per cent to 33 per cent, a rise in Kefauver's strength that George Gallup termed "phenomenal." [18] Stevenson was not yet out, but the professionals were re-evaluating the situation,[19] and another primary loss to Kefauver was generally expected to end Stevenson's hopes for the nomination. Stevenson himself became noticeably defensive and began to attack Kefauver's record directly instead of ignoring him, as had been Stevenson's strategy before Minnesota.[20]

The primary beneficiary of a Kefauver-Stevenson stand-off

in the primaries, or of a Kefauver sweep, however, was thought to be Governor Harriman of New York, who would inherit most of the machine support for Stevenson if the 1952 nominee should withdraw. Even Kefauver's impressive victory over Stevenson in Minnesota seemed to make little difference to the professionals, and the *New York Times,* analyzing the effect of the primary on the major contenders, observed:

> The opposition to Senator Kefauver among his Democratic colleagues in the Senate and in many of the state organizations is massive and apparently immovable. This opposition has a common basis in a feeling that he does not pull his oar in the galley-work of regular committees, but goes sailing off on investigations that make the headlines. More particularly, the Southerners will not forgive his "un-Southern" stand on civil-rights (he refused to sign the manifesto two weeks ago against the Supreme Court's desegregation ruling), and many Northern Democrats will not forget his crime-and-politics investigation which damaged some innocent Democrats as well as some guilty ones.[21]

Harriman backers, therefore, had everything to gain from continued Kefauver success, and, although most pro-Harriman support for Kefauver was discreet, some assistance was very obvious, as in the case of a Brooklyn textile firm president, slated to be a delegate to the convention favoring Harriman, who contributed $5000 to the Kefauver campaign.[22]

All eyes in the Democratic party were on the remaining primary battles. In spite of the fact that nineteen states plus Alaska and the District of Columbia held some form of presidential primary in 1956, there were only a few that would really influence the choice of the nominee. Kefauver entered fourteen, eight of which offered either no opposition or only token opposition—New Hampshire, New Jersey, Wisconsin, Maryland, Indiana, Nebraska, Montana, and South Dakota. In several of the eight, Kefauver's victory in the presidential preference vote did not automatically ensure his support by delegates elected at the same time; especially was this true in New Jersey, where Kefauver received 117,056 of the 122,228 votes cast but had almost no support among the pro-Stevenson delegation elected. In two states, Pennsylvania and Illinois, Kefauver declined to enter because of the overwhelming support for Stevenson among Democratic professionals. Since the delegates elected would be pro-Stevenson anyway, all that Kefauver could have accomplished in Pennsylvania and Illinois was an increase in his cumulative national primary vote, which might have been worth some effort, since it was vital for the Kefauver campaign to end up with statistics showing greater rank and file support for Kefauver than Stevenson. As it was, Kefauver allowed Stevenson to run up a total of 1,359,914 votes in the two states, to Kefauver's 70,644 write-ins.[23]

Stevenson had entered eight primaries, and faced Kefauver in six—Minnesota, Oregon, Florida, California, Alaska, and the District of Columbia. Of the post-Minnesota primaries, Oregon and California offered the best testing grounds for rank and file sentiment, but Oregon was complicated by Stevenson's and Kefauver's refusal to appear on the ballot there. Both had desired to avoid a party-splitting battle that might damage the re-election chances of maverick Senator Wayne Morse, who was seeking re-election as a Democrat in 1956 after having been elected as a Republican in 1944 and 1950. Morse, however, had written both Kefauver and Stevenson in early February:

> . . . I have absolutely no objections and I never have had any objections to a Presidential primary race in Oregon. . . . I have appreciated your concern which you have expressed to me in personal conversations as to whether or not a Presidential primary race in Oregon would interfere in any way with my race for the Senate. . . . I want to assure you again that if either one or both of you decide to enter the Oregon Presidential primary, I shall welcome you.[24]

Since Oregon was a small state and, therefore, much more compatible with Kefauver's personal campaign style, it was to Stevenson's advantage to prevent a head-on clash with Kefauver there. In the absence of an active campaign by Stevenson and Kefauver, Oregon Democrats favoring Stevenson outspent the Kefauver forces 25 to 1 and gave Stevenson a 98,131 to 62,987 victory in a purely write-in election that attracted only a small percentage of the state's Democrats.[25]

The climax of the primary campaigns, therefore, turned out to be Florida and California, which held their primaries a week apart—Florida, on May 29, and California, on June 5. These two primaries proved especially frustrating to both Kefauver and Stevenson, since the great distance between the two states was matched by the differing approaches each candidate attempted to take in each state in order to appeal to a winning combination of voters. In California, for example, both Stevenson and Kefauver pictured themselves as heirs to the great liberal tradition of the Democratic party; in Florida, on the other hand, both stressed the moderation, especially on the civil rights issue, that was thought necessary to win acceptance by Florida Democrats. It was not an easy assignment for either man, and the inconsistencies in their appeals and in their supporters in the two states opened the door to charges of opportunism and hypocrisy by both sides. Nothing else did more to disrupt the Democratic party in 1956 than the Florida and California primaries, and both men came out of the campaigns with their reputations somewhat tarnished, as Republicans and backers of Governor Harriman looked on approvingly.

The civil rights issue posed the greatest challenge to the two candidates, as it did to Democratic party unity in general. Although the civil rights movement was pressing forward on many fronts in 1956, the focus of its attention was on defending and implementing the school integration decision handed down by the United States Supreme Court in 1954. The stage was set for a donnybrook within the party between those who enthusiastically hailed the decision and those who saw the federally ordered integration as the gravest threat to states' rights and white supremacy since the Civil War.

Both Kefauver and Stevenson attempted to straddle the

issue, their public statements reflecting efforts to define a position acceptable to the entire party, alienating neither the liberals —which might cost them the California primary—nor the conservatives—who would turn the issue against them in Florida.

Kefauver, apparently feeling that his Southern background and his mixed record on civil rights [26] required him to remove any doubts the liberals might have about him,[27] outflanked Stevenson on civil rights in the early days of the campaign. Answering a question after his announcement of candidacy in December, Kefauver declared his support for the Supreme Court decision as "the law of the land" and termed it "high time people of both races got together and made their plans to comply with it." [28]

Kefauver stole a march on Stevenson in California in early February when, responding to Negro frustrations over the Emmett Till murder the previous September, he gave the impression of promising unqualified support to Negro leaders for legislation against mob violence in the South. Kefauver also won support among Negroes by attacking tuition grants used as a device to circumvent the school integration decision. Stevenson, in California at the same time, seemed to display much less concern over Negro problems, provoking William Rumford, San Francisco Negro assemblyman, to threaten that unless Stevenson spoke up more strongly on behalf of civil rights, "I'll have no alternative but to switch to Senator Kefauver." Similarly, the Reverend Mr. L. Sylvester Odom, pastor of one of California's largest Negro congregations, entered a conference of Negro leaders wearing a Stevenson button but left with a Kefauver button after hearing Kefauver explain his civil rights position.[29]

Kefauver was also aided when Stevenson stunned his liberal supporters by rejecting the use of troops to enforce desegregation. "I think that would be a great mistake," said Stevenson. "That is exactly what brought on the Civil War. It can't be done by troops or bayonets. We must proceed gradually, not upsetting habits or traditions that are older than the Republic." Walter

Reuther, one of Stevenson's most prominent supporters for the 1956 nomination, immediately called Stevenson "dead wrong this time," and the editor of two weekly Negro newspapers in Minnesota switched the endorsement of his papers from Stevenson to Kefauver.[30]

Kefauver's commitment to civil rights was not just a tactical maneuver but part of his general feeling that one of America's failures had been her reluctance "to stand up fair and square on the issue of colonialism and the right of self-determination and self-government for the differing peoples of the world." He saw the American Negro as just as much a victim of colonialism as the newly emerging nations in Asia and Africa and called upon the United States to recognize that:

> Winds of freedom are blowing all over the world and everywhere men are demanding freedom and dignity. They are going to find the answer and they are going to find it in this generation. These winds are blowing in America just as they are in Asia and Africa—everywhere.
>
> When we in America have learned that all men in their own nation are due the full dignity of their humanity, are due the right to equal opportunity in the life of their nation for themselves and their children, then we can face the world with pride and confidence.[31]

Kefauver's relations with Southern political leaders, never very warm, cooled even more as Kefauver pressed further to the left on the civil rights issue. His isolation from other Southern senators and congressmen was made especially obvious in early March, when he refused to sign the "Southern Manifesto," which announced that 96 members of Congress, including 19 senators, would seek every legal means of blocking the school integration decision. Kefauver advocated, instead, keeping "manifestoes and harsh words to a minimum." [32]

Of the three major contenders for the 1956 nomination, Southern Democrats found Stevenson by far the most acceptable. In spite of his prominent liberal support across the country, the Southerners preferred Stevenson to Kefauver because, as Florida Senator George Smathers expressed it, "the South is always more apt to go for a northerner who doesn't know any better than for a southerner who should know better, but doesn't."[33] Conversely, a history of the militantly liberal Americans for Democratic Action records that in 1956 " 'everybody in ADA was for Kefauver,' according to one ADA leader. (Kefauver is one of the few politicians for whom ADA members seem to have an almost unreserved admiration. As a Southerner, he is—by definition—a sinner, and the liberals like nothing better than to see a sinner get religion.)"[34]

But if Kefauver was unacceptable to the South, Governor Harriman of New York was anathema, because of his attacks on "moderation" and his emphasis on the Democratic party as a vehicle for dynamic, aggressive liberalism.[35] Southerners, therefore, saw Stevenson as by far the best of a bad lot and realized how important it was to block both Kefauver and Harriman. The only Southern presidential primary was that in Florida, and the clash between Kefauver and Stevenson there gave Dixiecrats their best opportunity to boost Stevenson at the expense of Kefauver.[36]

For a while, it appeared that the civil rights issue was going to be the only issue in the Florida presidential primary. When Kefauver arrived in Florida in February to begin campaigning, he held an hour-long press conference at which he received not a single question on any other topic. One reporter asked Kefauver if he supported segregation, as had been announced by his Eighth District chairman, Philip Barton. Kefauver did not repudiate his earlier pronouncements favoring civil rights, but he did express his attitude in terms more acceptable to a Southern audience. "The Supreme Court has spoken," he said, "and I would not condemn the Court." He implied that the Court's ruling had been misinterpreted somewhat and pointed out that the Court had shown that it recognized that "different conditions exist in different sections of the country" and that "customs can't be changed overnight." Ever the believer in the power of rational discussion, Kefauver expressed his faith that "this problem, too, can be solved if the people of both races sit down and discuss it calmly." [37]

Kefauver was especially disappointed in President Eisenhower's refusal to endorse the school integration decision as correct and found it difficult to understand why, "while part of our nation seethes with unrest in the relations between races, President Eisenhower has failed to use his good offices or the moral suasion which comes from the immense prestige of his position to promote the goodwill and understanding which will be basic to any solutions." In any event, Kefauver urged that the problem be approached "without passion, without revolution and without resorting to violence." [38]

The Florida Democratic organization, solidly behind Stevenson, sought to smear Kefauver with an integrationist tag, ignoring Stevenson's own remarkably similar civil rights positions and equally liberal reputation in the North and West. Sam Wilhite, political adviser to Mississippi Senator Jim Eastland, came into the state to aid the Stevenson campaign, and former Georgia Governor Herman Talmadge used his influence in north Florida against Kefauver. There was no doubt that most Southern leaders agreed with Mississippi Senator John Stennis's analysis that Stevenson was the "Southern candidate." [39]

It was with some basis, therefore, that Kefauver accused Stevenson of hypocrisy and irresponsibility in allowing segregationist attacks on Kefauver by Stevenson supporters to go unrebuked. Kefauver was especially provoked over a remark made by former Florida Governor Millard F. Caldwell, Jr., referring to Kefauver as a "sycophant for the Negro vote." What especially upset Kefauver was that Caldwell's attack came at a Stevenson rally featuring the 1952 nominee on the same platform. When Stevenson not only let the slur on Kefauver go unchallenged but also even denied hearing it, Kefauver accused him of utilizing a "smear and smile" technique and saw:

a remarkable parallel . . . in the attitude of Mr. Stevenson toward his delegate Caldwell and President Eisenhower in his atti-

tude toward Mr. Nixon. Mr. Nixon makes a vicious attack on the
Democrats which Mr. Eisenhower says he didn't read. Mr. Caldwell makes a vicious attack on me which . . . Mr. Stevenson says
he didn't hear.[40]

Not to be outdone, Kefauver supporters, without the knowledge
or consent of Kefauver himself, circulated material documenting
Stevenson's role as a champion of Negro rights.

It was not only the inconsistencies the two candidates exhibited over the race issue that undermined respect for both in
the minds of Democrats around the country but also the spec-
tacle of the two men chasing around all over Florida and California in what appeared to be a frantic, desperate search for
support that contrasted sharply with the image of Eisenhower,
whom both hoped to oppose in November, as above such pedes-
trian squabbling. The Minnesota primary had shaken Stevenson out of his complacency, and, although he said it made him
"disgusted and just plain mad" to be accused of being preoccupied with issues and not spending enough time shaking
hands, he began, after Minnesota, to attempt to match Kefauver's personal campaign style in an effort to counter criticisms
that his approach to the voters was too aloof and formal.[41]

Stevenson never admitted that he had been forced by Kefauver to adopt a style he found uncomfortable and, instead,
recalled that shaking hands with voters all across Illinois in 1948
was how he had been elected to office in the first place. However, he stressed his belief that a candidate should "find a balance between these personal conversations and the presentation
of important issues. I think a candidate owes both approaches
to the people and I'm trying to do it." [42]

The attempts of Kefauver and Stevenson to outdo each
other in personal campaigning in Florida and California
brought both to the edge of exhaustion and turned the campaigns more and more away from the issues.[43] The argument can
be made, however, that, since Stevenson's and Kefauver's positions on most of the major issues were practically indistinguish-
able anyway, there was really no basis on which they could ask

voters to choose between them except personality. Therefore, it may be that the emphasis on personalities in Florida and California was the effect of Stevenson's and Kefauver's lack of disagreement over issues rather than the cause of their tendency to ignore them. It was not without reason that the *New York Times,* seeing little difference between Kefauver and Stevenson, or, for that matter, Governor Harriman, on the important issues, described the task of choosing from among the three as like trying to distinguish "between a tittle, a jot and a scintilla." [44] Even Kefauver and Stevenson themselves were unable to enunciate the differences between themselves, as was dramatically illustrated when the two met on a nationally televised debate during the Florida campaign and found themselves agreeing with practically everything the other said.[45]

The routine of the campaign trail had so conditioned Kefauver and Stevenson to grab any loose hand that Stevenson once shook hands with a mannequin, and Kefauver, as a sleepy passenger in a car whose driver had been stopped for speeding, groggily reached for the hand of the policeman who was writing the ticket.[46]

The Florida results on May 29 indicated that Florida Democrats, too, had trouble choosing between Kefauver and Stevenson, and that many declined to make a choice. In a vote that fell from 674,634 (1952) to 446,834 (1956), Stevenson edged out Kefauver by 230,285 to 216,549, receiving, paradoxically, his strongest support from the segregationist Third District and Miami's Negro precincts. In spite of the close vote, however, the large number of at-large delegates, combined with narrow Stevenson victories in most of the congressional districts, gave Stevenson 22 of the 26 delegates.[47]

A week later Kefauver and Stevenson faced each other in the crucial California primary, which, as usual, saw the state organization lined up almost solidly against Kefauver. Whatever gains Kefauver had made with liberals because of his civil rights stand was more than countered by the array of big liberal names endorsing Stevenson, including Eleanor Roosevelt and Helen

Gahagan Douglas. Mrs. Roosevelt found Kefauver "a very nice man" but stressed that "at this point we need a world outlook . . . [which] Governor Stevenson has . . . [and] Senator Kefauver . . . does not have. . . ." [48] Stevenson also enjoyed the support of the ultra-liberal California Democratic Council, which, in spite of its warm regard for Kefauver, was overwhelmingly committed to Stevenson's nomination. [49]

The last ten days of the presidential primary campaign, which included the last days in Florida and the week before the California vote, saw Stevenson and Kefauver attacking each other in a fashion uncharacteristic of either man. Kefauver went to such lengths to attempt to distinguish differences between himself and Stevenson that a reaction set in against what were considered his irresponsible charges against Stevenson. One of the most controversial attacks made by Kefauver and his supporters had its origins in material circulated by a California old-age association, an offshoot of the Townsend movement of the 1930s, which charged that Stevenson, while Governor of Illinois, had vetoed a 10 per cent increase in "old-age and blind pensions." The attack ignored the fact that Stevenson had successfully urged raising such pensions while governor and had vetoed this particular bill because the Republican legislature had not passed an appropriation to cover the cost of the pension hike. The *New Republic,* almost always sympathetic to Kefauver, quoted "a reporter who admires Kefauver's liberal record" as "disheartened by this kind of attack," which "not even Nixon used . . . in '52." [50]

Stevenson himself reacted to Kefauver's accusation by suggesting: "The Senator's continued false charges remind me that there is such a thing as wanting to be President too much. The Senator seems to be confronted with the dilemma of how to win without proving that he is unworthy of winning." [51]

Kefauver was on more secure ground in questioning Stevenson's Southern support. In an attempt to drive a wedge between Stevenson and his liberal supporters almost on the eve of the California vote, Kefauver asked again and again:

Since his, Adlai's, statements are not unlike my own, why then is it that the Talmadges, the Ellenders, the Caldwells flock to his support?

Has anything been said in private to these segregationists that makes him more acceptable than I?

What representations have been made by spokesmen from my opponent's camp?

Have they been assured that the words of his supporters rather than his own personal words represent the correct position of his candidacy?

I think these questions are important. There comes a time when campaign promises—those made in public as well as those made in private—those made by the candidate himself as well as those made by spokesmen for him—must be dealt with.[52]

Kefauver also rode the bossism issue hard in California, warning that "one of the great dangers of the present campaign in California is that the old-guard politicians are using the campaign of Mr. Stevenson to climb back into power." "You can't teach an underdog new tricks," quipped Stevenson.[53]

The extent to which Kefauver realized that everything might very well hinge on his showings in Florida and California was illustrated by the stepped-up appearances of his wife Nancy, who had been such an asset to his 1952 drive but had not been very active in the 1956 campaign. The Kefauver family had been opposed to another bid for the nomination, and Kefauver's eldest daughter, Linda, had refused to speak to her father for two weeks after he announced he would run again. Nancy was less than enthusiastic about another campaign like the one in 1952, and her absence from the campaign trail reflected her own wishes as well as the calculation that Kefauver would come under criticism if he and Nancy both left their four children for any length of time. Thus, at his December announcement, Kefauver had informed the press that Nancy "would not be able to get away from home as much this time because our four children are older now, and badly need one of us, particularly their mother, with them." But the stakes in Florida and

California were so high that Nancy joined her husband during the last weeks of the campaigns and not only added strength to Kefauver's own appeal but subtly called attention to Stevenson's divorce, thereby scoring with those who felt the President's family life should be a model for the nation.[54]

The California primary on June 5 sank Kefauver's hopes for the nomination. Stevenson won a smashing victory in the most important presidential primary of the year, leading Kefauver by 1,139,964 to 680,722. The primaries were now over, and Kefauver's primary record was far from impressive enough to force antagonistic professionals to back him for the nomination as the choice of the rank and file. Although Kefauver had won nine primaries to Stevenson's seven, Stevenson had won five of the six in which he had faced Kefauver and had run up a total of 3,069,504 votes across the country to Kefauver's 2,283,172.[55]

In spite of Stevenson's strong primary finish, he had not yet recovered the strength he had gathered before the Minnesota primary. Both Kefauver and Harriman had substantial support, and several favorite sons held on to many more delegates. Former President Truman was known to be cool to Stevenson's renomination bid, and Kefauver, therefore, had gone all-out to achieve a reconciliation with his former antagonist. But Truman's dislike for Kefauver continued unabated, and by May, a Kefauver aide was joking that Truman's friendship for Kefauver was developing "with the speed of a retreating glacier." Truman confirmed this analysis by admitting that he was "very happy" over Stevenson's victory in California and that he was "inclined to anyone else besides Kefauver" for the 1956 nomination. Kefauver replied that "old sores never heal." [56]

In addition to Kefauver's failure to win support from anti-Stevenson professionals, especially Truman, Kefauver faced new problems in Tennessee as his enemies became bolder after the Florida and California defeats. Kefauver's stock among Tennessee Democrats had suffered as a result of the liberal positions he had staked out in his effort to line up support across the

North and West. A severe blow to Kefauver's chances to have his own state's support at the convention came on June 28 when the Tennessee state Democratic convention voted to support any Tennessean who "had an opportunity" for a place on the national ticket. Kefauver had given up the idea of a fight to instruct the delegation to support him and had left Nashville before the resolution was adopted after assuming that he had reached a compromise with the Clement forces. However, after adoption of the resolution, anti-Kefauver Democrats suggested that Kefauver's chances for the nomination were already so remote that he no longer "had an opportunity" to win the nomination; therefore, they felt that the resolution did not bind them to support Kefauver at the convention. It would be up to the delegates selected, however, to make the final decision about supporting Kefauver, and the Kefauver forces were in as much doubt as ever about the eventual course the Tennessee delegation would take.[57]

Kefauver had faced campaign financing problems from the beginning of his nomination bid, but after California, when his prospects for success had declined considerably, the specter of running up even more expenses with little hope of winning the nomination became a major concern. The Kefauver campaign had always been run on a shoestring, and Kefauver headquarters reported only $125,000 spent and collected by May 23. Kefauver later put his preconvention campaign expenses at $250,000, but a professional study estimated that the Kefauver forces spent at least $350,000. The amount spent was not as important to Kefauver as the deficit he would be left to pick up. He had gone into debt personally to the extent of $34,000 as a result of his 1952 campaign, which had enjoyed reasonable prospects for success up to the day of his convention defeat. By July 1956, however, his campaign deficit was already between $40,000 and $80,000, with little chance of a dramatic upturn in his fortunes that might bring in significant contributions.[58]

Although Kefauver had insisted after the California primary that he was in the race to stay, and that, in fact, he was the party's strongest candidate,[59] he, nevertheless, made several efforts to close the breach between himself and Stevenson which were interpreted as attempts to pave the way for a Stevenson-Kefauver ticket at the convention. Kefauver's most dramatic gesture to Stevenson was his admission on "Meet the Press" on June 17 that he "got mad and lost my head" in Florida after having been provoked by former Governor Caldwell, who "said a lot of bad things about me" without Stevenson's doing "anything about it." Kefauver wanted to make it clear that he considered Stevenson "a fine man" whom Kefauver could support if nominated. Stevenson replied that he was "very pleased by what Senator Kefauver said about the primaries. I am sure it will help immeasurably to restore unity to our party and strength to our common cause." [60]

After the California primary, Kefauver's managers had set up appointments with approximately thirty important Democratic leaders to discuss his political future. Their advice caused him to reconsider his candidacy. On June 18, the day after his "Meet the Press" appearance, Kefauver met with about seventy loyal supporters from all over the country to discuss what to do next. They considered possible deals with Stevenson and Harriman, as well as continuing through the convention and facing certain defeat. Kefauver himself was undecided. "My people went through hell for me. I can't withdraw—they went through hell for me." [61]

One of Kefauver's friends who took credit for finally convincing Kefauver to withdraw was Helen Fuller, managing editor of the *New Republic:*

> We worked on him every time he came to Washington. But then he would go out into the field and people there would unwork him. One day a mutual friend called me with the news, "I've got him to do it. Come on over." Estes was convinced all right, but I've never seen a man so down. What hurt him was that he was letting down all the people who had spilled their guts for him. He was finally agreeing to do this only because all the people whom he trusted best were insisting on it.[62]

Kefauver's withdrawal was the most logical step he could have taken after the California primary. After all, his argument had always been, "If I can't win before the people, then I don't deserve to win." But not only had Kefauver slipped in the primaries, he had continually lost ground to Stevenson in the Gallup polls after the Minnesota primary. A poll taken after the California primary showed Stevenson to be the choice of Democratic voters by the overwhelming margin of 45 per cent to 16 per cent.[63]

Kefauver realized that the only purpose he would serve if he remained in the race would be to prolong the division between his backers and those of Stevenson, who was sure to be nominated unless Kefauver co-operated with Harriman to block the man who had demonstrated his rank and file support. To be a party to such a strategy would have violated every principle Kefauver had stood for in his own campaign, and he would have no part of it.

On July 31, therefore, Kefauver called a news conference and made the announcement that he was withdrawing as a candidate for the Democratic presidential nomination:

> Surveying my present situation realistically, I have concluded that I can make a great contribution toward . . . unity and eventually victory for the party by withdrawing my name from consideration for the office of President at this time, and asking my supporters to whole-heartedly give their backing to Governor Adlai Stevenson, who alone, with me, was willing to take his cause to the people in almost as many primaries as I did myself.
>
> In these primaries he secured almost 3,000,000 votes, which was over 600,000 more votes than I secured. Furthermore, since the primaries have concluded, reliable, nation-wide polls show that most of the Democratic and independent voters want him to be nominated. He has the support of the majority of the Democratic party leaders. He has picked up additional support from several conventions since the primaries concluded.
>
> Governor Stevenson's delegate lead is such that he could be stopped only by throwing the convention into a deadlock. I

would not want to be a party to this. The nominee, whoever he might be, who secured his nomination as a result of the bitterness of a deadlocked convention would, I suspect, find it a hollow honor. Victory in November is more important than the victor in August. I am anxious that the resources of the party, of myself and of Governor Stevenson not be dissipated by continuing the contest. I am anxious that we begin now to unite the party for a vigorous, imaginative and resourceful campaign this fall.

. . . I do believe Mr. Stevenson has a good chance to lead the party to victory this fall. I once had my doubts that he could; I no longer harbor any misgivings. . . .

I intend to go to the Chicago convention, where I am a delegate from Tennessee, and be in contact with my supporters and do all that I can to persuade them that the course I have taken, and advise them to take, is in the best interest [of the party and the country].[64]

Kefauver's withdrawal was not completely unexpected, but his unqualified endorsement of Stevenson for the nomination was. Kefauver's move shocked the Harriman camp and upset their strategy of using Kefauver's strength to bring about a deadlock at the convention. Harriman's backers found out about the Kefauver withdrawal only 35 minutes before Kefauver announced it, and reports were that the frantic Harriman camp was willing to offer Kefauver almost anything to keep him in the race. After Harriman was unable to block Kefauver's withdrawal and endorsement of Stevenson, however, the Harriman forces adopted a cynical attitude toward Kefauver's exit and suggested that "Kefauver delegates and others are going to ask themselves 'what's the deal?' Has Kefauver traded out for the Vice-Presidential nomination, or what?" [65]

The blow to Harriman's hopes was indicated by a *New York Times* poll the Sunday before Kefauver's withdrawal which gave Stevenson 404½ delegates, Kefauver 200, and Harriman 141. With Kefauver actively working to deliver his delegates to Stevenson, it seemed that the contest was all but over. To Kefauver supporters who had felt betrayed by Harriman's switch to Stevenson at the 1952 convention, when Kefauver had expected support from the New Yorker, it was sweet revenge to watch the disintegration of Harriman's hopes for the nomination. Kefauver's announcement also caught Stevenson by surprise. The 1952 nominee quickly drove into Chicago from Libertyville, thirty-five miles away, to hold a press conference on the development. Of Kefauver, Stevenson said:

> I want to express to him my gratitude for his gracious and spontaneous expression of his support. He has often expressed his approval of the Presidential primaries and he has been as good as his word.
> I respect Senator Kefauver as a thoughtful, liberal Democrat. We share a grave anxiety about drift at home and deterioration abroad under a faltering leadership and a divided party.[66]

Under the circumstances, Kefauver's withdrawal was the wisest political move he could have made and, in addition, was a move which redounded to his personal credit, since it not only gave him an opportunity to join the Stevenson bandwagon but to do it in a way that caused his dedication to majority rule to completely overshadow any charges of opportunism that might be leveled at him. From the time of his withdrawal until Stevenson's nomination, he would be working with the consensus of the party against the threat to unity from Harriman on the left. And, while this was a new role for Kefauver, his success at it did much to heal the wounds caused by the bitter primary campaigns and was to make it possible for him to emerge from the convention as one of the leading figures of the national Democratic party.

chapter xv

TRIUMPH:
THE DEMOCRATIC
CONVENTION, 1956

To the casual observer, it seemed that Kefauver's July 31 withdrawal from the race for the 1956 Democratic presidential nomination marked a somewhat tragic end to his national political ambitions. Few suspected, therefore, that the Democratic convention which was about to meet would be the scene of the single most dramatic political victory of Kefauver's career.

Although Kefauver was more than ready for a rest after his withdrawal, he felt an obligation to rally as many of his former supporters as possible behind Stevenson. Some of the delegates who had been pledged to Kefauver felt that Governor Harriman of New York was a more attractive candidate than Stevenson, whom many had rejected in the first place because he was seen as not sufficiently dynamic and aggressively liberal. Kefauver went over the list of delegates who had once backed him but who were reluctant to switch to Stevenson, and agreed to make personal calls on each one. Stevenson was overjoyed at Kefauver's unexpected support and pledged that he would "never forget what you have done on my behalf with your delegates." Stevenson warned, however, that he could "make no promises" to Kefauver at that time because of the possibility that he might "have to deal with Senator [Lyndon] Johnson on an early ballot." If that need did not arise, Stevenson told Kefauver, "I can promise you the most careful consideration for whatever you want." [1]

Kefauver's backing of Stevenson seemed even more crucial when, on the eve of the convention, former President Truman announced his support of Harriman for the nomination and began to organize support for the New Yorker among the delegates. It was debatable whether the Truman-Harriman effort would have succeeded even with Kefauver still in the race, but there was almost no chance of a Harriman nomination once Kefauver joined the Stevenson forces. After a brief flurry of Harriman activity, the Stevenson bandwagon began to roll again, and Stevenson handily defeated Harriman on the first ballot, 905½ to 210.[2]

About the only suspense left in the convention was over Stevenson's choice for Vice-President. Kefauver had long been mentioned as a running mate if Stevenson were renominated, but Kefauver had, for obvious reasons, refused to show any interest in the Vice-Presidency as long as he was still an announced candidate for the Presidency. Even at his withdrawal press conference, Kefauver had stressed that "I am not a candidate for any other office," [3] a declaration which helped to blunt charges from the Harriman camp that Stevenson and Kefauver had agreed on a Stevenson-Kefauver ticket as the price of Kefauver's withdrawal. However, Kefauver's statements to his supporters and to the press over the next few days indicated that he was, indeed, very much interested in being offered second place on the ticket. He even went as far as asking Stevenson privately for the nomination; Stevenson made no commitment.[4]

Kefauver, of course, had a solid core of support in the Stevenson camp pushing him for the Vice-Presidency. Not only were his former delegates enthusiastically for him, but many who had always supported Stevenson for the nomination saw Kefauver as the running mate who could add the greatest strength to the ticket.[5]

There were others just as eager and willing as Kefauver to join Stevenson on the national ticket. Kefauver's two fellow Tennesseans, Governor Frank Clement and Senator Albert Gore, were widely discussed as possibilities, and both wanted the nomination. Clement had been keynote speaker, but his extra-long address, given in revival style, was generally thought to have damaged his prospects. Gore, however, was rated very highly by those close to Stevenson and was reported by the *New York Times* to be the choice of the nominee.[6] Other frequently mentioned possibilities included Senators Hubert Humphrey of Minnesota and John Kennedy of Massachusetts and Mayor Robert Wagner of New York City. Humphrey had been one of Stevenson's earliest and strongest supporters, although he had been unable to carry Minnesota for Stevenson against Kefauver. Kennedy, also an early supporter of Stevenson, had impressed the convention as a result not only of a film on the party's record he had narrated but also because he had delivered one of the best speeches of the convention in placing Stevenson's name in nomination. Both Wagner and Kennedy were, in addition, Roman Catholics, but this was not seen as an unqualified asset.

Since tradition dictated that a successful presidential nominee should choose his vice-presidential running mate, the delegates waited anxiously for word of Stevenson's choice. Instead, Stevenson asked to address the convention shortly after his nomination and electrified the delegates with the announcement:

> . . . I have concluded to depart from the precedents of the past. I have decided that the selection of the Vice-Presidential nominee should be made through the free processes of this Convention—(Applause)—so that the Democratic Party's candidate for this office may join me before the Nation not as one man's selection but as one chosen by our Party even as I have been chosen. (Applause)
> I add only this: In taking this step I am expressing my confi-

dence in your choice and in the many fine men whose prominence in our Party will command your consideration. The choice will be yours. The profit will be the Nation's. (Applause) [7]

It was almost midnight when Stevenson made his unexpected announcement. What followed was perhaps the most hectic seventeen hours in the history of American political conventions.[8]

Stevenson and his advisers had decided on the open convention selection of the vice-presidential nominee principally on the basis of three considerations. In the first place, the convention was in danger of becoming so dull that not only would the TV audience tune it out but the delegates themselves would go away from Chicago with little sense of accomplishment or participation. Second, Stevenson and his advisers were torn over which man to designate for second placee. The selection of any one by the nominee would have keenly disappointed several others. Some saw Stevenson's abdication of the responsibility to choose a running mate as a reappearance of the Hamlet in his personality; others, however, saw it as a clever way out of a sticky political problem. Third, the open convention idea was seen as a dramatic way to contrast the Democratic convention with the tightly controlled Republican convention which would meet a week later to rubber-stamp the renominations of Eisenhower and Nixon. Harold Stassen's abortive effort to dump Nixon from the 1956 Republican ticket had called to the attention of the public the centralized control of the Republican party by its national leadership, and Stevenson hoped to capitalize on public reaction against the monolithic Republican party organization by providing a real contest for second place on the Democratic ticket. In addition, the illnesses of Eisenhower had focused more and more attention on the Republican Vice-President, Nixon, as a likely successor to Eisenhower, if the President were unable to complete a second term. Naturally, therefore, it was necessary, if the Democrats hoped to take advantage of the succession issue, for the Democrats themselves to give special attention to the vice-presidential nomination of their own party.[9]

Stevenson's decision to allow an open convention did not meet with universal approval by party leaders. Speaker Sam Rayburn and Senate Majority Leader Lyndon Johnson were especially opposed to the idea on the grounds that it made Stevenson look indecisive. Humphrey was upset with the decision because he felt that he had little chance for the nomination unless he were designated for the slot by Stevenson. Kefauver and Kennedy were initially unhappy with Stevenson's announcement because they both thought the open convention proposal was more form than substance and that each was being set up for a humiliating defeat by the other, with the undercover support of the Stevenson forces.[10]

Pollster Elmo Roper was credited with changing Kefauver's mind about the sincerity of Stevenson's announcement. He had dropped by Kefauver's hotel room after Stevenson's appearance before the convention to find Kefauver angrily packing in order to return to Tennessee immediately. Roper began to argue strongly that Stevenson would never have made the announcement unless he meant it and urged Kefauver to stay and fight for the nomination Kefauver admitted he wanted. Kefauver aide Howard McGrath disagreed and warned Kefauver that he was "being sucked in . . . they're using you for a sucker . . . don't let them do it." Roper, however, persuaded Kefauver at least to meet with Stevenson and hear the candidate himself guarantee that the convention would indeed be open. Kefauver did so and then returned to his hotel room, where, over the continued objections of McGrath, he declared: "I've made up my mind . . . now let's get to work . . . contact my delegates and let's get going." [11]

Not only Kefauver had decided to "get going"; Kennedy, Humphrey, Gore, and Wagner also mounted serious campaigns during the night in frantic preparation for the nominations and balloting which were scheduled to take place within hours. Because of the core of delegates personally loyal to Kefauver and because of the prestige he had earned as Stevenson's principal challenger for the nomination, Kefauver was almost at once established as the man to beat.

At noon on Friday, August 17, one of the most exciting sessions of a national political convention ever held came to order, and almost immediately the roll call of the states began for the purpose of placing names in nomination for the Vice-Presidency. Alabama yielded to Tennessee, which had decided to back Gore. The nominating speech by Lt. Governor Jared Maddux of Tennessee and a seconding speech by former Representative Laurie Battle of Alabama, both considered reactionaries even in their own states, indicated that, as attractive a candidate as Gore was, he had been unable to win significant support outside the South and had become the Dixiecrat candidate. Alaska, with an endorsement of Kefauver, who was not yet nominated, passed. Arizona then yielded to Ohio, whose future Governor Mike DiSalle placed Kefauver in nomination in a brief speech giving appropriate attention to Kefauver's record and qualifications but concluding with emphasis on what was Kefauver's strongest appeal—that "the two Democratic candidates of highest stature, of widest acceptance, and the most popular approval . . . [were] Adlai Stevenson and Estes Kefauver" and that the party had a chance to offer two men of presidential caliber to the American people. To a party ready to question Vice-President Nixon's ability to succeed to the Presidency in the event of yet another Eisenhower illness, it was a persuasive argument. Kefauver seconder, Senator Richard Neuberger of Oregon, similarly pointed out that the party had not only an opportunity but an obligation to "give to the Nation the only two men in our Party who took their policies, personalities and issues to the people." Congressman James Roosevelt of California, son of the late President, also seconded Kefauver's nomination, reminding the convention that Kefauver was considered by the American people to be "one of our greatest symbols of rugged, plain, honest democracy." [12]

After Kennedy, Governor Leroy Collins of Florida, Humphrey, Wagner, and Governor Luther Hodges of North Carolina were placed in nomination, the balloting began almost immediately.

Kefauver got off to an early lead, which he maintained throughout the first ballot, based on strength from his own former delegates and Stevenson delegates from the Midwest and West. California, giving Kefauver 33 of its 68 votes, to Kennedy's 10½ and Humphrey's 23½, indicated the typical division of a pro-Stevenson delegation. The first indication of what was to be one of the most dramatic developments at the convention came when Georgia awarded its 32 votes to Kennedy. Louisiana and Virginia soon added their 56 votes to the Massachusetts senator's total. By the end of the first ballot, it was obvious that Kefauver and Kennedy were the only candidates with support widespread enough to hope for eventual victory:

Kefauver	483½
Kennedy	304
Gore	178
Wagner	162½
Humphrey	134½ [13]

Several patterns in the voting were quickly spotted. Kennedy's strength was drawn principally from New England (89½ of 104 votes; only New Hampshire, which had backed Kefauver in the March primary, did not cast a majority of its votes for Kennedy), the South (where Kennedy received 105½ votes to Kefauver's 20½ and Gore's 136½), and Illinois (46 of 64 votes). Kefauver's support had come principally from the West and Midwest. From the states west of the Mississippi River, Kefauver received 209 votes to Kennedy's 34½. Kefauver also did very well in the Midwestern industrial states, receiving 22 of 26 from Indiana, 40 of 44 from Michigan, 50½ of 58 from Ohio, and all 28 from Wisconsin. Pennsylvania, where Kefauver received 54 of 74, was the only large Eastern state to give him substantial support. Gore had come in third with 178 votes, but only one vote from Hawaii and twenty-eight from the border state of Oklahoma had come from outside the South. Humphrey had received 134½ votes, but many of his delegates, including most of the thirty from Minnesota who had been elected as Kefauver delegates the previous March, were restless to switch to the leading contenders. Mayor Wagner had received 162½ votes, but 129½ had come from New York and New Jersey, and there was little support for him elsewhere.[14]

The second ballot turned into a dramatic struggle between Kefauver and Kennedy. Kefauver jumped off to an early lead with Alaska and Arizona, but Kennedy went ahead 26 to 22 when Arkansas switched from Gore to Kennedy. Kefauver took the lead again briefly when Colorado gave him 15½ of its 20, and led Kennedy at this point, 37½ to 31. Kennedy jumped back in front with Connecticut's 20 and thereafter maintained a comfortable lead over Kefauver. By Illinois, Kennedy led, 155 to 82; by New Hampshire, Kennedy's lead had been narrowed to 42 votes, 271½ to 229½. Then came the switches in the urban East that reminded Kefauver supporters of the nightmare third ballot of 1952. New Jersey and New York, which had supported Wagner on the first ballot, switched 128 of their 134 votes to Kennedy. The Kennedy supporters roared their approval, and a Kennedy bandwagon seemed ready to roll, as his lead over Kefauver jumped to 402½ to 245½. However, four Kefauver delegations (North Dakota, Ohio, Oregon, and Pennsylvania) narrowed the margin again, 416½ to 387. South Carolina joined most of the rest of the South and raised Kennedy's lead 448 to 387. When the roll call reached Tennessee, there was a hush in the hall as Governor Clement announced the vote of Kefauver's home state. A roar of boos from Kefauver supporters cascaded across the convention hall as Clement indicated that Tennessee would stay with Gore even though the contest had narrowed to Kefauver and Kennedy, with Tennessee's senior senator needing all the support he could get. Under the instructions of the Tennessee convention, the delegation was bound to support a Tennessean if he had a chance for the nomination, and anti-Kefauver Tennessee delegates could hardly have defended a switch to Kennedy when a Tennessean was running a strong second. Therefore, even though Gore was out of the race for all practical purposes, anti-Kefauver Tennesseans had to continue to support him or allow a switch to Kefauver, which they definitely wished to avoid.

After Tennessee's vote for Gore, Texas continued the Southern parade toward Kennedy by switching its 56 votes from Gore to "the fighting Senator who wears the scars of battle, that fearless Senator . . . John Kennedy of Massachusetts." Kennedy's lead had now grown to 505 to 395. At the end of the regular roll call, Kennedy had edged up to 559½, while Kefauver was at 478½.

The clerk began the roll call of states that had passed earlier on the second ballot. Alabama, where party control was more diffuse than elsewhere in the South, still did what it could for Kennedy, giving him 12½ to Kefauver's 6, a dramatic increase over the 1½ Kennedy had received on the first ballot. California split 37½ to 25 for Kefauver, but a greater Kefauver plurality had been expected. Indiana, whose primary Kefauver had won in the spring, gave him 20 of 26, a drop of 2 from the first ballot. North Carolina split 17½ to 9½ for Kennedy. At this point all states had been recorded on the second ballot, and Kennedy led Kefauver, 618 to 551½. The magic number was 687, and Kennedy was only 69 votes away from the nomination. Acting Chairman Senator Warren G. Magnuson then recognized Kentucky, which switched its 30 votes from Gore to Kennedy, now only 39 votes short of a majority.

What happened then has been the subject of much discussion and controversy and has never been cleared up to the satisfaction of political observers. Sam Rayburn, permanent chairman of the convention, suddenly appeared and, claiming the gavel from Magnuson, proceeded to recognize Tennessee. Senator Gore was given unanimous consent to make a statement, in which he requested "that my name be withdrawn in favor of my colleague, Senator Estes Kefauver." [15] Overjoyed Kefauver supporters almost brought down the roof in the bedlam that followed Gore's announcement. The decision to withdraw had not been easy for Gore; anti-Kefauver leaders had encouraged him to hold out for a deadlock on the third ballot that might turn the convention to him after all. But Gore had finally bowed to constant pressure from Tennessee's National Committee-woman, Martha Ragland, a loyal Kefauver supporter, who warned Gore that he would be responsible for Kefauver's defeat if he did not immediately withdraw in Kefauver's favor. Gore was also influenced by several Kefauver supporters in the Tennessee delegation, as well as by well-to-do Tennesseans attending the convention who warned Gore that, if he continued to block Kefauver's vice-presidential bid, they would pull out all the stops to ensure Gore's defeat for re-election in 1958.[16] Governor Clement, himself torn between a desire to wreck Kefauver's vice-presidential ambitions and fear of home-state reaction to stabbing Kefauver in the back, was visibly upset when Gore came on the convention floor to tell Clement that he would withdraw and endorse Kefauver. "Oh, no, not Estes," Clement exclaimed.[17]

The great mystery, however, was not why Gore bowed out but why Rayburn stepped in at a crucial point in the balloting and made key decisions that ensured a Kefauver victory. It was not only Rayburn's recognition of Gore that stopped the Kennedy bandwagon and raised eyebrows around the hall among those who knew of Rayburn's intense dislike for Kefauver. It was also the order in which he extended recognition to state delegations in the wake of Gore's withdrawal. After Tennessee, Rayburn recognized Oklahoma, which switched its 28 votes to Kefauver. Then, Minnesota, which gave Kefauver all 30 of its votes. Then, Tennessee again, switching its 32 votes to Kefauver as it had not done at the time of Gore's withdrawal. Then, Missouri, giving Kefauver 37 of its 38 votes. At this point, Kefauver took the lead over Kennedy, 662 to 645½. But Rayburn was not through. Michigan was allowed to add 4 to Kefauver's total, South Carolina 3 to Kennedy's, the Florida ½ to Kefauver's, Illinois 5 to Kennedy's, but then Pennsylvania, Colorado, Iowa, and the District of Columbia enough to put Kefauver over the top. The final vote, after subsequent switches, gave Kefauver 755½ to Kennedy's 589.[18]

There was much speculation about whether Rayburn knew what he was doing or whether he had been misled by false rumors that Tennessee was switching to Kennedy. Or whether Rayburn's faithful lieutenant, John McCormack, bitter over Kennedy's takeover of the party machinery in Massachusetts, had arranged the series of recognitions which stopped his Massachusetts rival.

Those who found it difficult to believe that Rayburn had lost control of the convention will search in vain for any indication that Rayburn was not totally committed to blocking Kefauver. The Speaker had reportedly told the Texas delegation that "I don't care what the rest of you do, but I'm voting for Kennedy." [19] Both Congressman Wright Patman and former Texas Senator Tom Connally later expressed their disgust over Rayburn's and Johnson's attempt to beat the Texas delegation into line for Kennedy. A week after the convention, Patman wrote Stevenson:

> . . . when it was apparent that the race was between Kennedy and Kefauver . . . very much to my surprise, Speaker Rayburn and Senator Johnson were for Kennedy. This I could not understand because Kennedy was supporting the Eisenhower farm program, and it looked ridiculous to me to think about putting him on the ticket as Vice-President when the farm program would be one of the principal issues. So I again suggested Senator Kefauver's name. Senator Kefauver received 12 votes, which was large considering the opposition, but under the unit rule, we lost the 12 votes because Texas was obligated to vote as a unit.[20]

Connally's reaction to Rayburn's and Johnson's opposition to Kefauver and support of Kennedy was summed up by his comment that "Once again the Democratic Party has saved the nation from Texas." [21]

Kennedy biographer James MacGregor Burns later claimed

that Kennedy had reached his peak with the Kentucky vote and that there was no state from which Kennedy could have won more than a handful of delegates to go with his total at that point. There is evidence to the contrary, however.[22] Having Kennedy think that Texas did all it could for him would have been useful to a Lyndon Johnson hoping to put together a Johnson-Kennedy ticket in 1960. Perhaps Rayburn and Johnson had arranged it so that they would have the best of both Kennedy and Kefauver—Kefauver on the ticket, helping to win the farm vote, but Kennedy grateful for what he thought was an all-out effort on his behalf by Johnson's Texas.

The switch of the South to Kennedy became the talk of the convention. It seemed to defy all logic that the most fundamentalist Protestant area of the country would fall into line behind a New England Roman Catholic and reject fellow Southerner and Baptist Kefauver. The South's dislike for Kefauver was so intense that Southerners were willing to take anyone who had a chance to beat Kefauver. In addition, Southern leaders mistakenly thought of Kennedy as the protégé of Majority Leader John McCormack and former Governor Paul Dever of Massachusetts, who had worked successfully with the South against a liberal civil rights plank.[23]

The religious issue cut both ways. Although the Kennedy forces had unashamedly made much use of the Bailey Report (named for John Bailey, Democratic chairman in Connecticut) showing that the Catholic vote was essential to a Democratic victory and suggesting that it could best be rallied behind the Democratic ticket by putting a Catholic vice-presidential nominee on it, many Catholics, remembering the bitter campaign waged against Catholic Al Smith in 1928, were strongly opposed to the idea of taking a chance on stirring up religious prejudice once again. A Missouri delegate later recalled:

Kennedy had a lot of support in the Missouri delegation and he lost it not because of the Protestants but because of the Catholics. There were, I believe, eleven Catholics on the delegation and I believe that, to a man, they were not only against a Catholic getting the nomination, but violently against it. I have never seen such determined opposition in my life.[24]

Governor David Lawrence of Pennsylvania was perhaps the most important of the Catholic leaders of the party frightened by the prospect of a replay of 1928.

The issue that cost Kennedy the support of almost the entire West and Midwest was his stand on farm price supports. On April 11, Kennedy had been one of only four Democrats in the Senate voting against the Agriculture Act of 1956, which provided for 90 per cent mandatory price supports on basic crops.[25] Kefauver, on the other hand, had consistently advocated even higher price supports, especially for lower income farmers. Since falling farm prices were Western and Midwestern Democrats' biggest issue against the Eisenhower Administration, they would hardly be enthusiastic about putting an opponent of high supports on the national ticket. North Dakota's Quentin Burdick, who would be elected to the Senate in 1960, remembered Bobby Kennedy pleading with the North Dakota delegation for support for his brother during the chaotic second ballot:

> It didn't do any good. Jack had voted for sliding-scale supports and they don't like sliding-scale supports in our country. He stood there trying to explain his brother's voting position but we said we were sorry and the delegation wouldn't listen to him. . . .[26]

It was not only the farm issue that gave Kefauver an edge over Kennedy with many delegates. The very suddenness of the open contest for the vice-presidential nomination had prevented the careful, behind-the-scenes organization that had defeated Kefauver in 1952. Those who were his natural enemies in the party were at their best when they had time to deal privately and line up support systematically; during the vice-presidential contest, however, they were disorganized and lacked the time and facilities to co-ordinate a concerted drive against Kefauver. Events moved so fast that delegates had considerably more freedom from direction than is normal at a convention. This freedom worked to Kefauver's benefit, since he had been cultivating political contacts across the country for years. A vote for Kefauver at the 1956 convention seemed a small enough repayment for the personal attention Kefauver had given party workers during his many tours on behalf of the party's candidates in 1952 and 1954 and on his own behalf in 1952 and 1956. Kefauver had made a career of building personal ties with these party workers, and, while Kefauver's attentions to senators, governors, and party chairmen might not differ significantly from that accorded them by other figures in the party, the attention Kefauver showered on lower-level officials and party workers made him seem uniquely appreciative of them as individuals. Bobby Kennedy ran into this personal attachment to Kefauver time and again as he scoured delegations looking for support for his brother:

> It really struck me that it wasn't the issues which matter. It was the friendships. So many people said to me they would rather vote for Jack, but that they were going to vote for Estes Kefauver because he had sent them a card or gone to their home. I said right there that we should forget the issues and send Christmas cards and go to their homes next time.[27]

It was not without reason that the *New York Times* called Kefauver's victory "one for the rank-and-file delegates, achieved over the last-ditch opposition of most of the party's old-time professionals." [28] The coalition that put Kefauver across was, indeed, made up of the most idealistic and genuinely liberal elements in the party—those forces that truly represented the Democratic tradition. Opposing Kefauver were the worst elements in the party—the urban bosses and the reactionary South. In the ten Southern states outside Tennessee (whose vote for Kefauver was reluctant, to say the least), Kennedy received 249½ votes to Kefauver's 39 (23½ of which came from Florida, whose presidential primary and more liberal population made it clearly an atypical Southern state). Kennedy had the dubious distinction of having the unanimous support of the reactionary, racist delegations from South Carolina, Mississippi, Georgia, Louisiana, and Virginia. Kennedy also had the support of the Chicago machine of Mayor Richard Daley, who controlled Illinois, as well as the support of the infamous machines in New York City and New Jersey. It was also a commentary on Kennedy's support that the only state west of the Mississippi River, other than the Southern states of Texas and Arkansas, to give over half its vote to Kennedy on the second ballot was the gambling haven of Nevada. In Kennedy's defense it might be said, as one Deep South Democratic chairman did, in fact, say, that Southern support for Kennedy was based on a desire "to stop Kefauver and Kennedy seemed the most likely man to do it." [29] It was fortunate for Kennedy that he had a solid basis for rationalizing the kind of support he received at the 1956 convention; otherwise, he would have had great difficulty in assuming the liberal mantle in 1960 that was so much a part of the image he sought to project when seeking the Democratic presidential nomination.

Whether Stevenson was pleased with Kefauver's selection was never known; he was reported to have indicated initial displeasure, but two years later he insisted that "I expressed no preference and had none." Immediately after Kefauver's nomination, Stevenson told the press:

> what has occurred this afternoon is clear evidence of the great vitality and virility of the Democratic party.
> I am happy that Senator Estes Kefauver is to be my running mate. I know how formidable a candidate he will be, because I ran against him in several primaries. He is an old friend and an able leader. I welcome him on the ticket. [30]

Kefauver's victory on the second ballot marked his greatest triumph on the national political scene, and the conditions under which he won—fighting the traditional enemy, the bosses, as well as the most reactionary elements in the party—made his success all the more meaningful and certainly in the Kefauver tradition. Whatever Kefauver's nomination may have meant to the average delegate, it had a special, almost religious, significance to Kefauver's dedicated supporters in Tennessee and around the country. One of their most cherished memories of Kefauver would always be his dramatic entrance onto the convention platform immediately after his come-from-behind victory over Kennedy. The cheers began even before the candidate himself appeared, when the band struck up the melancholy "Tennessee Waltz," which had become widely associated with him during the 1952 campaign for the nomination. Then the candidate himself appeared, with Nancy by his side, and, as the roar of the crowd drowned out the band, Estes and Nancy silently acknowledged the outpouring of genuine affection and respect for a man whom not all delegates had supported but whom they recognized as having achieved a supreme personal triumph. To Kefauver loyalists the scene suggested the final triumph of good over evil, one of the few times in his career that Kefauver's integrity and determination were fully appreciated by the public he had served so well. It was a brief moment of illusion, but for many it would be sufficient to permanently endear Kefauver to them for the rest of his career.[31]

The convention concluded that evening, and, even with speeches by Truman, Kefauver, and Stevenson, the few remaining hours seemed anticlimatic. Kefauver's own brief acceptance speech was devoted principally to contrasting his view of the Vice-Presidency with what he felt Nixon had made it, and pledging, to the enthusiastic applause of the convention, not to imitate the Republican Vice-President by becoming "a political sharpshooter," providing "the smear under the protection of the President's smile," or sowing "the seeds of division and distrust." [32]

The convention thus ended on a harmonious note, as all the elements that had struggled for power united behind the Stevenson-Kefauver ticket and at least superficially patched up their differences in order to work for victory in November. Kefauver's prestige in the party, of course, had never been higher, and, as tired as he had been after the long drive for the presidential nomination, he seemed to look forward eagerly to the campaign ahead.

chapter xvi

THE CAMPAIGN WITH
STEVENSON, 1956

The 1956 election presented Kefauver, as the Democratic candidate for Vice-President, with an awesome challenge as well as a unique opportunity. He faced the voters with a prestige unusual for a vice-presidential nominee—not only had he been considered of presidential caliber for so long that even those strongly opposed to his political advancement had unconsciously come to regard him as one of the three or four most available men in the party, but his selection by the Democratic delegates, rather than by Stevenson himself, gave him a special standing as heir to the nomination that past running mates, placed on the ticket to achieve ideological or geographical balance, could never claim. Kefauver's very nomination for the Vice-Presidency was also psychologically important in giving his career the appearance of momentum—from crusader against bossism in 1948, to able young senator directing the crime investigation of 1950–51, followed by an incredibly successful grass roots drive for the nomination in 1952, a smashing re-election in 1954, a campaign for the nomination in 1956 that came close to overturning the overwhelming choice of the professionals, and, finally, his selection by an uncontrolled convention for second place on the national ticket. Thus, the opportunity—to participate at last in a national campaign as a spokesman of the party—and the challenge—to wage such an impressive and effective campaign personally that, even if the 1956 election were lost, Democrats would look to him for leadership in 1960, when the Twenty-second Amendment would retire the popular Eisenhower and Stevenson would be permanently labeled as a loser.

In spite of the advantages Kefauver took into the 1956 campaign, he was, on the whole, unsuccessful in making the most of them. Whether his unimpressive performance on the campaign trail was primarily the result of the secondary role to which he was relegated by Stevenson's advisers or due more to his own personal limitations, the fact remained that his 1956 campaign, while more than adequate as vice-presidential campaigns go, did little to enhance his presidential appeal to either the rank and file or the professionals.

Stevenson's advisers were at least partially responsible for Kefauver's failure to increase significantly his personal political influence during the campaign. They could never forgive or forget the bitterness of the primary campaigns, and, while they were grateful enough for Kefauver's help in the two weeks before the convention, there was little attempt to achieve real unity between the former Kefauver supporters and the Stevenson stalwarts.

Signs of strain in the relations between the Kefauver and Stevenson retinues, superficially united behind Stevenson after August 1, had not been long in coming. Even before his nomination for Vice-President, Kefauver had been disturbed over the extent to which his former supporters, most of whom followed his lead and began working for Stevenson, had been ignored by the professionals running Stevenson's campaign. The day after his nomination, he called on the regular Democratic organizations to take in his workers and stressed that "all my people want to cooperate, but in some states there has not been much cooperation with them." [1] The situation did not improve significantly throughout the campaign, and Kefauver himself was assigned to areas where the Stevenson brain trust thought he would prove least troublesome. Kefauver's role in the campaign, therefore, was ironic in the sense that he was not even given equal billing with Nixon, whose re-nomination by the Republican bosses was supposed to stand in such unfavorable contrast to the selection of Kefauver by the free choice of the Democratic delegates.

After Kefauver's plea for unity the morning after his nomination in Chicago, he flew to Nashville, where he was given a hero's welcome before almost immediately leaving the capital for a vacation on the farm of a friend in McMinnville. Three days later he emerged to be greeted by thousands of supporters in Chattanooga, Madisonville, Knoxville, and Gatlinburg. His stopover in Madisonville included a visit with his father, who had been too ill to follow his son's convention victory on TV; members of the family had gone next door to watch.[2]

From Gatlinburg, Estes and Nancy went to Blowing Rock, North Carolina, for what they hoped would be an extended rest before the grueling campaign ahead. However, the vacation was cut short after less than a week when Stevenson issued a call for the Democratic high command to meet with him at Libertyville to plan the campaign. Due to the scheduling of the Democratic convention in mid-August, there was less time than usual between the convention and the election in November. The campaign was officially kicked off on September 13, three days after the Maine elections, in which Democrats had made one of their strongest showings since the Civil War and had thereby given Democrats around the country renewed hope that the national ticket would also prove victorious.[3]

At least it can be said of Kefauver's vice-presidential campaign that he was allowed to concentrate on what he was known to do best—symbolizing the Democratic party's interest in the little man and carrying the Democratic message to his natural constituents in the Midwest (where he made Eisenhower's farm program the principal issue) and the West (where, in addition to the farm issue, his long association with public power insured a favorable reception).[4]

Kefauver's rhetoric on the campaign trail was reminiscent of the old agrarian populists, and, while attacks on Wall Street were popular in the rural West and Midwest, especially in a period of depressed farm prices, such attacks had the effect of casting Kefauver as somewhat of a radical outside farm country and creating the false impression that his grasp of economic matters was rather unsophisticated.

In rural areas, Kefauver ran more against Eisenhower's Secretary of Agriculture Ezra Taft Benson than against Eisenhower, whom Kefauver admitted was:

an honest, good man, a popular man.

But the point in this campaign is not whether he is an honest and good man, the question is whether his politics are what he promised the American people. The answer must be no.

The other question is whether his policies have been in the public interest. The answer is no.[5]

In Mitchell, South Dakota, Kefauver recalled:

All through 1953 and 1954 and 1955, President Eisenhower cheerfully watched Ezra Taft Benson slide farmers deeper and deeper in debt. He struck right by him and cheered him on. The economic disaster that fastened itself upon our farm families left President Eisenhower unshaken in his determination to keep his back turned against his own campaign promises.[6]

Kefauver also recalled that Eisenhower had accepted in principle the idea of 100 per cent of parity for farmers during the 1952 campaign, although the President had hedged by stipulating that farm supports should minimize government controls and protect the farmers' independence. But Administration policies had not led to farmers' receiving a "fair price" for their crops, and, Kefauver warned at Anderson, Indiana, they never would, because:

the food processors and meat packers and grain traders and big bankers and miscellaneous other millionaires who are running the Department of Agriculture under this Republican Administration . . . are going to be on guard as always to see that this kind of accident won't happen.[7]

In Milwaukee, Kefauver charged that farm income was down 27 per cent below 1952 levels, while General Motors' profits were up 113 per cent and United States Steel's up 158 per cent. The farmers' share of the food dollar was down 18 per cent, while farm mortgage debt had increased $2.4 billion in the last year—the largest increase since 1923.[8]

Kefauver's role as the champion of the lower-income farmer was not a tactic for the fall campaign. He had been attacking Eisenhower's farm policies for years and had become recognized as the farmers' best friend among the likely contenders for 1956. Throughout his primary campaigns, he had stressed that "if this outfit [the Eisenhower Administration] stays in power any longer, more and more of this country will belong to fewer and fewer people. . . . The farmer has taken it on the chin in these last three years, and the situation cannot be tolerated any longer." [9]

Kefauver's popularity in the rural Midwest was well known and, of course, had been one of the reasons Western and Midwestern Democratic delegates had supported him so strongly at the convention. A poll published in June 1956, by *Wallaces' Farmer and Iowa Homestead,* with a circulation throughout Iowa and some adjoining counties of other states, showed Kefauver leading Eisenhower, 51 per cent to 36 per cent, while the President led Stevenson, 49 per cent to 37 per cent. Similarly, a poll taken the previous fall by the *Rapid City Daily Journal* showed Kefauver to be the overwhelming favorite of South Dakota Democrats, with the support of 49 per cent, to Stevenson's 28 per cent and Harriman's 16 per cent.[10]

On June 23, Kefauver's strength in the Midwest was dramatically illustrated when he and Benson debated in Eldora, Iowa, with Kefauver the clear winner. The crowd of five thousand interrupted Kefauver with applause fourteen times and booed the Agriculture Secretary during his defense of the Eisenhower farm program. After Kefauver's nomination for vice-president, therefore, it was not surprising that the Democratic National Committee was swamped with requests for Kefauver to campaign in the farm belt. His value to the ticket there was indicated by an informal poll conducted by a *Newsweek* reporter in Iowa County, Wisconsin, which showed that over half of those who voted for Eisenhower in 1952 but were switching to Stevenson in 1956 cited Kefauver's presence on the Democratic ticket as the reason.[11]

Kefauver advocated exactly what the hard-pressed farmers wanted to hear—full parity for low-income farmers, government loans to farmers at low interest rates, expansion of the Rural Electrification Administration, and a food stamp plan which would distribute the farm surplus to the poor. Kefauver was against government support to agriculture that did not stress the objective of preserving "the small family farm rather than the big corporate type farm, absentee owned and absentee controlled." Thus, he supported 100 per cent of parity for farms earning less than a set dollar income if they were both owned and operated by the family living on them. He urged the establishment of a graduated scale of supports, with government subsidy declining as the absolute income of the farm increased.[12]

It was not only the plight of the farmer that Kefauver blamed on the special interests' control of the Republican party. Lower and middle income groups all over the country were seen as being exploited by the "readers of the *Wall Street Journal*" who were running the country. He saw it as no accident that the Eisenhower Administration, which "cut outlays to fight monopoly 16 percent below Democratic levels," was also an administration whose original cabinet contained "nine millionaires, including the president of General Motors, two big GM auto dealers, two Wall Street corporation lawyers, a bank treasurer, and two officials of corporations with assets of over $100 million." While the take-home pay of workers was going up 8 per cent, stockholder income was up 24 per cent, and "ninety-one cents of every dollar in tax cut went to the upper income families and to the corporations . . . only nine cents went to the rest of us." [13]

In the Pacific Northwest, Kefauver continually attacked the Dixon-Yates proposal as "one of the most rotten deals in all American history," and scored the Republican concept of private development of natural resources in "partnership" with government. "Despite four years of oratory about this program, the Republicans have not launched a single new Federal power project," Kefauver charged at Missoula, Montana.[14]

Although early in the campaign, Kefauver attacked Eisenhower personally for being "right down there with the rest of the boys as an aggressive fighter for the special interests" and urged that the real job of the Democrats would be "to explode the Eisenhower fiction, to confound the myth men, to tell the truth," Democratic strategy eventually placed more emphasis on Vice-President Nixon's role as, in Kefauver's words, "the darling of every reactionary in the Republican party," who was hiding behind the naïve Eisenhower and biding his time until Eisenhower's death in office or retirement in 1960 would bring Nixon to power. Eisenhower, while meaning well, had:

> exchanged a place of honor in history for a secondary role in politics, the role of a front man for Richard Nixon; he surrendered politically to reactionary Republicans and failed utterly, abjectly and miserably to do what he professed to set out to do four years ago, and must be feeling disillusionment in his secret heart.
>
> . . . Instead of being the President of all Americans, he gave us a government dominated by big business and the narrowest of special interests. And instead of liberalizing the Republican party, he submitted to the reactionary old guard.[15]

Kefauver was skeptical about the "new Nixon," who had supposedly evolved from the smear artist that had bedeviled liberals and Democrats for ten years. If the change in Nixon were sincere, Kefauver joked:

I want to say that I am delighted to hear about this new Nixon. I think we will all be glad to welcome him back to the company of civilized men, of men who believe that it is possible in this great democracy of ours to differ politically without assassinating each other and to campaign against each other without the necessity of impugning the motives, the patriotism, the decency and loyalty of our opponents or of the leaders of the other political party.[16]

Democrats hoped that voters' fears of Nixon as Eisenhower's successor would be one of their biggest issues in 1956 and would give them an indirect way of raising the issue of Eisenhower's health. Although Eisenhower had announced in February that he would seek a second term with his doctors' blessing, a major operation in June had put Eisenhower back in the hospital and had raised new fears that, however willing the President might be to seek re-election, his health would not hold up through another four years. The Democrats, therefore, sought to picture the choice as one between Stevenson and Nixon. "He [Nixon]—and not Eisenhower—is the man of the future in the Republican party," Kefauver warned:

Remember that Eisenhower cannot, under the Constitution, run for re-election if he should be re-elected. It is Nixon who will therefore be the real power in a new Eisenhower-Nixon Administration. It is Nixon with whom the Republican politicians will mend their fences and make their alliances. It will be Nixon who will call the signals and run the country.[17]

Once it became established that Eisenhower would definitely seek a second term, and voters were given a first-hand look at what appeared to be a healthy President, the Stevenson-Kefauver ticket's prospects for victory began to fade. The general prosperity of the country and the settlement of the war in Korea gave the Republicans an unbeatable combination of issues. In spite of the Republican emphasis on the peace issue, it was, ironically, the threat of a new war that damaged Democratic prospects at the same time that Stevenson and Kefauver were arguing that the quiet world situation was deceptive and that the Eisenhower Administration was following foreign policies that would be disastrous over the long run. In September, a Roper poll showed that the Eisenhower-Nixon ticket had only a slim 43 per cent to 37 per cent lead over Stevenson and Kefauver; a month later, the gap had widened to 50 per cent to 35 per cent. The reason, of course, was American concern over the unrest in the satellite countries which finally led to the Hungarian uprising, which, in turn, provoked the bloody Soviet occupation of the country. In addition, the attack on Egypt by the Israelis, acting with the support and cooperation of Britain and France, added to the feeling of apprehension and uncertainty among the American people and reinforced the idea that the country could not afford a change in such unstable times and, least of all, lose the service of a President who seemed to be so uniquely fitted to handle what might develop into a military crisis affecting the national security of the United States. The movement toward Eisenhower as a result of Hungary and Suez was so pronounced that the Gallup poll showed that the Republican lead on the question of which party could best keep the United States out of war had jumped from 26 per cent to 18 per cent (July 1954) to 42 per cent to 17 per cent (October 1956).[18]

The instability in Europe and the Middle East also made the Democratic emphasis on encouraging better relations with the Russians seem impractical. One of the fresh foreign policy initiatives attempted by Stevenson in the campaign had been his call for negotiations with the Russians on curbing nuclear testing, a proposal the Republican party, alert to evidence to document its stock charge that the Democrats were soft on communism, was quick to attack. While Stevenson and Kefauver simply advocated discussing the proposal with the Russians, Republicans attempted to picture Stevenson's suggestion as a call for unilateral disarmament. Kefauver sought unsuccessfully to limit the debate to Stevenson's original suggestion and argued:

While I do not have any great trust in the leaders of the Soviet Union and I do not like them, I feel that if there is real opportunity of taking a forward step that's going to lead to something better than an increase in the rate of detonation of hydrogen bombs, if there is a real chance to take steps that lead to peace in the world, I personally would sit down and talk to anybody, Mr. Bulganin or Mr. Khrushchev or whoever it may be. Certainly Mr. Eisenhower has had no hesitancy in writing letters to Mr. Bulganin.[19]

The Soviet move against Hungary which followed days later made Stevenson's nuclear test halt suggestion look naïve and was seen as a real blow to his election hopes. The Hungarian uprising and America's lack of significant aid to the rebels would have been a made-to-order issue for a Republican party out of power. As it was, the Democrats, who had argued against a hardline foreign policy that might lead to nuclear war, could scarcely call for intervention. The Democrats did attempt to exploit the Hungarian situation to the extent of pointing out that the efforts of the Nationalities Division of the Republican National Committee had raised the expectation of American aid for the people in the satellite countries by proclaiming throughout the campaign that the Republican party "stands firmly with the peoples of these countries in their just quest for freedom." This rhetoric contrasted sharply with the inaction of the Republican President when the Hungarian crisis arose. Kefauver later attacked the Republican party for "recklessly" playing "with the lives of these people for political purposes," and then "failing to take any positive action to aid the uprisings" in Poland and Hungary. However, since Stevenson and Kefauver criticized the Republican effort to foment counterrevolution rather than Republican inaction when it came, the American right found little appeal in the Democratic position.[20]

The political effect in the United States of the crisis in the Middle East, erupting simultaneously with the Hungarian uprising, was somewhat more complicated. Although the United States refusal to endorse the Israeli-British-French attack on

Egypt was hailed by newly emerging nations in Africa and Asia and was, on the whole, a plus for Eisenhower's State Department, Stevenson and Kefauver were provided with a unique opportunity to reap temporary benefits among Jewish voters who were unhappy with the United States' condemnation of Israel, Britain, and France. Kefauver had always been a staunch friend of Israel, so it was easy for him to term it a "sad commentary on our whole handling of the Middle East situation" if the United States sided with Russia and Egypt. In a distorted interpretation of the division between the United States, and Britain and France, Kefauver argued that "The Eisenhower-Nixon-Dulles foreign policy has so destroyed confidence in our Government that today we find ourselves without friends and our counsel disdained by the free powers of the world." Regardless of the merits of the argument that the United States could have prevented the Middle East crisis of 1956, there was little support in the United States for American aid, or even moral support, for the British-French-Israeli aggression against Egypt, and Eisenhower's refusal to condone the invasion was one of his more statesmanlike foreign policy decisions. The average voter interested in peace, therefore, could hardly have been impressed with the Stevenson-Kefauver position on the Middle East. Even Jewish voters acquiesced in the American position once it became obvious that the Israelis needed no American help and could take care of themselves. The Republicans thus came through the nuclear testing issue and the Middle East and Hungarian crises with a reinforced image of advocating peace through strength.[21]

In spite of the Democrats' difficulties with the major issues of the campaign, the opportunity nevertheless remained for Kefauver to broaden his appeal among party professionals, the Democratic rank and file, and the general public, and, therefore, emerge from the campaign with his own political reputation not only intact but actually enhanced. That he failed to do so was not due to any lack of effort on his part. Whatever might be said about its effectiveness, Kefauver's 1956 campaign for the

Vice-Presidency was a personal tour de force. *Time* called it the most vigorous campaign ever waged by a national candidate. In the eight weeks before the election, Kefauver traveled approximately 60,000 miles through 38 states and was estimated to have shaken 100,000 hands and given 450 speeches. By election eve he was so tired that he got the names of his daughter and the family dog mixed up on national TV.[22]

Nancy, who had stayed out of most of the primary campaigns, also tried to stay out of the national campaign as much as possible. "I'm not interested in politics one bit," she said later, "though I do enjoy people, and of course I'm interested in Estes's career. But the pleasure you get out of it is no compensation for what you miss by not being at home." What campaigning she did do she found:

> exciting but physically exhausting. The big problem is trying to live in two places. I was always flying home to keep in touch with a growing family. I never considered myself a politician but called myself a "family backdrop." I think that's the essential quality of a politician's wife.[23]

In spite of the incredible demands he made upon himself, Kefauver's health held up remarkably throughout 1956. His only major problem was a cold and an infected throat in early October that left him so hoarse that he had to cancel his speaking engagements.[24]

Whether Kefauver was effective on the campaign trail is a matter of opinion. Analyzed objectively, he certainly left much to be desired. There is no doubt that his lackluster performances before formal audiences did little to impress the cold-blooded professionals. Even Kefauver's close friends were under no illusions about his shortcomings as a public speaker. Immediately before the 1956 campaign, Edward J. Meeman, editor of the *Memphis Press-Scimitar* and a longtime Kefauver political ally, sent Kefauver aide Richard Wallace a copy of a book on public speaking for Kefauver's use and offered some frank comments on Kefauver's need for improvement:

. . . The fact is that Estes' friends think he should be a better speaker, and work harder at effectiveness in this field. Audiences like him so well, and his personality creates such a good impression, that the fact is often overlooked that the speech is not as good as it should be. . . . Since Estes' career is mostly ahead of him, regardless of the outcome of this election, the sooner he goes to work to be as good a speaker as he is capable of being, the better.[25]

But the orthodox approach to politics was never the foundation of Kefauver's career anyway. His support had been constructed from the bottom up, and it was his success with the average voter—the common man—that made him a political force to be reckoned with.

Kefauver's strength on the campaign trail was analyzed as his ability to leave the hundreds of voters he met and talked with each day with the feeling that they had a close personal friend who needed their help on election day. It was a style that many of Kefauver's critics could not understand and therefore were unable to appreciate. There is no doubt, however, that Kefauver was unusually good at turning a brief personal contact into a lasting commitment for support. More difficult to determine is what the contact meant to Kefauver himself. Even Nancy once remarked that she doubted if her husband was "much interested in individuals," and a fellow senator commented that Kefauver was:

so damned single-minded. He expects you to be interested in the things that interest him. Try to get him stirred up about something that interests you, he can barely hear you.[26]

Certainly most of the voters who met Kefauver along the campaign trails of his career would not have agreed with this analysis. In fact, his ability to communicate easily with people of all educational, social, and economic levels was universally admitted and admired. His sincerity was not always taken for granted, however. Another fellow senator called Kefauver "a political chameleon who is for whatever the man he's talking to is for. Behind that fumbling manner lies one of the best political brains in the country. His political sense is uncanny." [27]

In spite of the fact that Kefauver was so incapable of disliking anyone personally that it was often considered a political weakness, he never allowed himself the informality around other people, even his staff and family, which permitted intimate personal relationships to develop. Even those who were among his best friends in the Senate, Paul Douglas of Illinois and Joseph Clark of Pennsylvania, for example, were never taken into Kefauver's confidence and, like everyone else, thought of him as a "loner." [28]

It was therefore one of the great paradoxes of Kefauver's career—and his life—that the man who was so successful in quickly establishing a somewhat superficial personal tie between himself and a prospective voter should feel so little need for deeper personal relationships with those around whom he lived and worked year after year. There remained an emotional moat around Kefauver, and, as much as Kefauver's family, friends, and supporters came to admire and respect him, there was little feeling of sharing his personal hopes, fears, joys, and frustrations. Nancy herself once remarked, "Even in the family it's hard to tell what Estes is thinking." [29]

Kefauver's campaigns, whether for the Senate in Tennessee or for national office around the country, never showed signs of the obsession with "professionalism" that can usually be interpreted as a manifestation of calculating but cautious ambition. In short, if Kefauver was the scheming, unprincipled politician his most bitter critics accused him of being, his nonchalant attitude toward even the most elementary rules of politics gave no indication of it. Reporters covering Kefauver campaigns invariably wrote of chaotic organization, incredibly inefficient scheduling, and all the other disorder that afflicts a campaign being run with no one really in charge.

While every campaign Kefauver ever conducted was somewhat confused, the 1956 vice-presidential campaign offered maximum opportunity to compound the usual snafus. By October 1, *Time* correspondent Serrell Hillman, traveling with the Kefauver campaign, was writing, "Nothing seems to go right," and he offered example after example of lost suitcases, late campaign appearances, speeches on economic opportunity and full employment to the aged, and farm speeches in industrial centers. Yet, wrote Hillman, "the Kefauver campaign, for all its chartered plane, portable mimeograph and closed-circuit telephone speech, has developed a refreshingly American-primitive quality." [30]

Throughout it all, Kefauver appeared oblivious to the chaos around him and exhibited such placidity before his audiences that he won their hearts and their sympathy in a way a more polished speaker could never have done. Easterners who never understood his appeal in the rural areas were amazed at the ease with which Kefauver violated the most fundamental rules of politics. At one campaign stop, according to an astonished reporter at the scene, Kefauver:

> failed to bring up the name of a local candidate, and with an absence of embarrassment that was absolute he turned and asked simply, "What is Mister McGovern's first name?" Crowds show a smiling, possessive feeling for the big man. Bloopers that would ruin somebody else seem to endear him to other fallible mortals.[31]

It was not strange, therefore, that he was considered something of an eccentric in the sophisticated East and that there was little demand for him in the great urban centers. In fact, on a trip to upstate New York, Kefauver received no support from state Democratic leaders, who could not meet him "because of other commitments." An outcry from Democrats across the country at this snub of Kefauver, including a dig at Governor Harriman by Kefauver aide Howard McGrath that Harriman "must have a vested interest in having this ticket defeated," brought a superficial and temporary reversal by New York Democratic leaders. Even though Harriman sent Kefauver a telegram praising him for the "great campaign for the principles and policies we New York Democrats believe in," the incident still demonstrated not only the lack of enthusiasm for Kefauver among the urban leaders of the East but also the fact that his style and his message were somewhat alien to the Democratic faithful in the big cities.[32]

In spite of vigorous campaigns by both Stevenson and Kefauver, 1956 was not destined to be a Democratic year. Not only the relative satisfaction of the American people with Eisenhower's performance in office but also a 2 to 1 Republican advantage in campaign funds sank Democratic hopes.[33] The election on November 6 resulted in an Eisenhower-Nixon landslide, with the Republican presidential ticket amassing a popular vote margin of 35,585,316 to 26,031,322 and carrying 41 states (with 457 electoral votes) to the Democrats' 7 (and 74 electoral votes). That the victory was more a personal triumph for Eisenhower than for the Republican party was indicated by narrow Democratic majorities in the House and Senate.

After the election, Kefauver phoned Stevenson, telling him he should have no regrets, that he had "conducted a magnificent campaign." Kefauver said his only regret was "that I did not campaign in my home state of Tennessee." [34] The Volunteer State went to Eisenhower by the narrow margin of 462,288 to 456,507, a slight increase in the Republican margin of 446,147 to 443,710 of 1952.

About ten days later, Kefauver wrote Stevenson a consolation letter, saying:

> we were creeping up on them until that panicky stampede to Eisenhower for security from Eisenhower's mistakes. It was ironic, but I suppose not too surprising in view of the incredible state of euphoria and ignorance that they have managed to cultivate.[35]

However, when Kefauver, four years later, analyzed the effect of the foreign situation on the 1956 election, he minimized the influence the Hungarian and Middle East crises had on the election and complained instead that:

> too many Americans . . . were not concerned with foreign affairs. . . . Our veterans . . . were raising families and saving for chil-

dren or catching up in various ways with the years lost in service.
. . . The fact that President Eisenhower had ended the Korean
War and introduced a period of "peace" was sufficient for a
majority of American voters. . . . I doubt if either or both of
these incidents [Hungary or Suez] resulted in any considerable
switch of votes from one to the other party.[36]

Kefauver's contribution to the 1956 Democratic ticket was
a real one. The only states where Democratic percentages increased over 1952 were the farm states of the West and Midwest
where Kefauver had concentrated his campaign. The Democratic
share of the two party vote increased 10 per cent or more in
North Dakota, South Dakota, and Montana, and over 5 per cent
in Iowa, Idaho, Nebraska, Wisconsin, Minnesota, and Colorado
—and these gains came while the Democratic percentage nation-
wide was dropping.[37]

Although it was some time before either Kefauver or his
supporters across the country realized it, the 1956 election
marked the end of Kefauver's career, if not his ambitions, in
presidential politics. There were the obvious reasons—the interest
in fresher faces, such as Humphrey, Kennedy, and Johnson; the
Democratic landslide of 1958, which was to install Democratic
governors in so many important states that an anti-organization
candidate such as Kefauver could no longer come in from outside and hope for victory against a weak, ineffective Democratic
organization, as he had been able to do so many times in
1952 and 1956; the fact that he himself faced a re-election
battle for the Senate from Tennessee in 1960; all these were
to chip away at whatever hopes Kefauver harbored for another try for the nomination. But perhaps the major factor
in undermining Kefauver's future presidential hopes was the
general feeling that he had had an opportunity to demonstrate
the kind of national campaign he could conduct and that it
was simply not impressive enough for Democratic leaders to
believe Kefauver could rally the party for victory in 1960. Even
many of Kefauver's 1952 and 1956 supporters, while maintaining

their respect for Kefauver, began to drift to others being discussed as presidential contenders for 1960.

For the rest of his career, Kefauver would be, first and only, a United States senator. As soon as they realized the presidential campaigns were over forever, those who loved and respected Kefauver and had faith in his potential for public service breathed a sigh of relief that he had given up the exhausting quest for a hopeless goal and awaited the results of Kefauver's attention to the legislative matters that had always attracted him.

chapter xvii

SENATORIAL POLITICS, 1957

Kefauver might very well have expected the prestige he carried as the Democratic party's nominee for Vice-President and the gratitude he had earned among party workers for his physically exhausting national campaign to have dissipated some of the hostility the Democratic leadership in the Senate felt for him. Instead, he was almost immediately subjected to a public humiliation and came close to being the victim of power play which would have drastically curtailed his personal power on the subcommittee which would be his primary concern during the rest of his career.

Most of Kefauver's problems with his Senate elders derived from their feeling that he was using the Senate as a springboard for the White House. He was continually criticized, from 1951 until he definitely ruled himself out of the 1960 race, for devoting too much time and energy to the pursuit of national office and not enough to sharing the dull, routine work of the Senate. Since, after the 1956 election, there was no reason for Kefauver's Democratic Senate colleagues not to assume that he would try again in 1960, the hostility most of them felt toward his presidential ambitions meant that, contrary to seeing him as more of a party stalwart as a result of his campaign with Stevenson, they feared that his place on the 1956 national ticket had made his 1960 prospects brighter. Therefore, they not only continued to throw roadblocks in Kefauver's path but seemed to feel an even greater need to do so than ever before.

Kefauver himself did little to discourage speculation that he still had his eye on the White House. Even during the campaign, he had given cryptic answers to reporters who asked whether he and Nixon were running more for 1960 than 1956. "Not true in my own case; I'm just running in 1956," Kefauver had replied on one occasion; but, he quickly added, that did not "mean my Presidential ambitions are over." The extent to which Kefauver had spent his time on the campaign trail in 1956 seeking to build contacts with Democratic leaders helped to fuel rumors about a 1960 bid. A *New York Times* reporter, reminiscing on the eve of the election about Kefauver's vice-presidential campaign, had seen it as "notable that throughout his campaigning Mr. Kefauver exerted himself to meet the demands on his time and voice of almost every political leader on even the lowest level in the thirty-eight states he visited" and had interpreted Kefauver's behavior as a clear indication that he was laying the groundwork for yet another presidential drive.[1]

Once the election was over, Kefauver did give the stock answers to questions about his presidential ambitions, saying on November 18 that he had "no plans" to try again in 1960. His evasiveness, needless to say, was in sharp contrast to Stevenson's flat announcement that he would not seek the Democratic nomination again.[2]

Once Stevenson removed himself from consideration for 1960, Kefauver became the frontrunner for the nomination. A Gallup poll published in the summer of 1957 showed him enjoying the support of 29 per cent of Democratic voters, followed by Kennedy (23 per cent), Lyndon Johnson (8 per cent), Tennessee Governor Frank Clement (6 per cent). Senator Stuart Symington of Missouri (5 per cent), Humphrey (5 per cent), Michigan Governor G. Mennen Williams (4 per cent), and Maine Governor Edmund Muskie (2 per cent).[3]

Only one of Kefauver's prospective rivals—Majority Leader Lyndon Johnson of Texas—was in a position to undermine Kefauver's prestige and political influence, but he was more than ready and willing to do what he could to block what he feared were Kefauver's 1960 ambitions. Superficially, Kefauver and Johnson had much in common. Both had been elected to the House in the 1930s as staunch supporters of Franklin Roosevelt and had made reputations as Southern progressives regarded as a cut above the average Southern Democrat. Both had been elected to the Senate in the class of 1948, after primary victories over conservative opponents. Once in the Senate, both Kefauver and Johnson had sought to be more than typical Southern Democrats—and both had been notably successful in breaking out of the Southern mold; Kefauver, of course, had won wide support outside the South in his 1952 and 1956 presidential drives (in fact, his problem had been to regain Southern support), and Johnson, as early as 1951, had maneuvered his way into the Senate Democratic leadership, becoming Minority Leader in 1953, and, after the Democrats regained control of the Senate in 1954, Majority Leader. The difference in the two men was that, while Kefauver had elbowed senior senators out of the limelight and irritated them by his success at harvesting maximum publicity from the limited opportunities open to a junior senator, Johnson had cultivated the leadership, especially the powerful Southern committee chairmen, deferring to them, seeking their approval for his every move upward, and being careful to be on the politically safe side of every issue before the Senate. The older senators had rewarded him by backing his leadership ambitions with the same enthusiasm they attempted to torpedo Kefauver's.

The contrast between Johnson and Kefauver was simply that Johnson saw his national constituency as the Senate Democrats, whereas Kefauver's support lay with the Democratic rank and file across the country. In 1953, when Johnson was first chosen as the Senate Democratic leader, the Democratic contingent in the Senate was anything but representative of the national party. Of forty-seven Senate Democrats, thirty-two came from the South, the border states, and the Southwest (in contrast

to thirty from the same states in 1960, out of a total Democratic Senate membership of sixty-six). The problems that Kefauver, who was considered not only too liberal but almost a
traitor to the Southern way of life by most Southern Democrats,
would have with such a geographically unbalanced group of
Senate Democrats is obvious. Johnson, on the other hand, not
only rarely disagreed with the Democratic consensus in the
Senate but enjoyed warm personal relations with powerful
Southern leaders such as Richard Russell of Georgia and Harry
Byrd of Virginia. He could also rely on the influential support
of the Democratic leader in the House, fellow Texan Sam Rayburn, who after 1955 again served as Speaker and worked closely
with Johnson, who by this time was Senate Majority Leader.
The two, who were to dominate Congress until 1961, were an
almost unbeatable combination. Johnson, therefore, was the
complete team player, whereas Kefauver never hesitated to follow his personal judgment even if he isolated himself from a
Senate majority.

Although in Johnson's early years as Democratic leader his
antagonism toward Kefauver was basically a reflection of Southern Democratic dislike of Kefauver, after 1956 the Tennessean
was seen more and more as a threat to Johnson's 1960 presidential ambitions, and the Majority Leader therefore took a personal interest in causing trouble for Kefauver. There was simply
not room for two Southern Democrats in a presidential race, and
Kefauver's more liberal stance made Johnson, by contrast, seem
the candidate of the Dixiecrats, an image that would be fatal in
a Democratic convention where the North, Midwest, and West
were represented in much greater proportion than among Senate
Democrats. In short, there would be little future for Johnson's
presidential ambitions with Kefauver still in contention, and
Kefauver's elimination from the 1960 race became one of Johnson's primary objectives.

One of the first public disagreements between Kefauver and
Johnson after the 1956 election came over the attitude that Senate and House members should adopt toward the newly formed

Democratic Advisory Council, a group of twenty Democratic leaders chosen by the National Committee to debate and discuss, and then to define a Democratic position on, the major national issues. The Council was meant to include not only Stevenson and Kefauver, the party's 1956 nominees, but also the Democratic congressional leadership and representatives from state and local Democratic officeholders and party leaders. The establishment of the Council was pushed by liberals unwilling to let the moderately conservative Democratic congressional leadership, dominated by Rayburn and Johnson, speak for the party during a Republican Administration. Not unexpectedly, neither Johnson nor Rayburn would accept membership on the Council and both let it be known that they would not look favorably on any participation in the Council's activities by members of the Senate or House.[4]

The Democratic Advisory Council was, nevertheless, set up, but Rayburn and Johnson did manage to keep congressional participation to a minimum. Only Kefauver, as the party's 1956 vice-presidential nominee, and Humphrey, as a spokesman for the liberal wing, dared to oppose the Democratic congressional leadership and accept invitations to join. Kefauver, in responding favorably to the initial proposal for a Council, expressed the hope that it might help party leaders "keep in touch with the people at the grass roots"—a goal his own presidential primary campaigns had helped to accomplish.[5]

The Council, which was to function until the inauguration of the Kennedy Administration in 1961, never overcame the antagonism of congressional leaders and, therefore, dealt with national issues without the support or participation of those—the party's leadership in the Congress—who could do most to implement the positions taken by the Council.

In spite of the differences between Kefauver and Johnson over the Democratic Advisory Council—and many other issues as well—Kefauver was never so upset with Johnson that he joined other Democratic liberals seeking to oust Johnson as

Majority Leader or, at least, curb the powers he wielded so effectively. The Americans for Democratic Action were especially unhappy with the Johnson-Rayburn leadership and after the 1956 election called for Johnson to step down as Majority Leader because of his opposition to modification of the filibuster rule. Not only did Kefauver reject the ADA suggestion, but he also backed Johnson in opposing a more realistic move by Paul Douglas and Hubert Humphrey to have the Democratic Congress formulate a Democratic alternative to Eisenhower's program. Johnson was able to win Kefauver's support, as well as that of Massachusetts Senator John Kennedy, partially because Johnson controlled an appointment to the Foreign Relations Committee which both wanted.[6]

The struggle with Kennedy for the Foreign Relations Committee seat ended in one of the most bitter defeats of Kefauver's career. Since the Second World War, a place on the Foreign Relations Committee has been considered especially desirable for a senator who has presidential ambitions because it provides him an opportunity to acquire the expertise in the area of foreign affairs considered essential for a senator hoping to convince professional politicians and voters in general of his qualifications to handle the serious responsibilities of the modern presidency. Kefauver had long requested assignment to the Committee, but until 1956 each new Democratic vacancy went to a veteran senator who could claim seniority over Kefauver. However, by 1956 Kefauver had eight years' seniority himself, and it was just a matter of time until his request would have to be honored. Johnson, who had his own eye on the 1960 Democratic nomination, had no desire to see Kefauver go on a committee that would broaden his experience in foreign affairs and thereby increase his stature as a presidential contender. When a vacancy did open up after the 1956 election, Johnson moved to block what Kefauver expected would be his routine assignment to the Committee. There were other applicants for the vacancy, the most interested of whom was John Kennedy, but Kefauver had four years' seniority over Kennedy and, in fact, had had his application for the Foreign Relations assignment pending longer than Kennedy had been in the Senate.

It came as a great shock, therefore, when it was announced that the Democratic Steering Committee, headed by Johnson, had given the seat to Kennedy. Johnson's blatant favoritism to Kennedy was analyzed in Washington as an attempt to build a political alliance with Kennedy and lay the groundwork for a Johnson-Kennedy ticket in 1960.[7]

Whatever the real reason, it was necessary for the Democratic leadership to offer some logical defense of its snub of Kefauver, and one of the most frequently advanced rationalizations was that the Foreign Relations Committee needed a geographical balance which Kennedy, as a New Englander, could help give it. Congressional Quarterly scoffed at this explanation, pointing out that Foreign Relations had only three Southern Democrats, while Judiciary had five, Finance four, and Armed Services and Agriculture and Forestry six each. The Interior Committee was even more unbalanced, with Colorado the easternmost state represented![8]

Another argument used to defend Kennedy's selection was Johnson's announced policy of giving every senator at least one of his choices of a major committee before any other senator could claim seniority in requesting committee assignments. Kefauver, in an angry letter to Johnson after Kennedy's assignment was announced, rejected that explanation. "Frankly, Lyndon," he wrote, "this looks like a rule that was specifically made for me, and has not been applied to others." Kefauver then pointed out recent examples when Johnson did not apply the rule either to Russell Long or to Johnson himself. Kefauver recalled his consistent support of Johnson as Democratic leader and complained, "Notwithstanding all of this, I have been turned aside on every request for Committees that I have made since you became the Democratic leader." Kefauver then detailed the requests and cited the subsequent denial of each of them. "I want to refresh your memory about these," Kefauver continued, "to show how keenly I feel that I have been discriminated against and so there can be no misunderstanding about it when vacancies come up in the future." Kefauver then turned to what was the privately discussed reason for Kennedy's selection:

> . . . I know that rumors like this are probably not entitled to be given any credence, but there has been one around that you and others do not want me to have any build-up that might enable me to seek a National office in 1960. If this is in anybody's mind, I want to set the record straight that I am not and have no plans to be a candidate for any National office in 1960. My only plan is to remain in the United States Senate.[9]

Johnson, without the slightest hint of defensiveness, replied the next day to Kefauver's letter. The Majority Leader stressed that "in addition to seniority, the Steering Committee takes into account geography, political philosophy, the current status of a member desiring a change, and sometimes the estimate of a man's own colleagues toward him." Johnson pointed out that this was the first time it had been possible to accommodate Kennedy with a committee of his own choice, while Kefauver was the second ranking Democrat on Judiciary and fourth on Armed Services.[10]

Kefauver was so upset over the matter that he toyed with the idea of making an issue of it on the Senate floor; he went so far as to prepare some remarks but, after cooling off, decided against delivering them. In the statement, which went into his files rather than the *Congressional Record,* Kefauver emphasized that he felt no ill will toward Kennedy:

> But . . . it is important that the record clearly show that I was an applicant for this post. . . . I think it important for the record to show that I was not asked to waive my application for any other applicant. Therefore, the seniority rule did not enter into this decision.

Kefauver continued by recalling his long opposition to the seniority system, and detailed the criticisms and suggested re-

forms he had outlined in *A Twentieth Century Congress* ten
years before:

> However, up until today I thought that despite my criticism,
> seniority was the rule under which we were playing. I am making
> these comments merely to note that for committee assignments,
> seniority obviously is not a determining factor. And I make these
> comments not to complain, but to be certain that the record shows
> facts in order that the precedents may be clearly known, that this
> new situation does exist.[11]

In addition to Kefauver's problems with the Foreign Rela-
tions assignment, he also ran into unexpected trouble on the
Judiciary Committee. His problem there had its roots in the
death, on February 28, 1956, of West Virginia Senator Harley
Kilgore, who had been chairman of both the Antitrust and
Monopoly Subcommittee and the parent Judiciary Committee.
At Kilgore's death, Mississippi's reactionary Senator Jim East-
land, ranking Democrat on the full committee, took over as
Judiciary Committee chairman, and it was assumed that Kefau-
ver, as ranking Democrat on the subcommittee, would become
Antitrust and Monopoly chairman. However, at the time, Kefauver was busily engaged in the primary campaigns against
Stevenson and, unwilling to hamstring the subcommittee, agreed
that Wyoming Senator Joseph O'Mahoney would become Acting
Chairman until Kefauver could return his full attention to his
Senate duties. O'Mahoney had served in the Senate for years
before his defeat for re-election in 1952 cost him his seniority;
he had returned to the Senate by winning Wyoming's other seat
in 1954. Having been out of the Senate only two years, he was
psychologically a senior senator even though he was now practically at the bottom of the seniority list. The temporary chairmanship of Antitrust and Monopoly was almost his only opportunity to exercise prerogatives like those he had lost in
1952, and he, therefore, became more attached to the chairmanship than Kefauver was aware. Congress adjourned four days
before Kefauver withdrew as a presidential candidate, so the

issue of Kefauver's return as chairman of Antitrust and Monopoly did not arise until he took steps after the election to assume the chairmanship, only to find that O'Mahoney was reluctant to relinquish it, arguing, in effect, that Kefauver had waived his seniority. Kefauver immediately wrote Eastland to make it absolutely clear that he intended to be named subcommittee chairman and would not settle for any other arrangement. Acknowledging that O'Mahoney had been in charge of "hearings and some other matters which are of importance," Kefauver expressed his desire that O'Mahoney "carry these on as he has before and finish the hearings and report on these matters, but I shall of course insist upon my rights." [12]

Eastland, who would have preferred anyone in the Antitrust and Monopoly chairmanship to Kefauver, suggested that responsibility for the subcommittee be divided between Kefauver and O'Mahoney. Kefauver wrote the Chairman again, rejecting the suggestion and stating flatly:

> such a division would not be satisfactory since I have the required seniority both on the Subcommittee and the full Committee, as well as a long history of personal interest and work in this field, in both the House and Senate, I can see no reason why the principle of seniority should not be followed in this matter. . . . I shall, therefore, expect to be named chairman of the Subcommittee on Antitrust and Monopoly Legislation.[13]

Finally, the matter was resolved in Kefauver's favor. Since Eastland's own succession to the Judiciary Committee chairmanship had come under attack by liberals in both parties because of his unyielding opposition to civil rights legislation, it may be that the Mississippian did not care to do battle over a subcommittee chairmanship that required him to argue against the seniority rule that was his own greatest protection. In any event, O'Mahoney's Senate career was to run until 1961, which meant that, had Kefauver lost the fight to be named sole Antitrust and Monopoly Subcommittee chairman, he would have had only two years (1961–63) to direct the activities of the subcommittee, instead of the six years he was able to devote to its leadership as a result of becoming chairman in 1957. Since Kefauver's performance as subcommittee chairman was his single most important public service, the fight over the chairmanship in early 1957 might have had dramatic implications not only for Kefauver personally but also for his crusade against the concentration of economic power in the United States.

The Foreign Relations defeat and the threatened loss of the Antitrust and Monopoly chairmanship in early 1957 raised serious questions about the extent to which Kefauver's poor relations with the hierarchy of the Senate affected his effectiveness as a senator. The argument that Kefauver was not able, because of the antagonism important senators felt for him, to defend Tennessee's interests adequately was a standard campaign theme stressed in 1954 and 1960 by Kefauver's Tennessee opponents. There might have been much validity to the argument had not the Democratic membership of the Senate changed drastically after 1954, and especially after 1958, when more and more Democrats entered the Senate who were either former supporters of Kefauver or liberals who shared his concerns to the point of seeing him as a pillar of integrity against the old Republican-Dixiecrat coalition they had heard about so long and were determined to fight to a standstill. In addition to Paul Douglas of Illinois, Hubert Humphrey of Minnesota, and Wayne Morse of Oregon, who had been his closest allies since 1948, Kefauver was joined after 1954 by many other good friends and supporters, such as Richard Neuberger of Oregon (1954— and his wife Maurine, who succeeded him in 1960), Pat McNamara of Michigan (1954), Joseph Clark of Pennsylvania (1956), John Carroll of Colorado (1956), Frank Church of Idaho (1956), Ralph Yarborough of Texas (1957—the first liberal Southern Democrat besides Kefauver since Claude Pepper of Florida and Frank Graham of North Carolina were defeated in 1950), William Proxmire of Wisconsin (1957), Clair Engle of California (1958), Ed Muskie of Maine (1958), Phil Hart of Michigan (1958), Steve Young of Ohio (1958), Bob Bartlett and

Ernest Gruening of Alaska (1959), Quentin Burdick of North Dakota (1960), Tom McIntyre of New Hampshire (1962), and Gaylord Nelson of Wisconsin (1962). Most of these men would have agreed with Ralph Yarborough, who called Kefauver "one of my heroes at the time I came to the Senate." [14] Especially after the Democratic landslide of 1958 brought more Midwestern and Western Democrats to the Senate, there were simply too many Kefauvers for Lyndon Johnson and the Southern committee chairmen even to attempt to discipline. During the last four years of Kefauver's Senate career, he was considered a walking legend by at least a score of his Democratic colleagues, and, contrary to being without influence, could personally deliver at least ten votes on any issue by the sheer force of his reputation as a champion of the public interest.

Although Kefauver was second ranking Democrat on Judiciary behind Mississippi's Jim Eastland, he was never to head the committee. The conservative chairman outlived Kefauver and even now (1971) holds on to the Judiciary chairmanship. Kefauver's other committee assignment for the first ten years of his Senate career was Armed Services, where he had worked his way up to fourth position among Democrats by 1958. However, in anticipation of his 1960 re-election campaign, Kefauver decided to leave Armed Services and take advantage of an opportunity to go on the highly sought after Appropriations Committee, where he could be more effective on behalf of home state interests. In a letter to Johnson after the 1958 elections, a Democratic landslide which opened up every committee to new Democratic members, Kefauver wrote:

> . . . I have, as you probably know, a rough campaign coming up in 1960 and I need some real breaks to come through successfully. Also, you will remember that when I first came to the Senate I expressed a desire to get on the Appropriations and Foreign Relations Committees but Senator McKellar was on Appropriations and that was not possible. In our talks sometime back I understood you felt that I might get on either Appropriations or Foreign Relations this next term. I have thought it over a

great deal and I would like to apply for a place on the Appropriations Committee. I think I would enjoy the work and it would help my situation down home. I would, under these circumstances, reluctantly give up my place on the Armed Services Committee.[15]

The Democratic Steering Committee approved Kefauver's request, and his departure from Armed Services brought a letter from Chairman Richard Russell:

It has been good to work with you on the Committee and I regret to see you leave. In frankness, I am somewhat surprised to see you give up your seniority. You may have been much closer to the chairmanship than you thought.[16]

For the rest of his career, Kefauver concentrated on legislative work in his two committee assignments—Judiciary and Appropriations—and, more specifically, on the work in the two Judiciary Subcommittees on Constitutional Amendments and Antitrust and Monopoly, serving as chairman of both until his death. There was never any doubt that his heart and soul was in the Antitrust and Monopoly Subcommittee, but his other subcommittee assignments had their attractions, too. Constitutional Amendments gave Kefauver the reformer an opportunity to pursue some of the fundamental changes in the American political system he had long advocated, and under his chairmanship, the subcommittee was to approve one amendment which made its way successfully through the ratification process to become the Twenty-fourth Amendment to the United States Constitution (abolition of poll taxes in federal elections).[17] On the Appropriations Committee, Kefauver was especially fortunate in gaining assignment to two subcommittees that handled legislation of special importance to Tennessee. One was the subcommittee having jurisdiction over appropriations for both TVA and the Atomic Energy Commission. The other was the Public Works Subcommittee, whose routine responsibilities were not very interesting to Kefauver, but considered a prize nevertheless because of the ability to "deliver" on home state projects that membership on it gave.

Almost imperceptibly after 1956, Kefauver's image with his fellow senators, as well as the American public in general, underwent a dramatic change. No longer would he be thought of as the perennial presidential aspirant preoccupied with seeking national office at the expense of his Senate responsibilities. Indeed, he became recognized as one of the Senate's most dedicated and hardworking members. It would be in these final years, when the drama of the crime investigation and the excitement of the presidential campaigns had begun to fade at last in the public mind, that Kefauver, working now through the unglamorous legislative process, would make his greatest contributions to the public interest.

chapter xviii

ANTITRUST AND MONOPOLY
1957-1963

Kefauver's succession to the chairmanship of the Senate Antitrust and Monopoly Subcommittee in 1957 was one of the more fortunate accidents of the often reviled seniority system. Few men in either house of Congress were better qualified, either by experience or because of personal interest, to assume the responsibility for carrying forward, and, indeed, dramatically escalating, the congressional effort to prevent the excessive concentration of economic power which inevitably sets the stage for monopolistic practices. It was not surprising, therefore, that Kefauver's tenure as chairman of the subcommittee from 1957 to 1963 stands as one of the landmark eras in the battle to preserve the American free enterprise system.

Kefauver's serious and longstanding interest in antitrust investigation and legislation had been largely overshadowed during his rapid rise to national political prominence after 1950, but once the unsuccessful quest for national office was abandoned, he was free to devote more and more attention to what had been one of his continuing concerns since his early years in the House.

Service on the House Judiciary Committee and the Select Committee on Small Business had first exposed Kefauver to the national problems of economic concentration and had given him the opportunity to become one of the congressional experts on antitrust and monopoly. His reputation as a foe of monopoly was greatly enhanced by his performance as chairman, in 1946, of a Small Business subcommittee to investigate economic concentration in American business, which produced a report so thorough that it won wide praise even among economists.[1]

Kefauver's persistent efforts, both in the House and, after 1949, in the Senate, to close loopholes in the antitrust laws and to examine strictly all proposed legislation to determine its effect on intra-market competition led the *New Republic* to remark as early as 1952 that "what George Norris was in the public power field, Estes Kefauver is in the field of antitrust legislation." [2]

Kefauver had been one of the original members of the Judiciary Subcommittee on Antitrust and Monopoly, created in 1953 by its first Chairman, Republican maverick Senator William Langer of North Dakota, and from 1953 until Kefauver's death in 1963, the work of this subcommittee was to lead his list of legislative priorities.[3]

One can only conjecture about the influences that shaped the basically populist philosophy that guided Kefauver throughout his political career. Obvious explanations are simply not there. Kefauver's Southern aristocratic heritage and his parents' secure place in the upper middle class of his boyhood hometown of Madisonville, Tennessee, would have made it more natural for him to follow the Bourbon tradition within Southern Democracy. His success as a corporation lawyer certainly provided him with a greater understanding of the perspective of the business community than the typical Western or Southern populist usually exhibited. His education at Yale Law School and his opportunity to go to Wall Street after graduation furnished no basis for an underlying antagonism toward the Eastern business community with which Kefauver was to joust frequently after 1957. His family never suffered the serious financial setbacks at the hands of big business that could have made him especially sensitive to the economic power of large corporations. Nor was there a parochial identification with the South which might have led to a sectional antagonism toward Northern and Western business; in fact, Kefauver was one of the most national-minded Southerners in Congress. Even the most obvious influences around Kefauver during his first seventeen years ran counter to the liberal political and economic attitudes he was to avow later in life; his native Monroe County was (and is) staunchly Republican and has exhibited little sympathy for political parties or candidates which seem to question the belief that the individual is basically responsible for himself; no candidate (whether Bryan or Lyndon Johnson) offering government support or protection for economic or political rights has ever done well in Monroe County. In summary, while it is to some extent begging the question simply to describe Kefauver as a populist, ultimate causes are not to be found.

Whatever the side issues involved in Kefauver's attacks on monopoly, his real objection to the concentration of economic power lay in the resulting exploitation of the many by the few—an economic exploitation that he believed would lead eventually to political exploitation. Thus, Kefauver equated a society providing free competition between many producers as a prerequisite for a democratic political system, and he was never especially moved by arguments that property rights were somehow sacred and to be protected above all else.

Kefauver's special concern for a "public interest" led to his continually being charged, especially in the years during which his Antitrust and Monopoly Subcommittee seemed to train its guns on those areas of the economy where the greatest profits were being made, with being anti-business. Nothing was further from the truth. What Kefauver was trying to protect was a free market economy, and his concern was never over profits but the method by which they were made. "The best friend a business man has are the antitrust laws," Kefauver stressed over and over. "The time for business men to worry is when our antitrust laws are not enforced in the presence of a clear need for them to be enforced." [4]

Whatever big business was to think of Kefauver, small businessmen facing what they saw as cutthroat competition from the business giants considered Kefauver a hero, and Kefauver's career of fighting for an economy in which they could survive caused Senator Wayne Morse of Oregon to comment in 1956, "I do not know of anyone who has fought more persistently for the small-business men than has the Senator from Tennessee. . . ." [5]

Kefauver, in spite of charges that his airing of the dirty linen of American business allied him with the ideological enemies of the free enterprise system, patiently stressed that America's role as leader of the free world depended on her economic strength, and, contrary to weakening the free enterprise system, his criticisms of monopolistic practices were based on a desire to keep America powerful enough to shoulder the defense of the Western democracies. "This is the reason," he explained, "why I have devoted most of my efforts in the recent past to finding out how to make our capitalistic system work just as well as it can, and must, work." [6]

Kefauver had no faith in government control of prices and wages, terming such controls "a frightful thing" which would lead to a "regimentation which might have a tendency toward socializing our industries." He believed that the free enterprise system, operating under the law of supply and demand, was the best cure for the inflation that reflected wage hikes not based on increased productivity or price hikes not justified by increased costs. "This Nation was founded on the principles of free enterprise and individual liberty," Kefauver told the Young Democrats in March, 1957. "What we want to do, and what we must do, is save our freedom. . . ." Inevitably, Kefauver returned to the ultimate fear, that "it is only a step from the loss of economic freedom to the loss of political freedom." [7]

Kefauver was far too sophisticated about the problems of monopoly in the American economy to underestimate the difficulties he would have in alerting either Congress or public opinion in general to the dangers of excessive economic concentration. The modern battle against monopoly, in contrast to the crusades of the trustbusters at the turn of the century, could offer few ruthless villains ostentatiously scornful of public opinion; instead, a more subtle threat in recent decades has come from some of the most respected corporations in the country and in many instances has been the result of policies and practices whose relationship to the problem of monopoly was not clearly understood even by those executives responsible for their formulation and implementation.

Kefauver undertook, therefore, to turn the attention of the Antitrust and Monopoly Subcommittee to the general problem of identifying, defining, and analyzing both the extent and consequences of economic concentration in the American economy, and announced plans, in January 1957, to investigate concentration "industry by industry" to determine "the effect on free enterprise and especially small business." [8] This project—a systematic examination of monopoly in the American economy—was to become the famous "administered prices" hearings which occupied the subcommittee throughout Kefauver's six years as chairman. Although there were to be minor digressions in response to monopolistic practices that had for some reason suddenly attracted public attention and therefore offered a special opportunity to educate the public about the causes and dangers of monopoly, the subcommittee for the most part followed a pattern of exhaustive preliminary staff work, fair, although frequently dramatic hearings, and, finally, proposed legislation to deal with monopolistic practices identified in the hearings.

Basically, in investigating the problem of monopoly between 1957 and 1963, the Antitrust and Monopoly Subcommittee sought to examine the extent to which concentration of economic power within certain industries had made it possible for relatively few producers to defy the law of supply and demand by deliberately maintaining prices with minimum regard for the market forces that would normally affect the price at which goods are offered. These "administered prices" were defined by the subcommittee as prices "which are administratively set, administratively maintained, and are insensitive to changes in their markets, e.g., they are maintained when demand falls off through a curtailment in output. . . ." [9]

The hearings on "administered prices" began on July 9, 1957, with an explanation by Kefauver of the subcommittee's general objectives:

> In opening these hearings on "Administered Prices," the Subcommittee on Antitrust and Monopoly is trying to come to grips with what is probably the Nation's current No. 1 domestic economic problem—the problem of inflation. We are concerned particularly with the extent to which administered prices in concentrated industries may contribute to this problem.
> . . . All prices have not risen to the same extent, nor indeed have all prices even participated in the advance. . . .
> What are the reasons for these differences in price behavior? How can prices go up in the face of declining demand and excess capacity? To what extent are the increases centered in administered price industries? I hope that we can have sufficient staff to work at the problem and get up information on the question of the extent to which profits and wage increases may bear upon the high prices of certain products in industries today.
> These are among the questions to which the subcommittee will direct its attention.[10]

During the next six years, the subcommittee held hearings filling twenty-six volumes and issued comprehensive reports on administered prices in the steel, automobile, bread, and drug industries. In May, 1963, Kefauver summarized the general findings of the subcommittee:

> As a result of this investigation, a great deal has been learned concerning the historical development of these industries, their structural characteristics, their standards and methods of pricing, their patterns of price leadership and price followship, their break-even points, their profit rates, and many related characteristics.

Perhaps the most important finding of these investigations is that in these industries price competition which, under our system of free enterprise, is assumed to be the protector of the public interest, tends to be conspicuous by its absence. This in turn raises a serious question of public policy. Should efforts be made through stronger antitrust laws and other measures to restore price competition to these industries from which it has practically disappeared? Should some other course of public policy be followed and, if so, what should its nature be? Or should we be content to simply maintain the status quo under which the managers of our large corporations have the power to set prices, virtually unhindered by the restraining influence of price competition? [11]

At the time of Kefauver's death, therefore, the subcommittee had completed the basic task of confirming the reality of the problem of administered prices but was a long way from framing the comprehensive legislation needed to deal with the monopolistic practices it had uncovered. In the meantime, however, the subcommittee had developed a greater and greater concern for the safety and efficacy of products being produced by "administered price" industries. Although these questions lay outside the jurisdiction of the Antitrust and Monopoly Subcommittee except to the extent they could be shown to be directly related to a lack of competition, the airing of grievances of smaller companies in the same field and of the public in general set the stage for the mushrooming of consumer interest groups in the mid-1960s. Especially was this true of the drug hearings of 1959 to 1963, and the Kefauver-Harris Drug Act of 1962, the most famous legislative achievement of the Antitrust and Monopoly Subcommittee while under Kefauver's direction, had little to do with the problems of monopoly in the drug industry and was concerned almost entirely with drug safety.

Industries under investigation by the Antitrust and Monopoly Subcommittee were, of course, unhappy enough with Kefauver when he stayed within the jurisdiction of the subcommittee. They were especially irritated when he allowed the hearings to range widely and into areas that seemed to have little relation to the subcommittee's legislative responsibilities. Kefauver persistently defended the scope of the Antitrust and Monopoly hearings as not only necessary to make meaningful legislation within the jurisdiction of the subcommittee possible but also to educate the Congress and the public in general about important problems which would otherwise remain obscure:

> In recent years the argument has been made with increasing frequency that the hearings of congressional committees should be restricted solely to the consideration of legislation. Because of the flagrant abuses of some hearings, such as those of the late Senator Joseph R. McCarthy, this argument has found favor with many individuals of liberal persuasion who formerly would have opposed any restriction on the rights of congressional committees to get at the facts. Yet, throughout our history most reforms have been preceded by congressional investigations which were not directed toward any specific piece of legislation for the simple reason that no meaningful bill can even be drafted until the facts of the matter are known and understood.
>
> Each of the investigations made by the Subcommittee on Antitrust and Monopoly has been conducted for legislative purposes. Its inquiries have been focused principally on the questions of whether a need for new legislation exists and, if so, what form it should take. But even if they had not been directed to a legislative purpose, these investigations would still have been appropriate as part of what Woodrow Wilson called the informing function. Indeed, in his celebrated treatise on Congressional Government, President Wilson went so far as to say that "the informing function of Congress should be preferred even to its legislative function." With the emergence of big business, big labor, and big government as the central forces in our society, and with the pressures for greater secrecy and non-disclosure coming from everywhere, the need for the informing function today is far greater than in the simpler days of Woodrow Wilson.[12]

The Antitrust and Monopoly Subcommittee had never been popular with conservatives of either party, and even though it had been organized by Republican Judiciary Chairman William

Langer in 1953, it had to wait until 1955 to obtain full recognition by the Senate Rules Committee, which handled appropriations requests. Kefauver's first few months as chairman so frightened conservatives that on February 5, 1958, Republican Leader William Knowland of California moved to cut the Antitrust and Monopoly appropriation by over 30 per cent. The principal objections of the mostly Republican critics of the subcommittee centered on the fact that in spite of the considerable subcommittee expenses and lengthy hearings during the previous year, very little legislation had been reported to either the full Judiciary Committee or the Senate floor. In effect, Kefauver's critics argued, the subcommittee was a forum for attacks on American business and did not deserve the excessive financial support request by Kefauver. However, the most conservative senator on the subcommittee and the business community's fifth column throughout Kefauver's chairmanship, Senator Everett Dirksen of Illinois, broke with most of his fellow conservatives to back Kefauver's request and indicated the love-hate relationship he had developed with the subcommittee:

> . . . I think this particular subcommittee has burdened me, ever since I have been on it, more than have all the other subcommittees put together. I do not think that is an overstatement, as a matter of fact. . . . One would think that, since I am in disagreement with the subcommittee, I ought to be in favor of cutting off funds for it. I am not, because I think the work the subcommittee does is important, even though I disagree so generally with my able and affable friend from Tennessee. . . . [T]he subcommittee cannot be blamed for not wanting to fill the Senate Calendar with a lot of proposed legislation. I have used every parliamentary device and what feeble skill I have as a parliamentarian to keep these little brain children from seeing the light of day, if it is possible.
>
> I think that explanation is in order. It is owing to the distinguished Senator from Tennessee, because it has not been due to a lack of diligence on his part that a lot of measures have not come to this floor. . . . So even though at times I feel harassed

and even though I feel the subcommittee has burdened my time to the point where I had virtually a one-week vacation in the adjournment last year, because I came back for the hearings last fall in October and November, I still believe that the $365,000 [Kefauver's request] is a reasonable and very proper amount. . . .[13]

Most Democrats and sixteen Republicans united to defeat Knowland's motion, 61-28.[14]

Much of the conservatives' fire over the six years was directed at the subcommittee's chief economist, John Blair, who was to stay on in his position until 1970. Blair had first met Kefauver during the Second World War when Blair was with the Smaller War Plants Corporation and Kefauver was involved in antitrust matters as a member of the House Judiciary Committee. Blair was a disciple of Gardiner Means, who had developed the theory of administered prices in the 1930s, and it was Blair's observations during the war and, later, at the Federal Trade Commission that led him to urge an investigation of administered prices in general on Kefauver and to join the subcommittee staff as chief economist.[15]

Blair became the *bête noire* of senators not wishing to attack Kefauver personally. As early as December 1957, Maryland's Republican Senator John Marshall Butler identified Blair as the evil influence behind the Antitrust and Monopoly Subcommittee, and in a speech to the Merchant Club of Baltimore, expressed the hope that the Judiciary Committee, of which he was a member, would "have an opportunity to take the necessary action to prevent . . . abuse of the legitimate investigatory power of its anti-monopoly subcommittee." He revealed that "For many months I have endeavored to understand the apparent antibusiness bias of this subcommittee. I believe I have found the answer. Its chief economist is Dr. John M. Blair. . . ." Butler then launched into a vicious attack on Blair.[16]

Kefauver replied to Butler's attack on Blair by reminding the Senate that Butler, who had won his seat in 1950 by means of a Joe McCarthy-led smear campaign against Democratic Senator Millard Tydings, was a "past master of distortion. I would say that his speech indicates he has lost none of his techniques." [17]

The months and months of the administered prices hearings, resulting in over 18,000 pages of testimony, charts, analyses, and recommendations, were one of the most impressive and constructive uses to which the congressional investigative power has ever been put. Bernard Nossiter, a *Washington Post* staff writer who followed the Antitrust and Monopoly hearings for years, later described the new plateau in antitrust activity reached by the subcommittee after Kefauver took over as chairman in 1957:

> Before the subcommittee made its record, it was possible for policy makers to ignore the structure of industry. They could and generally did assume that prices were set and output determined largely by the forces of competition, that large firms were efficient engines of technological advance, that concentrated corporate power was diminishing.
>
> Today, these assertions are rarely made in earnest, apart from the handouts of the 200 largest manufacturing concerns who control 60 per cent of all manufacturing assets. The fact of corporate, and union, pricing power is a phenomenon with which every administration must cope, either openly or covertly.[18]

It is impossible to read more than a few pages of the transcripts of the hearings without being impressed by the extent to which the hearings were personal triumphs by Kefauver and chief economist Blair over a staggering collection of statistics and attempts at subterfuge by some of the sharpest corporate minds in America. Kefauver emerges from the testimony as a patient, persistent, and unfailingly courteous and fair chairman, whose incredible grasp of the complex policies and practices of America's industrial giants was to leave no doubt that his was one of the most able minds ever to battle in the halls of Congress on behalf of the public interest.

The record of the administered prices hearings of 1957 to 1963 stands as a quiet memorial to Kefauver's career-long efforts to preserve a competitive economy and fight the growth of monopolistic business practices. The foundation laid by the subcommittee during Kefauver's six years as chairman made possible more and more sophisticated examinations of monopoly in the years that followed, by both congressional investigators and economists in general who shared Kefauver's concern over the threat to free enterprise arising from excessive economic concentration.

But Kefauver deserves special credit for another of the subcommittee's major achievements—so dramatizing the problem of monopoly that the American public became more aware of the problem than at any time since the trustbusting era. Kefauver's knack for relating the lack of competition in major industries to consumer dissatisfaction with their products established an important bridge between the antimonopoly and consumer protection groups that was to have dramatic implications for consumerism in the late 1960s. Kefauver himself became a champion of all those who felt some grievance against American business which could even indirectly be tied to a lack of competition, and as a result, Kefauver's Senate office and the Antitrust and Monopoly Subcommittee became clearinghouses for complaints against big business in much the same way that Kefauver and the crime committee of 1950–51 served as a rallying point in the war against crime in the early 1950s.[19]

Kefauver's knack for cutting through elaborate rationalizations for monopolistic practices was invaluable in combatting the feeling of helplessness most investigators would have felt at taking on the executives and lawyers of some of America's largest corporations. One of the best examples of Kefauver's letting industry spokesmen trap themselves occurred when Kefauver asked Roger Blough, Chairman of the Board of United States Steel, why steel companies, for the most part, set identical prices for their products, regardless of the differing costs of individual companies and without concern for the relationship between supply and demand. Blough attempted to argue that only by offering purchasers products at identical prices could there be true competition—otherwise, the purchaser would be forced to buy at the lowest price:

> Mr. Blough. . . . My concept is that a price that matches another price is a competitive price. If you don't choose to accept that concept, then, of course, you don't accept it. In the steel industry we know it is so. . . .
> I would say that the buyer . . . has . . . this choice. He chooses to buy from one company at $5 higher. He chooses to buy from our company at $5 lower. Now if you call that competition and a desirable form of competition, you may have it your way. I say the buyer has more choice when the other fellow's price matches our price.
> Senator Kefauver. That's a new definition of competition that I have never heard.[20]

Similarly, George Humphrey, Board Chairman of National Steel and former Treasury Secretary under Eisenhower, was called on to explain why, even though his company was more efficient than United States Steel and was operating at only 80 per cent capacity, National did not lower its prices and take advantage of its greater efficiency to garner more of the market:

> Senator Kefauver. Mr. Humphrey, I have examined the prices submitted by your company and by all the other companies, and I can find no important instance where your price was lower than United States Steel.
> Mr. Humphrey. Of course you cannot, because if we made a lower price, everybody would meet it. They will do the same as we do.[21]

In other words, the relatively few companies dominating the steel industry were letting the most inefficient producer set the price, with other companies raising their prices to be "competitive." The social waste and the cost to the consumer seemed of no importance to the steel companies. That this situation could only exist in an industry lacking true competition was an insight

Kefauver was never able to communicate to steel executives, try as he might.[22]

There is no doubt that Kefauver's role as a foe of administered price inflation caused a more serious consideration of both price hikes and general corporate public relations. He served as a gadfly to the Eisenhower Administration, reluctant to interfere with business, and as a strong ally to the Kennedy Administration's efforts to hold back inflationary price and wage hikes.[23]

During his six years as chairman of the Antitrust and Monopoly Subcommittee, Kefauver led investigators into many areas of American life where economic concentration was an especially dangerous threat to competition. The steel probe, which was periodically revived whenever it seemed appropriate,[24] was followed by an examination of the automobile industry. The subcommittee finally concluded that "the hard core of the monopoly problem in the automobile industry is in the concentration of . . . power held by General Motors" and it recommended that the Justice Department move to break up GM, and possibly Ford and Chrysler, too. Six of the seven subcommittee members agreed with the report—only Dirksen dissented, finding it "regrettable that the majority has permitted the longstanding prejudices and biases of its staff to influence" its views.[25]

The subcommittee also looked into or threatened to investigate monopoly in sports,[26] hearing aids,[27] insurance,[28] railroads and airlines,[29] electrical equipment,[30] bread,[31] meat and dairy products, asphalt roofing,[32] and, of course, the drug industry.[33]

During these investigations, Kefauver was critical not only of inflation due to administered pricing by corporations but also of wage demands that were not based on gains in productivity. Although organized labor correctly thought of Kefauver as a friend, and he was even accused of providing Walter Reuther a forum to attack the automobile companies, Kefauver did not hesitate to turn the subcommittee's attention to the inflationary pressure exerted by the huge labor unions. He was critical of both management and labor when it seemed that either, or both working together, were guilty of monopolistic practices. When George Romney, President of American Motors, urged the breakup not only of the automobile industry's "big three" but also the huge United Auto Workers, Kefauver was obviously sympathetic and praised Romney for his "frank and courageous" testimony.[34]

On the whole, however, Kefauver sought to defend the unions from industry charges that wages alone were responsible for inflationary price increases. Kefauver was especially unsympathetic to the claim when it came from the steel industry and pointed out that Bethlehem Steel had eleven of the eighteen highest paid executives in the country, with a board chairman paid over $800,000 a year. But, Kefauver stressed, he did not think labor in the basic industries "should demand or receive any wage increase which management could justify as the basis for absolutely necessary price increases. To do so would add to the inflationary spiral." When Kefauver urged the Steelworkers Union and the steel industry to join in a move to curb inflation by keeping down wages and prices, Steelworkers President David McDonald showed his gratitude by commenting that "I wish Senator Kefauver would learn to keep his nose out of my business."[35]

The sustained efforts of Kefauver personally, and of the Antitrust and Monopoly Subcommittee as an institution, to turn the spotlight of public opinion on monopolistic behavior and a general disregard for the public interest by corporate giants led Henry Ford II to suggest to his fellow businessmen that they had better clean themselves up. "It is the job of our corporate executives to keep their own houses in order," he warned. If business did not respond, the job "certainly will be put in less friendly hands."[36]

Whatever big business or big labor might have criticized in Kefauver's antimonopoly investigations, his steadfast defense of the public interest made him a hero to millions of little people across the country who looked to him to defend their economic interest against the concentrations of economic power that left consumers practically helpless to affect the basic economic decisions that shaped their lives. To them Kefauver became a modern tribune of the people, and they would have found little with which to disagree in the judgment of the *New Republic*, in discussing yet another Kefauver investigation into an attempt by big business to gouge the American public:

> . . . it is not without cause that the felonious element in American business hates the man. And the force of this hatred has lifted him out of the ruck of anonymities whose period in Washington has benefited none but themselves and has put the Tennessean in the relatively short list of those whose membership in Congress has profited the country as a whole.[37]

chapter xix

CIVIL RIGHTS, 1957-1960

The civil rights revolution, which began to gather momentum after the 1954 Supreme Court decision against segregated schools, made the issue of Negro rights, always a burning issue across Dixie, of greater concern than ever to Southern whites. It was an indication of Kefauver's courage that he was willing to put his prestige, and even his career, on the line in support of most of the limited civil rights objectives of the late 1950s and early 1960s.

In spite of the attention he attracted as a Southerner who was willing to support some civil rights legislation, Kefauver's attitude toward Negro rights was widely misunderstood. He was never as liberal on racial matters as liberals hoped or conservatives feared. Liberals were willing to overlook or excuse Kefauver's mixed record on civil rights as the price he had to pay to stay in office as a Southern senator, and firmly believed that he wanted to go much further in support of civil rights than the Tennessee political situation would allow. Ironically, conservatives saw him the same way, interpreting every reservation Kefauver expressed about proposed civil rights legislation as an insincere public relations gimmick designed to help placate home state opposition to civil rights.

There is little doubt that Kefauver shared the liberals' dream of an America free from racial prejudice. His commitment to the ideal was reaffirmed many times throughout his career.[1] But his support or opposition to specific legislation designed to achieve that end was determined by his constantly shifting evaluation of what was possible—not possible in the sense of what would be defensible enough in Tennessee to allow him to win re-election, but possible for the people of the South to accept and adjust to. He believed very strongly that Southern white attitudes toward Negroes could not and would not be changed overnight, and opposed civil rights legislation which he felt was too far ahead of Southern opinion to gain widespread acceptance across the South. That he did have a mixed record on civil rights in general and, even in some cases, contradictory positions on the same issue, simply reflected his attempt to evaluate each issue on its merits and in the context of the times.

There was universal agreement among political observers that Kefauver's 1956 campaign for the Democratic nomination had not helped him at home. More than anything else, it had been Kefauver's appeal for Negro support in the North and West that had upset his fellow Tennesseans, and coupled with his refusal to sign the Southern Manifesto in early 1956, it appeared to many Southerners that Kefauver was indeed willing to sacrifice Southern interests for Northern support at the convention. Probably no position ever taken by Kefauver provoked more unfavorable mail from home than his rejection of the Manifesto. To the many letters (a majority of them bitterly critical) he received questioning his position on the Manifesto and segregation in general, Kefauver replied with the patient plea for understanding and goodwill that was so characteristic of his approach to controversy:

> In the case of the integration decision the Court has provided means by which the individual states and even the school districts can make the necessary adjustments over a period of time. At the time of the original decision I pointed out that these facts did exist and that it was a problem for people of good will of both races to work out in the various communities. My stand has not changed.

I realize that these conditions present many difficulties in some cases, but I am confident that we will solve these difficulties and reach a satisfactory conclusion. It is far better if we keep so-called manifestos and harsh words on both sides to a minimum and work instead toward assuring good will between the races which has been a product of hard and understanding effort by many leaders of both races throughout the years.[2]

Kefauver's bid for Negro support throughout the 1956 pre-convention campaign compounded already serious political troubles in Tennessee and might very well have cost him the support of his own state at the Democratic convention had he not withdrawn before the convention balloting. As it was, Tennessee's delegation supported him for Vice-President with the greatest reluctance. The national campaign with Stevenson repaired part of the damage by helping Kefauver achieve a more moderate image in Tennessee, but even so, once the election was over, Kefauver supporters aware of the state's negative attitude toward civil rights and already worried about Kefauver's renomination chances in 1960 were anxious that he minimize as much as possible his association with the accelerating drive for Negro rights.

Even if Kefauver had wished to avoid the civil rights issue after the election, however, he would have been unable to do so. The 1957 session of Congress opened with both Republicans and Northern Democrats determined to give civil rights the highest legislative priority—the Republicans because they had done unusually well with Negro voters in 1956, and Northern Democrats because they had not. Realizing that Kefauver would be making a civil rights record that they would have to defend in 1960, but also knowing better than to hope that Kefauver would sacrifice his principles for political expediency, Kefauver supporters at least hoped for a low profile on civil rights, especially if Kefauver ended up by voting for legislation before the Senate.

Liberals began the civil rights battle almost from the first day of the new Congress in January 1957, with an effort to have the Senate consider changes in the rules of debate which would make filibustering of civil rights legislation more difficult. The motion lost, 55 to 38, with Kefauver casting the only Southern vote in favor of the liberal-backed move.[3]

Many of those senators opposing a rules change were, nevertheless, committed to support of civil rights legislation and saw no need at that time to change the rules of the Senate. The more important battle would be over the proposals advanced by the Administration and Democratic liberals, the most significant of which were the establishment of a Civil Rights Commission, the appointment of an assistant attorney-general for civil rights, and increased federal protection for the right to vote, especially through an extension of the jurisdiction of the federal courts in civil rights cases. The Administration bill had little trouble in the House but in the Senate had been blocked in the Judiciary Committee, headed by Mississippi's Jim Eastland, who was, of course, determined to use all his powers as chairman to defeat or weaken the bill. Once the Constitutional Rights Subcommittee had reported the bill to the whole committee, Kefauver, as a member of the full Judiciary Committee, participated in the committee discussion and, on two key votes, indicated that his position lay between the liberals and the Southern die-hards. On May 20, Senator Sam Ervin of North Carolina moved to strike four of the five sections of the bill reported by the subcommittee, leaving only the section designed to protect Negro voting rights. Kefauver voted with five Republicans against four Southern Democrats to give the liberal position a 6 to 4 victory. However, on June 3, Kefauver voted with the majority on a 7 to 3 vote to allow jury trials for persons charged with criminal contempt for violating federal court injunctions.[4]

The "jury trial" amendment became the main point of contention between moderates and liberals, with Southern Democrats naturally supporting the modification because it placed a Southern jury between a federal judge and a person accused of violating an injunction against actions which threatened Negro rights. The Southerners made much of the right of trial by jury, but most observers recognized the jury trial amendment as a device to weaken federal protection of Negro rights. Republican Senator Clifford Case of New Jersey found it paradoxical that none of the senators fighting for trial by jury came from states that had "a provision for jury trial in contempt cases of the kind here involved." [5]

In spite of all the debate and discussion within the Senate Judiciary Committee, the Administration bill showed few signs of making it to the Senate floor. The committee continued to delay approval of the bill even after the House had considered the bill in committee, debated it on the floor, and passed it virtually intact. Liberals were beginning to fear that the bill would never reach the floor, or would reach it so late that a Southern filibuster in the closing weeks of the session would prevent a vote on the measure. The bipartisan civil rights coalition, therefore, decided to take advantage of a parliamentary maneuver which would allow the House-passed civil rights bill to go directly to the Senate floor, by-passing the Senate Judiciary Committee, which would otherwise have had control of the House bill as well as its own version of the Administration bill. Senator Russell of Georgia objected to the procedure, but the Senate upheld, 45 to 39, Vice-President Nixon's decision to put the House-passed bill on the calendar for consideration on the floor. Kefauver supported the move of the South to send the House bill to the Judiciary Committee but insisted that his concern was over following the proper procedure, not blocking the bill:

> The Senate will lose its stabilizing influence in the Nation if we place it in the power of a majority of the Senate, in connection with any particular bill, to vote not to refer a bill to a committee. Under such procedure, in my opinion, the Senate would lose its traditional stabilizing influence, which it has always had by reason of calmly considering questions while at the same time giving witnesses an opportunity to testify, while passions are allowed to cool. If we were to place it in the power of a majority immediately to send a bill to the calendar, and then act upon it with-

out the benefit of testimony before one of our legislative committees, in my opinion such action would substantially destroy
the committee system of the Senate.[6]

When the Senate got around to a vote on taking up the civil
rights bill, however, Kefauver voted with a 71 to 18 majority in
favor.[7]

The sentiment in favor of the Administration bill was so
strong that the South had no hopes of blocking the entire bill.
Instead, Southern efforts centered on amending the House bill
to include the jury trial provision written into the now abandoned Senate version. Southerners hoping for acceptance of the
jury trial amendment let Kefauver, Frank Church of Idaho, and
Joseph O'Mahoney of Wyoming lead the fight for it, and split
liberal ranks by writing the provision so that it applied to all
criminal contempt cases, not just those arising out of civil rights
litigation. By broadening the jury trial guarantee, Southerners
hoped to win support from pro-labor senators, since organized
labor had long advocated jury trials for criminal contempt to
protect labor from conservative federal judges. Most labor leaders were not impressed with the jury trial amendment, however,
and sought to dissuade senators from supporting it in the name
of protecting organized labor.

However, it was not primarily Kefauver's concern for labor
that led him to support the jury trial amendment but, more important, his emphasis on local responsibility for participation in
the protection of constitutional rights. Kefauver minimized the
liberals' concern that Southern juries would refuse to convict
fellow Southerners of contempt of a federal court order attempting to protect Negro rights but argued that even if that did
happen in some cases it would still be preferable to tampering
with trial by jury:

> . . . If there is any imperfection in the jury system, it will not
> be corrected by doing away with and surrendering the right to
> trial by jury. The cure for any imperfection is a better apprecia-
> tion of the responsibilities of government, of citizenship, and of

education, and by a greater use of the right to vote, the ballot box approach. These are the only workable means of correcting the imperfections of the jury system or any other system. Any miscarriage of justice will not be remedied by eliminating the important and hard won right of trial by jury.[8]

Kefauver's argument on behalf of jury trials got an important boost when, on July 23, in the midst of the debate over the amendment, a Knoxville jury returned guilty verdicts against racial agitator John Kasper and six of ten local defendants who were on trial for blocking court-ordered integration in Clinton, Tennessee. "I am delighted with the word from Knoxville today," Kefauver's immediate press release announced:

. . . [The jury] stood up like law-abiding citizens and convicted the violators. Their action should answer those who say Southern juries won't convict white defendants in civil rights cases. They showed that they took their oaths seriously and acted in a discerning manner, acquitting some and convicting others as they felt the facts justified.

Their action should show us that the kind of jury trial amendment I have proposed to the pending bill—one which grants a jury trial only in criminal cases—will not detract from the enforcibility of the bill.[9]

On August 2 the Senate voted 51 to 42 for the jury trial amendment, in what was hailed as a victory for the South. Kefauver supporters in Tennessee made much of his role in winning acceptance of the amendment, and the most important pro-Kefauver newspaper in the state, the *Nashville Tennessean*, continually hammered home the point that Kefauver's good relations with Northern and Western moderates and liberals had made him a more effective defender of Southern rights than the unreconstructed Dixiecrats who opposed even the most reasonable civil rights legislation. Kefauver's vote for the final bill was almost anticlimactic.[10]

Die-hard segregationists were, of course, outraged that Kefauver had not cooperated more closely with the South in trying to block the whole bill. As for his role in the adoption of the jury trial amendment, conservatives considered more significant such votes as Kefauver's opposition to making federal district court jurisdiction over voting rights cases permissive rather than mandatory when administrative remedies had not been exhausted. Thirteen liberal Democrats joined thirty-four Republicans to hand the South a key defeat, 34 to 47, and Kefauver was the only one of twenty-two Southern Democrats to vote against the amendment.[11]

The *Nashville Banner,* which spoke for the conservative wing of the Tennessee Democratic party, was as unhappy as ever with both Kefauver and Tennessee's junior senator, Albert Gore, and exhibited no appreciation for their efforts to work with Northern and Western senators to soften the civil rights bill. The *Banner* was especially unhappy with the suggestion that Kefauver deserved credit for the Southern victory on the jury trial amendment and bitterly attacked both Kefauver and Gore for their independence from the Dixie bloc:

> Senator Kefauver's performance was typical of the man and the politician—edging finally into the act, as into any act, when the chips fall to indicate what will get votes.
>
> Like Senator Gore, he is a Johnny-Come-Lately to the side demanded by Tennessee constituents, at which point both became suddenly vocal and vociferous. They elaborately refrained from any part in the "civil rights" dispute—so carefully evading participation, in fact, that the Southern bloc held its caucuses and strategy sessions week in and week out without them. They maintained that silence until in the closing days of the showdown it dawned that the people of Tennessee and the South were sick and tired of wilful sidestepping and representation that did not represent. So at that point they came alive, exploding like twin firecrackers, fused by the heat of public indignation.
>
> Tennessee's embarrassment at this conduct turned into nausea.[12]

Kefauver and Gore rarely disagreed on the explosive civil rights issue, but, although Gore's record over the years was as liberal, if not more so, than Kefauver's, the senior senator nevertheless remained the primary target of segregationists. Less than a year before his death, Kefauver commented on the moral support he and Gore gave each other on civil rights and noted, "Two senators is easier than one doing it alone." [13]

The fall of 1957 saw the confrontation between President Eisenhower and Governor Faubus of Arkansas over the integration of Little Rock Central High School. The resort to force especially upset Kefauver, who recognized it as a dangerous breakdown of the dialogue between the races and the sections that he believed would have to accompany any real Negro gains in the South. To constituents who wrote him of their concern about Little Rock, Kefauver replied:

> I was distressed by the Little Rock situation. It seems to me that mistakes were made by nearly everyone involved. In the first instance, I think Governor Faubus' use of the National Guard was most unfortunate. While there is no doubt that the President has responsibility to uphold the law and order, I think his use of the Airborne troops was equally unfortunate. There are many other things that could have been done and certainly the use of troops is no final solution of problems in human relations.[14]

Kefauver's rejection of force except as a last resort led him to oppose the nomination the following August of W. Wilson White as Assistant Attorney-General in charge of the newly created Civil Rights Division of the Justice Department. White had advised President Eisenhower in the Little Rock dispute and was blamed by Kefauver for sending in troops without exhausting other remedies, such as contempt citations:

> . . . I think Mr. White's nomination under these circumstances is questionable. He was asked, so far as the record shows, what the President could do. He said he listed alternatives, but he did not. His only thinking was about the use of troops. . . . Undoubtedly Governor Faubus made mistakes; but a much better situation would exist in the South today between the races and in the schools, and there would not be the sharp division which

is causing so much difficulty in eliminating discriminations against the races, if contempt proceedings had been used; if marshals had been deputized; if all the other alternatives had been used; or even, if the situation was completely out of hand, if military police, rather than armed combat troops had been brought in. . . . [T]he use of troops, without first trying all the other alternatives, should—as has clearly been shown by the resulting deterioration of relations—most definitely be a last resort, not the first one.[15]

The Democratic congressional landslide of 1958 dramatically increased the liberal forces in both the House and Senate and presented civil rights advocates with one of the most sympathetic Congresses in history. As always, one of the liberals' first objectives was modification of the cloture rule, and they eventually won a partial victory in altering the Senate rules to make it possible for two-thirds of those present and voting, rather than two-thirds of the entire Senate membership, to cut off debate. On earlier key votes on January 9 and 12, Kefauver had voted against more liberal proposals to allow a majority of three-fifths of the Senate to shut off debate, but he did support the slight change eventually passed.[16] In a letter to Senator Carl Hayden of Arizona, Kefauver explained why he had at last abandoned the position he had held ever since coming to the Senate in 1949 and had reaffirmed as recently as the rules change vote of 1957. Acknowledging that he had, in *A Twentieth Century Congress* a dozen years earlier, advocated allowing a majority of the Senate to cut off debate, and had generally favored the proposals to curb debate since then, Kefauver, nevertheless, admitted:

since I came to the Senate . . . I have observed times when lengthy debate in the Senate has prevented decisions in times of emotional stress and has also been a useful tool to secure better protection of the people in legislative enactments. I recall that I have participated in lengthy debate in connection with securing better rights of the people in the development of atomic energy and to prevent hasty enactments of the removal of regulations from the distribution of natural gas which I felt would bring increased rates. . . . [Therefore, Kefauver favored a two-thirds vote to impose cloture.] It is by this majority that treaties are ratified, impeachments [sic] are voted and constitutional amendments proposed.[17]

It was not only the vote on cloture that highlighted Kefauver's shift on civil rights. Later in 1959, he joined with Eastland in support of a constitutional amendment which would have guaranteed each state's control of its public schools and would, therefore, have, in effect, blocked integration of Southern schools. As chairman of the Constitutional Amendments Subcommittee, Kefauver presided over hearings on the amendment and must surely have felt considerable embarrassment by the support given the proposal by the lunatic fringe on the right. One witness predicted, "Naturally, every Communist and Socialist-infiltrated organization in the United States—and that includes most of the means of communication: press, radio and TV—will oppose this resolution." He went on to single out the *New York Times* and the *Washington Post* as the worst examples of Communist-infiltrated papers, provoking the soft-spoken Kefauver to object to such abusive language: "I'm sorry to hear you make the statement. It is repulsive to me. These papers are trying to do a good job in the public interest. I want no more testimony of this nature." [18]

The school amendment had little support in the Senate outside the Southern bloc, and Kefauver and Eastland were even unable to get it out of the subcommittee, which rejected it in a vote of 3 to 2.[19]

Kefauver also faced the problem in 1959 of deciding whether to support an extension of the Civil Rights Commission, which had been set up for two years under the Civil Rights Act of 1957. He finally decided to back the extension, but, in a newsletter explaining his vote to his constituents, Kefauver emphasized that his support for the Commission was not without qualification:

. . . The right of every qualified American citizen to vote is basic and sacred. Any intelligent investigation of voting privileges is worthwhile. I hope that the Civil Rights Commission will get back on the track of investigating the matter of voting, and, at the same time, it will get out of some of the other fields into which, unfortunately, it has wandered. . . .

While I am highly displeased with much of the Commission's report, especially its inaccuracies, I believe that continuation of the study with a revamped Commission may be the best defense against more drastic or even punitive legislation. While the study is going on, a telling argument can be made against the enactment of any punitive legislation. Therefore, I believe extension of the Commission's life is the best way to prevent legislation which could be harshly unfair to the South.

For these reasons, I voted for extension of the Commission. I was joined in this vote by 71 other Senators, including my colleague from Tennessee, Senator Gore, and the Democratic majority leader, Senator Lyndon Johnson.[20]

Kefauver was unhappy that the report of the Civil Rights Commission had contained what he called "inaccurate" references to two Tennessee counties and was especially upset with statements about Haywood County which alleged that Negroes, in spite of owning more land and paying more taxes than whites, were required to observe a strict curfew and not allowed to dance or drink beer. Kefauver also disagreed with many "carelessly conceived" recommendations of the Commission and found a recommendation for a federal voting registrar program "most unfortunate." "These are problems which we must solve locally," he warned; "they are not problems for which the solution can be imposed from above." [21]

Kefauver had hoped that Congress would delay further civil rights legislation until 1961, when a new study by the extended commission would have been completed.[22] However, sentiment in Congress was for some legislation before the 1960 election, thereby setting the stage for a civil rights battle in the months preceding Kefauver's re-nomination race in August.

Liberals hoped to move far beyond the 1957 civil rights act and provide extended federal protection of not only voting rights but also equality in housing and job opportunity. The Democratic Advisory Council gave such strong support to the liberals that Kefauver, dramatically illustrating the shift in his emphasis from a national to a Tennessee perspective, lined up with the Southern Council members in opposition to the majority's recommendations.[23]

Very early in the 1960 session of Congress, Kefauver was faced with a decision on one of the liberals' voting rights proposals, a bill to outlaw the poll tax as a requirement for voting. Kefauver opposed dealing with the problem by legislation, and instead, urged a constitutional amendment. His approach to the poll tax was eventually adopted, and the Twenty-fourth Amendment was passed by Congress in 1962 and finally ratified a few months after Kefauver's death.

The principal concern of a bipartisan congressional majority in 1960, however, was not to tamper with states' voting requirements but to make sure they were applied fairly to Negro applicants. Kefauver agreed that something should be done in this area and had justified his support for the 1957 civil rights act by arguing that "If we do what we can to assure all citizens the free exercise of the ballot, we shall have taken the major step necessary to solve the civil rights problem." [24] However, he was reluctant to see the federal government assume too great a role in the protection of Negro voting rights and went along with the Dixie bloc as never before when the civil rights package came first before the Judiciary Committee and then before the full Senate. On a delaying tactic on February 23, Kefauver voted with all other Southern Democrats except Senate Majority Leader Lyndon Johnson and Ralph Yarborough, both of Texas; the motion lost, 28 to 61. When liberals, on March 10, sought to impose cloture in the civil rights debate, Kefauver voted with all other Southern Democrats against the motion, which was defeated, 42 to 53.[25] Kefauver strongly emphasized his cooperation with the South in his weekly TV report to Tennessee following the cloture vote, but stressed that his opposition to limiting debate was based on a desire to have the issue fully debated rather than on opposition to all the provisions of the bill:

> . . . I think cloture should be used only in very rare conditions. I do not think the matter has been sufficiently debated. There has been more confusion than light shed on this issue thus far. Furthermore, here I would oppose "cloture" because we have not yet reached a point where we can clearly see just what the final bill will contain.

Why had Kefauver not joined the Southern filibuster? Because, Kefauver explained:

> a filibuster is designed not for full debate, which I favor on all issues, but rather to prevent the Senate from ever reaching a vote on particular legislation. I think that democracy will not long survive unless eventually a legislative body is able to vote. Otherwise, the whole legislative process may break down and we would not even be able to deal with situations affecting the safety of the nation. . . . I favor three proposals contained in the bill now before the Senate and expect to vote for them [right to vote protection, anti-bomb penalties, and a guarantee that schools would be provided for service personnel if local schools were closed to avoid integration]. . . . I think the vast majority of Tennesseans are for these proposals and would not want me to filibuster against them. They are basically right and therefore should be enacted into law.
>
> There are many other amendments and provisions of the bill which I shall vote against. I think that I am in a stronger position than some to oppose these harmful measures because I have tried to show that I am reasonable.[26]

Kefauver broke with the Southern bloc on March 24 when civil rights opponents sought to leave the bill in the Judiciary Committee with no deadline for reporting it to the floor; Gore, Johnson, and Yarborough also voted with the 72 to 19 majority.

The next week, the same four Southerners voted with a 71 to 17 majority to take up the bill on the floor.[27] The same day, however, Kefauver led a successful move in the Judiciary Committee to delete language in the bill which made it unnecessary for Negro voting applicants to confront local officials. Kefauver's substitute provided that the hearings before the referee had to be held in a public office, that the local registrar had to be given two days' written notice of the time and place of the hearing, and the registrar, or his counsel, might attend and make a transcript of the proceedings. The Senate Judiciary Committee adopted Kefauver's amendment by a 7 to 6 vote. The opportunity Kefauver's modification would provide for the intimidation of Negro voter applicants was so obvious that Republican Kenneth Keating of New York called the amendment "a devastating blow to the referee proposal" that "scuttles the program." [28] The outcry from liberals, and most moderates, was immediate, but Kefauver strongly defended the amendment on the Senate floor the following day:

> It was . . . my intention to try to have it be an open hearing, a public hearing—as all hearings should be—and not have it be a star chamber hearing. I wished the State and county registrars who would be charged with the responsibility in the first place to have an opportunity to be present. . . . In any event, my purpose was to have the registrars given a right to "appear" for the limited purpose of making a transcript of the proceeding. That is all the amendment would do. How anyone who wants to have a fair proceeding and an open proceeding and wants to avoid something which would be repugnant to our judicial system of procedure—to wit, star chamber proceedings—can object to this amendment is beyond my understanding. . . . [P]ublic business should be conducted in a public office. Public officials should not be allowed to conduct public business wherever they might wish to conduct it, at any hour of the day or night. The public would not long stand for such procedure. . . . I hope there will never be a repetition of the kind of thing that happened in days long ago. There was great political pressure in some presidential

campaigns, and in other elections, in various States, to get people registered. The referees or registrars went to people's homes and engaged in star chamber proceedings in which nobody could be present to make his own record. That happened. It was in many cases the rule rather than the exception. There is no protection in the bill as it stands, without the suggested language, to prevent that condition from happening again. . . . I think it is simply a matter of basic right that in any proceeding the person who is being accused of not having fulfilled his sworn obligation ought to have a right to at least be present. . . . He should be able to hear the dereliction of duty of which he is charged with being guilty.[29]

It was generally thought that Kefauver's amendment was a move to help him politically in Tennessee against the segregationist opponent already announced against him in the Democratic primary. Whatever Kefauver's personal motives for backing the amendment, there is little doubt that liberals were willing to help Kefauver out by giving him a temporary victory in committee against civil rights that would look good at home. The 7 to 6 Judiciary Committee majority for Kefauver's amendment included Wyoming's Joseph O'Mahoney and Colorado's John Carroll, both of whom were strong supporters of civil rights and had no intention of backing Kefauver's amendment on the Senate floor. In fact, one of the first amendments to the Judiciary Committee bill reported to the floor was a move by Carroll himself to restore the original language on voting referees and, thereby, knock out Kefauver's amendment; the Senate backed Carroll overwhelmingly, 69 to 22.[30]

Kefauver voted with the Southern bloc on most of the floor amendments to the Judiciary Committee bill, including a liberal proposal to establish a Commission on Equal Job Opportunity. The extent of Kefauver's support for the Dixie bloc was illustrated by a *Congressional Quarterly* analysis of individual senators' support for 19 amendments proposed by the South to weaken the bill. Outside the 18 Southern Democrats who supported every one, Kefauver had the highest percentage (83 per cent) of support for the amendments, ranking ahead of three other Southerners, Gore (74 per cent), Johnson (68 per cent), and Yarborough (53 per cent). On the final vote, however, Kefauver lined up with the three other Southern moderates and every non-Southern senator to pass the bill, 71 to 18.[31] Shortly before the final vote, he announced his support for the bill in a speech on the Senate floor:

> . . . I stated one month ago—on March 14—that I would vote for a civil rights bill which contained measures designed to strengthen the right of every qualified citizen in this Nation to vote.
>
> It was my feeling at that time that such a bill would evolve from the long hours of debate and the hard work of those who have aimed for this objective from the time when this legislation came before the Senate on February 15. This has been my objective.
>
> I shall, therefore, vote for this bill—the Civil Rights Act of 1960. I shall do so because I believe it is reasonable, constructive, and morally right. It contains the three elements which, from the beginning, I have said it should contain.
>
> It is primarily a voting rights bill. I have always been of the opinion, and shall continue to be of the opinion, that all qualified citizens—regardless of race or color—should have the right freely to register and vote. This bill strengthens the basic right, and its provisions on this subject are workable and fair.[32]

As in 1957, conservatives in Tennessee considered Kefauver's and Gore's refusal to join the Dixie bloc's co-ordinated effort to defeat the civil rights bill as the basest betrayal of Southern interests. Even Kefauver's well-publicized efforts to block some of the strongest provisions of the act were written off as an attempt to blind Tennessee voters to his past liberalism, and the *Nashville Banner* scoffed at what it called the "modified 'civil rights' stand for '60" that Kefauver was trotting out for the upcoming primary.[33] Kefauver had been keenly aware that his performance during the civil rights debate would be closely examined by Tennessee opponents and was sure to become an issue in the August primary. He had, nevertheless, tried to steer a course between dogmatic opposition to all civil rights legislation and impractical idealism for which the South was not psychologically prepared. No one could be sure how his stand would be received in Tennessee, but everyone did agree that Tennessee conservatives, disgusted not only with Kefauver's moderation on civil rights but also his liberalism on civil liberties, foreign policy, and economic matters, were gearing to give Kefauver the battle of his political life. It was time to go home.

chapter xx

THE BATTLE FOR SURVIVAL 1960

The 1960 Democratic senatorial primary in Tennessee was to be the last of the classic Kefauver campaigns, and because Kefauver elevated the battle from a contest over a Senate seat to a referendum on moderation versus reaction, perhaps the most meaningful of them all.

As Kefauver approached 1960, he was faced with somewhat of a dilemma in having to choose between another try for the Democratic presidential nomination and re-nomination to his Senate seat from Tennessee. No one familiar with the contrasting Democratic constituencies in Tennessee and the nation as a whole could have possibly advised that a simultaneous campaign for both was possible, especially since the competition for both was expected to be unusually keen.

Although Kefauver seems to have made the decision fairly early to forego another try for the Democratic presidential nomination, and instead, concentrate all his efforts on winning re-election to the Senate,[1] the polls continued to show him as the frontrunning Democrat throughout 1957; not only was he the first choice of Democratic and independent voters, but he also ran the best race against the expected 1960 Republican nominee, Vice-President Richard Nixon. Among Democrats, Kefauver led runner-up John Kennedy 29 per cent to 23 per cent in August and 26 per cent to 19 per cent in November. Against Nixon, Kefauver led 45 per cent to 41 per cent at the same time that Kennedy's lead over the Vice-President was 45 per cent to 43 per cent. Much of Kefauver's margin among Democratic voters (and, presumably, all voters) was due to the fact that he was much more widely known. An August 1957 poll showed that while 92 per cent of Democratic voters had heard or read about Kefauver, only 67 per cent recognized Kennedy. More revealing, however, was the fact that, among Democrats who had heard about both, the Massachusetts senator led Kefauver, 50 per cent to 39 per cent.[2]

As Kennedy became better known, therefore, he began to catch up with, and then passed Kefauver with the voters. By early 1958, Kennedy led Nixon, 49 per cent to 38 per cent, while the Vice-President barely edged by Kefauver, 45 per cent to 44 per cent.[3]

There was one way around Kefauver's dilemma of having to choose between the senatorial and presidential nominations in 1960. If Kefauver were willing to leave the Senate, he could run for governor of Tennessee in 1958, and because of the four year term, not only be free from a state-wide race in 1960 but also control his home state base, the lack of which had so handicapped him in 1956. Kefauver gave the idea some thought but finally announced that "it just isn't in the cards."[4] There is little doubt that Kefauver could have won the governorship, perhaps easily. Incumbent Governor Frank Clement was barred by the constitution from seeking re-election, and there was no prominent figure capable of beating Kefauver unless the anti-Kefauver vote were united behind one candidate, which was not destined to be the case in 1958. The Tennessee Democratic party was badly splintered, with several contenders expected to jump into the gubernatorial primary, and although Kefauver was thought to have slipped badly in the state, his core of followers was certainly more than enough to insure that he would lead the field, which would have given him the nomination, since

Tennessee does not provide for a runoff election if no candidate receives a majority.

Even without Kefauver, the field was crowded, and the final results confirmed the extent to which the party was divided. Buford Ellington, Clement's Commissioner of Agriculture, barely won the nomination with 213,415 votes, edging out Jackson Judge Andrew "Tip" Taylor, with 204,629, and Memphis Mayor Edmund Orgill, with 204,382. A fourth candidate received 56,854 votes. Ellington, therefore, was nominated with less than a third of the total vote.[5] Although Kefauver had not publicly endorsed any of the candidates, it was generally known that Orgill, an ally since the 1948 victory over Crump, was his private choice. An open Kefauver endorsement of Orgill would have most certainly given the Memphis mayor the nomination and helped Kefauver immeasurably in 1960, whether he sought the presidential nomination or re-election to the Senate. However, Kefauver's aversion to political organizations was so intense that he refused to establish one himself and never made the support of a candidate he favored a test of loyalty for his own backers.[6]

Kefauver's national support for the presidential nomination began to fall significantly in 1958. By December, polls showed that Stevenson, who had been left out of most earlier polls, was again the favorite among Democratic voters, leading (with 29 per cent) both Kennedy (23 per cent) and Kefauver (11 per cent); however, Kennedy (with 30 per cent) led Stevenson (20 per cent) and Kefauver (10 per cent) among independents.[7]

As 1959 opened, Kefauver was contacted by 1952 and 1956 supporters anxious to know his plans before they made their own decisions about 1960. The fierce Kennedy organizational activity put special pressure on Kefauver's New Hampshire backers, who finally were told in March 1959, that Kefauver would definitely not enter the 1960 New Hampshire primary. "My only plan for 1960 is to run for re-election to the Senate," Kefauver announced. "I shall have to forego the pleasure of seeing all my friends in New Hampshire." [8]

In spite of his disavowal, Kefauver held on to around 10 per cent of Democratic voters throughout 1959, until the polls quit listing him as a choice.[9] Kefauver's attitude toward the presidential primaries indicated that he was indeed serious about staying out of the 1960 presidential race. In September 1959, he refused to give his permission for his name to go on the Nebraska primary ballot. "I appreciate [Nebraska Democrats'] . . . thinking of me, but I am not a candidate," Kefauver said. Similarly, in early 1960, he notified the Oregon Secretary of State that he did not desire to be on the ballot there and would sign the required affidavit certifying that he was not a candidate.[10]

Meanwhile, Kefauver had stepped up his activity in Tennessee, announcing in the fall of 1958 a series of "workshops" to discuss national and local problems with Tennessee voters. He insisted, however, that he was not campaigning. Mending of Tennessee fences continued throughout 1959, and the extent to which Kefauver was running scared for 1960 is indicated by an order for an incredible 55,000 Christmas cards for 1959, up from the already staggering total of 40,000 in 1957.[11]

Almost no Tennesseans doubted that Kefauver would run again in 1960; most agreed that he might very well be "in trouble"; and practically everyone expected him to have stiff opposition in the August primary. Any candidate opposing Kefauver would pick up a hard core of anti-Kefauver voters, but the two most prominently mentioned Kefauver opponents had positive appeals to many other voters and, therefore, stood a better chance of unseating Kefauver. The most politically experienced, and the early frontrunner as Kefauver's opponent, was former Governor Frank Clement, whose organization had backed incumbent Governor Ellington and could, therefore, expect help from the state administration. In May 1959, the rumor circulated that Clement had decided to make the race against Kefauver and had lined up the necessary financial support. However, later in 1959, strained relations replaced the previous closeness between Clement and Ellington, and there was doubt that the governor would throw the full power of his administration behind Clement if he took on Kefauver.[12]

Clement finally decided to try for another term as governor in 1962 and left the 1960 field open to a second major figure, Judge Andrew "Tip" Taylor of Jackson. Taylor had attracted widespread and extremely favorable publicity as a result of his impressive race for governor in 1958, which he lost to Ellington in the primary by fewer than 9,000 votes; in a two-man race, Taylor would have won easily, since he was certainly the second choice of most of the 204,382 voters who backed Memphis Mayor Edmund Orgill. Taylor had had ties to both the old anti-Crump coalition and the Crump-McKellar machine, but after 1948, had been a strong supporter of Kefauver's anti-Crump ally, Gordon Browning; Browning, in turn, had backed Taylor in the 1958 primary.[13]

In 1958, Taylor had enjoyed support all across the political spectrum and had even had many Kefauver supporters behind him. In 1960, however, Taylor entered the race against Kefauver as the champion of conservative Democrats upset with Kefauver's alleged ultra-liberalism. From the time of Taylor's announcement in January until the primary voting in August, the Judge hammered home the theme that he was offering Tennessee Democrats a clear choice of philosophies—a marked contrast to 1958, when the three frontrunning gubernatorial candidates differed only slightly on the major issues.

Taylor's candidacy presented conservatives with the opposition to Kefauver they had long sought. They believed that Kefauver had never represented any more than a minority of Tennessee Democrats and had been especially lucky in twice winning election to the Senate. In 1948, conservatives pointed out, Kefauver had had the advantage of a conservative split and had gotten considerably less than 50 per cent of the primary vote; in 1954, conservatives had been stuck with Pat Sutton, who, by refusing to agree to get out in favor of a more attractive conservative candidate, had left conservatives no choice but to support him or again split the anti-Kefauver vote. In 1960, however, anti-Kefauver forces had an eminently respectable conservative candidate who faced Kefauver alone for the Senate nomination. At last they would be able to force an up and down vote on Kefauver's record, which they firmly believed was far to the left of Tennessee opinion.

The campaign began in earnest after Kefauver's formal announcement for re-election on May 21. Taylor had long before made it clear that he considered civil rights to be the number one issue in the campaign, and after the unsuccessful Southern filibuster against the 1960 Voting Rights Act, he had begun repeatedly to attack Kefauver's independence of the Southern bloc; in contrast, Taylor declared, "I would have definitely joined the Southerners." [14] Kefauver's final vote for the 1960 bill, coupled with his vote for the 1957 act, gave Taylor what he thought was his best issue against Kefauver. "This so-called civil rights bill which Estes Kefauver voted for this year will allow Federal referees or Federal agents to come into Tennessee and tell us who can and who cannot vote," Taylor charged. "They would simply take over our election machinery and deny to Tennessee the right of holding its own elections which is granted by the constitution." [15]

Kefauver did not try to evade the issue raised by his support of civil rights legislation. He wisely and accurately defended his pro-civil rights votes as support for the right to vote rather than of Negro equality. In connection with the 1960 act, Kefauver repeatedly stated, "I thought it was a fair and just bill, and I could not clear it with my conscience to vote against the right to vote. I don't know how we can hold our heads up in the world if we deprive people of this right." [16]

One of Kefauver's favorite campaign devices was to ask the crowd he was addressing if anyone there was "against the right to vote." If so, Kefauver continued, "maybe he'll raise his hand and tell us why." [17]

Even among Southerners who could swallow a moderate voting rights act, however, there was nagging doubt about the wisdom of stirring up the issue of civil rights at all. The South was especially edgy in the spring and summer of 1960 as a result of the first wave of sit-ins, and the voting rights act was seen by many frightened white Southerners as the beginning of the racial unrest that white supremacy had avoided for nearly a century. To these voters, Kefauver's support of the 1957 and 1960 civil rights acts was not seen as making the best of a bad but inevitable situation, but, instead, as the first steps down the road to the Negro equality they feared above all. Therefore, they considered it important to fight every civil rights advance tooth and nail, since blocking even a reasonable bill would help delay more drastic proposals which would surely follow.

Kefauver, to his credit, accepted the inevitability of eventual Negro political equality and pointed out to Tennesseans concerned about Negro unrest that barring Negroes from voting left them out of the system and made demonstrations and sit-ins more attractive as means of protest. "If we want to have more responsibility on the part of Negro citizens and others," Kefauver argued, "with that responsibility should go the right to vote." [18] In any event, Kefauver said in defense of his support of Negro voting rights, the South had no choice but to accept some civil rights legislation, and, therefore, was better off to face that fact and work to make the legislation as bearable as possible. For this reason, he said, "I voted for this bill [the 1960 act] to keep out bills that would require compulsory mixing of the races and other things." [19]

Taylor's appeal to the segregationist vote brought him the enthusiastic support of the white supremist groups, some of which were willing to sink to any level to defeat Kefauver. The extent to which Taylor was aware of the smear against Kefauver conducted in his behalf is unclear, but in any event, the race issue opened the door to one of the dirtiest campaigns in Tennessee history. John Kasper, convicted racial agitator, publicly endorsed Taylor and announced his determination to "get Kefauver out of the Senate." White Citizens' Councils and the Ku Klux Klan also gave Taylor their backing. Anti-Kefauver material was circulated showing Kefauver standing with or shaking hands with Negroes and implying that Kefauver's re-election campaign was a plot by Yankees, Jews, Communists, and Negroes to destroy the American way of life. One of the most widely circulated pictures was a doctored photograph of Kefauver and California Governor Pat Brown greeting a California Negro voter; Brown had been cropped from the picture before its use in Tennessee. "I plead guilty to shaking hands with Negroes," Kefauver humorously confessed. Taylor, in contrast, avoided Negroes during the campaign, sometimes to the point of outright discourtesy; at a Memphis plant, for example, Taylor campaigned at an entrance, shaking hands with white workers but turning aside when Negroes passed.[20]

Other anti-Kefauver material circulated by the lunatic fringe included a cartoon of a Negro man kissing a white woman ("The results of race mixing") and warnings that "hell-inspired Jews" were seeking "to destroy the white race," implying that Kefauver was their tool. This campaign literature in many cases violated federal law by not identifying its source, and the FBI, at the request of the Civil Rights Division of the Justice Department, finally opened an investigation of the anonymous hate literature flooding the state.[21]

Taylor sought to discredit Kefauver's claim that his support of civil rights was a matter of conscience. Instead, Taylor charged, Kefauver's pro-civil rights record was a result of his attempts to win Northern and Western support for his national political ambitions, at the expense of misrepresenting Tennessee. While admitting that there was nothing wrong in itself in seeking national office, Taylor argued that "when your ambition causes you to turn your back on your own people, as it has my opponent, then it is time for a change." Kefauver, in defense, pointed out the similarity between his record on civil rights and that of Senator Lyndon Johnson, the Southern candidate for the 1960 Democratic presidential nomination. "I wonder if the people down in Texas are giving Senator Lyndon Johnson as hard a time?" because he was seeking the Democratic nomination, Kefauver asked. Of course not, he pointed out. "Lyndon's a hero, and I'm a scalawag because I voted just like he did." "I wonder what . . . we are coming to in Tennessee when it is a disgrace to be a national figure. How does it disqualify you to be a senator because someone thought you were qualified to be a candidate for President?" Kefauver freely admitted that he had "friends all over the nation. I am glad I have friends I can call on when we need help in Tennessee." If he expected co-operation from other senators, Kefauver explained, he had to approach their problems, including civil rights, with an open mind. Especially was this true in regard to the TVA. At one time or another, Kefauver pointed out, more than half of the Southern senators had voted against TVA. Without support from senators from other sections, TVA would not exist. Taylor, however, relentlessly focused on Kefauver's independence from the Southern bloc in the Senate. "I am tired of furnishing New York an extra senator," he complained. "You will never find me playing post office with a bunch of Northern liberals." [22]

It was taken for granted that Taylor would score heavily in staunchly segregationist West Tennessee, where the large Negro population made local whites especially sensitive to the issue of civil rights. Kefauver had very little visible support in West Tennessee, outside of Shelby County, and it was considered an ominous sign that a Kefauver campaign appearance in Somer-ville, Fayette County seat, drew only two people. In adjoining, and equally segregationist, Haywood County—the home of Ke-fauver's Estes relatives—feelings were running so high against both Kefauver and the Civil Rights Commission that a deputy sheriff and a Commission representative got into a scuffle during Kefauver's visit to the county. While Kefauver watched, the two men fought verbally and physically over the deputy's charge that Kefauver had requested an investigation of Negro treatment in Haywood County. [23]

One of Kefauver's greatest assets throughout his Senate career, of course, was his image, in the old populist tradition, as a crusader against corruption and privilege. In 1960, he was fortunate in having an important forum from which to carry on his battle for the public interest—the chairmanship of the Antitrust and Monopoly Subcommittee probe into the drug industry. Normally, of course, a senator facing a hard fight for re-nomination would have taken leave of his Washington responsibilities in order to devote his full time to what was considered a difficult campaign. Kefauver knew, however, that the drug hearings, with their constant headlines about excessive cost and questionable efficacy and safety, were the greatest possible boosts to his re-nomination effort. Thus it was no accident that the Antitrust and Monopoly Subcommittee turned the drug investigation up full blast in early 1960, with a whole series of sub-investigations into the areas of the drug industry of greatest concern to the public—corticosteroids (December 7–12, 1959), tranquilizers (January 21–22, 26–28, 1960), physicians and other professional authorities (February 25–26, April 12–15), the Pharmaceutical Manufacturers Association (February 23–24, April 20), oral antidiabetic drugs (May 10–13), and conflict of interest in the Food and Drug Administration (May 17–18, June 1–3, 6).[24]

There was no doubt that the drug industry was extremely upset with Kefauver's investigations, and at least one company sent a man down to see if Taylor could be discreetly supported. Once reported in the press, this threat of outside interference in the Democratic primary gave Kefauver a valuable issue against Taylor, who, ironically, met with little success in rounding up contributions from the automobile, steel, drug, and other industries claiming to be harassed by the Antitrust and Monopoly Subcommittee. Nevertheless, Kefauver spoke of "a big slush fund . . . being raised by the big pharmaceutical manufacturers, and by some druggists who have been taken in by the manufacturers in an effort to defeat me. The reason is that they don't want the prices of drugs to come down." In attacking the drug industry, Kefauver always distinguished between the drug manufacturers and the local druggists. However, many local druggists interpreted Kefauver's investigation as a personal reflection on them and openly backed Taylor. The President of the Tennessee Pharmaceutical Association urged members—even Republicans —to vote in the Democratic primary for Taylor and claimed that 98 per cent of the membership was backing the Judge. Late in the campaign, Kefauver directed his fire at local druggists who were opposing him and suggested to voters, "Whenever you see a drugstore that is supporting my opponent, you know he wants to keep prices high. You just go to another drugstore." [25]

The last month of the primary was overshadowed by the Democratic convention in Los Angeles. Kefauver had come under heavy pressure to endorse Lyndon Johnson, but he had balked at getting involved in the nomination fight. In early June, he had told the Knoxville News-Sentinel:

> As of the present time, I'm not endorsing any candidate. As I've said before I've served a long time with Lyndon Johnson, and he is well qualified and would serve capably in any office to which he was elected. But I've told people who've asked my advice that they should use their own judgment about whom to support.[26]

Kefauver even decided against attending the convention. "I'm left with 55 counties yet to visit," he explained, and asked Governor Ellington to name someone to replace him as a delegate. When Nancy was suggested, she joked, "He better not. I just want to enjoy this one." She did, however, go to Los Angeles to represent the Kefauver "interests." [27]

After Kennedy's nomination, Kefauver received a telegram from the nominee inviting him to sit on the platform during the acceptance speeches; Kefauver replied with congratulations to Kennedy and Johnson but regretted that he could not attend; he promised, however, to campaign for the national ticket once his primary campaign was over.[28]

Kefauver hailed Johnson's selection as the vice-presidential nominee and predicted it would go "a long way to healing the wounds opened between the North and the South at the convention." He revealed that Johnson had been his personal choice for President, "but I feel sure that Senator John Kennedy as President will use to the fullest extent Johnson's wide, rough and tumble experience." [29]

Johnson's nomination for second place was a definite boost to Kefauver's re-nomination prospects. Since Johnson had been the choice of the Deep South, he was in a special position to lead Southerners into support for the national ticket, which meant advocating the kind of moderation that Kefauver had come to represent in Tennessee politics. On July 30, the Saturday before the primary, Johnson was the guest of honor at a gigantic rally in Nashville sponsored by the Young Democrats. The tension between Kefauver and Taylor supporters was high, and Johnson's obvious gestures in Kefauver's direction came as somewhat of a surprise to the supporters of both Kefauver and Taylor. In spite of the fact that Taylor's backers had been almost unanimously pro-Johnson before the convention and Kefauver's support, although also predominantly pro-Johnson, included what Tennessee strength Kennedy, Humphrey, and Symington had had, Johnson made it clear that Kefauver, not Taylor, spoke for the Democracy represented by the Kennedy-Johnson ticket. After introducing Kefauver as "my beloved colleage," thus setting off both boos and cheers, Johnson launched into a plea for party and national unity that was in stark contrast to the Southern chauvinism which characterized the Taylor campaign: "Wherever I may go, I will never speak as Southerner to Southerner or as a Protestant to Protestant or as a white to whites. I will speak only as an American to Americans—whatever their region, religion or race." [30]

Johnson's appearance, plus a telegram from Kennedy to Kefauver which spoke of the nominee's "counting strongly on your support and friendship during the coming campaign and during the years of our administration," left no doubt that Kefauver was the choice of the national ticket. Similarly, Adlai Stevenson announced a strong endorsement of Kefauver in a letter which declared that "no member of the Senate has served the people—and I mean all the people—more faithfully. . . . I view your re-election as absolutely imperative both from the standpoint of the country and of the Democratic party." [31]

Organized labor also considered Kefauver's primary fight to

be one of the most important campaigns of the year and threw its support solidly behind him. The $40,000 Kefauver received from labor was only part of its contribution to the campaign and was supplemented by a grass-roots effort that was exceptional by Tennessee standards. Not only was Taylor totally unacceptable to labor, but Kefauver was one of labor's best friends in Congress and had been one of only two senators to receive a 100 per cent labor rating in the 1959 session.[32]

Judge Taylor, meanwhile, continued to attack Kefauver as an ultra-liberal who had sold out the South for personal political advantage. Opinion differed on Taylor's strength across the state, but his campaign seemed to be well financed and appeared to be gathering momentum. The unanswered question was the extent to which white concern over civil rights would cut into Kefauver's moderate support, and political observers began to report alarming defections to Taylor. By July, the national press had called the race a tossup, and moving into the last three weeks of the campaign, Taylor was considered to have edged ahead. *Newsweek* entitled a late July analysis of the campaign "Kefauver—Is This It?" [33] and the *New York Times* painted an even darker picture of Kefauver's prospects:

> Senator Estes Kefauver . . . is waging a desperate fight to retain his Senate seat. His supporters conceded today that he had little better than an even chance. . . . The Senator faces a well-organized campaign supported and financed by a coalition of segregationists, business men, lawyers and druggists. He is largely dependent upon the backing of a corps of volunteer housewives and college youths and his traditional strength among organized labor, Negroes and other liberal groups.[34]

The smear against Kefauver seemed to be working, and the success that Arkansas Governor Orval Faubus had riding the race issue to a landslide victory in mid-July caused a step-up in the hate campaign against Kefauver in Tennessee. Kefauver was especially upset that Taylor did not denounce the tactics being used by anti-Kefauver racists. "There have been misrepresentations, lies, innuendoes, [and] smears," Kefauver charged. "Judge Taylor has said that he knows of it, but he has not lifted a finger to do anything about it. It looks to me like a planned part of the campaign. I have reached that conclusion reluctantly." [35]

Even among those aware that Kefauver campaigns always overestimated the opposition, concern began to mount that Kefauver was indeed in trouble, and there were subtle moves in Kefauver's direction by key leaders who, although they usually looked askance at Kefauver's liberalism, feared the repercussions of a Taylor victory. Former Governor Clement, aware that a narrow Taylor defeat might pit the Judge against him in 1962, let it be known that he favored Kefauver's re-nomination. Clement's father appeared at a Kefauver rally, and Kefauver, in turn, went as far as saying that Clement had "done much good for Tennessee." Governor Ellington, never a Kefauver sympathizer, also disappointed the Taylor campaign by withholding the support of his organization from Taylor, who had been led to believe that he would receive the governor's unqualified blessing. In fact, the *Chattanooga Times* reported after the election that Ellington had aided Kefauver behind the scenes.[36]

The driving force behind the Kefauver campaign, of course, was the candidate himself. By one estimate "he shook 700 hands a day, made six to eight speeches, dictated 100 letters each evening to people he had met, and covered 26,000 miles in seven weeks of campaigning." [37] Kefauver's key campaign technique was the personal contact, and his efforts on the campaign trail had, by 1960, made him a walking legend. His advice to fellow politicians, which he faithfully followed himself, was to:

> Shake every voter's hand you can shake—but you really have to mean it. Personal contact is priceless, but if you don't really like people and your association with them, it will show through. . . . A simple courtesy that means much to a constituent is a personal letter. If you enjoyed seeing him—even if it was for only a moment—drop him a brief line to say so. If you know him and missed him when you were there, a note saying so will be greatly appreciated.[38]

Kefauver drove himself to the point of exhaustion during the 1960 campaign, and an adviser who returned to Tennessee for the last weeks of the campaign was shocked to see that Kefauver "looked like death itself." [39] Even more than usual Kefauver was running scared, and the frantic Kefauver campaign pace heightened the sense of desperation his supporters felt at the prospect of his defeat. Liberals around the country were dismayed at the press reports coming out of Tennessee, and the *Nation* pleaded with Tennessee voters to:

> make an inventory of the interests actively arrayed against Senator Estes Kefauver—racial bigots, super-patriots, big-time crooks and corrupt politicians still angry about the Senator's crime investigations, professional instigators of "right to work" campaigns, interests incensed by his investigations of pricing policies in the drug, auto and steel industries, enemies of TVA, and other political miscreants. Then . . . ask themselves this question: with such a collection of splendid enemies arrayed against him, . . . isn't this . . . the best evidence of the fact that he has served the interests of the people of Tennessee well . . . ? [40]

The *Chattanooga Times* similarly warned that "torrents of money from well-heeled interests are flowing in to defeat" Kefauver, an incorrect report nevertheless echoed elsewhere in the press.[41]

Kefauver's re-nomination problems seemed so serious that even some of Kefauver's Southern colleagues in the Senate came to his aid against the rising tide from the right. Senators Talmadge of Georgia, Long of Louisiana, Hill and Sparkman of Alabama, Yarborough of Texas, Johnston of South Carolina, Stennis of Mississippi, and Smathers of Florida sent friendly letters which the Kefauver campaign publicized in huge newspaper ads in the days before the primary.[42]

On the eve of the primary, Kefauver's prospects were thought to have brightened somewhat and the race was considered a tossup.[43] The results on August 4, however, handed political observers across Tennessee and around the country one of the biggest shocks of the year. In a massive turnout, Tennessee Democrats gave Kefauver one of the most overwhelming victories in the state's history, 463,848 to 249,336. Much to the shock of the Taylor organization, Kefauver swept both East (where Taylor had hoped for a small margin) and Middle Tennessee (expected to go for Kefauver) by incredible margins and came into West Tennessee with a lead of 351,533 to 125,308. Taylor, as expected, carried West Tennessee, but by the slim margin of 124,028 to 112,315. All in all, Kefauver lost only sixteen of the state's ninety-five counties, including staunchly segregationist Fayette (368–2805) and Haywood (721–2991), but he easily carried Memphis. Negro voters came out in record numbers to vote almost en masse for Kefauver; sample Negro precincts showed margins of 648 to 6, 941 to 14, 901 to 16, and 650 to 7.[44]

Kefauver hailed the primary results as an overwhelming victory for Southern progressivism and as evidence that "the detractors of the South, who tried to say we are a backward people, have been proven wrong." He predicted that his victory would "give great encouragement to other Southern congressmen, men who have been wanting to get away from this blind opposition on civil rights, but who have been intimidated by some of the faces around them." [45]

Taylor backers were shocked at the outcome, which the anti-Kefauver *Nashville Banner* called "one of the most surprising votes in Tennessee's political history." Some Taylor supporters were bitter. "It's all right with me," one Taylor manager said as the returns had poured in. "I don't care. If they want to give the state and the schools and everything else over to the niggers, I don't care. No sir." Others were more philosophical. The *Memphis Commercial Appeal* admitted that it had "misjudged" Tennessee opinion and that "without rancor and in the best of humor we will continue to view his [Kefauver's] progress with a more thoughtful attitude. . . . [H]is victory serves to emphasize the need for some of us to examine more closely the things that brought it about as well as the things he advocates." [46]

National observers saw Kefauver's victory as an indication that opposition to civil rights in the South was not as strong as had been feared and as a good omen for the Kennedy-Johnson ticket's November prospects in the state and in the South generally. Kefauver agreed, calling his victory "an indication that the South wants to go ahead with the New Frontiers advocated by our Democratic candidate." Kennedy himself expressed delight "that he [Kefauver] is going to continue in the Senate." [47]

Kefauver's re-nomination in 1960 was generally regarded as having established him as unbeatable in Tennessee. But it had been more than a personal triumph; Kefauver had appealed to the best instincts of Tennessee voters, and they had risen to the challenge. His victory, therefore, became another small step away from the narrow sectionalism that has plagued the South for over a century.

A few days after the primary, Kefauver returned to Washington and walked onto the Senate floor to take his usual place among his colleagues. Senator Wayne Morse of Oregon, who had the floor, immediately interrupted his speech to congratulate and praise Kefauver for his overwhelming victory. As Morse finished his remarks about Kefauver, the senators present stood and applauded.[48] Kefauver was somewhat embarrassed at all this attention, but he must have known, better than anyone, that this tribute was not for him alone, but for the position of reason and moderation he had just defended so well. It was a proud moment, not only for Kefauver, but for Tennessee, and most of all, for the nation as a whole.

chapter xxi

TRIBUNE OF THE PEOPLE
1961-1963

Kefauver's last years in the Senate were the most enjoyable of his entire career. He was firmly established in Tennessee politics after his overwhelming victory in 1960; he got along exceptionally well with his colleague from Tennessee, Albert Gore; the Democrats had wide margins in both the Senate and the House; and, for the first time since 1950, there was a relatively friendly White House.

Kefauver had campaigned hard in the fall of 1960, devoting thirty-eight days in sixteen states to electing the Democratic ticket, and was singled out by Drew Pearson as one of the five men who worked hardest to elect Kennedy.[1]

Kefauver had no trouble in the campaign expounding on Kennedy's theme that the Democrats would "get the country moving again." Kefauver himself had been criticizing Republican inaction for years and pointed out the contradiction in the Republican Administration that

> Out of one side of its mouth . . . says that we are in a period
> of unparalleled prosperity [but] out of the other side . . . claims
> that the country cannot "afford" Federal aid for school construc-
> tion, cannot afford to raise the disgracefully low salaries of our

teachers, cannot afford adequate Social Security or effective unemployment insurance, or decent minimum wages for our working men and women.[2]

"Nixon may make vaguely liberal speeches in the campaign," Kefauver warned, "but he always votes the other way. His friends and colleagues are hard-shell conservatives, men who have fought almost every decent reform that has been proposed for the last thirty years."[3]

The anti-Catholic campaign against Kennedy, especially in Tennessee, upset Kefauver, and he strongly denounced as "hatemongers" those who peddled "messages of suspicion and falsehood," attempting "to rally prejudice in place of reason" and "using every smear technique in the book to invoke hatred in an effort to win elections by hiding the issues." Kefauver called on his fellow citizens to "publicly disown it. And, more important, . . . immunize ourselves against it. . . ."[4]

The Bible Belt reaction against Kennedy was strong, however, and Tennessee gave Nixon a plurality of over 70,000 votes, in contrast to Eisenhower's 1956 margin of 6,000. Nevertheless, Kefauver, as expected, won a landslide victory over his token Republican opponent in November, 594,460 to 234,053.[5]

Kefauver was favorably impressed with Kennedy's most important appointments, especially Dean Rusk as Secretary of State, Chester Bowles as Undersecretary, and Adlai Stevenson as United Nations Ambassador. He was even more pleased by Kennedy's naming of Antitrust and Monopoly counsel Paul Rand Dixon as Chairman of the Federal Trade Commission, Joseph Swidler (former TVA general counsel) as Chairman of the Federal Power Commission, and Aubrey Wagner (former general manager of TVA) to the TVA Board. Public power and antitrust matters were Kefauver's greatest concerns, and the Kennedy Administration provided him with exceptionally strong allies on the key regulatory commissions.[6]

There were rumors throughout the Kennedy Administration that Kefauver himself was in line for a Supreme Court appointment. In June of 1961, even the *New York Times* reported that Kefauver was being considered as a replacement for aging fellow Southerner, Hugo Black. Again, when Justice Whitaker announced his retirement the following spring, Kefauver figured prominently in the speculation about the vacancy. He finally felt compelled to tell the press, "There is no foundation to the talk about my being offered or considering such an appointment." [7]

Although Kefauver did find the Kennedy Administration much more compatible than the Eisenhower Administration or the last years of the Truman Administration, he was disappointed at Kennedy's failure to provide the kind of leadership, especially in domestic matters, that the President had promised during the 1960 campaign. Nowhere was this made more painfully obvious to Kefauver than in the maneuvering behind the drug reform proposals which finally led to the Kefauver-Harris Drug Act of 1962. [8]

The Antitrust and Monopoly Subcommittee had first begun an examination of the drug industry in 1959 as part of its comprehensive investigation of administered prices. The drug investigation, however, in contrast to earlier administered price probes, developed a momentum of its own and became the single most important focus of the subcommittee under Kefauver's chairmanship. Kefauver was concerned about the drug industry for two reasons—first, he was shocked at the tremendous profits drug companies were earning on products for which there was a captive market and among which there was little competition; and, second, he was disturbed that drugs were being made available to the public without adequate evidence that they were both safe and effective. Thus, the drug investigation was unique among the administered price hearings in that the Antitrust and Monopoly Subcommittee exhibited special concern over the quality of the product and the uses to which it was put. This latter concern, of course, lay outside the jurisdiction of the subcommittee, and its investigation could be defended only to the extent that it could be shown to be an aspect of the problem of monopoly. Ironically, however, the legislation which came out of the drug hearings dealt almost completely with safety and efficacy rather than economic concentration in the drug industry. The drug investigation was Kefauver's finest hour as a public servant. Few members of Congress contribute as much to the public interest in their entire careers as Kefauver did during the almost three years the drug investigation had first claim on his time and energy. Even with the aid of such courageous public servants as Antitrust and Monopoly economist John Blair and subcommittee members Phil Hart of Michigan and John Carroll of Colorado, the drug investigation was one of the most physically and intellectually exhausting and politically dangerous challenges Kefauver ever undertook. He faced general apathy from the Eisenhower and Kennedy Administrations and outright opposition from bureaucrats defending cosy relationships with the drug industry, from the American Medical Association, unwilling to admit that it had not lived up to its responsibility to protect the public from unsafe drugs, and from conservatives in general, opposed to what they considered yet another attack on business. Even on the subcommittee itself, Kefauver patiently endured the obstructionism of two of the most notorious champions of special interests in the Senate, Everett Dirksen of Illinois and Roman Hruska of Nebraska, the latter such an apologist for business that he proved an embarrassment even to drug industry lobbyists who were, in the end, willing to acquiesce in several of the most needed reforms.

The investigative hearings (December 1959 to September 1960) [9] and legislative hearings (July 1961 to February 1962) consumed hundreds of hours and thousands of pages of testimony. The picture of the drug industry that emerged from the hearings was enough to make even the most cautious conservative agree that the public interest demanded at least some protection against industry practices. Witnesses told of conflicts of interest in the AMA (whose *Journal*, for example, received millions of dollars in drug advertising and was, therefore, reluctant to challenge claims made by drug company ads) and the Food and Drug Administration (where the worst abuse was the collection of $287,142 by the director of the Antibiotics Division for work done on promotional outlays by drug companies). The drug companies themselves were shown to be engaged in frenzied advertising campaigns designed to sell trade name versions of drugs that could otherwise be prescribed under generic names at a fraction of the cost; this competition, in turn, had led to the marketing of new drugs that were no improvements on drugs already on the market but, nevertheless, heralded as dramatic breakthroughs without proper concern for either effectiveness or safety. Information on side effects of these new drugs was made difficult for doctors to obtain, and even the FDA was under an arbitrary deadline to make a case against a new drug or license it for manufacture, in facilities that were subject to loose government standards.

Everyone seemed to agree on the need for drugs that were both safe and effective, although there was wide disagreement over the role, if any, that the federal government should play in protecting the public. However, there was considerably less support for Kefauver's solution to what he considered the problem of excessively high prices of drugs. Kefauver was concerned about two aspects of drug pricing. First, he questioned the very concept of allowing seventeen-year patents on products that were of vital interest to the public and suggested, instead, that the patent laws be amended with respect to drugs to force licensing to competitors at a royalty tied to calculated cost after three years of exclusive right to produce. Second, he was disturbed by the extent to which current licensing agreements and patent infringement settlements acted to fix prices at the expense of the consumer. In short, Kefauver felt that, apart from the questions of safety and efficacy, the drug industry suffered from a lack of real competition.[10]

In contrast to the earlier administered prices hearings, the Antitrust and Monopoly Subcommittee's investigation of the drug industry was widely followed by the national press, and as a result, Kefauver's office and the Antitrust and Monopoly Subcommittee were swamped with mail from people across the country who, because of personal experiences or because of press reports of the subcommittee hearings, were convinced that drug reform was long overdue.[11] Public opinion in general, therefore, was overwhelmingly on the side of legislation to remedy at least some of the most obvious loopholes in consumer protection.

On April 12, 1961, Kefauver introduced a bill embodying his reforms of the drug industry. From July 5 until the following February, the Antitrust and Monopoly Subcommittee held hearings on the bill, which, for the most part, covered the same ground as the investigative hearings of 1959–60. On March 8, 1962, the Antitrust and Monopoly Subcommittee reported Kefauver's bill favorably to the parent Judiciary Committee, which, over Kefauver's objections, referred it to the Subcommittee on Patents, Trademarks and Copyrights, where most of Kefauver's patent provisions were stricken. Kefauver, however, had hopes of restoring the provisions in the whole committee or on the Senate floor, and was, therefore, generally optimistic that most of his reforms would eventually win congressional approval.

What happened next vividly illustrates how thankless is the role of a genuine reformer in Washington's legislative process. After the groundwork for drug legislation had been patiently laid, and public opinion had been successfully rallied, the Kennedy Administration, which had previously given lip service but no effective help to Kefauver in the area of drug reform, suddenly stepped in to seize credit for a drug bill which it was thought might help brighten an otherwise dismal record on domestic affairs. The Administration sent its own drug bill to the House, bypassing Kefauver's bill in the Senate and Emanuel Celler's companion bill in the House. Not satisfied with this disregard for the preliminary work already done by both House and Senate committees, the Administration shortly thereafter decided to shift gears again and speed passage of a drug bill by dropping all the previously introduced legislation and writing yet another bill, a compromise measure put together in a secret meeting of representatives of Dirksen, Eastland, HEW, and the drug industry. Although the HEW representatives fought to have the new bill meet the minimums of Kennedy's 1962 consumer message, the bill hammered out in the secret meeting was, on the whole, a triumph for the drug industry, and Kefauver later quipped that about the best that could be said for the new bill was that it did not repeal the Food, Drug and Cosmetic Act of 1938.[12]

At the time, Kefauver knew nothing of the meeting; three days later, however, when the Judiciary Committee met to consider Kefauver's bill, as reported from the Patents Subcommittee, he was shocked to find that what he thought was a coalition (including Eastland and John McClellan of Arkansas) on behalf of his bill had dissolved and that a committee majority was now lined up behind the weak compromise measure, which also claimed HEW's blessing. For the first time, Kefauver learned that the Administration had gone behind his back to sell out not only the pricing provisions but most of the safety and efficacy provisions as well. He was furious. "I've never been so disturbed by double dealing in all my life," he complained after the meeting:

> I trusted those people. They've obviously decided that it would be better to get *some* kind of a bill—the weakest possible—passed now. That way, it will be another twenty-five years before anything more is done. And if they get this new bill through, they can say to the public, "The industry was investigated thoroughly and Congress did such and such. Now you can have complete faith in drugs again." Also, I think it was the feeling on the part of the administration, especially the F. D. A., that they didn't want many reforms to start with. This new bill shows that they were content with the most moderate improvements. Now they can claim that they got legislation through to protect the people. At the same time, they can say to the industry, "See, we didn't do you much harm." [13]

Kefauver was so upset over his treatment that, later that afternoon, he asked Majority Leader Mike Mansfield to delay a vote on the Interior Department's annual appropriation so he could address the Senate, which had gathered in response to the quorum call. The White House, although barely aware of what had gone on at the secret meeting, was nevertheless nervous about a public relations setback to the Administration's consumer image, and presidential adviser Myer Feldman called to beg Kefauver not to embarrass the Administration. Kefauver's reply that he had not been "so shoddily treated in twenty-three years in Congress" left no doubt that he had no intention of keeping quiet. Even a last minute plea through Bobby Baker did not deter Kefauver.[14]

In a tone that was uncharacteristic of both himself and the Senate, Kefauver launched into an attack on not only Dirksen, Hruska, and Eastland but also the Administration's handling of the matter:

> . . . today a severe blow to the public interest was delivered in the Senate Judiciary Committee.
>
> Most of the drug manufacturing industry and its acolytes have been punching away for some time at S. 1522, which is designed to make vital prescription drugs available to the people at reasonable prices.
>
> Today they swung a "haymaker" and just about knocked this bill right out of the ring.
>
> I refuse to believe that my colleagues in the U. S. Senate will let this sorely needed legislation go down "for the count" in this way. . . .
>
> I think the time has come for the spotlight to be turned on so that the people of this country can see who is on which side. . . .
>
> Much to my amazement, at a meeting of the Judiciary Committee this morning, I discovered that there had been a secret meeting . . . of which I knew nothing, and no member of the staff of the Antitrust and Monopoly Subcommittee knew anything. . . .
>
> [T]here had . . . been an agreement to water down virtually every . . . feature of the bill. . . .
>
> [Although Dirksen and Hruska] have generally, and I think admittedly, taken the position on these issues set forth by the

pharmaceutical drug manufacturing industry, . . . I cannot believe that there has been any backing away on the part of the President of the United States.

In view of the fact that representatives of the Department of Health, Education, and Welfare participated in secret meetings to damage this bill seriously, I think the people are now entitled to know just how they happened to be there and what the administration's present position is.[15]

Eastland replied immediately to Kefauver's charge, taking full responsibility for the secret meeting:

It was my obligation to do what I think was needed, to get a realistic drug program, so I asked those who represent the administration to meet with the staff of the Judiciary Committee and to meet with the staffs of Senators who opposed the bill or who opposed parts of the bill, to see if . . . we could arrive at a drug bill both healthy and wholesome, which would be a step forward. . . .

I admit that I did not call in my friend from Tennessee for consultation, because I thought it would be a futile act. I did not think he would make any agreement with respect to anything.[16]

Kefauver's emotional speech on the Senate floor, recognized as extremely unusual for the quiet-spoken Tennessean, at least had the effect of blowing the whistle on the watered-down bill; and while his own bill was now considered dead, he was thought to have mobilized enough opposition to the compromise version to keep it from passing in its present form.

Kefauver had not given up on some meaningful reform, however, and voted with a Judiciary Committee majority on July 12 to report the compromise bill to the floor, where he hoped to restore his stronger language. Three days later, Kefauver's efforts to strengthen the drug bill received a dramatic boost when details of the soon-to-be famous thalidomide tragedy began to attract public attention. As more and more was learned about the deformed babies whose mothers had taken a drug which had not been adequately tested, public support for a stronger drug bill mushroomed, and even opinion in Congress began to retreat to the stronger provisions of the Kefauver bill. What was especially ironic about the thalidomide tragedy, however, was the fact that the drug had been blocked in the United States under existing regulations. Logically, therefore, the public could very well have seen the tragedy as evidence that the FDA was doing a better job than critics like Kefauver thought possible. Nevertheless, it was true that thalidomide had been kept off the market in the United States only because of the courageous efforts of an FDA medical officer, Dr. Frances O. Kelsey, who had to bend existing regulations to block manufacturers' demands for clearance. In any event, the thalidomide tragedy set off a public uproar that knocked the final props out from under the Dirksen-Hruska-drug industry compromise.

The Kennedy Administration, ever alert for favorable publicity and sensitive to criticism like that of the *New York Times*, which pleaded with the Administration to "give Senator Kefauver some real support on this issue and not confine itself to generalities about its concern for consumers," [17] reversed itself again and announced that it did not back its own compromise measure after all and asked instead for a whole set of strengthening amendments. Kefauver, as usual, was not consulted. At the President's request, the drug bill went back to the Judiciary Committee, where Kefauver led the fight which dramatically strengthened it, although even this new version fell short of his original bill. Once back on the Senate floor, the latest version of the drug bill faced little opposition. Kefauver made one last try to have his patent provisions restored, but lost, 28 to 53, in a vote observers considered remarkably close, considering the previous lack of sympathy in the Senate for Kefauver's drug patent restriction proposals.

The final version of the bill contained most of the safety and efficacy provisions Kefauver had fought long and hard for: a requirement that there be substantial evidence that a drug be both effective and safe before licensing; increased government inspection of drug manufacturing plants; immediate removal from the market of drugs found to be an "immediate hazard to the public health"; increased time (from 60 to 180 days) for government consideration of new drug applications; batch by batch tests for antibiotics; generic names on drug products (in letters at least half as large as trade names); and mandatory distribution to doctors of information on effectiveness, usage, and side effects.

Kefauver was generally pleased with the bill. "As far as getting safer, better tested, more accurately advertised drugs, it's an excellent bill," he remarked. "I'm highly satisfied with that part of it." However, he was "not at all satisfied with the pricing part which was stricken from the original bill—the part that would really lower drug prices." [18]

When the bill finally cleared both Houses in October, the *New York Times* hailed its passage and singled out Kefauver as "the hero of this victory . . . who doggedly continued to push for this needed legislation despite widespread public apathy, lack of administration interest and bitter opposition from some industry and congressional sources." [19] Nevertheless, Kefauver had to call the White House on October 9 to get an invitation to the signing ceremony the next day and was astounded to learn that Dirksen was to be invited. "My God," Kefauver said, "the Republicans fought us every inch of the way. Why give them public praise? I'd rather there was no ceremony at all." [20]

If Kefauver had felt ignored the day before the ceremony, he was certainly the guest of honor at the signing itself, to which, appropriately, Dirksen had not been invited after all. Kefauver was congratulated all around, and even Kennedy recognized his long fight for the drug bill by offering him the first pen used to sign the measure. "Here," the President said, "you played the most important part, Estes." [21]

Kefauver's role in the fight over the drug bill, which reporters immediately nicknamed the Kefauver-Harris Drug Act, established him as the outstanding defender of the public interest in Congress, and his reputation soared with liberals, who had almost come to take him for granted. "Nobody has found in this quarter anything resembling blind partisanship in favor of . . . Estes Kefauver," declared Gerald Johnson in the *New Republic*:

> His perennial aspiration for higher office has been viewed from this angle with a lack-lustre eye, and so have many of his ideas. But the trend of events is forcing a change of attitude. . . . It is astonishing what a variety of rapscallions this one investigator has exposed.[22]

Consumer groups, which were just becoming aware of how rare a champion of the public interest actually is in Congress, adopted Kefauver as their hero, and even Kefauver's Senate colleagues took pains to associate themselves with his efforts. Paul Douglas of Illinois, perhaps Kefauver's best friend and ally in the Senate, found it ironic: "Men who had openly and secretly fought him [Kefauver] now flock to get on the bandwagon, and pretend that they were always his supporters." [23]

While Douglas may have been right about the public relations advantage back home of standing with Kefauver for the public interest, there were few in the Senate who could be counted on, in the absence of the kind of public support enjoyed by drug reform, to withstand consistently the tremendous pressures of special interest lobbyists, as was made painfully clear in the dispute over the communications satellite bill, which, along with the drug bill, occupied the attention of Congress in the late summer of 1962. At issue was whether the proposed communications satellite system, which both liberals and conservatives agreed was desirable, should be established, owned, and operated by the government or by a private corporation.[24] Kefauver attacked the proposal for a private corporation, which had the support of most Republicans, as well as the Kennedy Administration, as a giant "giveaway of millions of taxpayer dollars": [25]

In the first place, any privately owned organization will receive, free of charge, the benefits of billions of dollars of taxpayer-financed research. The taxpayer will get no direct benefit from this research; indeed, he will ultimately have to pay again for the use of the satellite in rates passed on to him by communications companies using it.[26]

It was also charged by liberals, and admitted by many supporters of the bill, that AT&T, already one of the world's largest monopolies, would eventually dominate the private corporation. "In effect," Kefauver and other congressional opponents charged, "AT&T would be the chosen instrument of the United States Government to own and control civilian space communication. This would be intolerable from the standpoint of the public interest." [27]

Nevertheless, the pressure on Congress to accept the private corporation was intense, and only a handful of senators joined Kefauver in opposition to the Administration bill—Neuberger and Morse of Oregon, Yarborough of Texas, Clark of Pennsylvania, Gruening and Bartlett of Alaska, Burdick of North Dakota, Long of Louisiana, and Kefauver's Tennessee colleague, Albert Gore.[28]

The small band of liberals embarked upon a filibuster to block Senate passage of the bill. Supporters of the measure, therefore, moved to invoke cloture to force a vote on the proposal. Southern conservatives were somewhat frustrated by the situation; they supported the bill but hesitated to vote for cloture, since they were not anxious to strengthen precedents for limiting the freedom of debate that was their most powerful weapon against civil rights proposals. On August 14, however, cloture was voted, 63 to 27. Although only four Southerners supported the motion, five others stayed away so that the two-thirds present and voting would succeed in shutting off debate. It was the first time since 1927 and only the fifth time in history that cloture had been voted—earlier in the session, in fact, two votes to shut off debate on a civil rights bill had failed, providing a revealing commentary on the priorities of the 87th Congress. Once cleared for a vote, the communications satellite bill passed the Senate easily, 66 to 11, as Kefauver and his allies went down to final defeat on the measure.

Although the fights over drug reform and the communications satellite system thrust Kefauver into the public eye, he was also hard at work on other aspects of the monopoly problem that attracted far less publicity. One of his quietest successes was a law strengthening antitrust enforcement procedures by authorizing the Attorney General to demand corporate records for use in civil antitrust investigations without first convening a grand jury, making possible much more efficient and faster Justice Department action against monopolistic practices.[29]

Less successful was Kefauver's attempt to ride the wave of unfavorable publicity which rocked the steel companies in the wake of President Kennedy's forced rollback of steel prices in the spring of 1962. Kefauver had co-operated with the President's offensive against the companies by acceding to Kennedy's request that Kefauver issue a statement condemning the price hike and threatening an investigation by the Antitrust and Monopoly Subcommittee. Once the confrontation ended, however, Kennedy was relieved to be able to drop the matter after temporarily holding the line on steel prices. Kefauver, nevertheless, sought to plow ahead in a detailed investigation of steel pricing.[30]

Kefauver's 1962 campaign against administered prices in the steel industry led to one of the most politically awkward moments of his career. On April 14, subpoenas were issued to twelve steel companies for records from which the Antitrust and Monopoly Subcommittee hoped to determine steel costs in 1954 and 1961, to decide if the 1962 steel price hike had been justified. The steel companies were unanimous in opposing the request, although eight agreed to furnish the records under protest. Four companies, however, refused to comply with the subcommittee's order and announced that they would fight the subpoenas. On August 21, a week after the original deadline, the Antitrust and Monopoly Subcommittee voted a second set of subpoenas, this time including certain corporate officers; to meet objections that the original request asked companies to reveal confidential information, the subcommittee asked for the data in a more simplified form. When the new subpoenas were also ignored, the subcommittee voted, 5 to 3, along party lines, to cite the officials and companies for contempt.[31]

The steel companies, however, had been at work contacting their friends on the full committee, and when the committee met on September 25 to consider the contempt citations, Kefauver was overruled, 10 to 5, with only the five Democrats on the Antitrust and Monopoly Subcommittee supporting the citations. It was an almost unprecedented slap at Kefauver personally and the Antitrust and Monopoly Subcommittee collectively, and no doubt reflected some of the lingering hostility of committee members such as Dirksen, Hruska, and Eastland toward Kefauver as a result of the embarrassing turn of events in the drug reform fight over the past three months.[32] Kefauver, however, took his setback philosophically and turned the subcommittee back to the general question of administered prices.

Kefauver's 1962 battles over drug reform, the communications satellite bill, steel prices, and administered prices in general, indicated the extent to which he had settled into the role of a legislative specialist after 1957, in dramatic contrast to the presidential candidate of the early 1950s who was expected to and, in fact, did exhibit a serious concern over all the major issues of the day. After his 1956 defeat, however, Kefauver had devoted more and more time to antitrust matters and rarely played a prominent role in the resolution of issues that fell outside the jurisdiction of his committee assignments.

Even Kefauver's career-long interest in public power found little expression after 1957. The annual battle for TVA funds had been made unnecessary after 1959, as a result of a self-financing arrangement whereby TVA got the authority to float its own bonds in return for a limit on its service area.[33] And after the fight for government owned and operated dams on the Snake River at Hells Canyon between Idaho and Oregon was lost, there were few opportunities in the Senate to battle for public power generally.[34]

The attention Kefauver was willing to devote to foreign affairs likewise dramatically declined after 1957. Although he did continue his interest in Atlantic Union and faithfully attended the meetings of the Interparliamentary Union, his 1958 choice of the Appropriations Committee over a Foreign Relations vacancy symbolized his shift away from international affairs.[35] He did continue to favor the pursuit of a rapprochement with the Soviet Union and the Communist bloc in general, and hailed Khrushchev's 1959 visit to the United States, although he warned that Americans should "labor under no delusions that he is a great, friendly Santa Claus of some sort. He is a shrewd and tough opponent. We must be very alert when the talking takes place." [36] In line with Kefauver's interest in easing East-West misunderstanding, he urged lifting restrictions on American travel to Red China, especially for newsmen, pointing out, "It is better to get news from there through our own people than from canned information of some Communist bureau." [37] Similarly, he expressed great satisfaction with the Nuclear Test Ban Treaty of 1963. "This country cannot make all those years at Geneva seem pointless for the world," he pleaded in supporting its ratification.[38]

In spite of his desire to speed the thaw in the cold war, however, Kefauver nevertheless remained a champion of American preparedness. "It is dangerous to talk of balancing our budget with death and destruction waiting around the corner," he replied to critics of military spending who hoped to reduce the federal budget at the expense of the Pentagon.[39]

Kefauver continued to advocate a moderate approach to the growing civil rights movement and served as one of the few Southerners willing to defend the Kennedy Administration's handling of the touchy issue. When violence against freedom riders in the spring of 1961 prompted Attorney General Robert Kennedy to send deputies into Alabama to protect demonstrators' safety, Kefauver declared that Kennedy "had no alternative":

> Our Nation and our people will not be able to count, today, the depth of the damage that has been done the cause of freedom throughout the world by these days of shame in Alabama. . . .
> I suggest that some of the local officials of Alabama have been negligent of their obligations to control brutality brought about by hotheaded lawlessness. . . .
> [M]uch as we regret the need for using U. S. marshals to protect the rights of people and to prevent violence, it seems to me that the Attorney General had no alternative in this instance. He is to be commended for taking this necessary step.[40]

Similarly, Kefauver came to President Kennedy's defense during the rioting in 1962 at the University of Mississippi which led to federal troops being sent onto the campus to protect the right of James Meredith to enroll at the university. Kefauver was especially critical of the role of Mississippi's racist governor, Ross Barnett, in stirring up trouble over Meredith's admission. Rejecting Barnett's self-proclaimed defense of states' rights, Kefauver flatly declared, "The authority of the United States Government has got to prevail in this kind of situation. If Barnett had realized that, the sad and disgraceful situation could have been avoided." [41]

When Kennedy was rocked by Southern criticism of his decision to use troops to protect Meredith, Kefauver gave him firm support and wired the President:

> I want to congratulate you upon the calm, fair and yet positive way you have handled the tragic situation in Mississippi. You have carried out your responsibility in a conciliatory mood with dignity and firmness. The whole nation should appreciate the way you met this crisis.[42]

When Chairman Eastland of Mississippi threatened to have the Judiciary Committee undertake an investigation of the federal government's role in the rioting surrounding Meredith's admission, Kefauver acted quickly to undercut the chairman by sending him a letter, which Kefauver leaked to the press, warning that such an investigation "might have the effect of further inflaming emotions and precipitating more trouble, making an already tragic situation even worse, if such is possible." In any event, Kefauver reminded the chairman, "Before any such investigation is undertaken, I feel that it should be first considered and acted upon by the full Committee." [43]

Such dramatic involvement in general national issues was rare for Kefauver after 1957, however, and for the most part, he devoted himself to the work of the Antitrust and Monopoly Subcommittee and the needs or requests of his Tennessee constituents. Although by January of 1963 he had completed over twenty-three years of service in Congress, including fourteen in the Senate, and was practically a walking legend in both Washington and Tennessee, he was still, at fifty-nine, relatively young by Washington's seniority-conscious standards and could look forward to many more years of Senate service—perhaps even the Judiciary Committee chairmanship, for which he was so ably qualified. In the meantime, the chairmanship of the Antitrust and Monopoly Subcommittee, the solid support back home, and the warm regard in which he was held by the public made his political future and opportunities for public service appear brighter than ever.

EPILOGUE

Kefauver's death on August 10, 1963, came as a severe shock to his colleagues and friends in Washington, and even more so to his constituents in Tennessee. It had been generally thought that a man who could survive the grueling presidential and vice-presidential campaigns of 1956 and the re-nomination battle of 1960 would have no trouble coping with the routine demands of a Senate seat secure until 1966. For Kefauver, however, exhausting schedules had become a way of life, and his 1960 victory had shifted the direction but had not slowed the pace of his activity. He had seemed almost inexhaustible; yet there had been a few warning signs that his health was at last failing under the crush of years of incredible demands upon his physical reserves. After his return from an April trip to Europe to study antitrust problems in the Common Market, he had been hospitalized for two weeks during a bout with Asian flu. In June, he pulled a tendon and was again hospitalized for several days.[1]

Meanwhile, the Antitrust and Monopoly Subcommittee plowed ahead with a vigorous schedule—looking into truth-in-packaging legislation (March 6–7, 13, 19–22, April 24–26), Common Market monopoly problems (March 8–April 22), the insurance industry (April 2–May 15), general administered price theory (May 21–23), and the practices of American drug companies in Colombia (May 27–June 25). Kefauver's control of the subcommittee had been shaken somewhat by the appointment of John McClellan of Arkansas to the vacancy created by the 1962 defeat of liberal Democrat John Carroll of Colorado, one of Kefauver's most faithful allies, and there were rumors that Judiciary Chairman Eastland was determined to create a conservative majority on the subcommittee. The moderates on Antitrust and Monopoly still held the balance of power, however, and Kefauver could count on support for most of his efforts.[2]

In late July he had spent ten days on a dude ranch in Arizona and had joined some of his Senate colleagues on a visit to Yellowstone National Park, returning to Washington to participate in the debate over legislation affecting the communications satellite corporation authorized the previous year. He had planned a trip to Tennessee in the fall for a county-by-county tour of the state.[3]

In August, however, Kefauver was especially concerned over a proposed windfall for the newly created private communications satellite corporation. Legislation had been framed which would require the corporation to reimburse NASA only for research "requested" by the corporation, but making the benefits of unrequested research available without charge. Kefauver, in opposing the legislation, led the fight for an amendment requiring payment for any taxpayer-supported research made use of by the corporation.

It was in the midst of a speech on behalf of his amendment that Kefauver was first stricken on August 8. While Senator Clinton Anderson of New Mexico stepped in to protect Kefauver's right to the floor, Senator Joseph Clark of Pennsylvania rushed over to Kefauver. "I don't feel right," Kefauver said. "I've got a stomach ache." Clark urged Kefauver to seek medical attention immediately. "No," Kefauver insisted, "I've got to keep going." After a slight delay, Kefauver returned to his speech, which he concluded with a summary of his objections to the special interest legislation:

. . . the Communications Satellite Corporation is a private monopoly, created for the special purpose of relieving the taxpayers of heavy research expenditures and of operating the only satellite corporation that will be a communications satellite corporation in the United States. . . . The corporation will be the only private beneficiary of these expenditures. . . .

Because it is the only private entity in the commercial satellite communications field . . . a single monopoly would be the beneficiary. . . . [I]t is clear, Mr. President, that this corporation intends to contribute practically nothing. All we ask is that it pay its fair share. Could anything be more just?

We do not ask that research stop. We do not ask private corporations to pay for the benefits the military gets from it. We only ask that this corporation pay its proportionate fair share. . . .

This amendment seeks to make sure that the corporation pays its fair share.

Mr. President, I yield the floor.[4]

Kefauver was then admitted to Bethesda Naval Hospital, where his indigestion was diagnosed as a mild heart attack. Complete bed rest for three weeks was ordered. The next day, however, a more serious condition was discovered—a dissecting aneurysm, or ballooning, of the wall of the ascending aorta— and immediate surgery was recommended. Kefauver, however, wanted to postpone the operation until Nancy and two of their daughters could fly in from Colorado. It was a fatal delay. Just about the time Nancy and the children landed at National Airport, Kefauver's aorta burst, and he died "quickly and peacefully" around 3:40 A. M.[5]

Washington and Tennessee received the news with shock and disbelief. President Kennedy declared:

The death of Senator Estes Kefauver has deprived the nation of one of its most distinguished leaders.

Senator Kefauver was a public servant of energy, integrity and talent. His devotion to the public interest and the welfare of the people of his state and country made him a powerful influence for good in our nation's affairs. As a friend and former Senate colleague, I will miss him.[6]

Adlai Stevenson, with and against whom Kefauver had run during the 1956 campaign, called Kefauver "a modest gentleman, a colorful political figure, a tireless public servant and an implacable foe of privilege and monopoly. The people have lost a gallant champion and I have lost an old friend and a comrade in arms." Similar tributes came from across the country and across the political spectrum.[7]

Kefauver was buried in Madisonville on August 13, in the family cemetery on the grounds of the old plantation house built by his great-grandfather Cooke in the 1840s. The simple Baptist funeral service was held before a huge crowd including such dignitaries as Vice-President Lyndon Johnson, Adlai Stevenson, and scores of senators, congressmen, and political leaders from all across the nation, who had come to join thousands of Kefauver's friends and supporters in paying their last respects to the fallen leader.[8]

Just as it had seemed especially characteristic of Kefauver that he should be struck down on the Senate floor while fighting for the public interest, it was even more fitting that he should be buried in the little rural county seat, surrounded by thousands and thousands of the ordinary people for whom he had fought so long and so hard. For, although the delegation of Washington dignitaries was tacit recognition that Kefauver had indeed been a power with which to reckon in the capital, almost none of his Washington colleagues really knew the man or understood his appeal to the people across the nation—an appeal based not only on the populist philosophy he espoused but also on the special relationship he was able to establish with millions of average citizens. Since the form of Kefauver's appeal was never clearly understood by political observers, it was naturally the substance—Kefauver's populism—that figured most prominently in the evaluations after his death of his life and career. To the *New York Times*, Kefauver:

> epitomized all that was most valid in the old Populist tradition of concern for individual rights against the suffocating encroachments of bigness. The effervescence of his efforts made him something of an anachronism in the cool atmosphere of the New Frontier, but every American is the beneficiary of his dedication, his indomitability and the primacy he assigned human values.[9]

The even more sympathetic *New Republic* agreed that Kefauver hailed from simpler, more uncomplicated times:

> Estes Kefauver had neither the intellectual style nor the restrained manner valued on the New Frontier or elsewhere in an increasingly technocratic society. He was a legacy from the past —from the muckrakers and progressivism—when it was still fashionable to believe that the people were the ultimate repository of wisdom and virtue. His faith is today largely discredited. But the new age which is dawning has yet to discover a new faith to replace it. Until it does, Estes Kefauver should not be forgotten.[10]

The judgment that Kefauver's "faith is today largely discredited" is especially startling, even with the perspective of less than a decade, to one who can see in Kefauver's herculean efforts as Chairman of the Antitrust and Monopoly Subcommittee both the foundation and inspiration for the mushrooming consumerism of our own time. Not only has the battle been carried on by the Antitrust and Monopoly Subcommittee, but for the first time there are important lobbies of private citizens, including such apolitical champions of the public interest as Ralph Nader, who are able to stand shoulder-to-shoulder with the few members of Congress who consistently put the public interest ahead of other considerations. Similarly, Kefauver's appeal to the people over the heads of the professional politicians seems especially contemporary to Americans who have steadily lost faith in the

two major political parties as vehicles for the popular will. Indeed, Senator Eugene McCarthy's 1968 battle plan in New
Hampshire was lifted from Kefauver's 1952 script, and Lyndon
Johnson's subsequent retirement is testimony to the relevancy of
taking an issue to the people when the professionals fail to respond. Likewise is George Wallace's ten million votes in 1968
indicative of the passing of an age when voters left politics to
the politicians.

Kefauver, then, was anything but an anachronism. Indeed,
he was on many very obvious issues far ahead of his time. And,
of course, integrity, which was his principal stock in trade, is
never out of date.

An understanding of what Kefauver stood for and fought
for, however, furnishes only part of the explanation of his success as a political figure. Equally important is the recognition
that he possessed a special kind of charisma—dramatically enhanced, of course, by his appeal to the traditional American
sympathy for the underdog, whether fighting organized crime,
political bosses, or corporation presidents—but founded ultimately on Kefauver's uncanny ability to make an incredible
number of his fellow citizens feel that something very personal
was at stake when his career was on the line. It was a talent that
almost defies objective analysis and certainly cannot be explained simply in terms of hands shaken, letters written,
speeches made, or favors done in response to the avalanche of
requests for aid and assistance which flooded his Washington
office. It was a gift that perhaps found its most objective expression in a tone of voice that communicated a combination of concern, fairness, integrity, understanding, and, to a surprising degree, helplessness—not in a personal sense, but helplessness in a
political sense—as if the success or failure of the immediate
cause rested in the hands of each and every individual who was
exposed to Kefauver's appeal.

It is easy, therefore, to see how the qualities which led to
Kefauver's success with the "people" contributed to his problems
with the professional politicians. Perhaps no one better captured

the essence of Kefauver's difficulties with the pros, in contrast to his great success with the voters, than Victor Ferrall, who served under Kefauver on the staff of the Antitrust and Monopoly Subcommittee for three years and, therefore, had ample opportunity to observe the Kefauver style in operation in the Washington political jungle:

Politicians, living in a world of outstretched hands, are not comfortable with a person who helps them until they feel confident that they have identified his selfish motivation. Selfless support emanating from idealism rather than more pragmatic interests makes politicians nervous. Kefauver, though no exception to this rule, was himself guilty of obscuring his ends. Though he enjoyed enormous political autonomy in Tennessee, he had not become a patriarchal statesman or "taken the overview," remaining until his death actively political. He was clearly not running for President or the Supreme Court. Thus, "What is he up to now?" was the question which plagued the Senate each time Kefauver plunged into a new area of political unpopularity and danger.

It was his high political morality that compounded the Senate's discomfort with Kefauver. I suppose the ultimately politically moral man is the martyr. The martyr's credo—"No matter what you say or do, I will waver neither from the ends I seek nor the means which I have chosen"—defines the borderline between personal incorruptibility and political stalemate. Incorruptible dedication to both ends and means is philosophically attractive, but anathema to political action. Every effective politician must have his price: what matters is what the price is.

Kefauver had his price, but his rates were unfathomable. Offer him elaborate gifts, and they would be spurned; offer him money, and he would surely expose and denounce you. But, bring in one vote from Red Boiling Springs that he was sure to get anyway, loan him your briefcase, eat a ham sandwich with him on a plane to Knoxville, engage in any one of a myriad of apparently unrelated little friendships and you might win the friendship of a U. S. Senator that others would have paid hundreds of thousands of dollars to obtain. Kefauver sought and seriously considered the advice of a perfectly astonishing potpourri of corporation counsels and Capitol Hill policemen, laborers, and landowners. With respect to listening to advice, he was unalterably antifree competition. The highest bid always lost—the lowest often won. Whether this is good or bad from the longrun point of view of an effective legislature, I do not know. There can be no question, however, that Kefauver was unfailingly, unflinchingly honest.[11]

Kefauver, then, was the rarest of political animals—a politician, and a very successful one at that, who was never a true politician at all, but, rather, an advocate for his own legislative objectives, which, to an extent that made him even more unique in political life, bore a striking similarity to what was recognized, even by those who ignored it, as the public interest. His was an approach to issues that left little room for negotiation and compromise.

It is often said that no legislative body can afford too many men of principle—that the ability to work for a consensus is a noble end in itself and essential if the very concept of representative government is to survive. But if representative government cannot afford too much integrity, neither can it afford too little. That American political life during the middle third of the twentieth century set its sights a little higher was due in no small part to the courage and idealism of Estes Kefauver.

NOTES

Abbreviations for frequently cited sources:

CT	*Chattanooga Times*
CQA	*Congressional Quarterly Almanac*
CQWR	*Congressional Quarterly Weekly Report*
CR	*Congressional Record*
KP	Estes Kefauver Papers, University of Tennessee Library, Knoxville
KS	Jack Anderson and Fred Blumenthal, *The Kefauver Story* (New York, 1956)
NYT	*New York Times*

Chapter i

1. *Louisville Courier-Journal,* April 3, 1960.
2. *CR* 88:8068 (10/12/42).
3. *CQA,* III (1947), 500–502; however, in the ten other former Confederate states, there was only one affirmative vote in 1947; for a detailed, if biased, account of the poll tax issue in Tennessee politics, see Jennings Perry, *Democracy Begins at Home: The Tennessee Fight on the Poll Tax* (Philadelphia, 1944).
4. Charles Bartlett, "The Crusading Kefauver," *The Nation,* CLXXIV (May 3, 1952), 426.
5. *CT,* March 11, 1944.
6. *Ibid.,* March 17, 1946.
7. David E. Lilienthal, *The Venturesome Years, 1950–55* (Vol. III of *The Journals of David E. Lilienthal;* New York, 1966), 408.

8. *NYT,* June 29, 1946.

9. *CT,* April 7, 1944; for a good summary of McKellar's running battle with the TVA, see Joseph P. Harris, *The Advice and Consent of the Senate* (Berkeley, 1953), 155–77.

10. Letter from Alfred D. Mynders to George Fort Milton, undated, in George Fort Milton Papers, Container 86, May 1–28, 1942 folder.

11. Letter from George Fort Milton to Alfred D. Mynders, May 25, 1942, in *ibid.*

12. *CT,* July 18–22, 1944.

13. *Ibid.,* July 19–22, 1944.

14. *Official Report of the Proceedings of the Democratic National Convention* (Chicago, 1944), 240–41.

15. Letter from Kefauver to Thomas N. Schroth of the *Brooklyn Eagle,* June 13, 1951, in *KP:*66:1.

16. Letter from Henry Wallace to Kefauver, Aug. 1, 1944, in *KP:*91:2.

17. *CT,* July 22, 1944; also see William D. Miller, *Mr. Crump of Memphis* (Baton Rouge, 1964) for Crump's evolution, in his own eyes, from politician to statesman.

18. *CT,* July 22, 1944; *Official Report . . . Democratic National Convention* (1944), 270.

19. Letter from McKellar to Crump, in Crump Papers, quoted in Miller, *op. cit.,* 323.

20. *CT,* Aug. 2, 1944.

21. *NYT,* Oct. 29, 1944; undated clipping from *St. Louis Globe-Democrat,* in *KP:*91:2; the unfavorable publicity resulting from Kefauver's association with the One Thousand Club was probably the reason that Kefauver's 1944 Republican opponent made the strongest showing of any of Kefauver's general election opponents; in 1944, Kefauver received 32,497 votes; Republican Foster Johnson polled 11,541; *Tennessee Blue Book, 1945–1946,* 273.

22. Letter from Kefauver to Matthew Connelly, Nov. 7, 1945, in *KP:*Political, 1946.

23. Letter from Gordon Browning to Kefauver, Dec. 1, 1945, in *KP:*Political, 1948, A–C.

24. See letters in *KP:*Political, 1946.

25. Letter to Kefauver from Silliman Evans, Jan. 11, 1946, in *ibid.*

26. Letter from Kefauver to Adolph Ochs, Feb. 25, 1946, in *KP:*91:1.

27. Letter from Kefauver to Whitworth Stokes, April 29, 1946, in *KP:*91:2.

28. Letter to Kefauver from Milton B. Ochs, May 3, 1946, in *KP:*91:2.

29. See letters in *KP:*Political, 1946.

30. Letter from Kefauver to John Carson, May 4, 1946, in *ibid.*

31. Letter from Kefauver to R. W. Mehaffey, May 10, 1946, in *ibid.*

32. *KS*, 82–86; unidentified clipping in *KP*:1946; *CT*, Aug. 1, 1946.
33. *KS*, 85–86.
34. *Tennessee Blue Book, 1947–1948*, 251.
35. In the 1946 primary, McKellar defeated Carmack 188,805 to 107,363; McCord defeated Browning, 187,119 to 120,535; see *ibid.*, 248–50; *CT*, Aug. 1–7, 1946.
36. Undated clipping from fall, 1946, from *Chattanooga Free Press*, in *KP*:Political, 1948, A–C; Burch Biggs was the Polk County Democratic boss and an ally of the McKellar-Crump machine.

Chapter ii

1. Letter to the author from Mrs. Tom (Martha) Ragland, Jan. 11, 1970. Emanuel Celler recalled similar early impressions of Kefauver:

> When we served together on the Committee on the Judiciary of the House, I soon recognized in him the intellectual strength combined with a gentleness that made him unique. Listening to Estes then, it would have been difficult to predict that he could capture the hearts of millions of our people—so withdrawn and so reticent did he, at times, appear. (*Memorial Services . . . Carey Estes Kefauver*. 88th Congress, 1st Session. Government Printing Office, 1964, 133.)

2. A full treatment of the background and history of efforts to make cabinet officials directly responsible to Congress is provided by Stephen Horn, *The Cabinet and Congress* (New York, 1960).
3. *CR* 88:9310–17 (12/3/42).
4. Letter from Kefauver to John A. Vieg of Pomona College, April 3, 1945, in *KP*:91:1.
5. *CR* 89:378 (1/26/43), 8544 (10/19/43); Horn *op. cit.*, 137.
6. *CR* 89:9459–63 (11/12/43).
7. Horn, *op. cit.*, 139; *CR* 89:9677–79 (11/18/43).
8. *NYT*, Nov. 18, 21, 1943; *CR* 89:10.040 (11/26/43).
9. Horn, *op. cit.*, 152.
10. *Ibid.*, 139–57.
11. *NYT*, Nov. 21, 1943.
12. *Ibid.*, Dec. 22, 1943.
13. *Washington Post*, Feb. 3, 1944.
14. *CR* 90:A302 (1/19/44), 3272 (3/29/44).
15. *Ibid.*, 3272.
16. Editorial, *Life*, XVI (Feb. 21, 1944), 38.

17. Horn, *op. cit.*, 158–67; letter from Kefauver to Roosevelt, Feb. 1, 1944, in *KP:* Congress, II.

18. *CR* 93:49 (1/3/47), 1744–47 (3/6/47).

19. Quoted in "Should the Constitutional Treaty Process Be Preserved?" *Congressional Digest*, XXIV (April, 1945), 111.

20. *NYT*, Feb. 5, 1947.

21. Estes Kefauver, "I Oppose Limiting the Presidential Term," *Christian Science Monitor Magazine* (Jan. 5, 1946), 3, 16.

22. *NYT*, Feb. 5, 1947.

23. Estes Kefauver, "A Communication," *New Republic*, CXI (Nov. 6, 1944), 596–97.

24. Estes Kefauver, "Our Presidential Election System," *Vital Speeches*, XIV (May 15, 1948), 478–80.

25. Claude Pepper and Estes Kefauver, "Reform Congress Now," *New Republic*, CXIV (May 13, 1946), 676.

26. Estes Kefauver, "Did We Modernize Congress?" *National Municipal Review*, XXXVI (Nov. 1947), 552–57.

27. Estes Kefauver and Jack Levin, *A Twentieth Century Congress* (New York, 1947).

28. *Ibid.*, ix.

29. *Ibid.*, 133–42.

30. *Ibid.*, 96–113.

31. *Ibid.*, 44–205.

32. James MacGregor Burns, review of *A Twentieth Century Congress*, in *The Mississippi Valley Historical Review*, XXXIV (Dec. 1947), 513–14; see also Roland Young, review of *A Twentieth Century Congress*, in *Public Administration Review*, VIII (Spring, 1948), 141–46.

33. *New York Herald-Tribune*, March 20, 1947.

34. *NYT*, Sept. 30, 1946.

35. Coleman A. Harwell, "Estes Kefauver, Candidate for President" (pamphlet prepared for the 1956 pre-convention campaign by the *Nashville Tennessean*), available in *KP:*66:1.

36. *NYT*, Feb. 16, March 12, 1947.

37. *Ibid.*, March 12, 1947.

38. *Ibid.*, July 22, 1947.

39. *Ibid.*

40. *CR* 93:9111 (7/16/47).

41. Estes Kefauver, "The Sherman Act and the Enforcement of Competition: Needed Changes in Legislation," *American Economic Review*, XXXVIII (May, 1948), 182–202.

42. *CQA*, III (1947), 500–502.

43. Letter from Kefauver to Mr. R. L. Smith, President, International

Chemical Workers, Local No. 87, Chattanooga, March 16, 1945, in *KP*:1948 Campaign, C–L.

44. *CR* 94:9549 (7/29/48).
45. *CR* 94:9549 (7/29/48).
46. *Ibid.*
47. *CQA,* I (1945), 136.
48. *Ibid.,* II (1946), 248.
49. *Ibid.,* 130–31, 388–89.
50. *Ibid.,* IV (1948), 326–27.
51. *Ibid.,* III (1947), 480, 502–4; IV (1948), 46–49.
52. *Ibid.,* I (1945), 179, 187, 283, 287, 455; II (1946), 144–54, 601–13; III (1947), 304–7.
53. Letter from Kefauver to Henry Wallace, April 20, 1945, in *KP*:91:1.
54. Undated newspaper clipping in *KP*:1946, Political.

Chapter iii

1. *KS,* 100–101; letters and memoranda in *KP*:91:1.
2. *CT,* July 24, 1954.
3. Rough draft of an article by Charles L. Fontenay, in *KP*:61&71.
4. Announcement of candidacy, Nov. 9, 1947, available in *KP*:1948, Political.
5. *Ibid.*
6. Richard Wallace, "Defeat Comes to Boss Crump," *National Municipal Review,* XXXVII (Sept. 1948), 417; see also Charles Edmunson, "How Kefauver Beat Crump," *Harper's Magazine,* CXCVIII (Jan. 1949), 79.
7. Estes Kefauver, "The Best Advice I Ever Had," *Reader's Digest,* LXV (Aug. 1954), 134.
8. *NYT,* Nov. 10, 1947.
9. *Memphis Commercial Appeal,* July 4, 1948.
10. *CT,* Jan. 16, 1948.
11. *Nashville Tennessean,* Aug. 10, 1963; see also Charles L. Fontenay, "Estes Kefauver" (undated pamphlet published by the *Nashville Tennessean*), available in *KP*:61&71.
12. Estes Kefauver, "How Boss Crump Was Licked," *Collier's,* CXXII (Oct. 16, 1948), 24.
13. *Ibid.*
14. Edmundson, *loc. cit.*
15. *Ibid.*
16. *Ibid.,* 79–80; William Buchanan and Agnes Bird, *Money as a Campaign Resource: Tennessee Democratic Senatorial Primaries, 1948–*

1964 (Princeton, 1965), 17; interview with John Doughty, Aug. 2, 1969.

17. Edmundson, *loc. cit.*, 82–83; see also, for a summary of Crump's role in the 1948 Democratic primary, Ralph G. Martin, *The Bosses* (New York, 1964), 157–63.

18. *CT*, July 9, 1948.

19. *Ibid.*

20. Estes Kefauver, "How Boss Crump Was Licked," 25.

21. *NYT*, Dec. 14, 1947; William D. Miller, *Mr. Crump of Memphis* (Baton Rouge, 1964), 324.

22. Estes Kefauver, "The Best Advice I Ever Had," 133; see also excerpts from remarks by Kefauver at a panel discussion on political surveys, at Williams College, Sept. 22, 1962, in *KP:*Polls.

23. This explanation, never given during the campaign, was offered by Crump associate Judge Lois D. Bejach of the Tennessee State Court of Appeals in an interview Jan. 4, 1962, with Allen Hampton Kitchens, who referred to it in his paper, "Political Upheaval in Tennessee: Boss Crump and the Senatorial Election of 1948," *West Tennessee Historical Society Papers*, XVI (1962), 111–12; for a Crump quote and a different explanation of Crump's decision to back Mitchell, see Miller, *op. cit.*, 324.

24. *CR* 94:1164–66 (2/9/48).

25. *CT*, July 1, 1948.

26. *Ibid.*, July 4, 1948.

27. *Memphis Commercial Appeal*, July 16, 1948.

28. *CT*, July 16, 1948.

29. *Ibid.*, Aug. 3, 1948.

30. Letter from Will Gerber to Senator Kenneth McKellar, Feb. 19, 1948, in McKellar Papers, quoted in Miller, *op. cit.*, 323–24.

31. The ad became a news story itself and was first reported from Memphis, where the text of the ad was made available by the *Commercial Appeal*, a Crump ally, a day before its publication on June 10. The pro-Kefauver *Chattanooga Times* printed the text on June 10 as part of the coverage of the campaign, thereby saving Crump the cost of the ad in that paper.

32. *Memphis Commercial Appeal*, June 10, 1948.

33. Edmundson, *loc. cit.*, 82.

34. Radio speech by Kefauver over Station WDOD, Chattanooga, June 14, 1948, text in *KP:*State Senate Race, 1938.

35. Edmundson, *loc. cit.*, 82; an outdoorsman who happened to be in Kefauver headquarters in Nashville began talking by chance with Kefauver campaign manager Charles Neese, and they eventually got around to the All-American qualities of the coon; it did not

take Neese and other staff workers long to see the campaign possibilities of the coon image. After checking out coon "character traits" in the public library, the coon was officially adopted by the Kefauver campaign; see letter from Neese to Miss Lucile Myers (July, 1969), in possession of the author.

36. *Ibid.*

37. The cap had first been used in a Tennessee Bar Association skit on the election; it was after the TBA meeting that George Clark sent the cap to Kefauver; see letter to Miss Lucile Myers from Jere Tipton, July 30, 1969 (in the possession of the author); the quotation is from the above cited letter from Charles Neese to Miss Myers; one version, however, gives Jack Bailhe, a Kefauver press agent from New York, credit for the coonskin cap idea; see Jay Walz, "A Tennessee Crusader Tackles Crime," *New York Times Magazine* (July 30, 1950), 10.

38. Rufus Terral, "Southern Liberalism Gains a Hope," *Survey Graphic*, XXXVII (Dec. 1948), 503; Fontenay, *loc. cit.*

39. Edmundson, *loc. cit.*, 82.

40. *Ibid.*

41. Miller, *op. cit.*, 326–27.

42. *Nashville Banner,* July 21, 1948.

43. *Memphis Commercial Appeal,* July 9, 1948; "The Boss and the Editor," *Newsweek,* XXXII (July 19, 1948), 19–20; *CT,* July 8, 1948.

44. *Memphis Commercial Appeal,* July 8, 1948.

45. *Ibid.;* see also Edmunson, *loc. cit.*, 83.

46. Edmundson, *loc. cit.*

47. *CT*, Aug. 4, 1948.

48. *Ibid.,* July 6, 1948.

49. *Ibid.,* July 18, 1948.

50. Buchanan and Bird, *op. cit.*, 18.

51. *CT,* July 15, Aug. 1, 1948.

52. Edmundson, *loc. cit.*, 82.

53. *CT,* July 8, 1948.

54. *Ibid.,* July 9, 1948; Kefauver received very little financial help from labor; see Buchanan and Bird, *op. cit.*, 18.

55. *CT,* July 16, 1948.

56. *Ibid.,* July 12–15, 1948.

57. *Ibid.,* July 16, 1948.

58. Edmundson, *loc. cit.*, 83.

59. *CR* 94:9549 (7/29/48); however, after the primary, Kefauver told Mrs. Tom (Martha) Ragland that "I believe now I would have won even if I had come out for FEPC," indicating that he was

more sympathetic to Truman's civil rights program than his public pronouncements indicated; letter from Mrs. Ragland to the author, Jan. 11, 1970.

60. *CT*, July 30, 1948.

61. *Ibid.*, Aug. 3, 1948.

62. *Ibid.*, July 30, 1948.

63. *Ibid.*, July 27, Aug. 4, 1948; Terral, *loc. cit.*, 504.

64. *Ibid.*, Aug. 5, 1948.

65. *Nashville Tennessean*, Aug. 6, 1948.

66. *Tennessee Blue Book, 1949–1950*, 276.

67. *CT*, Aug. 7, 1948.

68. *NYT*, Aug. 8, 1948.

69. *Knoxville News-Sentinel*, Aug. 6, 1948; see also editorials in *CT*, Aug. 7, 1948, and *Memphis Press-Scimitar*, Aug. 6, 1948.

70. *CT*, Aug. 7, 1948. The substantial support Kefauver received in Shelby County was not due to a sudden disillusionment of Memphians with Crump but, rather, primarily to the temporary defection of Crump's traditional allies among the AFL in Memphis, whose support Kefauver won as a result of his opposition to the Taft-Hartley Act in 1947; interview with Mr. and Mrs. Stanton Smith, Aug. 1, 1970.

71. Quoted in Miller, *op. cit.*, 333.

72. *CT*, Aug. 8, 1948.

73. For a general discussion of how this relationship developed and affected Tennessee politics in the 1930s and 1940s, see William Goodman, *Inherited Domain: Political Parties in Tennessee* (Knoxville, University of Tennessee *Record*, Extension Series, III, 1954, No. 1), 1–48.

74. *Memphis Commercial Appeal*, April 16, Oct. 7, 1948.

75. Miller, *op. cit.*, 334.

76. *NYT*, Oct. 30, 1948; *Tennessee Blue Book, 1949–1950*, 293, 297; the final vote totals were: Kefauver 326,142 Reece 166,947; Browning 363,903, Acuff 179,957; Truman 270,402, Dewey 202,914, Thurmond 73,815. Crump did succeed in carrying Memphis for the States Rights ticket, 26,396 to Truman's 23,854.

Chapter iv

1. *Nashville Banner*, July 1, 1954.

2. *KS*, 123.

3. Letter from McKellar to Kefauver, quoted in *ibid.*, 123–24.

4. Letter from McKellar to Truman, quoted in *ibid.*, 124.

5. *Nashville Banner,* July 1, 1954.
6. Interview with Representative (and ex-Senator) Claude Pepper of Florida, Jan. 14, 1969.
7. Quoted in *KS,* 126.
8. *CQA,* VII (1951), 334.
9. *Ibid.,* V (1949), 52, 671.
10. *NYT,* Jan. 13, 1949.
11. Rowland Evans and Robert Novak, *Lyndon B. Johnson: The Exercise of Power* (New York, 1966), 32.
12. Letter from Truman to Kefauver, Jan. 21, 1949, in *KP:*General Correspondence, 1948–55.
13. *CR* 95:2238–41 (3/11/49).
14. *CQA,* V (1949), 52, 671.
15. *Ibid.,* VI (1950), 37, 355.
16. *CR* 95:105 (1/10/49).
17. *CR* 95:12,511 (8/30/49).
18. Celler said that if Kefauver had done nothing more during his twenty-five years in Congress than what he did on behalf of the Kefauver-Celler Act, he would, judged on that legislation alone, be one of the most effective members of Congress during the period during which he served; interview with Celler, Jan. 15, 1969.
19. For a political treatment of the basing point legislation, see Earl Lathan, *The Group Basis of Politics: A Study in Basing-Point Legislation* (Ithaca, N. Y., 1952). For an excellent summary of the issues involved, see *CQA,* V (1949), 705–14.
20. *CQA,* VII (1951), 119, 789.
21. *Ibid.,* VI (1950), 392.
22. *CR* 96:14,199 (9/5/50); *CR* 96:14,596–97 (9/12/50).
23. *CQA,* VI (1950), 397.
24. *Ibid.*
25. *CR* 96:15,553 (9/22/50).
26. *CQA,* VI (1950), 397.
27. *CR* 96:15,192 (9/20/50).
28. *CQA,* VI (1950), 397, 543.
29. *CQWR* (May 4, 1956), 502–3.
30. *CR* 96:3206 (3/13/50).
31. *CR* 96:6978 (5/12/50).
32. *CR* 96:3206 (3/13/50); *NYT,* April 26, Aug. 7, 1951; *CQWR* (May 4, 1956), 502–3.
33. Estes Kefauver, "What's to Be Done About Congress?" *New York Times Magazine* (Sept. 11, 1949), 9, 32–34.
34. *CQA,* VII (1951), 381; *NYT,* June 1, 5, 1949.

35. *NYT*, Jan. 6, 22, 1949; *CQA*, V (1949), 628; Estes Kefauver, "Political Competition Will Help the South," *Virginia Quarterly Review*, XXVI (Spring, 1950), 268–76; *CQA*, V (1949), 628.
36. *CT*, July 24, 1954; "The Senate's Most Valuable Ten," *Time*, LV (April 3, 1950), 20; "Who Are the Nation's Best and Worst Senators?" *Pageant*, V (Oct. 1949), 9–16, especially 15, 16.

Chapter v

1. *CR* 96:67–68 (1/5/50).
2. Paul S. Deland, "The Facilitation of Gambling," *Annals of the American Academy of Political and Social Science*, CCLXIX (May, 1950), 22.
3. "Politics Hides Gambling Rackets That Take Billions from Public," *U. S. News and World Report*, XXVIII (April 21, 1950), 12; "Kefauver Circus," *Newsweek*, XXXVII (March 12, 1951), 22.
4. Jay Walz, "A Tennessee Crusader Tackles Crime," *New York Times Magazine* (July 30, 1950), 10; *KS*, 140–41; Estes Kefauver, *Crime in America* (Garden City, N. Y., 1951), 1–2; *NYT*, July 12, 15, Sept. 12, 20, 1945.
5. Robert Coughlan, "How Stumping Kefauver Stumps the Pros," *Life*, XL (May 28, 1956), 177; *Crime in America*, 317; *Concord* (N. H.) *Monitor and New Hampshire Patriot*, Oct. 4, 1963.
6. *CQA*, VI (1950), 437; "We Who Serve," *Time*, LV (April 24, 1950), 25.
7. "We Who Serve," 25; see also Harry W. Kirwin, *The Inevitable Success: Herbert R. O'Conor* (Westminster, Md., 1962), 447–48; *KS*, 142–44; *NYT*, May 4, 1950.
8. Estes Kefauver, "Let's Cut Out These Congressional High Jinks," *American Magazine*, CXLV (April, 1948), 143–44.
9. *Congressional Quarterly Log for Editors*, VIII (April 14, 1950), 446.
10. *The Kefauver Committee Report on Organized Crime* (New York, 1951), 9–10.
11. *Ibid.*, 10; *Crime in America*, xiv, 12.
12. *NYT*, March 25, 1951.
13. Lester Velie, "Rudolph Halley—How He Nailed America's Racketeers," *Collier's*, CXXVII (May 19, 1951), 80–82; "Who's a Liar?" *Life*, XXX (April 2, 1951), 24.
14. "Quizzing Kefauver," *U. S. News and World Report*, XXX (April 20, 1951), 27.
15. Estes Kefauver, letter to the editor of *The Nation*, CLXXIII (Aug. 18, 1951), 140; *NYT*, March 27, 1951.

16. *Kefauver Committee Report*, 12–17.
17. *NYT*, June 27, Oct. 4, 1951.
18. *Ibid.*, Sept. 26, Oct. 5, 1950; "It Pays to Organize," *Time*, LVII (March 12, 1951), 23; "I'm Awfully Hot," *Time*, LVI (Oct. 9, 1950), 24–25.
19. *Chicago Sun-Times*, Nov. 2–8, 1950; *Chicago Daily News*, Nov. 2–8, 1950; *KS*, 166–67.
20. "Meet the Press," Nov. 12, 1950, available in the Motion Picture Division of the Library of Congress.
21. But in 1952, when he was trying to line up professional support for his Presidential bid, Kefauver stressed that "I don't believe it is fair, and I don't think the record will sustain the complaint that we were instrumental in swaying the elections anywhere"; see "The Rise of Senator Legend," *Time*, LIX (March 24, 1952), 23; *NYT*, Oct. 15, 1954.
22. "Gambling Proposals Lose in Four States," *Christian Science Monitor*, LXVII (Nov. 22, 1950), 1380–81. For two articles discussing the reaction of the religious community to the Kefauver Committee, see "Outlaw Organized Gambling," *Christian Century*, LXVIII (March 21, 1951), 358–59; "Kefauver Probe Stuns Cleveland," *ibid.*, 370.
23. William S. White, *Citadel* (New York, 1956), 260–63.
24. "Quizzing Kefauver," 26.
25. *St. Louis Post-Dispatch*, Aug. 1, Sept. 28–Oct. 1, 1950. *Washington Post*, July 16, Aug. 23–24, 1950.
26. "Keeping Kefauver," *Newsweek*, XXXVII (April 9, 1951), 18.

Chapter vi

1. Undated memo in *KP*:Congress, II.
2. Estes Kefauver, *Crime in America* (Garden City, N. Y., 1951), 313–14; memo in *KP*:"Crime in America." For another version of the origin of the idea to televise the Kefauver Committee hearings, see Blair Moody, "The United States Senate," *Holiday*, XV (Feb. 1954), 90.
3. "Quizzing Kefauver," *U. S. News and World Report*, XXX (April 20, 1951), 26.
4. Frank McNaughton, "Would a TV Congress Improve Democracy?" *Public Utilities Fortnightly*, LIII (Feb. 4, 1954), 150–51; *NYT*, March 20, 1951.
5. *NYT*, March 16, 1951.
6. *Ibid.*, March 13, 1951.

7. *Ibid.*, March 14–15, 17–18, 1951.
8. Lester Velie, "Rudolph Halley—How He Nailed America's Racketeers," *Collier's*, CXXVII (May 19, 1951), 80.
9. *NYT*, March 17, 1951.
10. *Ibid.*, March 20–22, 1951.
11. *Ibid.*, March 23–25, 1951.
12. Typical of the press coverage of the New York hearings were: "Mighty Interesting Visit," *Time*, LVII (April 2, 1951), 16–17; "Who's a Liar?" *Life*, XXX (April 2, 1951), 19–25; "Biggest Show Panics the Public," *Newsweek*, XXXVII (March 26, 1951), 21–24; "Crime Hunt in Foley Square," *Time*, LVII (March 26, 1951), 22–24; "Biggest Show on Earth," *Time*, LVII (March 26, 1951), 80–81; "The U. S. Gets a Close Look at Crime," *Life*, XXX (March 26, 1951), 33–39.
13. "Senate Probe Stopped New York's Clock," *Business Week*, No. 1125 (March 24, 1951), 19; "Biggest Show on Earth," 80–81; *NYT*, March 11, 1951.
14. According to one poll, 94 per cent of enrolled party members in the United States had a favorable reaction to the hearings; see G. D. Wiebe, "Responses to the Televised Kefauver Hearings: Some Social Psychological Implications," *Public Opinion Quarterly*, XVI (Summer, 1952), 189; *NYT*, March 20, 1951; McNaughton, *loc. cit.*, 150–51.
15. "Who's a Liar?" 22–23.
16. *NYT*, March 13–26, 1951.
17. *NYT*, March 25, 1951.
18. Letter from Herbert Monte Levy, Staff Counsel of the ACLU, to the editor of the *New York Herald-Tribune*, March 30, 1951.
19. Quoted in "The Biggest Show," *Newsweek*, XXXVII (March 26, 1951), 52; "In Passing," *ibid.* (June 18, 1951), 46.
20. McNaughton, *loc. cit.*, 147–53; "The Unanswered Questions," *Nation*, CLXXII (March 31, 1951), 292–93; "Millions Witness Crime Probe," *Christian Century*, LXVIII (April 4, 1951), 421; Robert Waithman, "Truth by Television," *Spectator*, CLXXXVI (March 30, 1951), 405–6; D. W. Brogan, "Kefauver and Crime," *ibid.*, CLXXXVIII (Feb. 15, 1952), 198–99; especially critical, in hindsight, was Charles L. Markmann, *The Noblest Cry: A History of the American Civil Liberties Union* (New York, 1965), 387. For one view of how the Senate itself looked at the investigation, see William S. White, *Citadel* (New York, 1956), 78, 260–63.
21. Thurman Arnold, "Mob Justice and Television," *Atlantic Monthly*, CLXXXVII (June, 1951), 69; Lloyd Cutler and Herbert Packer, "Make Them Tell Congress the Truth," *Harper's*, CCIV (March,

1952), 82–83; "Kefauver's Court: Trial by Camera," *Catholic World,* CLXXIII (May, 1951), 81–85; Allen T. Klots, "Trial by Television," *Harper's,* CCIII (Oct. 1951), 90–94; Waithman, *loc. cit.,* 405–6; Telford Taylor, "The Issue Is Not TV, But Fair Play," *New York Times Magazine* (April 15, 1951), 12, 67–68; Wilfrid Parsons, "Washington Front," *America,* LXXXIV (March 31, 1951), 742; Arnold, *loc. cit.,* 68–70.

22. Estes Kefauver, "What I Found in the Underworld," *Saturday Evening Post,* CCXXIII (April 7, 1951), 72; "Quizzing Kefauver," 26; *NYT,* Aug. 25, 1951; *CR* 97:10602–5 (8/24/51); see, for example, Kefauver's article, "A Fair Conduct Code for Congress," *New Republic,* CXXVIII (March 16, 1953), 14–15; *CR* 100:7223 (5/27/54); *NYT,* May 27, 1954.

23. "The Kefauver Show," *Newsweek,* XXXVII (March 12, 1951), 54; *NYT,* Feb. 27, 1951.

24. *U. S.* v. *Kleinman* et al., 107 F. Supp. 407.

25. *NYT,* Dec. 13, 1952; Feb. 17, June 25, 1953.

26. *Congressional Quarterly Log for Editors,* XI (May 8, 1953), 593.

27. Alan Barth, *Government by Investigation* (New York, 1955), 74–75.

28. "Quizzing Kefauver," 28.

29. "Meet the Press," April 1, 1951, available in the Motion Picture Division of the Library of Congress; *CQA,* VI (1951), 341; "Kefauver Findings," *Newsweek,* XXXVII (May 7, 1951), 27; *NYT,* April 18, 25, 1951; *Crime in America,* 318–20.

30. "Kefauver in Harness," *Newsweek,* XXXVII (May 28, 1951), 21; "The Luck of Bill O'Dwyer," *Newsweek,* XXXVII (May 14, 1951), 30; *NYT,* April 1, 1951.

31. *Ibid.,* March 21, 1951; "Who's a Liar?" 23.

32. Estes Kefauver, "What I Found in the Underworld," *Saturday Evening Post,* CCXXIII (April 7, 14, 21, 28, 1951), 7:19–21, 71–72, 76, 79; 14:23–25, 113–14, 116–18; 21:26–27, 107, 109–10, 112, 115; 28:30, 113–16.

33. *Ibid.* (April 7, 1951), 71.

34. *Ibid.,* 76.

35. *Chicago Daily Tribune,* April 6, 1951.

36. *Ibid.; NYT,* April 18, 1951.

37. Letter to Kefauver from Judge John J. Langenbach, Judge, Superior Court, South Bend, Washington, July 25, 1951; Kefauver's reply, Aug. 3, 1951; both in *KP:*"Crime in America."

38. Speech by Kefauver over radio Station WDOD, Chattanooga, June 14, 1948; transcript available in *KP:*State Senate Race, 1938.

39. Kefauver had been approached about writing books and articles from almost the beginning of the investigation—in fact, the first

suggestion for a book came in March, 1950, before the investigation had even begun. The most frequently emphasized point made by those seeking to sign Kefauver up was the political benefit he would receive as a result of the book or article. It was only a small step from getting Kefauver to agree to work with Shalett to then suggesting that the *Saturday Evening Post* articles should be an exclusive and that Kefauver should not grant writers and reporters interviews that would detract from the value of the *Post* articles. There is every indication that Kefauver lost control of the articles somewhere along the way; he had stressed from the beginning in his correspondence with Shalett and the *Post* that the report was to precede the articles. But with a reported $20,000 fee involved and *Post* competitors planning similar stories, he may have felt that he could not hold up publication of the articles. See letter to Kefauver from Charles A. Pearce, March 27, 1950, in *KP:*"Crime in America"; letter to Kefauver from Shalett, Nov. 10, 1950, in *ibid.;* other correspondence in *ibid.;* Robert Coon, "What Good Did the Kefauver Crime Committee Really Do?" *Cosmopolitan,* CXXXIV (April, 1953), 24.

40. Coon, *loc. cit.;* Estes Kefauver, *Crime in America* (Garden City, N. Y., 1951); *NYT,* July 28–Oct. 14, 1951; letter to Joseph Marks of Doubleday from S. George Little of General Features, Oct. 22, 1951, copy in *KP:*"Crime in America."

41. Coon, *loc. cit.;* Jack Gould, "Dismaying TV Trend," *NYT,* Dec. 9, 1951; however, another CBS-TV series which built on the Kefauver investigation, "The Nation's Nightmare," received widespread praise; see "Splendid Nightmare," *Newsweek,* XXXVIII (Aug. 13, 1951), 48.

42. Review of "The Enforcer," *Newsweek,* XXXVII (Feb. 5, 1951), 81; *NYT,* Jan. 21, 1951; *Boston Traveler,* April 3, 1952; the *New York Times* reported on Jan. 15, 1952, that Kefauver would receive $2,000 plus 2 per cent of the net for doing the epilogue to "The Tight Rope," which apparently was later renamed "The Captive City."

43. Statement by Bureau of Internal Information Office, July 23, 1954, in *KP:*Political, Tennessee, 1954 Sutton Material; Harry W. Kirwin, *The Inevitable Success: Herbert R. O'Conor* (Westminster, Md., 1962), 463; in addition, by 1955, of 79 persons the Commerce Committee thought should have been deported on the basis of Kefauver Committee revelations, five had been deported, six had had their proceedings dismissed by the courts, and suits were pending against 32; see "The Stay-at-Homes," *Newsweek,* XLV (May 9, 1955), 29–30.

44. Willard Shelton, "Cast No Stones," *The Nation,* CLXXII (March 31, 1951), 294; see also Robert Moses' comments in "The Minstrel Show," *Time,* LVIII (Aug. 20, 1951), 15–16.

45. "It Pays to Organize," *Time,* LVII (March 12, 1951), 24; interview with Kefauver on "Crime and the Committee" (CBS-TV, 1958), available in the Motion Picture Division of the Library of Congress.

46. "Kefauver Speaking: Gambling Corrupts as Much as Prohibition," *Newsweek,* XXXVII (April 2, 1951), 20

47. "Meet the Press," Nov. 12, 1950, available in the Motion Picture Division of the Library of Congress; see also "Quizzing Kefauver," 31; for an example of the committee's strong moral support for local cleanup efforts, see *NYT,* Aug. 29, 1951.

48. "Quizzing Kefauver," 33; "Kefauver Speaking," 20.

49. "Meet the Press," Nov. 12, 1950; "Kefauver Speaking," 20.

50. Kirwin, *op. cit.,* 463; *NYT,* June 25, Aug. 17, Sept. 10, 28, 1951; see also *CQA,* VII (1951), 351, 429, for Kefauver's major 1951 efforts to have the Senate act on his committee's recommendations.

51. "What Can an Angry People Do?" *National Municipal Review,* XL (May, 1951), 239–45; "Crime Up to States and Cities," *ibid.* (July, 1951), 354–59.

52. "In Passing," *Newsweek,* XXXVII (June 4, 1951), 40; *NYT,* May 23, 1951.

53. "Who Are the Nation's Best and Worst Senators?" *Pageant,* VII (Sept. 1951), 111–17, especially 114.

54. Memo in *KP:*61&71, Estes Kefauver, II; *CT,* July 24, 1954.

55. "Second Annual Look TV Awards," *Look,* XVI (Jan. 15, 1952), 44.

56. Letter to Kefauver from Mike Stokey, President of the Academy of Television Arts and Sciences, March 5, 1952, in *KP:*61&71, Estes Kefauver, II.

57. *Hollywood Citizen-News,* Feb. 19, 1952.

Chapter vii

1. "South's Plan to Beat Truman; interview with Senator Harry F. Byrd," *U. S. News and World Report,* XXXI (Nov. 30, 1951), 28–34.

2. "No. 1 Question at the Polls in '52," *U. S. News and World Report,* XXXII (Jan. 11, 1952), 26.

3. *Ibid.;* "MacArthur Approved," *Time,* LVII (April 30, 1951), 26.

4. *NYT,* Feb. 23, 1952.

5. "Kefauver in Seattle," *New Republic,* CXXV (Dec. 17, 1951), 6;

Congressional Quarterly Log for Editors, IX (June 1, 1951), 836; *NYT,* May 30, Aug. 5, Dec. 5, 1951; "Quizzing Kefauver," *U. S. News and World Report,* XXXII (April 4, 1952), 56; "Side Shows," *Time,* LIX (June 23, 1952), 20–21.

6. "Could Truman Win Again?" *U. S. News and World Report,* XXXI (Dec. 7, 1951), 47; "No. 1 Question at the Polls in '52," 26.

7. "Could Truman Win Again?" 48; *NYT,* March 4, 11, 14, July 19, 25, Dec. 30, 1951.

8. "People of the Week," *U. S. News and World Report,* XXX (Dec. 21, 1951), 44–45.

9. Thomas Stokes, "The Hats Begin to Fill the Ring for 1952," *New York Times Magazine* (Sept. 18, 1949), 62; *NYT,* March 4, 11, April 11, 1951.

10. Kefauver was the only major candidate of 1952 whose supporters ranked television above newspapers as the most important influence on their decision to support him for President; see Charles A. H. Thomson, *Television and Presidential Politics* (Washington, D. C., 1956), 47–48.

11. *NYT,* April 2, 1951; "Meet the Press," April 1, 1951, available in the Motion Picture Division of the Library of Congress.

12. *CT,* April 27, 1951; interview with Miss Lucile Myers; *NYT,* April 27, June 18, Aug. 20, 1951.

13. *NYT,* Nov. 7, 1951; statement issued by Kefauver, Oct. 29, 1951, copy in *KP*:66:1.

14. *NYT,* Nov. 17, 20, 30, Dec. 5, 8, 1951.

15. A poll of 150 national and international union presidents on their choices for President if Truman did not run showed Douglas a runaway winner with 47 per cent of the replies; Kefauver was second with 19 per cent; others receiving support were Eisenhower 16 per cent, Vinson 12 per cent, Stevenson 4 per cent, and William O. Douglas 2 per cent; in a separate poll for Vice-President (leaving out Barkley), Douglas and Kefauver each received the support of 34 per cent of those replying; others receiving support were Senator Brien McMahon of Connecticut 12 per cent, Governor G. Mennen Williams of Michigan 11 per cent, and Stevenson 4 per cent; *ibid.,* Dec. 27, 1951.

16. "People of the Week," 44–45.

17. *Pittsburg Post-Gazette,* May 3, 1952.

18. David Lawrence, "Taft—Weakness and Strength," editorial in *U. S. News and World Report,* XXXI (Oct. 26, 1951), 88; *NYT,* Sept. 6, Oct. 17, 18, Nov. 4, 16, 1951; "Could Truman Win Again?" 48.

19. *NYT,* April 16, November 9, 1951; in the spring of 1951, Gallup polls showed that Eisenhower was the first choice of Republican

voters, with 38 per cent preferring him to 22 per cent for the runnerup, Taft; Eisenhower was also the first choice of Democrats, with 42 per cent preferring him to 18 per cent for the runnerup, Truman; 44 per cent of independents favored Eisenhower, with only 17 per cent for Truman and Taft combined; see *Public Opinion Quarterly*, XV (Summer, 1951), 394–95; at this point, Kefauver was the choice of 3 per cent of the Democrats, 5 per cent of the independents. In the spring of 1952, Eisenhower led the list in Elmo Roper's survey of "most admired living Americans"; see Elmo Roper, *You and Your Leaders* (New York, 1957), 241.

20. *NYT*, May 11, Nov. 4, 1951.
21. *Ibid.*, Nov. 5, 1951.
22. See Arthur Krock's comments in *ibid.*, Jan. 20, 1952; "How a President is Chosen," *U. S. News and World Report*, XXXII (Feb. 1, 1952), 19–21.
23. *Concord* (N. H.) *Daily Monitor*, Jan. 9, 1952.
24. *Ibid.*
25. William L. Dunfey, "A Short History of the Democratic Party in New Hampshire" (unpublished master's thesis, University of New Hampshire, 1954), 216–17; interview with Hugh Waling, June 24, 1964; interview with Joseph Scott, June 23, 1964; Scott was a successful (pro-Truman) candidate for alternate in New Hampshire in 1952.
26. Waling interview.
27. Interviews with: Hugh H. Bownes, June 25, 1964; Alfred D. Rosenblatt, June 25, 1964; and Royal Dion, June 23, 1964; all were active on behalf of Kefauver in New Hampshire in 1952.
28. *NYT*, Nov. 24, 1951; Jan. 24, 1952; *Concord Daily Monitor*, Jan. 24, 1952; "The Rise of Senator Legend," *Time*, LIX (March 24, 1952), 24; "Gambling Doesn't Pay," *Newsweek*, XXXIX (Jan. 14, 1952), 46; *CT*, Jan. 2, 1952.
29. Letter from Charles Neese to Lucius E. Burch, Jr., April 26, 1951, copy in *KP*:General Correspondence, 1948–55; *NYT*, March 30, 1951; *CT*, Jan. 3, 1952.
30. *CT*, Jan. 4, 6, 1952.
31. *Ibid.*, Jan. 9, 1952.
32. *NYT*, Jan. 3, 4, 1952.
33. *Ibid.*, Jan. 9, 12, 1952.
34. *CT*, Jan. 16, 17, 1952.
35. *NYT*, Nov. 21, 1967.
36. Robert Wallace, "A Vote for Nancy," *Life*, XXXII (June 30, 1952), 104.
37. *CT*, Jan. 15, 21, 1952.

38. *Ibid.,* Jan. 24, 1952; see also, "Bosses Are Icy to Kefauver," *Newsweek,* XXXIX (Feb. 4, 1952), 17–18.
39. *CT,* Jan. 25, 1952.
40. The deadline to enter the preferential election was Jan. 30; delegate candidates could file through Feb. 9; see *Concord Daily Monitor,* Jan. 9, 11, 1952.

Chapter viii

1. "Preference Primaries for Nomination of Candidates for President and Vice-President," hearings before the Subcommittee on Rules of the Committee on Rules and Administration, U. S. Senate, 82nd Congress, 2nd Session, on S. 2570, March 28, 1952, 120–22; *Concord* (N. H.) *Daily Monitor,* Jan. 29, 1952.
2. *New York Herald-Tribune,* Feb. 1, 1952.
3. *NYT,* Feb. 1, 1952.
4. "The Primaries Are More Than Eyewash," *Life,* XXXII (Feb. 18, 1952), 42.
5. *Concord Daily Monitor,* Feb. 1, 1952.
6. *Ibid.,* Feb. 1, 2, 1952.
7. *Washington Post,* Feb. 1, 1952; see also Kefauver's defense of presidential primaries in "Indictment of the Political Convention," *New York Times Magazine* (March 16, 1952), 9, 59–61, 63.
8. Interview with Gail E. Bower, Jr., June 23, 1964; Bower was one of the delegate candidates in 1952 pledged to Kefauver; Bownes interview, June 25, 1964; Bownes later served as Democratic National Committeeman from New Hampshire.
9. *Concord Daily Monitor,* Feb. 1, 1952.
10. "No Contest," editorial in *Nashua Telegraph,* Feb. 4, 1952; "To Clear the Eyes," editorial in *Keene Sentinel,* Feb. 1, 1952; "The Political Week," editorial in *Exeter News-Letter,* Feb. 7, 1952.
11. *Washington Post,* Feb. 25, 1952.
12. *NYT,* Feb. 6, March 14, 1952; *Washington Star,* Feb. 10, 1952; *Concord Daily Monitor,* Feb. 5, 1952.
13. *NYT,* Jan. 25, 1952.
14. *Ibid.,* Jan. 6, 1952.
15. Elmo Roper, *You and Your Leaders* (New York, 1957), 146–47.
16. *Concord Daily Monitor,* Feb. 14, 1952.
17. *Ibid.,* Feb. 19, 1952.
18. Interview with Mario Vagge, chairman of the program committee and later an important Kefauver supporter in New Hampshire,

June 22, 1964; Dion interview, June 23, 1964; Dion later served as Executive Director of the New Hampshire Democratic party; interview with Conrad Bellevance, June 23, 1964; Bellevance was a field representative for the Kefauver campaign in New Hampshire in 1952.

19. *Concord Daily Monitor,* Feb. 13, 20, March 3, 1952.

20. Interview with Charles J. Griffin, June 24, 1964; Griffin was the second and permanent chairman of the 1952 Kefauver campaign in New Hampshire.

21. Interview with Leon W. Anderson, June 25, 1964; Anderson was a columnist and political reporter for the *Concord Daily Monitor;* Bownes interview; Rosenblatt interview, June 25, 1964; Rosenblatt was Kefauver's press secretary in New Hampshire in 1952; Griffin interview.

22. Griffin interview; Bellevance interview.

23. Dion interview; Vagge interview.

24. Bellevance interview; Vagge interview; Anderson interview; interview with Joseph F. Scott, June 23, 1964; Scott was a successful pro-Truman candidate for alternate in New Hampshire in 1952; Griffin interview; Bownes interview; Nyleen Morrison, "With N. H. Women," *Concord Daily Monitor,* Feb. 29, 1952.

25. *Concord Daily Monitor,* Feb. 25, 1952.

26. *Ibid.,* March 5, 1952.

27. *Ibid.,* Feb. 28, 1952; *Manchester Union-Leader,* March 6, 1952.

28. G. D. Wiebe, "Responses to the Televised Kefauver Hearings: Some Social Psychological Implications," *Public Opinion Quarterly,* XVI (Summer, 1952), 189.

29. *Manchester Union-Leader,* March 10, 1952.

30. *Ibid.,* March 6, 1952.

31. *Concord Daily Monitor,* March 7, 1952; *Manchester Union-Leader,* March 11, 1952; William L. Dunfey, "A Short History of the Democratic Party in New Hampshire" (unpublished master's thesis, University of New Hampshire, 1954), 217.

32. *Manchester Union-Leader,* March 1, 7, 8, 1952; *Concord Daily Monitor,* March 11, 18, 1952.

33. *Concord Daily Monitor,* March 12, 1952; *Manchester Union-Leader,* March 12, 1952. The final tabulation gave Kefauver 19,800, Truman 15,927; see James W. Davis, *Presidential Primaries: Road to the White House* (New York, 1967), 299.

34. *New York Daily News,* March 12, 1952.

35. *Concord Daily Monitor,* March 13, 1952; *NYT,* March 13, 14, 30, 1952.

36. *Boston Globe,* March 12, 1952; see also, Paul T. David, Malcolm Moos, and Ralph W. Goldman, *Presidential Nominating Politics in 1952* (Baltimore, 1954), I, 39.
37. Interview with Mrs. Estes Kefauver, July 11, 1964.

Chapter ix

1. Paul T. David, Malcolm Moos, and Ralph W. Goldman were editors of an exhaustive, five volume study of *Presidential Nominating Politics in 1952* (Baltimore, 1954), which included one general volume (Vol. I: *The National Story*) and four volumes of individual state studies done by local political scientists (Vol. II: *The Northeast;* Vol. III: *The South;* Vol. IV: *The Middle West;* Vol. V: *The West*). This work is by far the most important source of material on Kefauver's 1952 campaign for the Democratic nomination.
2. *NYT,* March 30, 1952; David, *et al., op. cit.,* I, 41.
3. A film of the "Presidential Timber" telecast is available at the Kefauver Library, Knoxville, Tennessee; see also "TV Timber," *Newsweek,* XXXIX (April 14, 1952), 62.
4. Douglass Cater, "Estes Kefauver, Most Willing of the Willing," *Reporter,* XIII (Nov. 3, 1955), 14–15.
5. "Professional Common Man," *Time,* LXVIII (Sept. 17, 1956), 25.
6. *Ibid.;* Charles Bartlett, "The Crusading Kefauver," *Nation,* CLXXIV (May 3, 1952), 427.
7. Interview with Dr. Paul Buck; see also "The Rise of Senator Legend," *Time,* LIX (March 24, 1952), 22.
8. John Hoving, "Campaigning with Kefauver," *New Republic,* CXXVI (April 21, 1952), 14.
9. James W. Davis, *Presidential Primaries: Road to the White House* (New York, 1967), 299; David, *et. al., op. cit.,* I, 55–66, 152.
10. Davis, *op. cit.,* 299; David, *et. al., op. cit.,* I, 55–66.
11. Arthur Naftalin, John E. Turner, and William R. Monat, "Minnesota," David, *et. al., op. cit.,* IV, 182.
12. *NYT,* April 1–2, 1952; "High v. Low," *Time,* LIX (March 31, 1952), 21; "Kefauver Knocks Out Kerr," *Life,* XXXII (April 14, 1952), 40–41; Robert J. Morgan, "Nebraska," David, *et. al., op. cit.,* IV, 295; Davis, *op. cit.,* 299.
13. *NYT,* March 3, 1952.
14. *Washington Post,* March 13, 1952.
15. Manning J. Dauer, William G. Carleton, W. Freeman Baker, and Swynal B. Pettingill, "Florida," David, *et. al., op. cit.,* III, 132–33.
16. "Duel in the Sun," *Time,* LIX (May 5, 1952), 25.

17. Dauer, *et. al., loc. cit.*, 133.
18. *Ibid.*, 132.
19. *NYT*, May 3, 1951.
20. Harold Lavine, "Kefauver's Stake," *Newsweek*, XXXIX (May 5, 1952), 25.
21. "Duel in the Sun," *loc. cit.*, 25.
22. *Ibid.*
23. Lavine, *loc. cit.*, 26; see also "Quizzing Kefauver," *U. S. News and World Report*, XXXII (April 4, 1952), 58–59.
24. *CT*, Jan. 4, 1952; *NYT*, Jan. 28, 1952.
25. The kind of Southern support Kefauver was likely to attract was illustrated by a pro-Kefauver endorsement by anti-Byrd Virginia Democrats; see Norman Parks, "Coonskin Candidate," *New Republic*, CXXV (Dec. 24, 1951), 15–16. See also William S. White's comments on Southern opposition to Kefauver, in *Citadel* (New York, 1956), 78–79.
26. Davis, *op. cit.*, 299.
27. H. Rowland Ludden, "District of Columbia," David, *et. al., op. cit.*, II, 336.
28. Robert T. Elson, "A Question for Democrats: If Not Truman, Who?" *Life*, XXXII (March 24, 1952), 119.
29. Davis, *op. cit.*, 299; Ludden, *loc. cit.*, 336.
30. David, *et al.*, I, 64.
31. *NYT*, March 20, 1952; Hoving, *loc. cit.*, 12–14.
32. *NYT*, April 7, 1952.
33. *CQA*, VIII (1952), 67.
34. *NYT*, May 14, 1951.
35. "Can Kefauver Break Through?" *New Republic*, CXXVI (May 19, 1952), 5; even through the convention the Kefauver campaign continued to stress the corruption issue and passed out to delegates a cake of soap with the slogan, "clean out corruption with Kefauver"; see *CT*, July 23, 1952.
36. *NYT*, March 5, 1952.
37. "The Rise of Senator Legend," *loc. cit.*, 24.
38. *Congressional Quarterly Log for Editors*, X (March 7, 1952), 197.
39. Theodore H. White, *The Making of the President 1960* (New York, 1961), 55.
40. "The Third Man," *Time*, LIX (April 21, 1952), 25.
41. Letter to Kefauver from Vincent M. Gaughan, Oct. 11, 1955, in *KP*:Elections.
42. "Quizzing Kefauver," 54.
43. Estes Kefauver, discussion/interview on Longines Chronoscope, reprinted in the *American Mercury*, LXXIV (June, 1952), 87.

44. Letter from Kefauver to Paul A. Theis of *Newsweek*, in *KP*:66:1.

45. "Quizzing Kefauver," 54, 56, 59, 60; but Kefauver's earlier call for a military victory under UN authority was withdrawn after General Ridgeway testified that UN forces lacked the capability to make good on a time-limit ultimatum regarding a negotiated settlement; see "Side Shows," *Time*, LIX (June 23, 1952), 20–21; *NYT*, April 10, 1952.

46. "Can Kefauver Break Through?" 5; Kefauver, however, had strong ties to the Eastern Jewish community; see *NYT*, June 30, 1950, and Estes Kefauver, "Need for Boldness," *Nation*, CLXXIV (June 7, 1952), 557. Kefauver's opposition to the infamous 1952 McCarran Immigration bill, passed over Truman's veto on June 27, certainly strengthened his appeal to Jewish leaders; see *CQA*, VIII (1952), 55, 154–59.

47. Douglas was ranked as the "best" senator in a poll of 128 correspondents covering the Senate in 1951. Kefauver was ranked second; see "Who Are the Nation's Best and Worst Senators?" *Pageant*, VII (Sept. 1951), 111–17.

48. *NYT*, April 18, 1952; see also Paul H. Douglas, "Why I'm For Kefauver," *Collier's*, CXXX (July 19, 1952), 20, 57; "Who's for Whom," *Time*, LIX (April 28, 1952), 23.

49. Elmo Roper, *You and Your Leaders* (New York, 1957), 241.

50. David, *et. al., op cit.*, I, 37.

51. *Washington Post*, March 19, 1952.

52. Roper, *op. cit.*, 212–13.

53. David, *et. al., op. cit.*, I, 64–65, 109.

54. *Ibid.*, 65.

55. *NYT*, July 15, 1952.

56. *Ibid.*, July 17, 1952.

57. "The Managers," *Time*, LIX (May 5, 1952), 25; see also Jack Redding, *Inside the Democratic Party* (Indianapolis, 1958), 39; letter to the author from Mrs. Tom Ragland, Jan. 11, 1970; letter from Kefauver to Marshall McNeil, Jan. 10, 1956, in *KP*:Elections.

58. Letter to Theis.

59. David, *et. al., op. cit.*, I, 101–56.

60. *Ibid.;* interview with James A. Farley, March 13, 1970; *CT*, July 21, 22, 1952. For a lengthy account of one Kefauver delegate's disgust with the management of the convention, see Vera Shultz, "Delegate in a Draft," *Ladies Home Journal*, LXIX (Nov. 1952), 54–55, 114–19.

61. Kurt Lang and Gladys Engel Lang, "The Television Personality in Politics: Some Considerations," *Public Opinion Quarterly*, XX (Spring, 1956), 108–9. Kefauver wrote later that "I have always

felt that he [Rayburn] did an excellent job as Speaker but that in the political arena he was not so judicious"; see memo of June 27, 1962, in *KP:*Miscellaneous; see also David, *et. al., op. cit.,* I, 141–42.

62. *Official Report of the Proceedings of the Democratic National Convention, 1952,* 350; David, *et. al., op. cit.,* I, 103, 144–45; J. M. Arvey, "The Reluctant Candidate—An Inside Story," *Reporter,* IX (Nov. 24, 1953), 24.

63. For example, Massachusetts switched from 32 to 4 *against* to 19 to 16 *against;* Iowa, from 14½ to 9½ *against* to 17 to 7 *for;* Missouri, from 34 *against* to 34 *for;* North Dakota, from 8 *against* to 8 *for.* On the convention's third ballot, the above states cast 65 votes for Stevenson and only 15 for Kefauver.

64. Of the 296 Southern votes cast on the motion to seat Virginia, only Tennessee's 28 opposed the motion, setting the stage for charges that Tennessee's delegation had "betrayed the South"; see David, *et. al., op. cit.,* I, 144–45, 150.

65. Letter to Theis.

66. David, *et. al., op. cit.,* I, 150.

67. *Proceedings,* 276.

68. *CT,* July 24, 1952.

69. *Proceedings,* 287–89.

70. *Ibid.,* 289–92.

71. *Ibid.,* 456, 484.

72. *Ibid.,* 538.

73. Kefauver's 1956 campaign biography gives Truman most of the credit for Stevenson's nomination; see *KS,* 190–91. President Truman also gave himself credit for the decisive support that resulted in Stevenson's nomination; see his *Memoirs,* II (*Years of Trial and Hope;* Garden City, N. Y., 1956), 496–97; however, Truman says that Barkley, not Kefauver, would have been the nominee if the President had not intervened. Mrs. Tom Ragland, Tennessee's National Committeewoman, offered this view of the draft: "You have accepted their story that the Truman forces just came along after the fact. I do not believe it. I think Truman bulldozed the switch and the liberal rationalization followed. I remember the expression that my liberal and labor friends used at the time, that they had to go along 'to clean it up' "; letter to the author, Jan. 11, 1970.

74. David, *et al., op. cit.,* I, 150–51.

75. That the Stevenson campaign was based overwhelmingly on support for the Illinois governor rather than opposition to Kefauver is clearly indicated by the two most intimate published accounts of

the pro-Stevenson efforts; see Arvey, *loc. cit.*, 19–24, 26, and Walter Johnson, *How We Drafted Adlai Stevenson* (New York, 1955). Massachusetts was a key Northern delegation that can be taken as typical of those which eventually "drafted" Adlai Stevenson. Extensive interviews with political figures in that state indicate that Stevenson's support there came principally as a result of the high regard in which he was held by Governor Paul Dever, who, because of the respect he commanded from most Massachusetts delegates (and not because of their fear of political reprisal) was able to swing most of the Massachusetts delegation to Stevenson, without any pressure whatsoever from Truman. In fact, those in the Massachusetts delegation closest to the Administration (House Majority Leader John McCormack, for example) supported Vice-President Barkley to the end.

76. Just before the voting, Kefauver had told Boston Mayor John Hynes that everything was set for a Kefauver victory on the third ballot. Hynes remained convinced that Kefauver was still confident of eventual victory even at that late hour; Hynes interview, March, 10, 1967.

77. Estes Kefauver with Sidney Shallet, "Why Not Let the People Elect Our President," *Collier's*, CXXXI (Jan. 31, 1953), 39. Jake Arvey, Illinois National Committeeman and Stevenson intimate, agreed that Rayburn had acted unwisely; Arvey, *loc. cit.*, 26.

78. *Proceedings*, 535–36.

79. Interview with Senator John Sparkman, Jan. 18, 1969.

80. For the view of the Kefauver camp, see, again, *KS*, 190–94.

81. "Why Not Let the People Elect Our President," 35.

82. *CT*, July 27, 1952.

83. *NYT*, July 26, 1952.

84. *CT*, July 27, 1952.

85. Arvey, *loc. cit.*, 22; Kenneth S. Davis, *The Politics of Honor: A Biography of Adlai E. Stevenson* (New York, 1967), 232.

86. *KS*, 195–96; *CT*, July 27, 1952; David, *et. al., op. cit.*, I, 156.

87. *NYT*, July 29, 1952.

88. Robert Wallace, "A Vote for Nancy," *Life*, XXXII (June 30, 1952), 107.

89. "Secret Weapon," *Time*, LIX (April 28, 1952), 22. Nancy's lack of enthusiasm for the role of First Lady was also evident in an earlier interview; see "Candid Comment," *Newsweek*, XXXIX (Jan. 28, 1952), 44. For another very favorable reaction to Nancy by a figure cool to Kefauver's presidential campaign, see David E. Lilienthal, *The Venturesome Years, 1950–55* (Vol. III, *The Journals of David E. Lilienthal;* New York, 1966), 361.

90. "What's Behind the Handshake?" *New Republic*, CXXVI (June 9, 1952), 13; "Duel in the Sun," 25; interview with Senator Ralph Yarborough, Jan. 28, 1969.

91. *KS*, 198–99; interview with Lucile Myers; interviews with Kefauver's sisters, Nora Kefauver, Aug. 1, 1969, and Nancy Kefauver Fooshee, Aug. 2, 1969.

Chapter x

1. *Nashville Banner*, July 25, 1952.
2. Norman L. Parks, "Tennessee Politics Since Kefauver and Reece: A 'Generalist' View," *The Journal of Politics*, XXVIII (Feb. 1966), 149; *CT*, Aug. 4, 1950.
3. *Tennessee Blue Book, 1951–1952* (Nashville: Rich Printing Co., 1951), 289. Browning even carried Shelby County, 31,189 to 20,570.
4. *CT*, July 26, 1952.
5. *Ibid.*, Aug. 1, 1952.
6. *Tennessee Blue Book, 1954*, 313, 317.
7. "Hometown Girl," *Newsweek*, XL (Oct. 20, 1952), 57; "Holiday," *Newsweek*, XL (Sept. 22, 1952), 54; *NYT*, Aug. 23, 28, 1952.
8. David E. Lilienthal, *The Journals of David E. Lilienthal* (New York, 1964), III, 361.
9. *NYT*, Sept. 25, 26, 1952.
10. *Ibid.*, Sept. 13, 1952.
11. *Ibid.*, Oct. 9, 1952.
12. *Ibid.*, Nov. 4, 1952.
13. *Ibid.*, Oct. 9, 25, 31, 1952.
14. *Ibid.*, Oct. 26, 31, 1952.
15. Alfred de Grazia, *The Western Public, 1952 and Beyond* (Stanford Univ. Press, 1954), 34.
16. *NYT*, Aug. 23, 1952.
17. See Jack Anderson and Fred Blumenthal, *The Kefauver Story* (New York, 1956), 199–202, for Kefauver's view of the 1952 election results. On the other hand, President Truman thought one of Stevenson's major campaign errors was his attempt to disassociate himself from the Truman Administration; see Harry S Truman, *Memoirs* (Garden City, N. Y., 1956), II, 498–500.
18. Estes Kefauver, "Man—Not Principle," *New Republic*, CXXVII (Nov. 17, 1952), 10–11; *NYT*, Dec. 17, 1952.
19. An example of Kefauver's attempt to rally public opinion behind a nationwide system of presidential primaries was the article he

wrote with Sidney Shalett, "Why Not Lct the People Elect Our President?" *Collier's*, CXXXI (Jan. 31, 1953), 34–35, 38–39.

20. *CQA*, IX (1953), 34; *Nashville Tennessean* article of April 10, 1960, reprinted in *CR* 106:9072 (5/2/60).

21. *CQA*, IX (1953), 93.

22. *NYT*, May 24, 1953; "The Ammo Report," *Newsweek*, XLI (June 1, 1953), 23.

23. For a concise summary of the tidelands oil issue, see *CQA*, IX (1953), 388–96; see also *CQWR*, XI (May 1, 1953), 575.

24. *CQWR*, XI (April 24, 1953), 537; *NYT*, April 21, May 2, 1953.

25. *CR* 99:1722 (3/9/53); *CQA*, IX (1953), 388–96.

26. *CQA*, IX (1953), 233–37, 258; X (1954), 254–62, 294; *NYT*, Feb. 14, 1954. A film of an unidentified debate over the amendment between Kefauver and Senator John Bricker of Ohio, sponsor of the amendment, is preserved in the Kefauver Library.

27. *NYT*, June 18, 1953; *CQA*, IX (1953), 145–48.

28. *CQWR*, XI (Oct. 23, 1953), 1271.

29. *Ibid.* (Nov. 20, 1953), 1356; (Nov. 27, 1953), 1382.

30. "What Kefauver Said About the Republicans," *U. S. News and World Report*, XXXVI (June 8, 1954), 80.

31. For a summary of the issue, see *CQA*, X (1954), 334–37.

32. *Ibid.*, 336–37.

33. *CR* 100:15108 (8/19/54).

34. *CQA*, X (1954), 336–37.

Chapter xi

1. *NYT*, Nov. 1, 1953; see also, "Mr. TVA," *New Republic*, CXXIX (Aug. 10, 1953), 4–5.

2. William Buchanan and Agnes Bird, *Money as a Campaign Resource: Tennessee Democratic Senatorial Primaries, 1948–1964* (Princeton, 1965), 22; Alexander Heard, *The Costs of Democracy* (Chapel Hill, 1960), 330.

3. Buchanan and Bird, *op. cit.*, 22; *KS*, 203; *CQWR*, XI (Oct. 23, 1953), 1261.

4. Interview with Lucile Myers; Howard Whitman, "Our Worst Congressmen," *Redbook*, XCIX (Oct. 1952), 36, 72. The ranking was based on confidential talks with six senators, one ex-senator, five representatives, thirteen congressional assistants, nine newspapermen, ten leaders of better government organizations, and eight others.

5. Heard, *op. cit.*, 33, 330.

6. *Ibid.;* Buchanan and Bird, *op. cit.,* 22.
7. *NYT,* Jan. 24, 1954.
8. *Ibid.,* April 4, 1954.
9. Poll dated June 2, 1954, in *KP:*Elections.
10. Buchanan and Bird, *op. cit.,* 22–23.
11. *Ibid.,* 23; *NYT,* June 20, 1954. The author himself recalls spending several hours watching Sutton's Knoxville performance.
12. Buchanan and Bird, *op. cit.,* 24–25; Heard, *op. cit.,* 25.
13. *L'Italia,* Jan. 28, 1954; translation printed in *Nashville Tennessean,* Feb. 7, 1954.
14. *Nashville Tennessean,* Feb. 7, 1954.
15. Paul Healy, "Capital Circus," *New York Daily News,* July 31, 1954; *CT,* July 12, 18, 28, 1954; "Sutton's Friends," *New Republic,* CXXXI (Aug. 2, 1954), 4; letter from Kefauver to deLesseps Morrison, July 20, 1954, in *KP:*Personal, 1955–57.
16. Kefauver letter to Morrison.
17. Robert G. Venn vs. Tennessean Newspapers, Inc. (Federal District Court, Middle District of Tennessee, Feb. 2–9, 1961), quoted in Buchanan and Bird, *op. cit.,* 25–26; Healy, *loc. cit.;* "Poison Brewing," *New Republic,* CXXXI (July 19, 1954), 4; *Nashville Tennessean,* June 18, 1963.
18. Healy, *loc. cit.*
19. Copy in *KP:*Political-Tennessee-1954-Sutton Material.
20. Press release of July 27, 1954, in *KP*-Political-1954-General.
21. *Nashville Banner,* July 16, 1954.
22. *CT,* July 28, 1954.
23. Letter to the author from Mrs. Tom Ragland, Jan. 11, 1970.
24. *CT,* July 28, 1954.
25. *Ibid.,* July 3, 1954.
26. Buchanan and Bird, *op. cit.,* 25.
27. *CT,* July 11, 1954.
28. *Nashville Banner,* July 9, 24, 1954; *NYT,* Jan. 24, 1954.
29. *CT,* July 24, 1954.
30. *Nashville Banner,* July 12, 16, 1954; *CT,* July 6, 31, 1954.
31. *CT,* July 7–9, 1954.
32. *Ibid.,* July 11, 1954.
33. *Ibid.,* July 23, 1954.
34. "Tempest in Tennessee," *Newsweek,* XLIV (Aug. 9, 1954), 19–20; *CT,* July 24, 1954.
35. *CT,* July 24, 1954.
36. Letter from Walter White to Mrs. Ruby Hurley of Birmingham and Z. Alexander Looby of Nashville, April 23, 1954, copy in *KP:*Personal, 1955–57.

37. *CQWR*, XII (Oct. 22, 1954), 1296–97.
38. *Memphis Commercial Appeal*, March 31, 1954.
39. Buchanan and Bird, *op. cit.*, 22–25, 33; *CT*, Aug. 4, 1954; see also William D. Miller, *Mr. Crump of Memphis* (Baton Rouge, 1964), 349–50; *Memphis Commercial Appeal*, 19, 1954.
40. *Knoxville Journal*, July 11, 1954.
41. *CQWR*, XII (Oct. 1, 1954), 1220.
42. Buchanan and Bird, *op. cit.*, 25; *CT*, July 14, 26, 27, 1954; "Sutton's Friends," *loc. cit.*, 4; *NYT*, April 19, July 30, 1958; *Knoxville News-Sentinel*, July 25, 1954; *CR* 109:14926 (8/14/63); Jack Anderson, "The Tall Man from Tennessee," *Washington Post*, Aug. 14, 1963.
43. See, for example, "Poison Brewing," *loc. cit.*, and most *New York Times* stories on the primary; Drew Pearson's columns in the *Washington Post*, June-Aug., 1954; Buchanan and Bird, *op. cit.*, 31; *Reader's Digest*, LXV (Aug. 1954), 132–34; letter from Kefauver to Blake Clark, in *KP:*61&71.
44. Buchanan and Bird, *op. cit.*, 28.
45. Interview with Alfred Rosenblatt, Kefauver's press secretary in the 1952 and 1956 New Hampshire primaries, June 25, 1964.
46. *CT*, July 28, 1954.
47. *Tennessee Blue Book, 1956* (Nashville, 1956), 375–76; *Nashville Banner*, Aug. 6, 1954; *Washington Post*, Aug. 6, 1954.
48. "Politics," *Newsweek*, XLIII (May 17, 1954), 29.
49. "Familiar TV Faces," *Newsweek*, XLIII (June 28, 1954), 22.
50. *NYT*, Sept. 3, 1954; "One Will Be Missing," *Newsweek*, XLIV (July 12, 1954), 23; "Kefauver vs. Whom?" *Newsweek*, XLIV (Aug. 16, 1954), 18; *Tennessee Blue Book, 1956*, 397.

Chapter *xii*

1. *NYT*, Oct. 7, 1955.
2. "Calculating a Risk," *Newsweek*, XLIII (April 19, 1954), 24.
3. *CQWR*, XIV (Aug. 24, 1956), 1054.
4. *CR* 100:7603 (6/13/54).
5. *Ibid.*, 7919 (6/9/54); *NYT*, June 9, 1954.
6. *CQWR*, XIII (Jan. 28, 1955), 102.
7. *Ibid.* (Feb. 4, 1955), 120; *CQA*, XI (1955), 279; *NYT*, Feb. 10, 1955.
8. Estes Kefauver, "Let's Talk About Peace," *Nation*, CLXXX (April 16, 1955), 317.
9. *NYT*, May 4, 1955.
10. *CR* 101:4044 (3/30/55).
11. *CR* 101:4216 (4/1/55).

12. CR 101:4264 (4/1/55).
13. CQWR, XIV (Aug. 24, 1956), 1054.
14. "Professional Common Man," Time, LXVIII (Sept. 17, 1956), 26–27.
15. Kefauver seems to have been determined not to repeat the political mistakes of the crime investigation; he wrote key leaders, including Chicago's Richard Daley, informing them of the probe and asking confidential advice; see letters in KP:Personal, 1955–57.
16. NYT, March 27, 1955.
17. NYT, Aug. 26, 1955. The major subcommittee reports issued under Kefauver's chairmanship were: "Comic Books and Juvenile Delinquency" (Senate Report No. 62, March 14, 1955), "Television and Juvenile Delinquency" (Senate Report No. 1466, Jan. 31, 1956), "Motion Pictures and Juvenile Delinquency" (Senate Report No. 2055, May 25, 1956), and "Obscene and Pornographic Literature and Juvenile Delinquency" (Senate Report No. 2381, June 28, 1956). The most important hearings were: comic books (April 21, 22, June 4, 1954), television (April 6, 7, 1955), obscenity and pornographic materials (May 24, 26, 31, June 9, 18, 1955).
18. "Mr. TVA," New Republic, CXXIX (Aug. 10, 1953), 5.
19. CQWR, XII (Jan. 8, 1954), 35.
20. NYT, July 22, 1954.
21. Quoted in Emmet John Hughes, The Ordeal of Power (New York 1963), 152.
22. CR 100:5862 (5/3/54); Nashville Tennessean, April 18, 1954.
23. For much more thorough treatments of Dixon-Yates, see the following: CQA, XI (1955), 533–52; Jason L. Finkle, The President Makes a Decision: A Study of Dixon-Yates (Michigan Government Studies, #39, 1960); Aaron Wildovsky, Dixon-Yates: A Study in Power Politics (New Haven, 1962); David A. Frier, Conflict of Interest in the Eisenhower Administration (Ames, Iowa, 1969), 54–77.
24. CQA, XI (1955), 534.
25. CQWR, XII (July 9, 1954), 887; (Feb. 26, 1954), 262–63; NYT, Sept. 30, 1954.
26. CQA, XI (1955), 535.
27. Finkle, op. cit., 300–301; see "Power Policy: Dixon-Yates Contract," hearings before a Subcommittee of the Committee on the Judiciary. United States Senate. Eighty-third Congress, Second Session, on Investigation Concerning the Charges of Monopolistic Influences in the Power Industry, Pt. 1 (July 1, 2, 1954) and Pt. 2 (Sept. 28-Oct. 1, 5–7, 21–22, 29–30, 1954).
28. CQWR, XII (Oct. 1, 1954), 1236.
29. CQA, XI (1955), 534.

30. St. Louis Post-Dispatch, Dec. 6, 1954.
31. NYT, Nov. 10, Dec. 19, 1954.
32. Ibid., Nov. 19, 1954; Jan. 24, 1955.
33. Wildovsky, op. cit., 226, 251; CQWR, XIII (July 1, 1955), 782.
34. Estes Kefauver, "What's Wrong with Dixon-Yates," Atlantic Monthly, CXCV (Jan. 1955), 69.
35. Statement by Kefauver on Dixon-Yates, Feb. 17, 1955, in KP:61&71.
36. "Power Policy: Dixon-Yates Contract," hearings before the Subcommittee on Antitrust and Monopoly of the Committee on the Judiciary. United States Senate. Eighty-fourth Congress, 1st Session. Pursuant to S. Res. 61 on Investigation Concerning the Charges of Monopolistic Influences in the Power Industry. Pts. 1 and 2 (June 27, 30, July 6-8, 11–13, 18–21, 27, 29, Aug. 1–3, Nov. 12, Dec. 5, 1955).
37. CQA, XI (1955), 535–36; NYT, July 1, 1955.
38. CR 101:10196–97 (7/11/55).
39. Antitrust and Monopoly hearings on Dixon-Yates, July 11, 1955, 322.
40. CQA, XI (1955), 536.
41. Clarence Manion, Let's Face It (South Bend, 1956), 196.
42. Antitrust and Monopoly hearings on Dixon-Yates, July 11, 1955, 322.
43. CQA, XI (1955), 536; Antitrust and Monopoly hearings on Dixon-Yates, July 8, 1955, 268.
44. CQA, XI (1955), 537; NYT, July 22, 1955.
45. CQA, XI (1955), 537.
46. CQWR, XIII (Dec. 2, 1955), 1252.

Chapter xiii

1. CT, July 27, 1952.
2. NYT, Oct. 20, Nov. 26–28, 1954.
3. Edward F. Cox, Voting in Postwar Federal Elections: A Statistical Analysis of Party Strengths Since 1945 (Ann Arbor, 1966), 336.
4. "The Man in Command," Newsweek, XLV (Feb. 28, 1955), 21; one of the last polls taken before Eisenhower's heart attack showed Stevenson, the strongest Democratic candidate, losing to Eisenhower, 61 per cent to 39 per cent; see "Walkaway," Newsweek, XLVI (Sept. 26, 1955), 38.
5. NYT, Sept. 25, 26, 1954; KS, 224.
6. NYT, July 31, Aug. 26, 1955.
7. Ibid., Sept. 12, 13, 1955; copy of undated article by Kefauver in the Philadelphia Record, in KP:61&71; KS, 222–23.

8. *NYT,* Sept. 15, 1955; *KS,* 224.
9. *KS,* 224–30; *NYT,* Sept. 24–27, Oct. 2, 7, Dec. 23, 1955.
10. *NYT,* Aug. 14, Sept. 27, 1955.
11. See the immediate reaction to Eisenhower's illness among political commentators, in *NYT,* Sept. 25, Oct. 21, Dec. 30, 1955.
12. Ralph G. Martin, *Ballots and Bandwagons* (Chicago, 1964), 379; *NYT,* Oct. 30, 1955.
13. *NYT,* Nov. 14, 16, 19, 23, 1955; *CQWR,* XIII (Dec. 2, 1955), 1250.
14. James L. McConaughy, Jr., "It's Adlai versus Stevenson for the Democratic Nomination," *Life,* XXXIX (Nov. 28, 1955), 118 ff.
15. *KS,* 236.
16. *NYT,* Dec. 17, 1955; *Washington Post,* Dec. 17, 1955; *Washington Star,* Dec. 16, 1955.
17. *NYT,* Dec. 21, 1955.
18. *Ibid.,* Dec. 17, 1955.
19. *Ibid.,* Oct. 10, 1955.
20. " 'Coonskin' in the Ring," *Newsweek,* XLVI (Dec. 26, 1955), 15; *KS,* 237; "Up and Down Hill," *Time,* LXVII (Jan. 23, 1956), 16; *NYT,* Jan. 16, 1956; Harold Lavine, "Kefauver's Campaign: Can It Be Stopped?" *Newsweek,* XLVII (Feb. 27, 1956), 26; "The Man in the Coonskin Cap," *New Statesman and Nation,* LI (June 2, 1956), 619.
21. *NYT,* Jan. 16, 1956.
22. Theodore H. White, "Kefauver Rides Again," *Collier's,* CXXXVII (May 11, 1956), 28.
23. *NYT,* April 11, May 5, 1956.
24. Robert Coughlan, "How Stumping Kefauver Stumps the Pros," *Life,* XL (May 28, 1956), 178.
25. *Nashville Banner,* Dec. 16, 1955.
26. Kefauver defeated Pat Sutton, 440,497 to 186,363; Clement defeated Browning, 481,808 to 195,156; see *Tennessee Blue Book, 1956,* 376.
27. Wilma Dykeman, "Too Much Talent in Tennessee?" *Harper's,* CCX (March, 1955), 48–53; *CQWR,* XIII (July 29, 1955), 910.
28. *NYT,* Oct. 21, 1955; *KS,* 209–10.
29. See, for example, *NYT,* Oct. 2, 1955.
30. "Enough for Adlai?" *Newsweek,* XLVII (Jan. 16, 1956), 22.

Chapter xiv

1. *NYT,* Feb. 26, 1956; James W. Davis, *Presidential Primaries: Road to the White House* (New York, 1967), 92.
2. The most important of Kefauver's 1956 advisers are discussed in "Those Who Would Be President," *New Republic,* CXXXIV (Jan.

2, 1956), 4–5; Charles Alexander Holmes Thomson and Frances M. Shattuck, *The 1956 Presidential Campaign* (Washington, 1960), 32; Douglass Cater, "Estes Kefauver, Most Willing of the Willing," *Reporter*, XIII (Nov. 3, 1955), 14–18; *NYT*, Dec. 21, 1955; May 8, 1956. The author is also indebted to Joseph Donohue, Kefauver's 1956 campaign manager, for discussing the 1956 campaign in depth and at length at an interview, June 18, 1970.

3. Defections from Kefauver's 1952 New Hampshire supporters were few; Sullivan, the most prominent, acquired a wide reputation as an opportunist among New Hampshire Democratic leaders as a result of his switch to Stevenson. Kefauver backers were especially angry with him, since his election as National Committeeman had been by the Kefauver delegates elected in 1952.

4. For the 1956 New Hampshire Democratic presidential primary, see: "Unhappy Moments," *Newsweek*, XLVII (Jan. 30, 1956), 25; *NYT*, Jan. 30, Feb. 2, March 2, 7, 12, 13, 14, 1956; *Concord* (N. H.) *Daily Monitor*, March 12, 15, 1956; *CQWR*, XIV (March 30, 1956), 384; Davis, *op. cit.*, 301.

5. *NYT*, Dec. 17, 19, 1955; Jan. 1, 1956.

6. *Ibid.*, Feb. 25, 26, 1956.

7. *Minneapolis Morning Tribune*, March 16, 1956.

8. *NYT*, March 17, 1956; John McDonald, "Kefauver Passes the Plate in Minnesota," *New Republic*, CXXXIV (March 5, 1956), 7.

9. Thomson and Shattuck, *op. cit.*, 38–39.

10. "Whistle-Stopping," *Newsweek*, XLVII (March 19, 1956), 34. Ralph G. Martin, *Ballots and Bandwagons* (Chicago, 1964), 377, records that former Republican Governor Harold Stassen helped turn out 125,000 Republican votes for Kefauver.

11. *NYT*, March 22, 1956; Theodore H. White, "Kefauver Rides Again," *Collier's*, CXXXVII (May 11, 1956), 27. In an obvious bid for the farm vote, Kefauver had flown back to Washington on Sunday, March 18, to vote for high price supports; *NYT*, March 19, 1956.

12. " 'Plot' or 'Panic'?" *Newsweek*, XLVII (May 21, 1956), 37; Martin, *op. cit.*, 377.

13. "Minnesota Miracle," *Time*, LXVII (April 2, 1956), 18; see also, Patrick O'Donovan, "How Kefauver Made It in Minnesota," *Reporter*, XIV (April 5, 1956), 22–23; "The High & Low Roads," *Time*, LXVII (March 24, 1956), 24.

14. White, *loc. cit.*, 26.

15. "Little Promise in Those Who Promise All," *Christian Century*, LXXIII (April 4, 1956), 412.

16. "Hand That Shook the Democrats," *Life*, XL (April 2, 1956), 23–29; *CQWR*, XIV (May 4, 1956), 517.

17. "One Man's Meat," *Time*, LXVII (April 9, 1956), 31–34; *NYT*, March 22, 1956; "'After You, Estes,'" *Time*, LXVII (April 16, 1956), 22.
18. "The Tennessee Whiz," *Time*, LXVII (April 23, 1956), 27.
19. For example, Philadelphia Mayor Richardson Dilworth wired Kefauver two days after the Minnesota primary, strongly urging that Kefauver:

> contact Jim Clark and Bill Green by telephone as soon as possible. Green intends to ask Governor [George Leader] to release delegation from Stevenson commitment. If situation is dealt with promptly, I think majority of Pennsylvania delegates can be in your corner. (Telegram of March 22, 1956, in *KP:*Elections)

20. Stevenson came down so hard on Kefauver's Senate record in the days after the Minnesota primary that the very attention he paid to Kefauver increased the Tennessean's prestige among Democrats; Stevenson's interpretation of Kefauver's record, including a blast at Kefauver for missing a Senate vote on a reciprocal trade bill in 1948 (before Kefauver was even elected to the Senate), caused Kefauver to picture Stevenson as a poor loser, unable to accept his Minnesota defeat. Kefauver pointed out, "I didn't cry after I lost . . . in 1952. I got out and worked to help Mr. Stevenson and the Democratic Party. I'm sorry that Mr. Stevenson feels he now must engage in mudslinging. He's not in character doing it. . . . We'll turn the other cheek." See "Family Squabble," *Newsweek*, XLVII (April 16, 1956), 33–34.
21. *NYT*, March 25, 1956.
22. *CQWR*, XIV (April 27, 1956), 488.
23. Davis, *op. cit.*, 301; Thomson and Shattuck, *op. cit.*, 33–34.
24. Letter to Kefauver and Stevenson from Morse, Feb. 21, 1956, in *KP:*Elections; Thomson and Shattuck, *op. cit.*, 33–34.
25. Davis, *op. cit.*, 210, 301; "Oregon," *Newsweek*, XLVII (May 14, 1956), 37–38; "On to Florida," *Newsweek*, XLVII (May 28, 1956), 30.
26. The Americans for Democratic Action evaluated Kefauver's 1947–52 civil rights votes as two "right" and five "wrong"; see "The Civil Rights Squeeze on the Democrats," *New Republic*, CXXXIV (Feb. 20, 1956), 3.
27. Although Kefauver was always considered a "liberal," he declined to so label himself; in a letter to Eric Goldman at Princeton, responding to Goldman's letter asking if Kefauver considered himself a liberal and, if so, what that meant, Kefauver replied that he had:

. . . never felt it was necessary or proper to place myself in a category of general classification, particularly one capable of numerous and divergent interpretations and definitions. It is my belief that a man in public office need only conduct himself in a manner consistent with his genuine belief in what is good for his country, regardless of what the public may see fit to classify him as. (Letter of Feb. 16, 1955, in *KP*:9:2&12:1, Estes Kefauver, III).

28. *Washington Post*, Dec. 17, 1955.
29. "Playing Politics with the Negro Vote," *New Republic*, CXXXIV (Feb. 13, 1956), 3; *NYT*, Feb. 6, 1956; "'Imagine That,'" *Newsweek*, XLVII (Feb. 20, 1956), 31.
30. "The Race Issue Explodes," *Time*, LXVII (Feb. 20, 1956), 18–19.
31. *NYT*, April 21, 1956.
32. *Ibid.*, March 12, 29, 1956.
33. Quoted in Martin, *op. cit.*, 411.
34. Clifton Brock, *Americans for Democratic Action: Its Role in National Politics* (Washington, 1962), 185; Kefauver's popularity with the ADA, which Brock greatly exaggerated, was due to a large extent, of course, to the absolute as well as the relative nature of Kefauver's liberal voting record, especially after 1952; during the last session of Congress before the 1956 campaign, Kefauver was one of four senators with a 100 per cent ADA rating; *CQWR*, XIII (Sept. 16, 1955), 1060.
35. Kefauver supporters were aware that, with Stevenson out, the South might be forced to turn to Kefauver in order to block Harriman, who was perhaps the one candidate who was more objectionable to the South than Kefauver. An attempt to exploit Southern fears of Harriman was evident in a letter written by a Kefauver aide on Sept. 10, 1955, to Judge "Red" Townsend, a segregationist leader in Georgia, warning:

. . . the South is going to be caught napping if we aren't careful. Harriman, rather than Stevenson, will emerge as the nominee even without the South unless we move quickly to back a Southerner who is acceptable to the rest of the country. And you will remember Harriman beat Estes in the District of Columbia perference in 1952 *solely* on the 'force' FEPC issue. That ought to convince you 'Crackers' as to where your solace lies. (*KP*:Personal, 1955–57)

Similarly, Kefauver aide Charles Neese wrote in late 1955:

. . . This upsurge for Harriman is working well for our side, because we are now able to convince the South that Harri-

man may come up with the marbles unless the South gets behind a Southerner right now who has support in the remainder of the country. (Letter to Frank L. Bowron, Casper,
Wyoming, Oct. 7, 1955, in *KP:*Elections)

36. William A. Emerson, Jr., "The Peculiar State of Florida Politics,"
Newsweek, XLVII (May 7, 1956), 30–32, furnishes a good summary
of the Florida political situation in which Kefauver and Stevenson
had to operate in the presidential primary campaign there; see
also, *NYT,* March 26, April 9, May 14, 30, 1956.
37. Harold Lavine, "Kefauver's Campaign: Can Stevenson Be Stopped?"
Newsweek, XLVII (Feb. 27, 1956), 26.
38. *NYT,* Feb. 15, March 30, 1956.
39. "The Great Boz-Woz," *Time,* LXVII (June 11, 1956), 28–29; *NYT,*
March 26, May 15, 1956.
40. "Duel in the Sun," *Newsweek,* XLVII (June 4, 1956), 29.
41. Thomson and Shattuck, *op. cit.,* 34; "One Man's Meat," *loc. cit.;*
NYT, March 29, 1956.
42. *NYT,* March 29, 1956.
43. In spite of Kefauver's announcement the previous fall, "I'm not
going to kill myself this time," he so exhausted himself during the
1956 campaign, especially in Florida and California, that some
of his friends believe he never fully recovered his strength; see
James L. McConaughy, Jr., "It's Adlai versus Stevenson for
Democratic Nomination," *Life,* XXXIX (Nov. 28, 1955), 118 ff.;
E. W. Kenworthy, "Shall the Best Handshaker Be Nominated?"
New York Times Magazine (May 27, 1956), 11, 68–70; Davis, *op.
cit.,* 258–59. Stevenson, later evaluating presidential primaries as
"almost . . . useless," also complained that they were "exhausting
physically"; *CQWR,* XVI (June 6, 1958), 710.
44. *NYT,* May 14, 1956.
45. Thomson and Shattuck, *op. cit.,* 54; a film of the "debate" is preserved at the Kefauver Library, Knoxville, Tennessee.
46. Thomson and Shattuck, *op. cit.,* 53.
47. Davis, *op. cit.,* 301; *Miami Herald,* May 30, 1956; "The Great Boz-
Woz," *loc. cit.; NYT,* May 31, 1956.
48. *NYT,* May 29, 1956; Thomson and Shattuck, *op. cit.,* 60; "Duel in
the Sun," *loc. cit.,* 28.
49. In appearances before the CDC in February, Kefauver had been
interrupted by applause 43 times to Stevenson's 23, but Stevenson
received the personal endorsement of 86 per cent of the delegates
to the CDC convention; see "Bosses and a 'Wigging,' " *Newsweek,*
XLVII (Feb. 13, 1956), 28; *NYT,* Feb. 5, 1956.

410 : Kefauver: A Political Biography

50. "Washington Wire," *New Republic,* CXXXIV (June 4, 1956), 2; *NYT,* June 1, 1956.
51. *Washington Post,* May 25, 1956.
52. *Ibid.,* June 4, 1956.
53. *NYT,* May 31, 1956; "Washington Wire," *loc. cit.*
54. *Washington Star,* Dec. 16, 1955; Thomson and Shattuck, *op. cit.,* 45–46; "Professional Common Man," *Time,* LXVIII (Sept. 17, 1956), 27.
55. Davis, *op. cit.,* 301.
56. White, *loc. cit.,* 29; *CQWR,* XIV (July 13, 1956), 849; *NYT,* July 18, 1956.
57. "Preview Conventions '56," *Newsweek,* XLVIII (Aug. 13, 1956), 24; *NYT,* June 28, 29, 1956.
58. Alexander Heard, *The Costs of Democracy* (Chapel Hill, 1960), 336; Davis, *op. cit.,* 210; "Preview Conventions '56," *loc. cit.;* Martin, *op. cit.,* 383; McConaughy, *loc. cit.,* 128.
59. *NYT,* June 14, 1956; the Kefauver apology for Florida and California centered around the argument that if Kefauver did as well as he did with no money and no organization, then he certainly would be unbeatable if the party, with all its resources, got behind him as the Democratic candidate in November; this was the view expounded at length by Kefauver manager Donohue in an appearance on ABC's "Town Meeting of the Air," June 10, 1956, a transcript of which is in the author's possession.
60. "Is This It? Stevenson and Kefauver," *Newsweek,* XLVIII (July 30, 1956), 19–20; *NYT,* June 18, 1956.
61. Martin, *op. cit.,* 382–83.
62. Quoted in *ibid.,* 383.
63. Speech at Vernon City, Minnesota, quoted in McDonald, *loc. cit.;* Davis, *op. cit.,* 92.
64. *NYT,* Aug. 1, 1956.
65. *Ibid.,* Aug. 1, 2, 1956. Harriman had reportedly already offered to pick up Kefauver's campaign deficit if Kefauver would get behind a Harriman bid for the nomination; see "Preview Conventions '56," *loc. cit.;* Heard, *op. cit.,* 338. George Backer, director of the Harriman for President Committee, had thought that the Kefauver and Harriman camps were on the verge of an anti-Stevenson coalition at the time of Kefauver's withdrawal; *NYT,* Aug. 2, 1956.
66. *NYT,* Aug. 1, 1956.

Chapter xv

1. Harold Lavine, "After Four Years . . . Squaring Off Again," *Newsweek*, XLVIII (Aug. 27, 1956), 24, 26.
2. *NYT*, Aug. 15–17, 1956; *Official Report of the Proceedings of the Democratic National Convention . . . 1956* (Richmond, 1956), 418 (hereafter cited as *Proceedings*). Kefauver met with mixed success in attempting to win his delegates for Stevenson; the New York governor did pick up some support among former Kefauver supporters, winning 11 of 26 Kefauver delegates from Minnesota, 5 of 28 from Wisconsin, and 6 of 16 from Montana; however, Stevenson got all 18 Kefauver delegates from Maryland, 21½ of 26 from Indiana, 5½ of 8 from New Hampshire, 8 of 8 from South Dakota, and, of course, all 32 from Tennessee, which Stevenson might have gotten even in the face of Kefauver's opposition but which probably would have stayed with Kefauver at least through the first ballot.
3. *NYT*, Aug. 1, 1956.
4. Ralph G. Martin, *Ballots & Bandwagons* (Chicago, 1964), 387.
5. *NYT*, Aug. 15, 1956; Charles A. H. Thomson and Frances M. Shattuck, *The 1956 Presidential Campaign* (Washington, 1960), 126.
6. *NYT*, Aug. 15, 1956.
7. *Proceedings*, 420.
8. Martin, *op. cit.*, 372–455, provides an exhaustive and most exciting account of the open fight for the 1956 Democratic vice-presidential nomination. Essentially the same account was published earlier in Ralph G. Martin and Edward Plaut, *Front Runner, Dark Horse* (Garden City, N. Y., 1960), 17–109.
9. Martin, *op. cit.*, 373–99, gives a detailed account of the background to Stevenson's decision to leave the vice-presidential nomination to the delegates.
10. *Ibid.*, 401–4; *NYT*, Aug. 18, 1956.
11. Martin, *op. cit.*, 402–4.
12. *Proceedings*, 427–35.
13. *Ibid.*, 435–65.
14. *Ibid.*, 464–65.
15. *Ibid.*, 476.
16. Martin, *op. cit.*, 438–39; Lavine, *loc. cit.*, 28–29.
17. Martin, *op. cit.*, 440.
18. *Proceedings*, 476–78, 481.
19. Martin, *op. cit.*, 443.

20. Letter from Wright Patman to Adlai Stevenson, Aug. 23, 1956, copy in *KP:*Elections.
21. Robert Sherrill, *The Accidental President* (New York, 1967), 104.
22. James MacGregor Burns, *John Kennedy: A Political Profile* (New York, 1960), 190; but, see Martin, *op. cit.,* 444–45.
23. Martin, *op. cit.,* 405–6, 411.
24. *Ibid.,* 385, 447.
25. *CQA,* XII (1956), 162.
26. Martin, *op. cit.,* 448; concern over the farm vote was also given as the reason for Humphrey's important switch to Kefauver during the second ballot; see *ibid.,* 431, 434–35; see also, Allan H. Ryskind, *Hubert* (New Rochelle, N. Y., 1968), 215–16.
27. Ralph de Toledano, *R. F. K.: The Man Who Would Be President* (New York, 1967), 142.
28. *NYT,* Aug. 18, 1956.
29. *NYT,* Dec. 14, 1956.
30. Martin, *op. cit.,* 452; *CQWR,* XVI (Dec. 5, 1958), 1511; *NYT,* Aug. 18, 1956.
31. A CBS-TV film of the dramatic Kefauver-Kennedy battle on the second ballot and Kefauver's subsequent appearance before the convention is available at the Kefauver Library, Knoxville, Tennessee.
32. *Proceedings,* 499–503.

Chapter xvi

1. *Chicago Tribune,* Aug. 19, 1956; *NYT,* Aug. 19, 1956.
2. *NYT,* Aug. 18, 19, 22, 1956.
3. *Ibid.,* Aug. 22, 27, Sept. 2, 11, 14, 1956.
4. Charles A. H. Thomson and Frances M. Shattuck, *The 1956 Presidential Campaign* (Washington, 1960), 253.
5. *NYT,* Sept. 23, 1956.
6. *Ibid.,* Sept. 25, 1956.
7. *Ibid.,* Sept. 27, 1956.
8. *Ibid.,* Sept. 19, 1956.
9. *Ibid.,* Feb. 21, 1956.
10. *Wallaces' Farmer and Iowa Homestead,* June 16, 1956; *Rapid City* (S. D.) *Daily Journal,* Nov. 13, 1955.
11. *NYT,* June 23, 1956; "Tennessean on a Hayride," *Newsweek,* XLVIII (Oct. 15, 1956), 45–47.
12. "Fluffs and Farmers." *Newsweek,* XLVIII (Oct. 1, 1956), 24; *CQWR,* XIV (March 9, 1956), 263.

13. *CQWR,* XIV (Sept. 28, 1956), 1185; *NYT,* Feb. 28, Sept. 23, Oct. 17, 1956. Perhaps the most comprehensive statement of Kefauver's political philosophy presented during the 1956 campaign was his September 13 speech, carried over TV and radio from Harrisburg, Pennsylvania; see "The Essence of Democracy is Equality: Political, Economic Opportunity, Voting and Education," *Vital Speeches,* XXII (Oct. 1, 1956), 763–64.

14. *NYT,* Sept. 21, Oct. 17, 1956.

15. *Ibid.,* Sept. 11, 22, Oct. 30, 1956.

16. *Ibid.,* Sept. 20, 1956.

17. *Ibid.,* March 1, June 10, Sept. 25, 1956.

18. Elmo Roper, *You and Your Leaders* (New York, 1957), 231; *CT,* July 15, 1960.

19. *NYT,* Oct. 23, 1956.

20. *NYT,* Oct. 28, Nov. 6, Dec. 30, 1956.

21. *Ibid.,* Oct. 31, Nov. 1, 1956.

22. "He Just Can't Stop," *Time,* LXVIII (Nov. 12, 1956), 21; memo by Richard Wallace, in *KP:*Elections.

23. *Washington Star,* Nov. 21, 1967; *CT,* Nov. 21, 1967.

24. *NYT,* Oct. 9, 13, 1956.

25. Letter from Meeman to Wallace, in *KP:*General Correspondence, 1948–55.

26. "Professional Common Man," *Time,* LXVIII (Sept. 17, 1956), 25; "The Man in the Coonskin Cap," *New Statesman and Nation,* LI (June 2, 1956), 620.

27. Martin, *loc. cit.,* 89.

28. Letter to Kefauver from Welburn Mayock of Washington, Jan. 19, 1954, in *KP:*Personal, 1955–57; interviews with: Paul Douglas, April 1, 1970, and Joseph Clark, June 4, 1970; Charles Bartlett, "The Crusading Kefauver," *Nation,* CLXXIV (May 3, 1952), 427.

29. "Tennessean on a Hayride," *loc. cit.,* 46.

30. Serrell Hillman, "On a Fast-Moving Tour, Only Estes Is Unmoved," *Time,* LXVIII (Oct. 1, 1956), 20.

31. " 'Bundle of Calm,' " *New Republic,* CXXXV (Oct. 8, 1956), 2. William S. White wrote of Kefauver that "His memory for first and last names—and a keen memory is supposed to be a politician's special requirement—is so bad as to be almost unbelievable"; *Boston Traveler,* June 2, 1958. Stevenson himself rarely appeared with Kefauver during the campaign, but, when he did, got a taste of the Kefauver campaign style. At a regional meeting in Knoxville, Kefauver's late arrival held up the whole program, provoking Stevenson to ask irritatedly, "Where's Estes?"; see Leonard Slater, "At the Grass Roots," *Newsweek,* XLVIII (Sept.

10, 1956), 33; see also, "The Campaign Trail," *Time*, LXVIII (Oct. 8, 1956), 55–56.

32. Thomson and Shattuck, *op. cit.*, 275; "The Absent Treatment," *Time*, LXVIII (Oct. 22, 1956), 20.

33. Republicans spent about $21 million, Democrats about $11 million; see Thomson and Shattuck, *op. cit.*, 326.

34. *NYT*, Nov. 7, 1956.

35. Letter from Kefauver to Stevenson, Nov. 17, 1956, in *KP*:Miscellaneous Material, 175, p. 2.

36. Letter from Kefauver to Robert Hamilton of Geneva, Switzerland, Jan. 20, 1960, in *KP*:Elections.

37. Thomson and Shattuck, *op. cit.*, 352.

Chapter xvii

1. *NYT*, Oct. 19, Nov. 4, 1956.

2. *Ibid.*, Nov. 18, 1956; "He Just Can't Stop," *Time*, LXVIII (Nov. 12, 1956), 21.

3. "Who's for Whom," *Time*, LXX (Aug. 19, 1957), 13.

4. *NYT*, Dec. 6, 1956. See Rayburn's opposition to the Council, in *NYT*, Dec. 9, Johnson's, Dec. 14, 1956.

5. *CQWR*, XIV (Dec. 28, 1956), 1476.

6. *NYT*, Dec. 7, 1956; Samuel Shaffer, "Power Play," *Newsweek*, XLVIII (Dec. 17, 1956), 42, 44.

7. Rowland Evans and Robert Novak, *Lyndon B. Johnson: The Exercise of Power* (New York, 1966), 101; "Restless Estes," *Time*, LXIX (Jan. 21, 1957), 14.

8. *CQWR*, XV (Jan. 18, 1957), 76.

9. Letter from Kefauver to Johnson, Jan. 9, 1957, in *KP*:9:2&12:1, Estes Kefauver, III.

10. *Ibid.*, letter from Johnson to Kefauver, Jan. 10, 1957.

11. *Ibid.*, copy of remarks, with personal notation that they were not delivered.

12. *Ibid.*, letter from Kefauver to Eastland, Dec. 20, 1956.

13. *Ibid.*, letter from Kefauver to Eastland, Jan. 16, 1957.

14. Letter from Senator Ralph Yarborough to the author, Dec. 27, 1968. Some of Yarborough's affection for Kefauver derived from the fact that Kefauver was the only Democratic senator who would brave Johnson's wrath and speak at liberal (and mostly anti-Johnson) fundraising dinners in Texas.

15. Letter from Kefauver to Johnson, Nov. 14, 1958, in *KP*:9:2&12:1, Estes Kefauver, III.

16. *Ibid.*, letter from Russell to Kefauver, Jan. 17, 1959.
17. The Twenty-third Amendment (presidential vote for the District of Columbia) was also proposed, passed, and ratified while Kefauver was chairman of Constitutional Amendments, but it was one of the few amendments not handled by the Judiciary Committee, being assigned, instead, to the District of Columbia Committee.

Chapter xviii

1. It was Kefauver's chairmanship of this committee that first brought him to the attention of Paul Douglas, who, impressed by Kefauver's performance, selected him to address a convention of the American Economic Association; see Harry Conn, "What's Behind the Handshake?" *New Republic*, CXXVI (June 9, 1952), 12; interview with Paul Douglas, April 1, 1970.
2. Conn, *loc. cit.*, 13. One of Kefauver's most persistent legislative efforts over the years was the strengthening of the Robinson-Patman fair trade law; see *CQWR*, XIII (March 25, 1955), 297–98, and *ibid.* XV (March 22, 1957), 367.
3. Kefauver's zeal for antitrust activity frequently exceeded that of the executive departments and regulatory agencies charged with the enforcement of antitrust laws. In 1955, for example, resigned Federal Trade Commission Chairman Edward F. Howrey complained that congressional interference was a major hindrance to the FTC's functioning and accused Kefauver and House Judiciary Chairman Emanuel Celler, two of the most outspoken foes of monopoly in Congress, with "standing over our shoulders and attempting to dominate our opinions"; *CQWR*, XIII (Aug. 12, 1955), 989. Responsible for Howrey's irritation had been statements from Kefauver such as one earlier in the year warning that 3,000 mergers had taken place since 1950 and criticizing the fact that the FTC had issued only three complaints; *NYT*, Jan. 27, 1955. Similarly, Kefauver attacked the report of the Attorney General's Committee on Revision of Antitrust Legislation as "a gigantic brief for the non-enforcement of the anti-trust laws"; *CQWR*, XIII (May 13, 1955), 556.
4. *NYT*, Oct. 28, 1961.
5. *CR* 102:15134 (7/27/56).
6. *CR* 105:5340 (3/26/59).
7. *CR* 103:6230 (5/1/57), 105:3152 (3/2/59), 4338 (3/25/59).
8. *NYT*, Jan. 24, 1957.
9. "Administered Prices: A Compendium on Public Policy," Committee

Print of the Antitrust and Monopoly Subcommittee of the Senate Judiciary Committee. Eighty-eighth Congress, 1st Session, 1963, 3. Throughout this chapter, unless otherwise noted, hearings and reports cited will be those of the Antitrust and Monopoly Subcommittee of the Senate Judiciary Committee.

10. *Hearings,* Administered Prices, Part 1 (Opening Phase—Economists' Views, July 9, 11–13, 16, 1957), 1–2.

11. *Hearings,* Administered Prices, Part 29 (Public Policy on Administered Prices, May 21–23, 1963), 17967–68. The twenty-six volumes to which Kefauver referred, plus three additional volumes, were as follows: Part 1 (Opening Phase—Economists' Views, July 9, 11–13, 16, 1957); Part 2 (Steel, Aug. 8–10, 12, 15–16, 20–22, Oct. 21–22, 1957); Part 3 (Steel, Oct. 29–30, Nov. 4–5, 1957; Steel, Appendix A); Part 4 (Steel, Appendix B); Part 5 (Asphalt Roofing, March 25–27, 1958); Part 6 (Automobiles, Jan. 28–31, Feb. 4–7, 10, 20, April 29–30, May 1–2, 6, 1958); Part 7 (Automobiles, Appendix); Part 8 (1958 Steel Price Increase, Aug. 5–6, 1958); Part 9 (Administered Price Inflation: Alternative Public Policies, Jan. 23–24, 26, 1959); Part 10 (Alternative Public Policies—con't., March 10–13, 1959); Part 11 (Advance Notice and Public Justification for Price Increases in Administered Price Industries, April 23–24, 28–30, May 1, 5, 21, 1959); Part 12 (Bread, June 16, 18, 30, July 1, 2, 7–10, 1959); Part 13 (Identical Bidding, TVA, Sept. 28–30, 1959); Part 14 (Drugs —Corticosteroids, Dec. 7–12, 1959); Part 15 (Drugs—Corticosteroids, Appendix); Part 16 (Drugs—Tranquilizers, Jan. 21–22, 26–28, 1960); Part 17 (Drugs—Tranquilizers, Appendix); Part 18 (Drugs— General: Physicians and Other Professional Authorities, Feb. 25– 26, April 12–15, 1960); Part 19 (Drugs—General: Pharmaceutical Manufacturers Association, Feb. 23–24, April 20, 1960); Part 20 (Drugs—Oral Antidiabetic Drugs, April 26–28, May 3–4, 1960); Part 21 (Drugs—General: Generic and Brand Names, May 10–13, 1960); Part 22 (Drugs—Food and Drug Administration: Dr. Henry Welch, May 17–18, June 1–3, 6, 1960); Part 23 (Drugs—Food and Drug Administration: Dr. Henry Welch, Appendix); Part 24 (Drugs— Antibiotics, September 7–9, 12–14, 1960); Part 25 (Drugs—Antibiotics, Appendix); Part 26 (Drugs—Antibiotics, Appendix B); Part 27 (Price Fixing and Bid Rigging in the Electrical Manufacturing Industry, April 13–14, 17–20, 25–28, May 2, 1961); Part 28 (Price Fixing and Bid Rigging in the Electrical Manufacturing Industry, cont'd., May 3–5, 10–11, 16–18, June 5–6, 22–23, 1961); Part 29 (Public Policy on Administered Prices, May 21–23, 1963). At the time of his death, Kefauver had largely completed the first draft of a book about administered prices and monopoly in general, *In*

a Few Hands: Monopoly Power in America (New York, 1965). The book was finished by Dr. Irene Till, who worked with Kefauver on the administered prices hearings.

12. *CR* 107:11560 (6/28/61).
13. *CR* 104:1739–40 (2/5/58).
14. *CQA,* XIV (1958), 417.
15. Bernard D. Nossiter, "A Staff Man Leaves His Mark on the Hill," *Washington Post,* April 11, 1970.
16. *CR* 104:1768 (1/9/58).
17. *NYT,* Dec. 12, 1957.
18. Nossiter, *loc. cit.;* see also Nossiter's earlier evaluation of the Antitrust and Monopoly Subcommittee under Kefauver, "Kefauver and the Price-Makers," *Nation,* CXCVII (July 6, 1963), 12–13.
19. Kefauver's experiences on the Antitrust and Monopoly Subcommittee no doubt played a major part in his sponsorship of a bill in 1959, 1961, and 1963 which would have created a Consumers Office; *CR* 109:10324 (6/6/63). Kefauver said the office was needed to serve as a "daily burr in the hides of Government officialdom to get important consumer issues raised, and to aid in their settlement in such a fashion that consumer interest will be heard and taken account of"; *NYT,* June 7, 1963.
20. *Hearings,* Administered Prices, Part 2 (Steel), 311–12 (Aug. 12, 1957).
21. *Hearings,* Administered Prices, Part 3 (Steel), 871 (Nov. 5, 1957).
22. See the amusing attempts of Blough and Humphrey to argue the logic of their positions and their frustrations when Kefauver seemed unable to fathom their incredible definitions of competition; *Hearings,* Administered Prices, Part 2 (Steel), 298 ff.; *ibid.,* Part 3 (Steel), 866 ff.
23. See, for example, *CR* 105:5197 (3/25/59), praise for Eisenhower's urging restraint in steel wage negotiations; *NYT,* June 20, 1958 (when Kefauver was counting down the days before a threatened steel price hike on July 1): "Here we have an industry in which for more than six months about half of the capacity has been unutilized and in which, following the price increase, more than half of the capacity is expected to be idle. Nonetheless, it seems bound and determined to go through with its planned price advance which, in the end, can only aggravate further the already depressed levels of steel demand." *NYT,* July 31, 1958 (on steel price rise: "I am disappointed the President has not acted. I urge him to do so. I think he might even now be able to secure a price rollback.); *NYT,* Aug. 30, 1959 (Kefauver urging steel companies to lower prices and increase wages—an attempt by

Kefauver to offset steel companies argument that a wage hike would bring a price hike).

24. The first phase of the steel probe began on July 9, 1957, and concluded on Nov. 5 (see above, Note 14); the subcommittee's findings were issued March 13, 1958, in Senate Report 1387. The subcommittee reopened hearings on steel in Aug. 1958, in response to the 1958 steel price hike; see *Hearings,* Administered Prices, Part 8 (Aug. 5–6, 1958). For Kefauver's later attacks on the steel industry, see below, Chapter XXIV.

25. *CQA,* XIV (1958), 704; *NYT,* Nov. 7, 1958, Feb. 25, 1959; "Administered Prices: Automobiles," Committee Print, 85th Congress, 2nd Session (1958); *Hearings,* Administered Prices (Automobiles, see above, Note 14).

26. *NYT,* Feb. 4, July 2, 28, Aug. 1, Nov. 14, 1959; Jan. 9, 30, April 24, May 6, 18, June 15, 16, 29, Nov. 16, Dec. 15, 18, 1960; March 30, May 1, June 1–3, 1961; March 28, 1962; Feb. 9, March 26, 1963; *CQWR,* XVII (Aug. 4, 1959), 1208; XVIII (May 27, 1960), 945; (June 24, 1960), 1106; XIX (June 9, 1961), 949–50. The subcommittee's most comprehensive look at a sports monopoly, an investigation into professional boxing, began June 14, 1960, and continued intermittently through the rest of the year; see *Hearings,* Professional Boxing.

27. *NYT,* March 4, April 19, 1962; the investigation of the hearing aid industry began April 18, 1962, and concluded April 25; see Senate Report 2216 (1962).

28. *NYT,* Aug. 14, 1961; the insurance investigation began May 13, 1959, and concluded June 17, 1960; see Senate Reports 1753 and 1834, 86th Congress, 2nd Session.

29. *NYT,* Jan. 25, Feb. 19, April 4, Aug. 28, 1962; March 1, June 24, 1963; "One from Two?" *Newsweek,* LIX (Feb. 5, 1962), 61–62.

30. *CR* 105:3550–52 (3/9/59), 8423 (5/19/59), 107:1918 (2/9/61), 8431 (5/19/61); *NYT,* Sept. 29–30, 1959; April 14, June 19, 21, July 14, 16, Sept. 26, 1961; "Who Gave the Crucial Order?" *Newsweek,* LVII (May 8, 1961), 73–74; "Now the Bloom of Recovery," *Newsweek,* LVII (May 15, 1961), 79–80; " 'No Excuse,' " *Newsweek,* LVII (June 19, 1961), 72. An investigation of identical bids on TVA electrical equipment was held on Sept. 28–30, 1959; see *Hearings,* Administered Prices, Part 13. A second investigation into general price-fixing in the electrical industry began April 17, 1961, and concluded Aug. 29, 1961; see, *Hearings,* Administered Prices, Parts 27 and 28; see also, *CQA,* XVII (1961), 1007.

31. "Administered Prices: Bread," Senate Report 1923, 86th Congress,

2nd Session; see also, *Hearings,* Administered Prices, Part 12 (Bread, June 16, 18, 30, July 1, 2, 7–10, 1959).

32. *CQA,* XIV (1958), 704; *Hearings,* Administered Prices, Part 5 (Asphalt Roofing, March 25–27, 1958); "Administered Prices, Asphalt Roofing," 85th Congress, 2nd Session, 1958.

33. For a discussion of the drug investigation and Kefauver's role in passing the Kefauver-Harris Drug Act of 1962, see below, Chap. xxi.

34. *NYT,* Jan. 30, Feb. 8, April 6, 1958; *CQWR,* XVI (Feb. 14, 1958), 208; *CQA,* XIV (1958), 704; "No Collusion," *Newsweek,* LI (Feb. 17, 1958), 77–78.

35. *NYT,* Oct. 22, 1957; Dec. 30, 1958; Feb. 28, 1959; *CQA,* XIII (1957), 795.

36. " 'Find the Bad Apples,' " *Newsweek,* LVII (May 1, 1961), 69.

37. "Kefauver and the Swindlers," *New Republic,* CXLV (Aug. 7, 1961), 12.

Chapter xix

1. There is no evidence that Kefauver's private views on racial equality differed from his public position. Kefauver's only uncharacteristic response to a racial topic was his evaluation of a racist statement, sent to him for comment by a Memphis constituent and containing the declaration that "White people are smarter than Negroes," as "fundamentally right"; letter from Burton H. Johnson to Kefauver, July 20, 1957; Kefauver's reply, July 24, 1957; both in *KP:*401:1. When, in late 1957, Kefauver was questioned about a racial covenant in the deed to his home, Kefauver went to great lengths to explain his position on such restrictions:

> The fact is, the original developer of Spring Valley had included a restricting clause, which was quite obviously unconstitutional. Several of us, including Senator John Sparkman and Vice President Nixon, bought houses in this section. In my case, and I dare say, in theirs, I did not even know the restrictive covenant existed. When I found out about it, I wrote the developer and stated I refused to abide by it.
>
> I have since sold that house and bought another. The second time I carefully examined the deed and refused to sign it until the restrictive covenant was removed.
>
> I appreciate your writing to me about this and assure you

that I would never knowingly be a party to any such un-democratic and discriminatory arrangement. (Letter from Kefauver to Lyman A. Kasselberg of Memphis, Nov. 25, 1957, in *KP:Civil Rights,* II.

2. Kefauver's form letter, in *KP*:Civil Rights, II.
3. *CQA,* XIII (1957), 284.
4. *CQA,* XIII (1957), 561; *CQWR,* XV (May 24, 1957), 620; (June 7, 1957), 690.
5. *CQWR,* XV (June 7, 1957), 690.
6. *CR* 103:9816 (6/20/57). The Republican leadership managed to rally almost all Republicans against Russell's move to send the House bill to the Judiciary Committee; several pro-civil rights Democrats, including John Kennedy, Wayne Morse of Oregon, and Mike Mansfield of Montana, voted with Russell, and rumors circulated about a Democratic agreement whereby Southern Democrats would support a federal power project at Hell's Canyon in return for Northern and Western support for sending the House bill to the Senate Judiciary Committee. President Eisenhower, in his memoir of the 1957 civil rights battle, spoke of such a coalition; see *Waging Peace, 1956–61* (Vol. II of *The White House Years;* Garden City, New York, 1965), 155.
7. *CQWR,* XV (July 19, 1957), 854.
8. *CR* 103:11984 (7/17/57).
9. Press release, July 23, 1957, in *KP*:401:1.
10. *CQA,* XIII (1957), 564; "Civil Rights—Backstage Drama," *Newsweek,* L (Aug. 12, 1957), 25–26; see both news stories and editorial opinion in the *Nashville Tennessean,* July 17 ff., Aug. 31, 1957. Four other Southern Democrats (Gore of Tennessee, Lyndon Johnson and Ralph Yarborough of Texas, and George Smathers of Florida) also voted for the bill on final passage; *CQA,* XIII (1957), 307.
11. *CQA,* XIII (1957). 307.
12. *Nashville Banner,* Aug. 2, 1957.
13. Norfolk-Portsmouth (Va.) *Virginian-Pilot,* Sept. 16, 1962.
14. Form letter, fall, 1957, in *KP*:Civil Rights, III.
15. *CR* 104:182202–2 (8/18/58); *CQWR,* XVI (Aug. 15, 1958), 1081.
16. *CQA,* XV (1959), 398.
17. Letter to Hayden from Kefauver, Jan. 6, 1959, in *KP*:Congress II.
18. *NYT,* May 14, 1959.
19. *CQWR,* XVII (Aug. 7, 1959), 1077.
20. *CR* 105:19817 (9/14/59).
21. *CR* 105:19555 (9/14/59).

22. *NYT*, Dec. 1, 1959.
23. *NYT*, March 16, 1960.
24. *CR* 103:11982 (7/17/57).
25. *CQA*, XVI (1960), 476, 481.
26. Transcript of weekly TV report, March 12, 1960, in *KP*:401:1.
27. *CQA*, XVI (1960), 483, 485.
28. *NYT*, March 30, 1960; *CQA*, XVI (1960), 194.
29. CR 106:70252–57 (3/31/60).
30. *NYT*, March 30, April 2, 1960; *CQA*, XVI (1960), 486.
31. *CQA*, XVI (1960), 204, 486.
32. *CR* 106:7810 (4/8/60).
33. See, for example, a Jack Knox cartoon in the April 11, 1960, *Banner*.

Chapter xx

1. See Kefauver's unequivocal promise to Johnson, above, Chapter xvii; one of Kefauver's strongest and earliest public denials of interest in the 1960 presidential nomination was reported by *CQWR*, XV (July 26, 1957), 894.
2. Polls in the *Nashville Tennessean*, Aug. 11, 1957, and the *Memphis Commercial Appeal*, Nov. 17, 1957, filed in *KP*:Polls.
3. "Young Man Running," *Newsweek*, LI (Feb. 24, 1958), 26.
4. *CQWR*, XV (Dec. 6, 1957), 1296.
5. *Tennessee Blue Book, 1960*, 175.
6. In a letter to his aunt, Mrs. J. C. Johns, Kefauver wrote, "I am not taking any public position in connection with the Governor's race by Mayor Orgill. He has always been a consistent friend of mine. If you want to pass around a good word for him, I would appreciate it"; letter of June 13, 1958, in *KP*:General Correspondence.
7. Nov. 29, 1958, Gallup poll, in *CQWR*, XVI (Dec. 5, 1958), 1511.
8. *CQWR*, XVII (March 27, 1959), 460; see also, *NYT*, March 22, 1959.
9. Kefauver's standing in the Gallup poll of Democratic voters stayed fairly constant in 1959—10 per cent (May), 9 per cent (June), 11 per cent (July), 9 per cent (Sept.), 10 per cent (Nov.); *CQWR*, XVII (June 19, 1959), 829; (July 17, 1959), 968; (Oct. 9, 1959), 1385; (Nov. 27, 1959), 1510.
10. *NYT*, Sept. 15, 1959; March 3, 1960.
11. *NYT*, Dec. 20, 1957; Sept. 7, 1958; May 3, 1959; bill of Dec. 11, 1959, from Prince Lithograph Company, in *KP*:General Correspondence, 1959.
12. *NYT*, May 3, 1959; William Buchanan and Agnes Bird, *Money as*

a *Campaign Resource: Tennessee Democratic Senatorial Primaries, 1948–1964* (Princeton, 1966), 40.

13. Buchanan and Bird, *op. cit.*, 41. Kefauver had met Taylor and apparently had gotten to know him fairly well during Kefauver's tenure as finance commissioner in 1939. In 1943, Taylor sent Kefauver a postcard from "somewhere in the Middle East" telling Kefauver that "I often think of the good old days in Nashville. Remember me to Nancy"; Feb. 3, 1943, in *KP*:91:1.

14. *NYT*, April 10, 1960.

15. *Nashville Banner*, July 15, 1960.

16. David Halberstam, "The 'Silent Ones' Speak Up in Tennessee," *Reporter*, XX (Sept. 1, 1960), 29.

17. *Ibid.*, 28–29; "Kefauver's Victory," *New Republic*, CXLIII (Aug. 15, 1960), 5.

18. Nashville *Banner*, July 13, 1960.

19. *CT*, July 12, 1960.

20. *Ibid.*, July 26, 30, Aug. 5, 1960; *Nashville Banner*, July 23, 1960; Robert Bendiner, "Tennessee," *New Statesman*, LX (Aug. 20, 1960), 231; *Louisville Courier-Journal*, July 24, 1960.

21. *NYT*, July 24, 1960.

22. *CT*, July 20, 21, 27, 1960; *Nashville Banner*, July 22, 27, 1960; "Kefauver—Is This It?" *Newsweek*, LVI (Aug. 1, 1960), 33.

23. *CT*, July 16, 1960; *NYT*, June 15, 1960.

24. See Note 14, Chapter xviii.

25. Buchanan and Bird, *op. cit.*, 43; *CT*, July 26, 28, 1960.

26. *Knoxville News-Sentinel*, June 6, 1960.

27. "Where's Estes," *Time*, LXXVI (July 18, 1960), 13; *Nashville Banner*, July 7, 1960.

28. *CT*, July 20, 1960.

29. *Ibid.*, July 15, 1960.

30. *Ibid.*, July 31, 1960.

31. *Ibid.*, Aug. 3, 1960.

32. *NYT*, July 5, 1959; letter from Walter Bartkin, COPE accountant, July 29, 1960, in *KP*:Tennessee, I; Buchanan and Bird, *op. cit.*, 44.

33. *Loc. cit.*

34. *NYT*, July 24, 1960.

35. *CT*, July 23, 1960; *Nashville Banner*, July 27, 1960.

36. *Nashville Banner*, July 6, 1960; Buchanan and Bird, *op. cit.*, 40–41; *CT*, Aug. 11, 1963.

37. Buchanan and Bird, *op. cit.*, 43.

38. Kefauver's comments on effective campaign techniques, response to Democratic Senatorial Campaign Committee inquiry, May 4, 1961, in *KP*:61&71.

39. Buchanan and Bird, *op. cit.*, 43, 45; interview with Mr. and Mrs. Stanton Smith, Aug. 1, 1970.
40. "Senator Kefauver," *Nation*, CXCI (Aug. 6, 1960), 62.
41. *CT*, July 23, 1960; Buchanan and Bird, *op. cit.*, 42.
42. *Nashville Banner*, Aug. 3, 1960.
43. *NYT*, July 31, 1960.
44. *Tennessee Blue Book, 1961–62*, 190–91; *CT*, Aug. 5, 1960; Halberstam, *loc. cit.*, 30; *NYT*, Aug. 6, 1960.
45. Halberstam, *loc. cit.*, 28; Bendiner, *loc. cit.*
46. *Nashville Banner*, Aug. 5, 1960; Halberstam, *loc. cit.*, 28; *Memphis Commercial Appeal*, Aug. 6, 1960.
47. "South Wins with Kefauver," *Christian Century*, LXXVII (Aug. 17, 1960), 940–41; *NYT*, Aug. 6, 17, 1960.
48. *CR* 106:16152 (8/10/60).

Chapter xxi

1. Letter from Kefauver to Pearson, Nov. 19, 1960, in *KP:*Estes Kefauver, IV; *NYT*, Sept. 11, Oct. 25, 1960.
2. *NYT*, Oct. 25, 1960.
3. *Ibid.*
4. *CR* 106:18312 (8/30/60); *NYT*, Sept. 25, 1960.
5. *Tennessee Blue Book, 1961–1962*, 205.
6. *CR* 107:2652 (2/24/61); *NYT*, Dec. 13, 1960.
7. *NYT*, June 15, 1961; letter from Black to Kefauver, June 21, 1961; Kefauver statement of March 29, 1962, both in *KP:*9:2&12:1, Estes Kefauver, III.
8. The discussion of the drug bill which follows draws heavily on Richard Harris' remarkably well done account, *The Real Voice* (New York, 1964); *CQA*, XVI (1960), 743–49, XVII (1961), 290–92, XVIII (1962), 197–210; scores of articles from the *New York Times*, which gave extensive coverage to the drug bill from the first hearings in Dec. 1959, through final presidential approval in Oct., 1962; and, Kefauver's own book, *In a Few Hands: Monopoly Power in America* (New York, 1965), 8–79.
9. See Note 14, Chapter xviii.
10. Although Kefauver spoke often and at length on his patent provisions, for a brief summary of his position, see Estes Kefauver, on "Should the Patent and Antitrust Laws Be Substantially Changed in Regard to the Drug Industry?" *Congressional Digest*, XLI (Feb. 1962), 42 ff.
11. Harris, *op. cit.*, 141.

12. *Ibid.*, 165.
13. *Ibid.*, 166–69.
14. *Ibid.*, 169–70.
15. *CR* 108:10105–57 (6/11/62).
16. *Ibid.*, 10107.
17. *NYT*, July 27, 1962.
18. Bruce H. Frisch, "Kefauver's Last Interview," *Science Digest*, LIV (Nov. 1963), 13.
19. *NYT*, Oct. 5, 1962.
20. Harris, *op. cit.*, 245.
21. *Ibid.* When Kefauver died in 1963, his estate included seventy-five shares of American Home Products and 100 shares of Chas. Pfizer, leading Philip Meyer of the Knight newspapers to charge that Kefauver's ownership of drug stocks "cast a shadow on the respected Senator's career." A serious examination of the charge, however, led even Austin Smith of the Pharmaceutical Manufacturers Association, Kefauver's longtime antagonist during the years of the drug investigation, to dismiss "allegations about the late Senator's having played hanky-panky with drug share holdings . . . [as] ridiculous." The charge was laid to rest permanently by a detailed defense of Kefauver by John Blair, Chief Economist of the Antitrust and Monopoly Subcommittee. In a letter to the *Washington Post*, Blair pointed out that Kefauver's drug holdings had been purchased six months after the passage of the Kefauver-Harris Drug Act of 1962 and that, far from receiving special treatment by the Subcommittee since then, "these two companies have been more directly and adversely affected by the drug investigation than any of the other major drug companies." *The Nation*, after a look at the facts, agreed that the charge of conflict of interest was unsupported; indeed, said *The Nation*, "from such stockholders [as Kefauver] the drug companies may pray to be delivered." Nevertheless, the *Washington Post* editorialized, "if these holdings had been known at the time, questions would have been raised about his investigation of the drug industry." See *Washington Post*, Nov. 3, 10, 1963; *CR* 109:24045–46 (12/10/63); "Kefauver's Reward," *Nation*, CXCVIII (Jan. 6, 1964), 23; Austin Smith, letter to the editor of *The Nation*, CXCVIII (Feb. 10, 1964), 1; *NYT*, Nov. 2, 1963; *CT*, Oct. 31, Nov. 3, 1963.
22. Gerald W. Johnson, "Kefauver and the Swindlers," *New Republic*, CXLV (Aug. 7, 1961), 12.
23. *CR* 108:17422 (8/23/62).
24. For a brief summary of the issues involved in the communications satellite dispute, see *CQA*, XVIII (1962), 546–58; for a condensed

version of Kefauver's position, see Estes Kefauver and William Fitts Ryan, "Big Business in Space," *New Republic*, CXLVI (June 11, 1962), 18–20.

25. *NYT*, June 21, 1962.
26. Kefauver, in a letter to the *New York Times*, April 1, 1962.
27. Letter to President Kennedy from Kefauver, two other senators, and 32 congressmen opposed to the private corporation, *NYT*, Aug. 28, 1961.
28. *NYT*, June 24, 1962.
29. *CQA*, XVII (1961), 496–97; *CQWR*, XX (Sept. 14, 1962), 1527.
30. Grant McConnell, *Steel and the Presidency* (New York, 1963), 84; *NYT*, April 11, 17, 1962; see also, Kefauver's letter to the *New Republic* defending Kennedy's action, CXLVI (May 14, 1962), 13–14.
31. *NYT*, Aug. 15, 31, Sept. 1, 13, 1962; *CQA*, XVIII (1962), 1019.
32. *NYT*, Sept. 13, 26, 1962; *CQA*, XVIII (1962), 1019; see also the *Hearings* before the full committee on the contempt citations, Committee on the Judiciary, 87th Congress, 2nd Session, Sept. 12–20, 1962.
33. *CR* 104:289 (1/13/58), 105:15266 (8/6/59), 106:A6400 (8/26/60); *CQWR*, XVII (July 17, 1959), 962; *CQA*, XIII (1957), 310; XV (1959), 261–65.
34. *CR* 102:13470 (7/19/56), 103:9947 (6/21/57), 12800 (7/26/57); *NYT*, Feb. 14, 1954; June 1, 6, 25, July 4, 6, 1957; *CQWR*, XV (June 28, 1957), 785; "Return of the Hound-Dog," *New Republic*, CXXXVI (June 10, 1957), 2; "No News and Good News," *ibid.* (June 17, 1957), 2.
35. *CQWR*, XVIII (Feb. 26, 1960), 306; *NYT*, Sept. 24, 1957; Nov. 13, 1962; *CQA*, XVI (1960), 421.
36. *CR* 105:15272–73 (8/6/59).
37. *NYT*, April 25, 1957.
38. *CT*, Aug. 11, 1963.
39. *NYT*, March 16, 1959.
40. *CR* 108:8603 (5/23/62).
41. *NYT*, Oct. 1, 1962.
42. Telegram from Kefauver to President Kennedy, Oct. 2, 1962, copy in *KP*:401:1.
43. Letter from Kefauver to Eastland, Oct. 4, 1962, copy in *KP*:401:1, with note that a copy was also sent to Jim McCartney of the *Chicago Daily News*.

Epilogue

1. *NYT,* April 15, May 4, 1963; *Nashville Tennessean,* Aug. 10, 1963.
2. *NYT,* March 27, 1963.
3. *Nashville Tennessean,* Aug. 10, 1963; *Memorial Services Held in the Senate and House of Representatives of the United States, Together with Remarks Presented in Eulogy of Carey Estes Kefauver, Late a Senator from Tennessee.* 85th Congress, 1st Session (Government Printing Office, 1964), 57.
4. *CR* 109:14554–55 (8/8/63); interview with former Senator Joseph Clark, June 4, 1970.
5. *Nashville Tennessean,* Aug. 10, 1963; *NYT,* Aug. 11, 1963.
6. *NYT,* Aug. 11, 1963.
7. *Ibid.*
8. *CT,* Aug. 14, 1963.
9. *NYT,* Aug. 11, 1963.
10. "Estes Kefauver," *New Republic,* CXLIX (Aug. 31, 1963), 5.
11. "Carey Estes Kefauver, 1927," *Yale Law Report,* X (Fall, 1963), reprinted in *CR* 110:644 (1/20/64).

INDEX